PD

D0261893

The Great Dan

The Great Dan

A Biography of Daniel O'Connell

Charles Chenevix Trench

JONATHAN CAPE
THIRTY BEDFORD SQUARE LONDON

First published 1984
Copyright © 1984 by Charles Chenevix Trench

Jonathan Cape Ltd, 30 Bedford Square, London WC1

British Library Cataloguing in Publication Data

Trench, Charles Chenevix
The Great Dan.
1. O'Connell, Daniel   2. Politicians—
Ireland—Biography   3. Lawyers—Ireland—
Biography
I. Title
941.5081'092'4   DA950.22

ISBN 0-224-02176-1

Printed in Great Britain by Butler & Tanner Ltd
Frome and London

To my neighbours, who owe much
to Daniel O'Connell

Contents

Illustrations

The author and publishers are grateful to the following for permission to reproduce black and white plates: *Punch* Publications Ltd, nos 5 and 6; Trinity College Library, University of Dublin, nos 1–4.

Acknowledgments

My gratitude goes first to Professor Maurice R. O'Connell, whose help and advice have been of more value than I can readily express. I also received much help from Dr Fergus O'Ferral, who made available to me his PhD thesis on O'Connell and the Catholic Association, product of much original research.

For permission to use the Anglesey papers, which are of great interest in relation to O'Connell, I am indebted to the Marquess of Anglesey, DL, FSA, Hon. FRIBA, FRSL and the Deputy Keeper of Records, Public Records Office, Northern Ireland. I am also most grateful to the Librarian and Board of Trinity College, Dublin, for permission to quote extracts from the Crampton Mss; and to the Council of Trustees of the National Library of Ireland for permission to quote from the Wyse and O'Neill Daunt papers. Mr Brian McDermot very kindly let me have a copy of an important letter from Sir William Parnell to Denys Scully.

Finally I must thank the staff of the National Library of Ireland, the Public Records Office, Northern Ireland and the Library of Trinity College for their help throughout.

Foreword

Charles Chenevix Trench has chosen as his subject one of the three Irish political leaders to achieve an international reputation, the others being Charles Stewart Parnell and Eamon De Valera. Parnell belonged to the age of romantic nationalism when men's vision was bound by the needs of their own country. De Valera was likewise subject to this limitation but he had the advantage of being the head of a government. O'Connell had interests of universal validity.

Born into the Enlightenment, he shared to the full that age's interest in the universal. He based the struggle for Catholic emancipation on his own theory of religious freedom for all, Jew as well as Gentile, and on the separation of Church from state. It was not until the final session of Vatican II in 1965 that the Catholic Church endorsed a definition of religious freedom that could be described as consistent with O'Connell's.

He ranks as a great European democrat. The Catholic Association was the first democratic mass organisation of modern times; by initiating the penny-a-month plan for membership he brought the poor man into politics. His humanitarianism and his belief in democracy induced him to take up the cause of negro emancipation in both the British Empire and the United States of America. In Britain he played an essential part in the passing of the Great Reform Bill, and in movements for the repeal of the Corn Laws, for introducing a secret ballot and for a more democratic suffrage in parliamentary and municipal elections. For

Foreword

more than a decade he was the principal radical in British politics.

His third contribution of universal significance was his commitment to non-violence and constitutionalism and to the rule of law. It is these principles which are most vital for the world today, but they are also the ones most under attack. The rule of law is ignored in large areas of the world while constitutional methods are derided, and violence is praised as the surest road to freedom and justice. O'Connell stands with Gandhi and Martin Luther King as a political leader devoted to non-violence; and his life is a practical example of the hard thinking and hard work that are essential to the constitutional method of grappling with a nation's problems. By invoking these principles and using these means he gave to Irish Catholics, a subject people inured to failure, their first taste of victory.

1st July 1983   Maurice R. O'Connell

History Department
Fordham University
New York City

Preface

The greatest demagogues the English-speaking world has produced were a Londoner and a Kerryman, John Wilkes and Daniel O'Connell. Each in his own way represented that curiously attractive phenomenon in politics – the gentleman revolutionary, the man of the people who flaunts an aristocratic or affluent life-style. They aroused paroxysms of rage among those who saw them as traitors to their class, and adulation among the mobs who cheered and demonstrated for them.

They developed a new technique in politics, which had hitherto been the preserve of well-mannered gentlemen debating in well-rounded phrases and hurling Greek and Latin quotations at one another. Wilkes and O'Connell could exchange quips from Virgil with anyone, but also understood and exploited the untapped power of the bawling, rowdy, unlettered multitudes, which could be marshalled by middle-class activists. Both pulled the Establishment's nose and reduced its overweening power. Both were offensive in speech far beyond current usage, but clever at keeping just to windward of the law. Both abhorred violence, but exploited the fear of it. The worst any Wilkite mob ever did was to up-end the Austrian Ambassador to chalk political graffiti on the soles of his shoes. The worst O'Connell's muscle-men ever did was to rough up the occasional Trinity College undergraduate who picked a fight by ignoring their cries of 'Hats off!' as the Liberator walked down the street. Both suffered the usual fate of revolutionaries in old age, to be outdone in militancy and discredited by the next generation of zealots.

They were radicals of the eighteenth century: that is to say, their radicalism was essentially negative; they were against landlord-power, arbitrary acts by the executive, press censorship, governmental interference of all kinds. 'Positive discrimination', in the widest sense, is a concept of twentieth-century radicalism. They did not hold it to be any business of government to make the poor richer, or even the rich poorer. So long as rich and poor, Englishmen, Irishmen and Americans, had the same constitutional rights and the same liberty within the law, the state's and the reformer's duty was done. 'Seek ye first the political kingdom,' said Kwame Nkrumah, 'and the rest shall be added unto you.' Wilkes and O'Connell would have agreed. They were instinctively conservative and traditionalist, using radical methods to restore what they imagined had been the felicity of the good old days before 'Whig principles' and 'Irish liberties' had been betrayed.

Neither made the smallest attempt to adjust his expenditure to his means. They lived extravagantly and were saved from debtors' prisons only by hundreds of thousands of admirers who for years kept the Patriot and the Liberator beyond reach of want, never grudging their pennies and their pounds.

O'Connell's reputation has suffered from adulation by early biographers who accepted him at his own valuation, and denigration by later writers who accepted him at the Young Irelanders'. For most of the twentieth century the latter view has prevailed and O'Connell has been in disrepute mainly because his lifelong rejection of violence for political ends runs counter to the received version of Irish history that freedom was won only by the 'armed struggle'. (It is arguable that, but for the armed struggle, all thirty-two counties of Ireland would now be free, but this is not the place to argue it.) Nor does his lack of interest in the Irish language (which he spoke fluently) commend him to present-day nationalists who must pledge themselves to promote the use of Irish however little they may actually use it. Lastly, his dislike of trade unions puts him on the Progressive's black list.

So, while dozens of O'Connell statues tower over dozens of O'Connell streets, the Liberator himself is damned by socialists as a union-basher and by republicans as a West Brit.

In recent years, however, academic historians have been presenting a more balanced view of O'Connell. It is time for a non-academic to do likewise. In Catholic emancipation O'Connell achieved the first and most important step towards Irish freedom. To condemn him for not achieving more is like denouncing Columbus for not going on to discover Australia.

1

First Performance

In September 1798 the Court House at Tralee was packed with
country people cramming in for a day's free entertainment. Here
they could watch their friends and enemies in the dock and the
witness-box, sentenced, perhaps, to be 'taken to the place of
execution and there hanged by the neck until you are dead', or
else fencing warily, with truth, lie and half-truth, against prosecution and defence counsels, some of them much more famous
in Tralee than any Dublin play-actor. From the crowded public
benches rose a pungent, not unpleasant, aroma of plug-tobacco,
potheen, damp frieze, sweat and the all-pervading turf-smoke.
But the case now before the court was a petty one, of common
assault resulting from a faction-fight, and the point at issue was
whether the principal prosecution witness was, at the time of the
incident, drunk or sober.

In such a small affair none of the star turns took part, and the
dock brief was allocated to a newcomer to the Munster Bar, a
burly young man with a plump face, curly black hair and rolling
blue-grey eyes. Although it was his very first brief, he showed no
nervousness. Genial, confiding, his eyes twinkling with good humour, he asked the witness, as one man of the world to another,
'On your oath, now, how much drink had you taken before the
fight began?'

The witness was confident that he could handle this young
fellow. 'Troth, not very much.'

'Did you not have a pint of potheen a man?'

'Well, I had my share of a pint.'

1

'How much was your share?'

' 'Twas a good sup.'

'On your solemn oath, now, did not your share of a pint of potheen consist of it all except the pewter?'

If the question had been put in a more obvious way, 'Did you consume the whole pint?', the witness, his solemn face unmoved, would have solemnly denied it. But the unexpected wording surprised him into a smile. 'Well, then, dear knows, but that's true for you, sir!'

The court and the prosecution case collapsed in laughter (not for the last time in one of Daniel O'Connell's cross-examinations), and Jerry Keller, doyen of the Munster Bar, clapped him on the shoulder. '*You'll do*, young gentleman, *you'll do*!'

With this single question Daniel O'Connell edged out of the ruck of young barristers; when next he came to Tralee, his face would be known. But he had a long way to go, for in his first year at the Bar he had only one more brief, and earned precisely £2 5s 6d.

But the Munster circuit, even for a very insignificant tyro, was fun. Judges and counsels rode or drove by easy stages from one comfortable inn to another. The best on the circuit was at Millstreet, a day's ride from Tralee, kept by a distant cousin of O'Connell's. (Kerry was full of his distant cousins.) In a clean, well-furnished parlour, their muddy boots hauled off, the barristers toasted their feet before a roaring fire, called for the best of claret and madeira, or punch on a cold day, and watched the servant girl lay the long table with 'the whitest table-linen, the best beef, the sweetest and tenderest mutton, the fattest fowl'.

Riding on next day, they might practise their pistol-shooting at trees or rocks beside the road. O'Connell became a dead shot, a useful accomplishment for a young gentleman in a country where duelling was so common that the first question asked about a young man, perhaps by a prospective father-in-law, was, 'Does he blaze?' – with a black mark against him if he did not. Angry words between lawyers in court often resulted in pistols for two next morning. 'A lawyer', wrote O'Connell's colleague, Richard Sheil, with some exaggeration, 'was almost a gladiator by profession: his pistols were the chief implements of reasoning.' A savage old hanging judge, Lord Norbury, was said to have 'shot his way to the Bench'.

2

The Kilworth Mountains were notorious for robbers. O'Connell and a friend, Standish Grady, resting at an inn in Fermoy before venturing through them, discovered that they were out of ammunition, which was not easy to buy in a strange town. In came a patrol of dragoons, commanded by a corporal, whom Grady approached.

'Soldier, will you sell me some powder and ball?'

'Sir, I don't sell powder,' replied the corporal curtly.

'Will you then have the goodness to buy me some?' said Grady. 'In these unsettled times the dealers in the article are reluctant to sell it to strangers like us.'

'Sir,' replied the corporal, 'I am no man's messenger but the king's – go yourself.'

'Grady,' said O'Connell in a low tone, 'you have made a great mistake. Did you see by the mark on his sleeve that the man is a corporal? You mortified his pride by calling him a soldier, especially before his own men, amongst whom he doubtless plays the officer.'

After a few minutes, O'Connell bought the corporal a drink.

'Did you ever see such rain as we had today, sergeant? I was very glad to find that the regulars had not the trouble of escorting the judge. It was very suitable work for those awkward yeomen.'

'Yes, indeed, sir,' returned the corporal, 'we were very lucky in escaping those torrents of rain.'

'Perhaps, sergeant, you will have the kindness,' continued O'Connell, 'to buy me some powder and ball in town. We are to pass the Kilworth Mountains, and shall want ammunition. You can, of course, find no difficulty in buying it; but it is not to every one they sell these matters.'

'Sir,' said the corporal, 'I shall have great pleasure in requesting your acceptance of a small supply of powder and ball. My balls will, I think, just fit your pistols. You'll stand in need of ammunition, for there are some of those outlying rebelly rascals on the mountains.'

'Dan,' said Grady, in a low tone, 'you'll go through the world fair and easy.'

But in this Standish Grady prophesied less truly than Jerry Keller. Although he maintained that 'more flies are caught with a spoonful of honey than with a tun of vinegar', O'Connell's career was to be by no means 'fair and easy'.

2

The O'Connells of Kerry

Daniel O'Connell belonged to a family of Gaelic gentry based on Kerry. As Catholics, the O'Connells of the day had fought, and two had died, for King James II against William of Orange. After the ruin of their cause at Limerick, they made a dignified retirement from public life (from which, as Papists, they were perforce excluded) and Captain John O'Connell, in about 1702, built on the north shore of the Kenmare estuary, on land leased from the Earl of Cork, a sound, plain, two-storeyed house at Derrynane. It was slightly outside traditional O'Connell country which began with the barony of Iveragh, seven miles to the north, but by that time such concepts meant little. As an old, Catholic, landed family they retained much unofficial authority and universal respect among the mountain men, peasants and fishermen of Kerry, who were a tough breed, bold, clannish and independent, wretchedly housed (with their sheep and pigs) in stone and mud hovels roofed with turf-sods through which dripped the rain, but well fed on potatoes, milk and the fish with which the local seas abounded.

A Catholic's life in the early eighteenth century was governed by the anti-Papist Penal Laws, enacted by the Irish parliament which was composed of, and elected by, Protestants. Some of the laws deprived Catholics of rights they had been specifically granted by the Treaty of Limerick. The objects of the Penal Laws were to safeguard the Protestant Ascendancy; to ensure that the Catholic Irish could not effectively rebel in the Jacobite cause while the British army was locked in a death-grapple with the strongest military power in the world, Louis XIV's France; and to convince the deluded Irish of the errors of Popery.

Catholicism was not made illegal, but much ingenuity was devoted to making it inconvenient and expensive, while encouraging conversions to the established Church. But although the Penal Laws were harsh, their implementation was mitigated by personal friendships, inefficiency and sheer lack of zeal for law enforcement – a situation not unknown in Ireland today.

The key piece of legislation was an Act of the English parliament in 1691,[1] applying to Ireland two previous Acts which had hitherto applied only to England, viz. the Test Act of 1678 and that commonly known as the Bill of Rights of 1689. This excluded from the Irish parliament all who would not take the Oaths of Allegiance to the King and of Supremacy, which denied the Pope's temporal *and spiritual* authority within the realm, and who would not make a declaration denouncing the Catholic doctrine of transubstantiation, the sacrifice of the Mass and the 'idolatry' of the invocation of the Virgin Mary and the Saints Thus purged of Papists, the Irish parliament proceeded to exclude them altogether from public life. A series of Acts[2] barred them from all offices under the Crown, from commissioned ranks in the army and navy, from the Grand Juries which performed the functions of local government in the counties, from all learned professions except medicine, and from Trinity College. Finally, in 1727, they were deprived of the parliamentary franchise.[3] Dozens of charters granted by the Stuart kings to cities and boroughs confined municipal office, municipal government and the freedom of cities and boroughs to Protestants. All these laws were strictly enforced.

Other laws were not. After the Treaty of Limerick the 'regular' clergy (i.e. monks and friars) were all expelled, subject to hanging if they returned.[4] None was hanged. However, 1,089 'lay' clergy, parish priests, were licensed to remain and minister to their community, which then numbered about 800,000. When the long French wars were over, those who had been expelled started coming back, in increasing numbers after 1716, and no one tried to stop them, except in the fiercely Presbyterian north-east. Long before mid-century the full hierarchy was functioning – keeping a low profile, but not in hiding and seldom molested. In 1731

5

there were at least 1,445 parish priests and 245 regular clergy besides uncountable itinerant friars; there were nine nunneries. The ancient places of worship had fallen into ruin or been taken over by the established Church and the main difficulty in replacing them was the expense; but a House of Lords Committee inquiring into the state of Popery found that there were – besides fifty-four private chapels, huts, sheds and movable altars – 892 'mass houses', some of them – oh, horror! – 'large and pompous' erections. All towns, except in the north-east had Catholic 'chapels'.[5] If rural areas were less well served, it was because they found it difficult to raise the money. Moreover Protestants who by mid-century, owned about 90 per cent of the land, were reluctant to make any available for a purpose of which they disapproved. In a widespread parish it might be easier for the priest to ride round visiting the flock than for the flock to walk to the priest's dwelling, so Mass was often celebrated in private houses, barns, and even at the old Mass-rocks which were re-membered from Cromwellian times – but now with no risk of interruption from a patrol of dragoons.

It was unlawful for Catholics to be guardians of children. It was also unlawful for them to run schools,[6] but after 1716 the law was seldom implemented. The Committee found in 1731 sixty-eight Catholic schools, including three convent girls' schools, in and around Dublin; and a further 481 outside. There were, of course, fewer Catholic schools in the countryside, because there were fewer people to pay for them. A family like the O'Connells would employ as tutor the parish priest, or an itinerant schoolmaster, or perhaps send the younger boys to the local 'hedge school' (generally housed in a building of some kind) where they would learn the three Rs and a smattering of Latin. But to put a polish on a young gentleman required that he go either to a boarding school where he would be exposed to a sustained effort to wean him from Popery, or abroad, preferably to France which was illegal[7] (but the law was winked at) and expensive. Catholics were not, of course, admitted to Trinity College, the Ascendancy's Holy of Holies.

A Papist could inherit and own land, but if he died without a Protestant heir his estate had to be 'gavelled',[8] that is to say divided equally between all his sons; and if his eldest son became a Protestant, the whole estate automatically became his and the father was merely tenant-for-life. A Papist could not buy land. If one were bold enough to do so, any Protestant could file a 'bill of discovery' (the technical term for this legalised plunder) and take the land off him for nothing. There were other ways of acquiring land, some legal, some not so legal. It could be leased from a powerful Protestant, as Derrynane was from the Earl of Cork, who would protect his tenant and, in exchange for a fair rent, be spared a lot of trouble. A common way round the law was for a Catholic who wanted to buy land to arrange for a Protestant friend to purchase it, ostensibly for himself. This friendly office was performed for the O'Connells by a Protestant cousin named Hugh Falvey who, threatened with 'discovery', was 'ready to swear the print out of the Bible' that he bought the land for himself.[9] O'Connell once remarked that there would be no Catholic gentry if individual Protestants had not been a great deal more honest than their laws. At least one O'Connell probably emulated a gentleman who, asked by the Protestant Archbishop of Dublin to explain his grounds for embracing the reformed religion, replied, 'Faith, my lord, I can tell you easily – two thousand and five hundred acres of the best grounds in the County of Roscommon.'

Catholics, unless licensed to do so, were not allowed to carry arms.[10] In 1713, when England was still at war with France and Louis XIV supported the Stuarts' claim to the English throne, 134 Papists were licensed to carry sword, pistols and gun.[11] Thereafter the laws seemed to have been progressively relaxed for families like the O'Connells, on good terms with Protestant magistrates and Grand Jurymen: they could shoot pheasants, duck and grouse with impunity; blaze away at one another with duelling pistols to their hearts' content; and might without difficulty obtain a licence for musket or blunderbuss to protect their property.

There were laws similar to the 'petty apartheid' of South Africa, which served no purpose but to humiliate and annoy. No Catholic church – or 'mass house' as it was offensively called – might have a steeple. If a Protestant found a Catholic riding a horse worth more than £5, he could buy it for £5.[12] Perhaps this was not a great grievance in the extreme south-west where the terrain was inimicable for fox-hunting and racing and the only horses were mountain cobs and ponies. More serious was the

7

requirement that Catholic farmers pay tithes to support the Protestant clergy.

Catholics' sole political power was through (Anglican) Parish Vestries. The Vestry was an assembly of all solvent householders resident in the parish, including Catholics and dissenters. It had modest responsibilities, including Poor Relief and the upkeep of (Anglican) churches, for which purposes it could levy a cess from local landholders. Catholics sometimes packed a Vestry meeting to block some project of which they disapproved. Ironically, they were sometimes elected churchwardens, a somewhat unwelcome distinction as it carried the responsibility for collecting the cess. O'Connell in his maturity knew well how to manipulate a Vestry.

For families like the O'Connells of Derrynane the effect of the Penal Laws was mitigated by their good relations with the Protestant gentry of Kerry. These were invariably given the honorary title of 'Colonel', however tender their years or meagre their military experience. When 'Colonel' Blennerhasset's lady was brought to bed, a neighbour made a polite inquiry about the Colonel's health. 'Do you mean the old Colonel, or the young Colonel?' he was asked. The young 'Colonel' was less than a week old. These friendly relations were vital for the O'Connells, for the Colonels, as Justices of the Peace, Grand Jurymen and officers of the yeomanry and Volunteers, really governed the country. In contrast to the Colonels, most low-class Protestants were intolerant and many were intolerable.

Of course personal friendships did not open to Catholics professions which were Protestant monopolies. They could not obtain commissions in the army and navy; the Bench, the Bar and parliament were closed to them.[13] So, in the Seven Years' War, one grandson of John O'Connell (who built Derrynane) died for King George as an officer in a privateer, while the other fought for King Louis as an officer in the Irish Brigade. The latter, Daniel O'Connell, was one of the most distinguished of thousands of Kerrymen in the French, Spanish and Austrian services. After fighting in Germany, India and the Mediterranean, as Inspector General of Infantry he initiated reforms in tactics and administration of which the ultimate benefactor was Napoleon. By 1789 he was a full General in the French service and a Count in the French nobility. He was completely devoid of resentment against the English whom he was paid to fight, and

was as likely to spend his leave in London as in Paris or Derrynane. Indeed his fondest hope, when the Seven Years' War was
over, was to 'get into the English service without injury to my
religion', though he would 'never bear arms against France where
only I found an asylum when refused one at home'.[14]

A Catholic in England was subject to similar restrictions:[15] in
one respect he was even worse treated, for he could not inherit
land if his nearest Protestant relative chose to claim it.

Irish Catholics who stayed at home could advance themselves
only by agriculture and trade. The second half of the eighteenth
century was a period of increasing prosperity for Ireland. Population expansion, wars and the beginning of the industrial revolution in England provided a growing market for Irish agricultural produce, the prices of which rose steadily from mid-century,
and in 1758–9 the Westminster parliament suspended the laws
which had banned the import of Irish beef, mutton and pork.
Between 1750 and 1790 Irish linen exports to Britain more than
trebled in quantity. There was a similar story in corn exports, in
the woollen trade, glass manufacturing, distilling and brewing.
To cope with this expansion, roads were vastly improved and a
network of country fairs and markets developed. Catholics took
a fair share of this prosperity, often making loans to Protestant
landlords who were better at spending money than making it.
One Catholic who thus re-established his family fortune was
Maurice O'Connell of Derrynane, elder brother of the General
and the privateer.

He was a man who generally got the best of a bargain and was
notoriously parsimonious. Although he had no official position,
his word was law in the barony of Iveragh, especially when the
bearer of it displayed a little crooked pruning knife which served
the purpose of a mediaeval monarch's ring in proving that an
order came from him. He was a tall man, over six foot, and his
portrait shows a narrow face with a long nose and dark, wary
eyes which seem to be watching for the main chance. Out of
doors he always wore a hunting cap rather than pay the tax on
beaver hats, and was known as 'Muiris an Chaipín' or 'Hunting
Cap' through all the county. (His grand-daughter, Ellen Fitz-
Simon, says he wore the cap in consequence of a bad fall from
a horse when hunting.) He thought that women should be kept
in abject submission and on a maximum allowance of £20 a year.

He married Mary Cantillon, whose principal charm was her dowry. He added to the estates which the family had been able to keep, mainly at Glencara, and those which they rented at Derrynane. He farmed intensively, exporting cattle, sheep, hides, wool, meat and salt; he made a good thing of cargoes salvaged from many ships wrecked on the Kerry coast; he imported, without the tiresome formality of paying customs duties, wine, brandy, tea, tobacco, silk and lace for which he found a ready market among the 'Colonels' and their ladies. His younger brother, Morgan, was partner in these enterprises. No more in Kerry than in Cornwall were 'free traders' in disrepute: indeed they were regarded rather as public servants than as criminals.

Such was the world in which Morgan O'Connell married Catherine O'Mullane of Whitechurch, Mallow, in the Anglican Church of Holy Trinity, Cork, in 1771. Why they were married in a Protestant church is not clear, for no law required it; presumably it was a sort of extra insurance against any kind of attempt on their property. Catherine was a lively young lady, of good family, who introduced 'a cock nose and bad teeth' into the O'Connell family. They lived at first in brother Maurice's house at Derrynane, but it was not a happy arrangement for the two wives, so Morgan moved to a farmhouse at Carhen, near Cahirciveen, twenty miles west of Derrynane.

But it was a changing world. The ruin of the Jacobites at Culloden in 1746 and their failure to raise even a whimper of rebellion in Ireland reduced their cause from deadly danger to nostalgic song and legend. In 1766 James Edward, the 'Old Pretender' to Hanoverians and King James III to Jacobites, died. The Pope did not recognise his son, Prince Charles Edward, as king of England, so Catholics were free to recognise King George III, as most people of property and the parish clergy did. The O'Connells' Jacobitism thereafter amounted to no more than a picture of the Prince on a wall in Derrynane. In 1774 Catholics were permitted to swear allegiance to King George and probably most of the gentry did so, including Hunting Cap.

In 1778 England was at war not only with the American rebels but with France, and later with Spain and Holland. It became necessary to conciliate Ireland so that regular troops could be sent overseas. In that year[16] Catholics were permitted to acquire land on perpetual leases, though not freehold, and to inherit land on the same terms as Protestants provided they took the oath of allegiance; the requirement that Catholic-owned estates be gavelled was repealed. So gratified was Colonel Daniel O'Connell of the Irish Brigade in the French service that he wrote to his brother, 'One step more still remains to be made ... I mean the liberty of spilling their blood in defence of their King and country.'[17] (In 1793 even that privilege was granted.) In 1778 many regiments of Volunteers were raised, for local defence against French invasion.[18] Theoretically all were Protestants but the rule was not observed. In 1780 Maurice O'Connell of Derrynane was invited by the Knight of Kerry, M.P. for the county, to help form a mounted corps in which Catholics would serve alongside Protestants. But Hunting Cap, although loyal to King George and all for 'purging the land of Outlaws and Vagabonds' and 'repelling the Pillagings of scampering Privateers,' had better things to do than play, unpaid, at soldiers, and replied austerely:

the Roman Catholic gentlemen of Iveragh would readily unite with their Protestant neighbours ... to form a corps did they think such a measure would meet the approbation of the Legislature. They would, in common with every Catholic of standing in Ireland, be exceedingly happy by every means in their power to give additional weight and strength and security to the kingdom; but what can they do while the laws of their country forbid them the use of arms? Under such circumstances I look upon it to be their duty to confine themselves to that line of conduct marked out for them by the Legislature, and with humility and resignation wait for a further relaxation of the laws which a more enlightened and liberal way of thinking, added to a clearer and more deliberate attention to the real interests and prosperity of the country will, I hope, soon bring about.[19]

The discipline of the Volunteers might fall short of perfection; the companies were so independent of their 'ostensible leaders' that their behaviour was impossible to predict; and 'these whom Volunteers call their commanders must obey their orders'. But 40,000 Irishmen in arms, with 130 cannon, constituted a political factor which could not be ignored. Irishmen – Protestants as well as Catholics – had many grievances, and across the Atlantic the American Revolution acted as a catalyst to them. In political

11

background, religious beliefs and family associations the Protestants who had settled in Ulster during the seventeenth century were very close to those who had settled in New England at the same time; Ireland was then, no less than Pennsylvania, a new frontier. Thereafter many 'Scots-Irish' from Ulster had emigrated to the Thirteen Colonies, and were among the most militant rebels. Irish and American grievances were similar. The Irish parliament and the colonial assemblies were equally subject to overruling by Westminster. 'No Taxation without Representation' was a slogan well understood by Irish Catholics and Presbyterians, who were taxed but not represented. They did not, in general, side with the rebel colonists; they volunteered in thousands to repel a possible French invasion, and passed resolutions of loyalty to the Crown. But the American revolution stimulated Irish liberalism and nationalism, particularly among northern Protestants and the rising Catholic merchant class.

Like the Americans, these bitterly resented the restrictions, imposed by Westminster, on direct trade between Ireland and other countries: trade had to be channelled through England. The Dublin Volunteers paraded – perhaps 'demonstrated' would be a better word – with two cannon on which were hung placards saying FREE TRADE – OR THIS. By 'free trade' they meant the right to trade direct with other countries, as English merchants could do. Promptly – well, fairly promptly – Irish merchants were allowed to trade with anyone, except of course the enemy. In 1782[20] Catholics were permitted to be the legal guardians of their own children, to open schools, to bear arms, to buy land outright and to own horses of any value. In 1782 also came the repeal of the old laws by which the Westminster parliament could not only legislate for Ireland, but overrule any Act of the Irish parliament. In 1884 Catholics were admitted to membership of the Volunteers, and in some southern corps they were soon a majority.

The Irish executive was still appointed by and responsible to the British ministry, not to the Irish parliament; that parliament was wholly Protestant and could readily be controlled by a judicious distribution of the loaves and fishes. Catholics did not have the vote. They were still excluded from the commissioned ranks of the armed forces and from the learned professions. Nevertheless within half a dozen years the most objectionable and humiliating of the Penal Laws had been repealed.

Born on 6th August 1775, eldest son of Morgan and Catherine of Carhen, Daniel O'Connell had no personal experience of the rigours of the Penal Laws or of their less than rigorous implementation. But the former, burnt deep into the Catholic Irish consciousness, were and are remembered from one generation to another – with 'advantages'.

Daniel was soon put out to nurse with a peasant family named Moran. One of the objects of fosterage was to toughen up the sons of the gentry. There was plenty of potatoes, milk and fish, but meat was so scarce that when Morgan, on his son's return home, asked if he had ever eaten mutton, the boy answered the big, burly, snuff-taking stranger in Irish, 'Whenever my father killed one of Morgan O'Connell's sheep.' Like all peasants' small boys in Kerry, he wore always a *caulac* (girl's dress) because fairies are jealous of small boys and sometimes steal them away. Morgan thought this all wrong and, when Dan left the Morans, presented him with a boy's suit. A few hours later Dan was nowhere to be seen. He was eventually found tramping sturdily back to his foster-home, having resumed the *caulac*. At his parents' home, the first thing he had to do was to learn English.

He seems to have absorbed with his foster-mother's milk, and while playing and squabbling with his foster-brothers on the dung-smeared floor, while the rain drip-drip-dripped through the roof and the turf smoke stung their eyes, an understanding of their hopes and fears, loves and hatreds, which one day was to make him a great lawyer and a greater agitator, a leader of his people. He was not one of them, but once upon a time he had been, almost, and he could speak to them and for them, in their language or in his.

In the first half of the nineteenth century it was agreed among well-informed observers that the Irish peasant was the most wretched, in modern jargon 'deprived', in Europe. This was due mainly to sub-division of holdings caused by the inexorable pressure of population growth. There were no reliable demographic statistics, but most historians agree that during the latter part of the eighteenth century the population grew rather fast. The reasons for this are much debated (early marriage and higher birth-rate owing to increased potato cultivation, lower death-rate owing to the fading out of killer diseases), but there is no debate about its pernicious effect. In many cases competition for holdings and a whole series of middlemen, 'deputies of deputies of deputies', each taking his cut, between the cultivator of the land and the owner, who was often resident in Dublin, London or Bath (about a third were absentees), raised rents until many tenancies were marginal, only just better than landless destitution. But these conditions hardly applied during O'Connell's boyhood. The sub-division of holdings would not have become prevalent before the end of the century; the Kerry peasants could add fish to their potato and milk diet; most of their landlords, Protestant and Catholic, lived on their estates or in town houses no further away than Killarney. O'Connell was to give evidence before a parliamentary commission (in 1825) that in Cork landlord-tenant relations were bad, but in Kerry they were good. With rising agricultural output, and rising prices in Britain for agricultural produce, it is probable that in his boyhood the Kerry peasants were better off than at any time in the eighteenth and first half of the nineteenth centuries. But they would not have been human if they had not resented a rule which was more alien to them than to the semi-anglicised gentry; the law was not softened on their behalf by personal friendship with the Colonels; they *must* have hoped that one day, however distant, the Saxons would be packed off, bag and baggage, the old families and the old faith would prevail, and there would be no more rents to Protestants, nor enclosures of common land, nor tithes to Protestant parsons. But there was at that time no spirit of conscious nationalist revolt. Kerry was not a county notorious for attacks on landlords and rent-collectors, and even in 1798 there was not a whisper of rebellion there.

Morgan farmed on a fairly large scale, on his own land and on land rented from Trinity College and Lord Lansdowne. He also kept a general store in which could be bought anything from an anchor to a needle. A modern politician would have sought political credit by claiming to be the son of a grocer; not so O'Connell, who said of a detractor, 'The vagabond lies when he says I am of humble origin. My father's family was very ancient and my mother was a lady of the first rank.' The most that he would admit was that his father was a grazier or gentleman farmer.

Hunting Cap, rich and childless, had adopted Dan as his heir, so the boy spent more time at Derrynane than at Carhen. It lies

14

on the north shore of the Kenmare estuary, about two hundred yards from a long strand stretching from Derrynane harbour to Cahirdaniel Bay. Although the sea was close, it was out of sight except from the upper windows. Sand dunes sheltered the house against southerly gales, while woods and the steeply rising hillside protected it from other directions. There was no carriage road to the house: it could be reached only on foot or horseback, the baggage carried by pack-horses. It had the distinction of the only slate roof in the neighbourhood, but was solid and comfortable rather than grand, a family house rather than a 'gentleman's seat'. Built at the turn of the century, it had been altered, knocked about, a room built on here, a partition wall removed there, with no particular plan or architectural taste, so that it was neither Queen Anne, Georgian, nor any other distinctive style. A modern 'holiday home' would face the sea and the sun, but the O'Connells had to live there all the year round and think more of the winter rains beating at their windows; so the older part of Derrynane house turns its back to the sea and faces across a courtyard towards the hillside covered with indigenous forest – oak, beech, chestnut, birch, ash and rowan. The walls were thick, the windows small. It was three storeys high, the top floor rooms lighted by dormer windows. Offices, stables and outhouses were built round the courtyard, but there was no need for a coach-house.

Hunting Cap's tenants lived in scattered cabins and cultivated a strip, a quarter to a half mile wide, of agricultural land between the sea and the mountains. The fields are small, won by the labour of generations clearing away the rocks and building them into drystone walls out of which grow brambles, wild roses, blackthorns and fuchsias. Manured by black Kerry cattle and with seaweed brought up by donkeys, it is good land, but there is little of it. Above it towers for a thousand feet the steep mountainside, heather, gorse and bracken broken by smooth rock faces, supporting only long-legged, agile sheep and goats, grouse and strong mountain hares.

The nearest hamlet is Cahirdaniel, a couple of miles to the east across sand dunes and marshes which are now a wildfowl sanctuary. More important to Derrynane was its own harbour, a quarter mile to the west, much used by smugglers. Yachts now lie moored in its smooth water, a small trawler is often made fast

15

to the quay. The rocky Abbey Island – a peninsula except at high tide – breaks the force of the Atlantic storms. On the island are the ruins of a Cistercian abbey, in the graveyard of which lie many O'Connells. In the days of sail it was a hazardous job to bring in a ship of any size through the narrow, rockbound entrance, with no margin for error.

Only a glutton for boredom would wade through apocryphal tales of Dan's childhood, most of which make him out an insufferable little prig. He was, in fact, a brave boy: when attacked by a savage bull, instead of running away, which would have been fatal, he stood his ground and hurled a stone in the bull's face, thus giving himself time to clamber over a ditch to safety. As a boy Hunting Cap, heir to the estate, had been told, 'Visit the workmen, fish in a boat, ride and see herds and cattle, see waste grass and corn. Run, leap, play ball. You'll inform yourself and do your family a service.' Who can doubt that he brought up his nephew and heir on the same lines? On the flat meadow between the house and the sea the boys must have played hurley and football. At Carhen he caught many a trout in the stream at the back of the house. Off-shore, twenty-eight kinds of sea-fish could be caught, including oysters (sold at threepence a hundred) and fine turbot. Of course he went out with the fishermen and helped haul in their nets or pull cod and bass up on a hand line. When he was old enough to handle a gun, Hunting Cap's keeper took him out after grouse on the mountain, duck and snipe in the bog and woodcock which in winter flitted ghost-like between the trees in the woods round the house. Beagling became his favourite sport, hunting the hare on foot (since no one could ride there) on the steep mountainside. It was an incredibly tough sport, requiring tremendous strength of wind and limb to follow hounds uphill, and reckless courage in bounding down after them in great leaps, like a boulder falling down the mountain, trusting to luck that one would land on sound ground and not on stone or in a hole with a broken ankle. In later years he became a scientific 'hound man', studying problems of line, scent and breeding. He surely learned his hunting as a boy. In the evenings on festive occasions there would be *ceilidhs*, jigs and reels and songs to the music of pipe and fiddle.

3

Young Dan

After a grounding in the three Rs, Latin and Greek by an itinerant schoolmaster and the parish priest at Derrynane, and two years at Father Harrington's school in Cork, Dan's father and uncle had to consider his career. They would have been disappointed had he wished to be a priest, but fortunately he had no vocation and perhaps rather an eye for a pretty girl. The Irish Brigade was no longer an option, for in the early 1790s the French king's foreign mercenaries, traditionally royalist, were in disrepute with the men in Paris who were dismantling the *ancien régime*. Dan's uncle, General Count O'Connell, volunteered to use the Irish, Swiss and Swedes to end all this revolutionary nonsense with a whiff of grape-shot, but the placid, indecisive Louis XVI could not bring himself to sanction anything so drastic. However the General advised his brother that the schools in France still offered the best available education to the sons of Irish Catholics, and he himself would keep an eye on the progress and (very important to Hunting Cap) the finances of Dan and his younger brother, Maurice. So they left home in 1790 for France.

The O'Connells might be conservative in their political attitudes and thoroughly loyal, for one reason or another, to King George III; but they were indubitably Irish. So, on the Channel crossing, the two boys heard unmoved a French passenger trying to get a rise out of them by abusing the perfidy of the English. Irritated by what he thought to be *le flegme britannique*, he rounded on them.

17

'Do you hear? Do you understand what I am saying?'

'Yes,' replied Dan placidly, 'I hear. I comprehend you perfectly.'

'Yet you do not seem angry.'

'Not in the least. England is not my country. Censure her as much as you like, you cannot offend me. I am an Irishman, and my countrymen have as little reason as yours have to love England – perhaps less.' It was his first recorded declaration of political principle.

At Dr Stapleton's school at St Omer the boys were taught Latin, Greek, English, French, Geography, music, drawing, dancing and fencing, with an emphasis on English and rhetoric; mathematics was an extra, at a guinea a month. There was a small stage on which the boys acted plays. The threepence a week which Hunting Cap allowed them as pocket-money did not go far, but on the credit side there was no ban on eating meat during Lent, perhaps because the revolutionary ferment made it difficult to obtain fish. On the whole, however, Dan approved of Dr Stapleton's academy, and certainly Dr Stapleton approved of Dan – second in Latin, Greek and English examinations, eleventh in French. Reporting on Maurice as a decent, run of the mill, extrovert sort of lad, he prophesied that Dan was 'destined to make a remarkable figure in society'.

After nineteen months at St Omer, in August 1792 the brothers moved on to the English College at Douai. Dan's first letter from Douai mentions what was to be a recurring theme in his correspondence for the rest of his life – shortage of money. However much he had, it was never enough. Second helpings at dinner cost four guineas a term extra.

> We would be much obliged to you for leave to get them, but this is as you please. I hope, my dear uncle, that you will not think me troublesome in saying so much on these heads; you may be convinced it is only a desire of satisfying you and letting you know in what way your money is spent that makes me do so.

Although the laundry was also an extra, soft soap was evidently not in short supply, and Dan did not spare it.

It was a bad time to be at a seminary with clerical associations.

A hostile crowd of soldiers and civilians shouted opprobrious epithets at them, *'Jeunes Jésuites! Capucines!'* When Louis XVI was beheaded in January 1793, the General, who had joined the royal forces in exile, decided it was time his nephews made a bolt for it. This they did, sporting large tricolour cockades which they threw into the sea as soon as they were clear of Calais. On board were two Irish brothers named Sheares, lawyers, scions of an Ascendancy family from Cork, who entered the saloon in a high state of exaltation from watching the king's head being cut off. 'By bribing two of the National Guard to lend us their uniforms, we obtained a most excellent view of the entire scene.'

'But in God's name,' asked an English passenger, 'how could you endure to witness such a hideous spectacle?'

'From love of the Cause!'

In 1798 both were to be hanged for love of the cause.

O'Connell* in middle age used to tell the story with revulsion, and most biographers attribute to his experiences at this time his horror of violence for political ends. This seems rather far-fetched, as he did not actually see anything horrid in France. The atrocities and reprisals in Ireland must have made a far greater impact upon him.

The boys arrived in London with nothing but the clothes they wore, so Hunting Cup was put to the expense of buying them complete new outfits, itemised to the last penny by Dan. Within two months he had to apologise for their 'foolish and ungrateful conduct' in spending, without permission, *nine guineas* of their dear uncle's money.

> You have seen [by a previous letter] only a part of that sorrow which I was not able to express as I wished. No one can be more convinced than I am of the justice of your anger against us. You have done everything for us, and we have shown no advantage from it. I shall not, my dear uncle, take up your time in making promises. That would be childish. I shall only beg to assure you of my regret.

But the problem of the boys' future had again to be faced.

* In future, whenever reference is made to 'O'Connell', it must be understood as applying to Daniel O'Connell, the Liberator; other members of the family will be designated by their Christian names, ranks or nicknames.

It was more easily solved than in 1790. With the outbreak of war, the government had shown an almost indecent haste in propitiating Catholics, not only to buy off trouble in Ireland but to enable a Protestant Britain to appear in French, Austrian and Spanish eyes as the defender of the Faith against republican atheism. The Irish parliament's Catholic Relief Acts of 1792 and 1793[1] extended to Papists the forty-shilling freehold franchise, which was more than English Catholics had. The term 'freeholder' was applied to both owner-occupiers and a far larger class of leaseholders for one or more lives.* To qualify for the franchise a man had to swear either that he owned land worth forty shillings a year, or that he leased freehold land worth forty shillings a year after payment of rent.[2]

More relevantly to O'Connell's immediate interests, the Acts allowed Catholics to hold commissions up to and including the rank of Colonel in the army and Captain in the navy; to become Justices of the Peace, jurymen and Grand Jurymen; to bear arms; to take degrees at Trinity College; and to be called to the Bar. Although a long clause enumerated the prizes still withheld – Papists could not sit in either House of parliament or be judges, Privy Councillors, Generals, Admirals or King's Counsel – most Catholic gentry thought this handsome, including Hunting Cap who was made a J.P. and Deputy Governor of Kerry with authority to call out the militia after he had taken the new and not objectionable (although distasteful) Oath of Allegiance.

Maurice, it was decided, at the age of seventeen was perfectly good cannon-fodder. He was commissioned into one of the Irish regiments which were being raised at the instigation of his uncle, the General (now a Colonel in the British army), for service in the West Indies. Within four years he was dead, an item in the appalling statistics of casualties from yellow fever. Dan would read for the Bar.

He would have preferred to study in Dublin where (he explained to Hunting Cap) the cost of living was much lower than in London, and from where he would have been able to spend his vacations in Derrynane, studying without urban distractions

---

* The Encyclopedia Britannica defines 'freeholder' as 'the owner of a substantial interest in land of indefinite duration'. A lease for a number of years would not constitute a freehold, but a lease for a number of lives would.

and with ample opportunity to profit from his dear uncle's example. He enclosed a list of absolutely essential London expenses, calculated to the last halfpenny. However there were as yet no facilities for reading for the Bar in Dublin, so he entered Lincoln's Inn, and Hunting Cap must have come up to scratch to receive

> the most heartfelt thanks for the additional instance ... of that more than paternal goodness with which you have incessantly honoured us ... I have not gone to one single place of entertainment since I came to London ... P.S. It may be necessary to remark that I am perhaps the only law student in London without a watch, but this is a thing which may be done without.

He prudently omitted to mention that he had joined the Honourable Society of Cogers, a radical social and debating club. Since bald old Jack Wilkes was a senior member, it can be assumed that club meetings were convivial occasions. O'Connell spoke often in debates, and acquired great fluency, but reproached himself for the time and money it cost him. However, he did not give it up – he was never one for self-denial – and with John Philpot Curran also a member, the debates must have been lively.

O'Connell had arrived in London, from France, almost a Tory, but then he attended the trial for treason of the radical Thomas Hardy, secretary of the London Corresponding Society. The trumped-up charge, sympathy for the underdog and the spectacle of reactionary Toryism running scared and turning nasty made him almost a radical.

There was no formal instruction for law students, no lectures, no required course of reading. He had to eat his quota of dinners; get all four volumes of Blackstone's Commentaries almost off by heart; read, mark, learn, and inwardly digest dozens of more weighty tomes – *Coke on Littleton* and Hale's *Pleas of the Crown*, Gilbert's *Law of Evidence* and Jacob's *New Law Dictionary*, volume after volume on case law, constitutional law and abridged statutes. 'I see a very wide field before me and no landmarks to guide my steps.'

He would go mad if he read nothing but law, so he joined a

21

circulating library (one guinea) which gave him the use of more than 30,000 books. 'By this means I relax my mind with the study of history and Belles Lettres.' Most young men of nineteen would not find Tom Paine's *Age of Reason* and *Rights of Man*, Godwin's *Political Justice*, Rousseau's *Confessions*, Hume's *Works*, Voltaire's *Essays* or Mary Woolstonecraft's *Rights of Women* markedly relaxing to the mind. Compared to these, Gibbon's *Decline and Fall* and the Bible were positively light, to be devoured a dozen chapters at a sitting. But O'Connell, a child of the eighteenth century and a glutton for punishment, steeped himself in progressive literature.

His journal abounds in disquisitions on virtue, vice, happiness, justice, crime, punishment, religion, together with self-reproaches for staying up until the small hours, and in bed until noon. Nevertheless he found time, between sleeping, working and reading, to begin a novel about George III's rumoured son by Hannah Lightfoot, the 'Fair Quakeress'. How many bad novels have been written about that non-existent person? Fortunately O'Connell's was never completed. Judging by the style and content of his journal, it would have been unreadable; the journal is painfully introspective, for O'Connell never tired of examining his thoughts, feelings and imperfections – notably indolence, unpunctuality, a tendency never to do anything today which can be put off till tomorrow.

After two moves, he settled in a boarding house near Chiswick in which (he assured his dear uncle) the other lodgers were prudent, middle-aged people of respectable rank. The only one of his own age, who became a friend for life, was a Protestant law student from Co. Wexford, Richard Newton Bennett, who was, he told Hunting Cap, a paragon of virtue, besides being of good family and fortune. 'I hope, nay I flatter myself, that when we meet again the success of my efforts to correct those bad habits which you have pointed out will be apparent.'

Each lodger had a large, commodious apartment to himself. The landlady was 'extremely deformed, with a hump before and behind' and no teeth in her upper jaw. But she was highly intelligent, spoke French and Italian, was competent at history, knew a great deal about the stage and everything about the English Peerage. She had a problem: 'She is at all times familiar, but when heated with drinking, she is rude in her familiarities.' It is when O'Connell stops being introspective and philosophical, and turns his pen to describing people and events, that his journal comes to life.

He made the long journey to Derrynane for the 1795 summer vacation, and Hunting Cap's characteristic observations to his mother indicate that, for all his reading, he had not lost his capacity for enjoyment.

Your son left this house ten days ago and took with him my favourite horse. Had it not been for that, I might have dispensed with his company. He is, I am told, employed in visiting the seats of hares at Keelrelig, the earths of foxes at Tarmons, the caves of otters at Bohus, and the celebration of Miss Burke's wedding at Direen – useful avocations for a nominal student of law! The many indications he has given of a liberal mind in the expenditure of money has left a vacuum in my purse, as well as an impression on my mind not easily eradicated.

Just under six foot tall, big-boned, with dark curly hair, blue-grey eyes and a boyish smile, O'Connell was a striking young man. As he did not take the exercise available to young gentlemen in London, riding, rowing, fencing, boxing, he was rather plump; only in Kerry did he keep his figure under control. He was a good talker, full of humour, anecdote and fun, the life and soul of a party. But though he would go along with any diversion or escapade, he was at this stage a follower rather than a leader; and Hunting Cap was to reproach him (of course Hunting Cap would) for being too easily led astray by cronies. Like most country gentlemen of his day, he spoke with a marked provincial accent, in his case the soft, sing-song brogue, not unlike Welsh, of Kerry, on which was sometimes superimposed the trace of a French accent. He was attractive to women. His most pious biographer admits that before marriage he was not a model of virtue, and he himself described his affections as ardent, but capricious and wavering. But he kept his successes to himself: his journal contains none of the sexual adventures and misadventures which put Boswell's London diary into the best-seller lists. Only once does he admit to being even tempted, by the mistress of a friend with whom he dined.

She is a fine young woman. She seemed to be partial to me, and I endeavoured to improve that partiality. She is a most debauched woman ... she acted the part of the inamorata ... However, I have little chance of ever being able to profit by her good graces, did I possess them, for want of an opportunity.

Holding hands with another young lady at a party led to angry words with a young brewer's son named Thompson. Words led to blows, blows to Bennett being sent to Thompson 'with a message'. But Thompson's father, a respectable bourgeois, called a constable and O'Connell was obliged to give security to keep the peace. He reflected at length in his journal:

I know that duelling is a vice, yet there is a certain charm in the independence which it bestows on a man ... The General scolded me very much.... He spoke of my folly in being a democrat, of my absurdity in displaying my political opinions. He railed at me for not having returned the blow. Now, if I had struck Thompson, he certainly would have blamed me as much, if not more. He would then say with justice that there was a more gentlemanlike method of revenging an injury than that of fighting with cudgels like common porters etc. etc.

There were other dangers in wait for a young Irishman in London. A smooth citizen named Hobson tried to persuade him to join in signing a post-obit bond for £1,200 for the benefit of a youth named Fullarton who was due to inherit £30,000 from an uncle. For the first, and indeed last, time in his life O'Connell displayed the rudiments of financial prudence.

Now Fullarton is only 17. He may die before he comes of age. After he comes of age, he may refuse to pay on a plea of non-age. Hobson may, and I suppose he will, become a bankrupt; so thus I should possibly be saddled with the debt. Add to this, the chance of the transaction coming to my uncle's knowledge ... Any intimacy with this man [Hobson] is dangerous. I must therefore shun him.

Like any young radical law student, he took an enlightened

view of crime and punishment, pointing out that the full weight of the law fell upon the poor while the misdemeanours of the rich were subject only to mild reprobation.

> On Friday I attended at the Old Bailey. Two highwaymen were tried and found guilty. Now if these unfortunate individuals are hanged, will one more virtue be infused into the bosom of any individual? Will one crime less be committed? Certainly not ... Oh Justice, what horrors are committed in thy name!

He had just read sixty pages of Godwin's *Political Justice* which denounced not only punishment but laws, property and marriage too. Heady stuff!

He had a taste for good claret, which on at least one occasion resulted in his spending an uncomfortable night in the watch-house. This was not, unfortunately, matched by a strong head or, rather, stomach, which was awkward, for the social mores of the day still required a host to ply his guests with wine until they vomited. But O'Connell rebelled against custom, and found that many of his contemporaries agreed with him. The age of really heavy drinking, when William Hickey, Colonel Arthur Wellesley and six 'as strong headed fellows as could be found in Hindustan' each put away at a single sitting over thirty bumpers 'in glasses of considerable magnitude', was coming to an end. Nevertheless two years later, in deep penitence during an excruciating hang-over, O'Connell resolved yet again to remember the weakness of his flesh:

> Many find a vicious pleasure in drinking, but punishment soon awaits them; stupidity, sickness and contempt are in the train of this gratification. How feelingly ought I to write on this subject – I, whose head aches, whose stomach is nauseated, and whose reflections are embittered in consequence of last night's debauch. Oh ... let me forever retain the salutary hatred which I now feel against this odious vice!

Experience of the world and of the Irish Bar was to develop the critical, indeed cynical, side of his mind. But in London he swallowed whole all the political and religious claptrap fashionable in his circle. He was, of course, a Deist, writing platitudes about the First Cause, the Supreme Being, the God of Nature. This was certainly incompatible with being a Catholic, for the God of the Deists – in Voltaire's words, the great geometrician, the architect of the universe – would never have countenanced a business so bungled as a virgin giving birth in a stable.

He was never a slave to the truth, but was inclined to say one thing to Smith, another to Ryan, one today, another tomorrow. He recognised this fault in himself, and wished 'it was within my power to get rid entirely of all propensity to falsehood ... I now form the resolution of not departing from the truth in any instance tomorrow.' A modest enough resolution, one might think.

By the end of the Lenten Term of 1796 he had consumed enough dinners to convince the luminaries of Lincoln's Inn of his aptitude for the Bar. He must think of returning to Dublin to continue his studies at the King's Inn. But first there was a problem – his insolvency, debts and travelling expenses, which he must confess in full to his dear uncle: 'with you all low cunning would be as base as it is useless. Your liberality takes away the will as your penetration does the means of deceit.'

4

Dublin and 1798

Dublin, where he arrived on 12th May 1796, was no mean city. Indeed it was one of the finest capitals in Europe with a population of about 180,000, more than any British city except London. It had a magnificent range of public buildings – the Four Courts, the Royal Exchange, Trinity College, the Rotunda, Parliament House, the great Customs House beside the Liffey. Forty years of labours by the Wide Streets Commission had given it roomy, well-planned thoroughfares on a north-south axis down what is now O'Connell Street, over what is now O'Connell Bridge to St Stephen's Green. The supremely elegant Merrion and Rutland Squares were nearly complete, and progress was being made on the equally satisfying Fitzwilliam and Mountjoy Squares. Parliament – a Protestant parliament for a Catholic people – attracted most of the 247 peers, 22 bishops and 300 members of the House of Commons during the sessions; they were housed in fine terraced houses, and no fewer than ninety-six wealthy peers had splendid town mansions filled with the souvenirs of Grand Tours, with products of English factories designed by Wyatt and Adam and Chippendale and Angelica Kauffman, and with handsome, rather more ornate, Irish furniture. To cater for the needs of the elegant upper crust there were forty coach-building factories and a hundred firms employing craftsmen specialising in decorative plasterwork. There were silversmiths, glass factories and flourishing theatres, though perhaps not quite as flourishing as in the days when Garrick and Mrs Siddons had appeared there.

27

Through the middle of the city from east to west ebbed and flowed the Liffey, not yet a public sewer. (Indeed Dublin did not boast a public sewer.)

There was another side to it. Dublin was notorious for its bucks and its gamesters and for duellists who would shoot a man, or be shot, for the most frivolous reasons. There were slums as dreadful as any depicted by Hogarth, and beggars so numerous that it was a convention to include at least one in every print or engraving of the Dublin scene. To refresh the notoriously thirsty population there were 2,000 ale houses, 300 taverns, and 1,200 grog shops.

Dublin's traditional seat of learning was Trinity College. It was also a seat of drinking, whoring, advanced radical politics and rioting so uninhibited that on one occasion, when the lads were ducking a bailiff, the plaintive voice of a professor was heard: 'Gentlemen! I implore you not to nail his ears to the pump!' Learning of a more restrained kind was promoted by the Royal Irish Academy and the Royal Dublin Society, the former specialising in the study of Irish history and antiquities, the latter in the training of artists and sculptors.

Dublin had never been a Gaelic Irish city. It was built by Danes, Normans, English, Dutch and Huguenots, and until the Restoration the population had been mainly Protestant. Now it was perhaps four-fifths Catholic, but it was still governed by and largely for Protestants. Every member of parliament was a Protestant; the Mayor and every member of the Corporation; all the judges; nearly all the members of Trinity College, senior and junior; and nearly all barristers.

There was nothing about Dublin which a young man newly arrived from London could disparage as provincial – except, perhaps, that the Irish parliament was hardly a galaxy of talent. Henry Grattan, the Whig Opposition member, eloquent, witty, generous, popular and respected, was nearly a great parliamentarian; the Tory Lord Chancellor, John Fitzgibbon, was a singularly crafty and ruthless political bruiser. Otherwise the Irish peers and M.P.s were of modest parts, and their parliament was described as being to the Westminster parliament as a monkey is to a man. Really able Irish politicians like Edmund Burke and, in his eccentric, alcoholic way, Richard Brinsley Sheridan, were more likely to be found at Westminster than in College Green.

But these imperfections were not, perhaps, apparent to young O'Connell, who retained in retrospect a sentimental attachment to 'Grattan's Parliament' (as it was called in tribute to its most distinguished member) which it did not deserve, especially after it had been induced by bribes to commit suicide.

O'Connell had hitherto shown very little interest in politics; or, rather, his interest was general and theoretical, not practical; he was zealous for the Rights of Man, but not particularly interested in the rights of the freeholders of Iveragh. There is hardly a reference to practical, everyday politics in his London journal. But in Dublin he was in the thick of politics of the most exhilarating kind, with no one acting quite as posterity thought he should.

Grattan's parliament had, by the Catholic Relief Acts of 1782, 1792 and 1793, defused, temporarily, Catholic discontent. However, the fact that Catholic forty-shilling freeholders had the vote did not mean that they – any more than Protestant forty-shilling freeholders – could use it as they pleased. Freeholders were expected, as in Britain, to vote according to their landlord's instructions. A landlord, like a present-day T.U.C. baron, had a sort of block vote, large or small depending on the number of his tenants who held freehold landed property worth forty shillings a year after payment of rent; and the first reaction of politically-minded landlords to the Catholic Relief Act of 1793 had been to convert as many leases as possible from a term of years to a term of one or more lives.[1] In 1430, when an income from land of forty shillings a year had been judged by parliament to be a proper qualification for the vote, it had conferred on the freeholder a degree of independence; but three hundred and fifty years later a 'forty-shillinger' could be a very poor man, vulnerable to landlord pressure. Since a landlord's political power depended on the number of voters he could produce at elections, 'forty shillings' was liberally interpreted. A landlord used his block vote to further a political cause, or to advance his own and his family's interests, or both. This arrangement was part of the normal landlord-tenant relationship, and most people in the 1790s thought there was nothing much wrong in it, political power being based essentially on the ownership of land. Even fifty years later, after the passing of the 1832 Reform Act, O'Connell expected a landlord who favoured the Liberal cause to order his tenants to vote for it: 'he can *command* them.'[2]

Two out of three Irish M.P.s sat for boroughs,[3] of which there were a wide variety, each clinging jealously to rights conferred by a charter granted by the Stuarts or earlier. Of thirty-three Irish boroughs, eighteen were 'closed' or 'pocket' boroughs, untroubled by elections of any kind. Fifteen were so-called 'open' boroughs which were not infrequently contested, but many of these were more or less controlled by the 'interest' of some local, generally Tory, magnate. Each was run by a Corporation, wholly Protestant since common counsellors and aldermen had to take an oath denouncing the doctrine of transubstantiation, and describing as impious and idolatrous invocations to the Blessed Virgin Mary and other Saints. Some Corporations were elected on a very restricted franchise, others were virtually self-elected. The Corporations chose the Freemen (who had a parliamentary vote) and the Sheriffs (who 'pricked' jurymen, very important in cases with political implications). The franchise, both for the Corporations and for parliament, was infinitely varied. In some boroughs only Freemen had the vote; in others, all substantial householders; in yet others it extended to all 'potwallopers', i.e. anyone with a cooking hearth. Often the franchise was restricted to men residing within the boundaries of the borough as they were when the charter was granted. But in one way or another, every borough was run by a small, self-perpetuating Protestant oligarchy. In 'open' boroughs that oligarchy selected the M.P.; in 'closed' or 'pocket' boroughs they were told whom to select by the borough-owner, a neighbouring county magnate, perhaps, or the owner of most of the borough's house property.

Grattan would have liked to remove all disabilities imposed on Catholics, but this was too much for parliament to swallow: the gentlemen of the Ascendancy would do almost anything to gratify their Catholic friends and neighbours except share power with them. Catholics like Hunting Cap, his brothers and most of his friends were suitably grateful, and confident that if they made no trouble and were assiduous in showing their loyalty, sooner or later they would be allowed to enter parliament.

The other achievement of Grattan's parliament had been to end its subordination to the British parliament. The parliament at Westminster had been able to annul Acts of the parliament at Dublin and even to legislate directly for Ireland. That was so no longer. Britain and Ireland were now two independent states, equal in status, linked only by their common allegiance to King George III. That was the theory, that was Grattan's ideal, and to that O'Connell was later to dedicate himself. It was a concept with which we have become familiar in our own day, for before the character of the British Commonwealth changed after the 1939–45 war, Canada, Australia and New Zealand were perfectly satisfied with this 'dominion status'. It worked rather well.

In the eighteenth century the reality was quite different. The governing factors in politics were not principles, policies or public opinion, but personal friendship, family relationships, appointments and sinecures, favours given and received – all that the eighteenth century termed 'interest', by which those who controlled the voters, particularly in 'closed' boroughs, could be influenced. Some boroughmongers as a matter of principle always supported the king's government; others were obdurate in opposition; but there were a large number of floaters who might be induced, by 'civility', 'bustle', 'management' or, as a last resort, 'expense', to side with the Crown, whose resources of patronage were unrivalled. There were other centres of patronage – for instance those with church livings in their gift – but the Crown's patronage was infinitely greater, since it included naval and military promotions, Lord Lieutenancies, peerages, jobs and sinecures at Court, appointments in the civil service, post office and revenue, Admiralty contracts, and bishoprics. So the theory and practice of eighteenth-century government was that the king chose the Prime Minister and then, to enable him to manage parliament and run the country, put the Crown patronage at his disposal. A Prime Minister with the confidence of the king need fear no adverse vote in parliament save in the most extraordinary circumstances, such as defeat in America, when public indignation overcame patronage. To us, cleansed and purified by universal suffrage, these practices are very shocking; but even politicians must live, and in O'Connell's day they had no parliamentary salaries, allowances, expense accounts, directorates or trade union pensions to sustain them.

In Ireland the Crown patronage was exercised at second hand. The Prime Minister at Westminster chose the Lord Lieutenant and Irish executive who governed the country by the judicious use of the Irish patronage. From Church of Ireland bishops and

judges to postmasters, surveyors and tidewaiters, the Castle*
appointed them all, invariably with a view to political advantage.
Of the 300 members of Grattan's parliament, about one-third
were placemen or pensioners of the Crown, which gave the executive its hard core of reliable support. Furthermore, 172 members represented more or less rotten boroughs, with few or no
electors, the property of about one hundred boroughmongers.
Provided these one hundred gentlemen could also be gratified by
attentions, civilities, places and pensions for themselves, their
friends and relations, the Castle need fear no evil. Parliamentary
management in Dublin was child's play compared to Westminster, where fewer than one in ten of the Commons were placemen,
and the proportion of members for rotten boroughs was less than
one in three. The Lord Lieutenant and the executive were responsible not to the Irish parliament but to the British government, which appointed and could at any time dismiss them.

It was, complained Grattan, a 'creeping union'. Only once did
the Irish parliament make a bid for freedom, with unhappy
results. During the Royal Malady of 1788-9 it offered the Re-
gency to the Prince of Wales before the Westminster parliament
made the offer. Alas, before its emissaries arrived in London, the
royal patient recovered and the gentlemen from Dublin were
made to look rather foolish as they were dismissed by His Royal
Highness with urbane thanks.

Middle-class Protestants with radical leanings, especially the
Presbyterians of Belfast who were inclined to republicanism, were
outraged at their position. Not being of the Ascendancy, they
benefited little from the patronage. They, like O'Connell, were
steeped in the works of Tom Paine, Rousseau, Voltaire, Godwin.
They took very much to heart the fact that they had no say in
the way their country was governed. Parliamentary reform was
their panacea, i.e. widening the franchise even as far as one
(middle-class) man one vote in order to destroy the power of the
boroughmongers, together with such stock radical nostrums as
annual elections and the elimination, root and branch, of sinecures and pensions. Just as the American revolution had stimulated their fathers, so they were given a tremendous boost by the

* The executive was commonly known as the Castle, because its headquarters
and secretariat were in Dublin Castle.

French Revolution which brought their class to power overnight; and while Whigs like Burke were horrified by the Terror, radicals like O'Connell's shipboard acquaintances, the Sheares brothers, accepted that you could not make an omelette without breaking eggs.

So here was the basis of a radical, even a republican, revolutionary party. They were nearly all Protestant and middle class, many were lawyers. Parliamentary reform, many thought, should include giving the franchise to all respectable people, and emancipation to Catholics. This was very much in the tradition of the Volunteers, only more so, and many leading lights of the movement were or had been Volunteers.

Typical of these radical Protestants was a spirited, lively young Dubliner named Wolfe Tone, a lightweight, perhaps, but a brave and attractive one. Disappointed in his hopes of a commission in the British army or the army of the East India Company, he threw himself with zest into political agitation, and in 1792 accepted the post of secretary to the Catholic Committee which from time to time petitioned (in the most respectful way) for Catholics' disabilities to be lightened. Up to that time, he admitted, he was not socially acquainted with a single Catholic.

It obviously made sense for radical and republican Protestants to make common cause with Catholics, who had their own reasons for discontent. To this end was formed the Society of United Irishmen, which held its first meeting in Belfast on 18th October 1791. Its objects were parliamentary reform, equal rights for Catholics and Protestants, and (after 1794) an independent republic separate from England. What it lacked was mass appeal outside its homeland, Counties Down and Antrim. It was strong in intellectual eminence, but weak in muscle.

Through the eighteenth century Ireland had learned to live with gangs of peasant terrorists to whom were given the generic name of Whiteboys. (This was the name of one terrorist society: there were dozens of them.) Bound to secrecy by horrific oaths, they shot a few landlords, pitchforked a few bailiffs, drowned a few tithe-proctors in bogs, burned houses and ricks, and houghed cattle and horses belonging to those whom they saw as oppressors. Their outrages were localised and spasmodic; nowhere did they constitute more than a tolerable nuisance (except, of course, to their immediate victims). They were not really political, and

33

not consciously nationalist. In modern terms, they were against 'the system' but not against the government, to which, indeed, they looked in an incoherent way (and in vain) for protection against the system. They often proclaimed their loyalty to King George. But in the north-eastern counties rural terrorists had more political and sectarian motivation. The Protestant Peep-o'-Day Boys conducted sporadic guerilla warfare against the Catholic Defenders, and the latter acquired the character of an anti-Protestant, anti-English resistance movement. It was to them that the United Irishmen began to make approaches.

It was a curious and complicated situation. The Defenders were linked to the United Irishmen, who were linked to the Volunteers, who were linked to the Peep-o'-Day Boys, who were fighting the Defenders.

To the Castle the United Irishmen were at first no more dangerous than the radical clubs and corresponding societies which proliferated in England in the early 1790s. The Defenders were a minor nuisance, but no more so than the Whiteboys and similar groups of homicidal peasants. A greater danger was perceived from the Volunteers, a pale shadow of the proud Volunteers of 1782, but nevertheless armed, so in 1793 they were disbanded. In their place were raised a militia, for which recruits were taken by compulsory ballot, and a volunteer cavalry, known as the yeomanry, formed by local magnates and composed mainly of better-off farmers, disproportionately Protestant, who owned horses and were considered politically reliable.

War with France broke out in February 1793. Again there rose the spectre of French invasion supported by Irish dissidents, who this time would be not Jacobites but Jacobin republicans. Both the United Irishmen and the Defenders now seemed, and indeed were, dangerously subversive. In July 1793 there was a battle between Defenders and militia in County Wexford.

Through 1794 and 1795 Defenderism spread southwards, together with the administration of republican oaths, all the paraphernalia of secret recognition signs and passwords, the intimidation of juries, the cutting down of trees to make pike-shafts and raiding for arms. The Lord Lieutenant, Lord Fitzwilliam, favoured Catholic emancipation, but in February 1795 Fitzgibbon's representations in London bore fruit and Fitzwilliam was replaced by Lord Camden who took a much harder line.

A development ominous for the future occurred in September 1795 when the Peep-o'-Day Boys reformed as the Orange Society.

In March 1796, just before O'Connell arrived in Dublin, parliament passed the Insurrection Act, the main effect of which was to make it easier for troops – there were, it must be remembered, virtually no police – to ransack houses in searches for arms, a freedom of which they took full advantage. Links between the United Irishmen and the Defenders became closer, and the former were developing a military organisation and chain of command. Throughout, the government was well informed about the United Irishmen by a founder member, a lawyer who, while briefing the Castle about their every move, was also briefed to defend in court any who were prosecuted. The French were less well informed, suggesting to Wolfe Tone, who was in Paris trying to expedite a French invasion, that Fitzgibbon might be helpful to the Cause. Besides Tone, the most prominent United Irishman in Leinster and Munster was Lord Edward FitzGerald, son of the Duke of Leinster, a former officer of the British army who had fought with great gallantry against the Americans but, before resigning his commission, had taken to calling himself 'Citizen FitzGerald' and had suggested that the army adopt the *Marseillaise* as its march.

On 21st December 1796 the great day dawned. Thirty-six French ships, carrying about seven thousand troops including Wolfe Tone in French Colonel's uniform, beat into Bantry Bay. Very glad they were to reach it, for an Atlantic gale had sunk one ship, scattered the rest and sent the Admiral, the general officer commanding and half the troops ignominiously back to France. So there they lay anchored off Beare Island, buffeted by the gale, sodden, cold and sea-sick, wondering what to do next. Opposed to them were only four hundred men of the Galway militia stationed in Bantry and the local yeomanry called out by Mr Richard White. From Bantry, and from Hunting Cap in Derrynane, messengers galloped all night over the snow-bound roads to Cork. If the French had landed, and marched quickly on Cork, nothing could have stopped them reaching it before regular reinforcements arrived. But they did not land, and by 3rd January they had all departed. As Tone noted in his diary, the English had not had such an escape since the Armada.

The most interesting and, to the Castle, encouraging feature of the whole business had been the attitude of the West Cork and Kerry peasantry. Not only had they not risen as Wolfe Tone had promised they would, but 'their good will, zeal and activity', wrote General Dalrymple to the king, 'exceeds all description.' Somehow – could it have been through crafty government propaganda? – the Catholic peasantry associated the French with those who, it was understood, had invited them over – the Peep-o'-Day Boys and Orangemen of Ulster.

O'Connell's views on the United Irishmen were mixed. He thoroughly approved of their ideas on franchise reform and, of course, on Catholic emancipation. But he was no republican. His family and all their Kerry friends and neighbours had always been royalists, though differing perhaps on the delicate subject of which king should command their loyalty. We do not know what he thought, at this time, of the link with England; later he was to advocate the policy of Henry Grattan – that Ireland and England should be equal, independent, separate countries linked by common allegiance to one king. He viewed with horror the increasing violence by troops and Defenders. In his ideas about Ireland there was certainly no place for French soldiers.

On 29th December 1796 he wrote in his journal, almost casually, after expatiating for a page or two on Dr Johnson, jealousy, genius and patriotism:

> The French fleet is arrived in Bantry Bay.... The French will perhaps meet with a greater resistance than they have been in all probability led to believe ... Liberty is in my bosom less a principle than a passion. But I know that the victories of the French would be attended with bad consequences. The Irish people are not yet sufficiently enlightened to be able to bear the sun of freedom. Freedom would soon dwindle into licentiousness. They would rob; they would murder. The altar of liberty totters when it is cemented only with blood, when it is supported only with carcases.

Besides, the invasion, as he wrote in a later letter, would have 'shook the foundations of all property and destroyed our profession root and branch'. He ended this day by attending a meeting of the Historical Society where he denounced the partition of ancient Greece. 'I spoke pretty well.'

Dublin took it less calmly. The streets were full of regulars, militia and yeomanry, marching and drilling and guarding government buildings. There was a rush to volunteer, which produced even a company of gouty old gentlemen who paraded in Merrion Square in sedan chairs, their muskets sticking out of the windows. A crack corps of yeomanry was the Lawyers' Artillery Corps, and O'Connell, infected like everyone else by the prevailing excitement and desire to have a shot at the French, queued up to join it. On 2nd January he was enlisted: 'I have this day written to my uncle to get leave – that is in fact money – to enter into this corps.'

No letter required more careful drafting. After a general description of all the alarms and excursions, he brought up his own wishes.

Every man capable of bearing arms has taken them up. In the midst of this general fermentation you must not be surprised if my inclinations tend to run with the current .... I am now the only young man as far as I can learn of the body of lawyers or students of the law who has not entered into some corps. [Actually he already had.] It is for you to say what I am to do. It has been industriously propagated that such men as did not enter the corps would be marked by government ... Tho' a man should escape the notice of government he cannot avoid that of his companions. I am young, active, healthy and single. What excuse can I then possibly make? ... I need not add that your decision will be religiously obeyed. Yet I must suggest the necessity of my quitting Dublin should your decision be contrary to my wishes. If I remain here, I may perhaps incur the disgrace of being forced to march as a common soldier in the ... militia for which they are going to ballot. But the whole of my conduct rests with you, should you consent to my going into any corps it will be necessary to inform you that I could not afford the expense attending it out of my allowance; and that the corps into which I should wish to enter would be the Lawyers' artillery as the best regulated and the least expensive. On the uniform coat there is no lace at all so that it is made up for about £4 whereas the coat of the Lawyers' infantry, all

37

bedaubed with lace, costs £9!! I could not enter into the latter without incurring an expense of about £30 whereas, in the former, the expense should not exceed £20. I shall expect your instructions with impatience.

After remarking that the French fleet had sailed to the north-ward where 'they will meet with many friends' (i.e. Ulster Presbyterians), he concluded:

If I should have expressed myself with too much ardour on the subject of taking up arms, I hope, my dear Uncle, you will pardon me. Surrounded as I am with young men whom the moment has inspired with enthusiasm; with the blood of youth boiling in my veins, you will not be surprised that I should be more than usually animated ... P.S. I could quit any corps I now entered as soon as the danger of invasion was over and, the coat of the artillery corps being blue, by taking off the facings it would be serviceable.

No letter of O'Connell reveals more clearly the mixture in his character of enthusiasm, follow-my-leadership, cool calculation, knowledge of human nature and a tendency to be economical of the truth. If his dear uncle realised that he had joined up *before* asking permission ... !

All was in vain. No one could desire more than Hunting Cap the defeat of the Jacobin French but he was supporting his nephew in Dublin to qualify for a profession, not to play expensively at soldiers. Curtly he refused permission.

O'Connell was in despair. By omitting to join up he would have put himself in danger (he wrote in another letter) 'of being looked upon by the men who are to be my companions and fellow labourers through life as a coward or a scoundrel or both'. He had already in his zeal, wearing plain clothes, put in two drill days, and to quit the corps now would be infinitely worse than never joining. What a despicable fool he would look! How lamentably it would damage his career!

Then, for some reason - perhaps a talk with Morgan or a letter from his brother the General - Hunting Cap relented. All was well. 'My uncle gives me leave,' wrote O'Connell on 23rd January 1797, 'with as much harshness as he last week refused to permit me.' To 'the old gentleman' he wrote next day 'most humbly and heartily to thank you for the permission ... By a change in the dress of the corps, £17 will be sufficient.' In his journal next day he confided, 'I am well satisfied with my letter to my uncle, but that is no proof that he will be.'

On 6th February he appeared for the first time on parade in the full glory of his new uniform, blue coat, red facings, gilt buttons, white breeches and all. Whatever his motives in joining, he became a keen part-time soldier, though proficiency in arms was very time-consuming. Frequently he was under arms all day, being taught the exercise of the cannon, to the detriment of his studying and his social life. However, it would be a great thing thereafter to be able to say, 'I was a Volunteer.'

Educated men, serving unpaid from a sense of duty, soon mastered the artillery drill, carried their three-pounders about the city, sponged, loaded, rammed and fired as well (in their own estimation) as any regular.

In March 1797 General Lake arrived in Ulster with orders to disarm all civilians, which the troops took to mean, essentially, the United Irishmen. Martial law was imposed on the greater part of the province. This meant that cases of offences against the state were tried not by a magistrate or judge but by an army officer who had no training in assessing evidence, let alone in legal procedure, and could hardly take an objective view of the case. During the next six months the Defenders were stamped down. The soldiers were not gentle. Their main object was to search for arms and discover the oath administrators. The simplest way was to burn down a few houses in a village to show you meant business, set up the triangle in the main street, grab someone – anyone – who looked as though he might be up to no good, and flog him with a cat-o'-nine-tails until lumps of flesh were torn from the writhing body and his ribs and internal organs were exposed. By that time he was probably ready – if he knew anything – to talk; either to tell where were the hidden pikes and muskets, or to name someone else who might know, who was then in turn brought to the blood-sticky triangle.

Orangemen, former Peep-o'-Day Boys, enlisted in yeomanry corps or acting as unofficial vigilantes, participated zealously in these transactions. Two years ago the authorities had regarded them as 'lawless banditti', now they were viewed with favour. To the Castle the United Irishmen were now the greatest danger. As they professed to unite Protestant and Catholic in rebellion, it made sense to encourage the Orangemen whose aim was to keep Protestant and Catholic divided.

The newly appointed Commander-in-Chief, Sir Ralph Abercrombie, a humane man, resigned because he got no support from the government in his efforts to stop these horrors. In a private letter he wrote, 'every crime, every cruelty that could be committed by Cossacks or Colmucks has been transacted here.' The Castle's attitude was to close an eye to the troops' cruelties, not specifically sanctioning them but allowing senior officers to take the responsibility. It worked. By August martial law in Ulster could be lifted, but the situation in north Leinster was deteriorating.

The Leinster Directorate of the United Irishmen now began to assume the character of a general staff for the republican movement. It improved liaison with the Defenders, who began to call themselves United Irishmen, but tried to stop any premature rising before the French made another landing. Its headquarters were in Dublin and its leader was Lord Edward FitzGerald. For the rest of 1797 the situation on the surface was comparatively quiet.

O'Connell in Dublin improved his artillery training, pursued his legal studies and became a Freemason. Of his private life the journal reveals nothing, except a few references to 'sweet Eliza', but who she was, whether whore or milliner, actress or young lady, we do not know. A note in his journal for 22nd June 1797 may indicate success in this amour: '*Satis - superque* - Oh sweet Eliza!' Six days later he offered up to her 'the tribute of his silent wishes' and reflected on her 'with satisfaction and delight'. There is not a shadow of evidence to support the legend that, then or later, by his personal exertions he kept a whole street of brothels in business. (And would Hunting Cap have paid?)

For four weeks in April, while Bennett was on circuit, he slept in Bennett's house. 'His wife was brought to bed on the 3rd ... On the 9th I thought it was impossible for her to recover.' No one, surely, could do more for a friend.

He made up his mind to enter parliament when that became possible for a Catholic.

I too will be a member. I will steadfastly and perseveringly attach myself to the real interests of Ireland. I shall endeavour equally to avoid the profligacy of corruption and the violence of unreasonable *patriotism*. Of real patriotism, moderation is the chief mark.

A few days later he observed, 'A revolution would not produce the happiness of the Irish people.'

Many of his friends were more or less United Irishmen, including Bennett (far from activist). 'I was myself a United Irishman,' he told O'Neill Daunt many years later. But the remainder of his recollections imparted to Daunt suggest that his connection with the society was intermittent, that he attended an occasional meeting more from curiosity than dedication and was soon disillusioned.

One lesson he learned in those times and never forgot – that political agitation should be open, legal and above board. Those who worked in secret were in perpetual danger of treachery. 'You saw men on whose fidelity you would have staked your existence playing false when tempted by the magnitude of the bribe on one side, and on the other by the danger of hanging.'

But even mildly radical opinions in a young Catholic lawyer might be dangerous at such a time. He must be discreet: 'It would be a devilish unpleasant thing to get *caged*.' But only six days earlier he had written of the future Lord Castlereagh, fiercely High Tory, 'Stuart seems to me to be a very valuable man.' So did his opinions veer. It is significant that, from 1st May 1797, two pages are torn out of his journal. In June he departed for the long summer vacation to Derrynane.

He returned to Dublin in the autumn to take up his law studies and volunteer duties. During the winter and spring the government's campaign against the United Irishmen and Defenders in Kildare, Meath and Carlow was warming up. To flogging with the cat-o'-nine-tails (which brutality was also frequently practised on English soldiers and sailors) were added two new methods of interrogation in depth. The first was 'half hanging', with the suspect being pulled up, half throttled and let down several times before he was hauled up for good. The second was the 'pitchcap'. A paper bowl was filled with hot pitch and gunpowder and clapped on the victim's head. When the pitch was half set, it was set alight. The result was most diverting to the soldiery, and often elicited information. It was considered to be an amusingly appropriate treatment for 'croppies'.* Four out of five of the soldiers were Irish (65,598 out of 76,791 in December 1797), and of these the majority must have been Catholics since the militia were selected by ballot.

Most of these appalling atrocities were inflicted by Catholic Irishmen (many of whom, in western militia regiments, could speak not a word of English) upon Catholic Irishmen, who in Leinster could speak not a word of Irish. The pitch-cap was invented by a militia sergeant called Tom the Devil. The barbaric ferocity of the militia horrified liberal-minded officers: 'Murder', wrote General Cornwallis, 'appears to be their favourite pastime.'

Sectarian divisions deepened. There was, O'Connell told Hunting Cap, an odium against Catholics, and the Lord Chancellor, Fitzgibbon, did not conceal his hatred of them. They were blamed for conditions which were partly the result of the ferment in Europe but mainly due to the government's weakness and cruelty. Such was the prejudice that he doubted he would ever be called to the Bar.

A common feature in every age and every country of situations such as that in Dublin in 1798 is the ubiquitous activity of amateur, would-be professional, sleuths bombarding the authorities with every snippet of gossip they can pick up or invent. Some are in it for what they can get, hoping to be paid at piece-rates; others see themselves as patriots and deliberately fabricate plots in order to stir the government out of its inertia. Typical of the mercenaries was a flamboyant Dublin character, Francis Higgins, known as the Sham Squire from his attempt to delude an heiress by posing as a gentleman of good family and fortune. There is, or was, in existence a report by him dated 2nd March 1798 and addressed to the Under-Secretary at the Castle. The son of Napper Tandy, he wrote, had waited on Mr Connell with a letter. 'Connell holds a commission from France (a Colonel's). He was to be called to the Bar to please a rich old uncle, but is one of the most abominable and bloodthirsty Republicans

---

*Rebels who proclaimed their faith by cropping their hair short in French Jacobin fashion. This torture was last applied in the Irish Republic in 1979 to a man who had given information to the Garda Siochana on an armed robbery.

I ever heard.' Whether the authorities identified 'Connell' with
the young lawyer, or with his uncle, formerly General in the
Irish Brigade but now a Colonel in the British army, we do not
know. But they had their own very reliable source of information
on the United Irishmen and knew how much credence to place
on the Sham Squire's report. They ignored it.

Information, more accurate than the Sham Squire's, poured
into the Castle. On 12th March 1798 the entire Leinster Directorate was put in the bag except for Lord Edward FitzGerald,
who went on the run in Dublin. It was about that time that
O'Connell attended a convivial party at the house of Hugh Fitzpatrick, a radical printer and bookseller but not a United Irishman. *Plenus Bachhi*, O'Connell called for a prayer book and
proceeded to 'swear in' some of the company as United Irishmen.
One can picture the scene – the wine-dabbled table, the half-
empty bottles and overturned glasses, the laughing young bucks,
stocks awry, faces flushed, treating the ceremony with bibulous
solemnity. According to legend, Fitzpatrick* suddenly sobered
up, realised how dangerous this might be if the zealous town
major, Sirr, and his yeomanry were to pay a call, and persuaded
O'Connell to escape arrest by departing on a turf-boat. Nonsense.
Whether O'Connell took passage in a turf-boat for a joy-ride in
a mood of unusual elevation, or was shanghaied by his pot-com-
panions, it was certainly not to escape arrest. A few days later he
was back in Dublin – not on the run, pursuing quite openly his
normal business, and on 12th April he was called to the Bar.
Clearly he was on no suspects' list. His name is not among the
hundreds mentioned in Sirr's papers.

On the 26th he took the required Oath of Allegiance. There
was nothing in it specifically repugnant to a Catholic of that time:
Papal infallibility had not yet been declared a dogma of the
Catholic Church. But it was humiliating to be obliged to swear
that one was not a murderer. No one called upon Orangemen to
swear such an oath, or the Sheares brothers, or Wolfe Tone.

I, Daniel O'Connell, do swear that I abjure, condemn and
detest as un-christian and impious the principle that it is lawful
to murder, destroy, or anyways injure any person whatsoever,

---

* In another version of the story, O'Connell's landlord, a Mr Murray.

for or under the pretence of being a heretic; and I do declare solemnly before God that I believe no act in itself unjust, immoral, or wicked, can ever be justified or excused by or under pretence or colour that it was done either for the good of the Church or in obedience to any ecclesiastical power whatsoever. I also declare that it is not an article of the Catholic faith, neither am I thereby required to believe or profess that the Pope is infallible, or that I am bound to obey an order in its own nature immoral, though the Pope, or any ecclesiastical power, should issue or direct such order; but, on the contrary, I hold that it would be sinful in me to pay any respect or obedience thereto. I further declare that I do not believe that any sin whatsoever committed by me can be forgiven at the mere will of any Pope or any priest, or of any person whatsoever; but that sincere sorrow for past sins, a firm and sincere resolution to avoid future guilt, and to atone to God, are previous and indispensable requisites to establish a wellfounded expectation of forgiveness; and that any person who receives absolution without these previous requisites so far from obtaining thereby any remission of his sins, incurs the additional guilt of violating a Sacrament; and I do swear that I will defend to the utmost of my power the settlement and arrangement of property in this country as established by the laws now in being. I do hereby disclaim, disavow, and solemnly abjure any intention to subvert the present Church Establishment for the purpose of substituting a Catholic Establishment in its stead, and I do solemnly swear that I will not exercise any privilege to which I am or may become entitled to disturb and weaken the Protestant religion and Protestant Government in this Kingdom. So help me, God.

During May the pace hotted up. On the 19th Lord Edward was taken, fighting desperately, in his bedroom. During the struggle he was shot in the shoulder. The wound was not thought serious – he would surely be saved for the hangman – but it turned gangrenous and he died fifteen days later. The Sheares brothers tried to form a National Committee to control the rebellion, but were themselves arrested on the 21st, and later hanged. All the leaders of the United Irishmen were now in custody or dead, and the rebellion, with no co-ordination and no

French landing, hung fire. In Carlow, where the rebels half-heartedly mobilised, some four or five hundred were shot down by troops who surrounded them, and about two hundred (one tended to lose count) were later executed. But at Prosperous, in County Kildare, twenty-eight men of the Cork militia were trapped by the rebels in blazing barracks and roasted alive or piked as they tried to break out.

The Lawyers' Artillery Corps were called up for full-time duty on 23rd May. There being no targets for its three-pounders, the corps was employed, no doubt to its disgust, as mere infantry, on guarding public buildings and strategic points, cordons and house searches. O'Connell was in less danger from 'croppies' than from over-enthusiastic comrades, for a state of emergency breeds not only amateur sleuths but innumerable amateur soldiers in whom patriotic zeal and the glory of bearing arms far outrun discretion and common sense. Such warriors, avid to justify their uniforms and weapons, believe any rumour and arrest or shoot on the flimsiest evidence. House-searching in particular goes to the heads of the most respectable citizens once they are in uniform. Suddenly private property need no longer be respected; they can ransack drawers, read private correspondence, turn up carpets, prod cushions and mattresses for arms. But Private O'Connell did not lose his sense of proportion and observed the law while doing his duty.

By the end of May the worst seemed to be over. An assembly of 2,000 rebels on the Curragh, offered pardon if they surrendered their arms and handed over their leader, dispersed homewards with shouts of joy, leaving thirteen cart-loads of pikes behind. In a fight on the hill of Tara some 350 rebels were slain, the Catholic Lord Fingall's yeomanry particularly distinguishing themselves. A few days later a loyal address was signed by four Catholic peers, the entire Catholic college of Maynooth and some two thousand respectable Catholics of Leinster. In Dublin the law courts and most business houses were closed because all able-bodied lawyers and businessmen were in uniform. Outside the Castle, gunners stood to their guns with lighted matches. If the rebels ever had an opportunity, they had missed it.

There was nothing to keep O'Connell in Dublin. He must have obtained leave of absence from the corps because on his return in the autumn he resumed duty without being put on a

charge of absence without leave. It is usually suggested that he
departed to Derrynane 'discreetly', lest he get into trouble. It is
far more likely that he went on his usual summer holiday during
the law vacation.

In his absence the rebellion flared up in a final blaze of frantic
fury, and then fizzled out. The scene of the last act was County
Wexford, hitherto so quiet that the government had few troops
there. The rebels, virtually leaderless, routed a few penny-packets
of yeomanry and militia and seized Wexford. They then accepted
the leadership of a rather reluctant and not markedly effective
Protestant landowner named Beauchamp Bagenal Harvey; set up
a fortified camp on Vinegar Hill; and were checked at New Ross
and Arklow. They roasted alive about two hundred Protestant
men, women and children in a barn at Scullabogue; they hoisted
a hundred or so on pikes and tossed them writhing off Wexford
Bridge into the river Slaney – thus, they doubtless felt, evening
the score for innumerable suspected rebels, and surrendered rebels, and persons suspected of sympathy with the rebellion, who
had been butchered by militia and yeomanry. On 21st June they
were finally routed by vastly superior forces at Vinegar Hill. After
the usual slaughter and executions, they were reduced to a few
scattered outlaws in the Wicklow Mountains. In the same month
a rising by mainly Presbyterian United Irishmen collapsed in
Ulster. The rebellion of 1798 was over.

Two months too late the French did arrive, landing 1,000 men
under General Humbert at Killala in County Mayo. Hoping to
find the Irish peasantry rising en masse to help them, they
brought 5,000 muskets. But there was no mass rising. A few
thousand devout peasants arrived (so they told the puzzled, atheist French) to take up arms for France and the Blessed Virgin,
but they seemed unresponsive to discipline and instruction. After
an initial success at Castlebar (the French veterans were very
good soldiers), Humbert's small army was surrounded and surrendered on 8th September at Ballinamuck. The French were
taken to Dublin and there lionised before repatriation. Their
Irish allies were slaughtered.

Unaware of Humbert's misfortune, another small French expedition, carrying few troops but many muskets, artillery pieces
and saddles for Irish rebels, to say nothing of a veteran and
rather bibulous Protestant Dublin republican named Napper

Tandy, landed on Rathlin Island off the Donegal coast, and promptly re-embarked when informed by the local postmaster of Humbert's surrender. (Napper Tandy had celebrated his return to the old sod to such effect that he had to be carried on board, pissing copiously down the shoulders of his bearers.) A third expedition was roughly handled by a British squadron off shore – all ten ships were captured. On board, jaunty and indomitable, was Wolfe Tone in French uniform. He was tried for waging war against the king and in the course of a spirited address said, 'I have done my duty, and have no doubt that the court will do theirs.' The court did, but Wolfe Tone cut his throat to cheat the hangman and died in agony a week later, leaving a legend of gallantry in adversity which has inspired Irish patriots ever since.

The year of liberty was over.

It had one immediate and three long-term results.

It linked for the first time republicanism with militant anglophobia. Before 1798 Irish anglophobes had proclaimed allegiance to another king, not to a republic. O'Connell was never a republican.

Viewed in retrospect it enshrined in Irish republicanism a tradition of violence and the concept of the blood sacrifice. Without the shedding of blood, theirs *and ours*, runs this dogma, freedom from Britain will never be won; and if it is won, it will not be real freedom. To people in the United Irishmen-Young Ireland-Fenian-Irish Republican Brotherhood-I.R.A. tradition of physical force, this provides both an intellectual justification for killing, and an excuse if killing does not immediately achieve its object: 'You may think we failed, but our blood shed today, on the battlefield and the scaffold, is the price for freedom to-morrow – or the day after.' To O'Connell politics was a matter of persuasion, agitation and compromise, totally incompatible with bloodshed. Besides, if it came to fighting, England being the stronger was sure to win.

It polarised the sectarian divisions in Irish politics. Leaders of the United Irishmen were nearly all Protestants; indeed there was only one Catholic in the Leinster Directorate, W.J. Mac-Neven, who purchased a pardon and a passage to America by telling the Castle much of what he knew (but without naming his colleagues). The government forces were mainly Irish, and Catholic Irish at that. Wolfe Tone, a Protestant, whose blood sacrifice

47

was the most moving before those of 1916, constantly pleaded for Catholics and Protestants to forget their differences and consider themselves only as Irishmen. Yet '98 very soon became in legend, and still remains in the minds of most people, Catholic Ireland's rebellion against Protestant England. It exacerbated old sectarian hatreds and added new sectarian grievances. O'Connell, though his greatest achievement was Catholic emancipation, was the least sectarian of men: he always insisted that Irish Protestants were just as Irish and just as entitled to political and religious liberty as Catholics.

The immediate result of the rebellion was that William Pitt, the Prime Minister of the day, began to take seriously an idea already mooted in political circles, that the best way of ensuring that Ireland would not provide an easy objective for French invasion, and also of giving a fair deal to Catholics, would be a legislative union with England such as that which had proved so beneficial to Scotland.

O'Connell's final verdict on 1798 was given over forty years later in a public altercation with the Young Irelander, John Mitchel: 'He speaks of '98. Their struggle was of blood and defeated in blood. The means they adopted weakened Ireland and enabled England to carry the Union.'

During O'Connell's short life there had been three major revolutions – the American, the French and 1798. They were of enormous influence in forming the opinions which made him a great demagogue. In O'Connell's early days there were few Catholic Irish-Americans; in so far as there was an American dimension in Irish politics, it stemmed from Protestant Scots-Irish who had emigrated from Ulster. In his journal and early letters there is hardly a mention of America. Nevertheless he, like any other English-speaking radical, must have known the Declaration of Independence almost off by heart, and agreed with most of it. In fact he might almost have drafted it himself. Of course a Catholic Kerryman with a royalist family background could not join Ulster Presbyterians in applauding the republicanism inherent in the American revolution, but with everything else he would have been in wholehearted agreement. It was a political, not a social revolution. It did not destroy the structure of society, or the rights of property, or undermine the rule of law (and lawyers); and that, to O'Connell, was as it should be.

He would have approved the early stages of the French Revolution, of Lafayette and Mirabeau and those liberal clergy who
voted away their own wealth and privileges. But the Terror; the
militant, dogmatic atheism; the persecution of the Church, the
destruction of property and the homicidal mobs roaming round
Paris turned him for a while almost into a Tory, so that even the
Revolution's contribution to political ideas and democratic practice did not reconcile him to it. As for 1798, except that it was
not atheist, it displayed all the worst characteristics of the French
Revolution and was, moreover, damned by utter failure.

More formative for O'Connell was the English Revolutionary
Settlement of 1689. Of course he deplored the ejection of a legitimate Catholic king by a usurper, and the consequent Protestant
Ascendancy in Ireland. Nevertheless liberalism was based on the
premise, not entirely false, that the Glorious Revolution had
replaced arbitrary Stuart despotism by the supremacy of parliament, democracy, individual liberty and the rule of law. What it
had in fact done was to provide the conditions from which these
desiderata would eventually emerge; otherwise Wilkes, Fox,
Adams and O'Connell would have had short shrift.

The Williamites, Americans, French and 1798 rebels had all
taken up arms. O'Connell was no pacifist. He thought the military
profession the most honourable for a gentleman. He paid for the
uniform and equipment of a young cousin in the 43rd Regiment
who, volunteering twice for the 'forlorn hope', was wounded at
Badajoz and killed at San Sebastian. He sent his son to South
America to fight for Bolivar, which was in the best liberal tradition, and then into the Austrian army, which wasn't. His views
on Napoleon and the Napoleonic wars, rather a touchstone for
pacifism, varied. He took great pride in, and frequently exaggerated, the part Irishmen played in the war, 'at least three fourths
of our army and navy'. Napoleon at the height of his power was
'the great enemy of the world, who threatens us with the invasion
from a thousand ports of his vast empire'; he was the 'mighty
foe of freedom, the extinguisher of civil liberty who rules the
Continent from St Petersburg to the verge of Irish bayonets in
Spain'. Now was a time, when 'that splendid madman made the
Catholics of Ireland essential to the military defence of the Empire', peculiarly appropriate for pressing Irish claims. But after
Waterloo he lamented the fall of 'that great man', and grieved

that 'liberty was forever curbed in France'. He would never have condemned the American colonists for taking up arms, but in the Irish context he thought that violence was a blunder worse than a crime, because it would surely fail against the might of the British Empire. Moreover the mere theoretical advocacy of armed rebellion should persuasion fail would lay one open to a charge of high treason.[4] But his objection to violence, at least in the Irish context, was also a matter of principle. Again and again, for nearly fifty years, in speeches and private conversations, public and private letters, he denounced the resort to violence for political ends, and declared that it would be better to forego repeal than to achieve it by physical force. The classic argument against terrorism was put in a letter from his friend Tom Steele, in the last year of his life.

> You could not permit William Smith O'Brien or Tom Steele or every Whitefoot or Molly Maguire or Tipperary Disturber or Terry Alt to select a *casus belli* for himself and act on it and wage war *at his own time and in his own judgement*.[5]

From June to October O'Connell stayed at Derrynane, hare-hunting, grouse-shooting, trout-fishing, dancing and dining with friends and relatives. Then, riding sixty miles in a day and dancing up to three in the morning, he rode off to Tralee to seek his fortune.

5

Paterfamilias

Back in Dublin he took up his old routine, with the trifling difference that he was no longer a law student but a practising barrister. But not very practising: 1799 produced only sixteen fees worth £27 3s 6d even though the General (busy raising an Irish Brigade in the British service, officered by former officers of Louis XVI) put some business in his way. Bennett had escaped the notice of Major Sirr. He and O'Connell sat up late deploring the 'unhappy rebellion ... May every virtuous revolutionist remember the horrors of Wexford!'

But he did not allow them to prey unduly on his mind. Claret was good and cheap, and he did not need much to elevate him. Coming home late, considerably elevated, he came across a fire in a timber-yard and some workmen trying to uncover the stopcock in a water-pipe. O'Connell was in a mood to help, seized a pick and in no time had exposed the plug. Fired by honest zeal, he kept working away, *con amore*, until he had dug up half the street. A militia patrol arrived, but was unable to persuade him to desist from his excavations. 'I was rather an unruly customer,' he admitted, 'and one of the soldiers ran a bayonet at me which was intercepted by the cover of my hunting-watch. If I had not had the watch, there was the end of the Agitator!'

In 1800 he had twenty-seven fees, worth £205 - not a bad income for a young bachelor of economic habits. (Unfortunately his habits were never economical.) One of his cases involved a young sprig of the Segerson family, Catholic Kerrymen of Norse descent. O'Connell cross-examined Segerson so severely that he lost his temper, jumped up and called O'Connell a purse-proud blockhead. O'Connell replied, 'In the first place, I have no purse to be proud of; and secondly, if I be a blockhead, it is better for you, as I am counsel against you. However, to save you the trouble of saying so again, I'll administer a slight rebuke.' Whereupon O'Connell whacked him with a cane. The result was a challenge; but soon after it was received Segerson wrote to O'Connell to say that he could not proceed in the affair, as he had ascertained that O'Connell was one of the lives in a valuable lease. 'Under these circumstances,' he wrote, 'I cannot afford to shoot you, unless you first insure your life for my benefit. If you do, then I'm your man!' O'Connell saw no reason thus to oblige him, so the duel never took place.

Hunting Cap thought it time he married, and made preliminary arrangements for an advantageous alliance with a young – well, youngish – lady noted for short stature, long purse and longer nose. O'Connell, however, had other ideas: he had fallen precipitously in love with his third cousin once removed, Mary O'Connell.

Mary was twenty-two, three years younger than Dan. Her portrait by John Gubbins, painted seventeen years later, does not show a beauty. She had fair hair, a healthy complexion, a good figure; but a snub nose and slightly protruding teeth deprived her of classic beauty. However, sexual attraction often has nothing to do with classic beauty, and O'Connell found her overwhelmingly attractive. Although she was one of eight impoverished orphans of an impecunious physician and his own financial position was far from secure, although he could have known very little about her character, temperament and tastes, within three weeks of their first meeting on 7th November 1800 he asked, 'Are you engaged, Miss O'Connell?'

'I am not.'

'Will you engage yourself to me?'

'I will.'

It was as easy as that — except for the problem of Hunting Cap. In his first letter to her O'Connell wrote, 'You know as well as I do how much we have at stake in keeping the business secret.' Why? Hunting Cap had to know sooner or later, and there was no obvious advantage in it being later. However, elaborate precautions were taken. For the next two years, while he spent most of his time in Dublin or on circuit and they met only briefly at Tralee, where she lived with her mother, he wrote to her every few days, the letters going under cover to her sister, Betsy; his sister, Ellen; Ellen's future husband, a rather erratic lawyer named 'Splinter' O'Connell; or Mary's mother, who were all in the secret. They were fated to spend a great deal of their lives apart, but Dan in hundreds of letters assured her again and again of his undying devotion. 'I *so* doat on you, my darling little woman.' He started as he was to continue:

I have told you before and I delight in repeating it that you are my first and only love ... I read your letters over and over again, I sleep with them in my bosom. Do not laugh at me, Mary. I was born with strong feelings ... Darling of my heart, my sweet tender love, Adieu.

And so on, week after week, with repeated warnings that she looked after her delicate health (she was slightly asthmatic, addicted to coughs, colds and nerves, and inclined to hypochondria), and reminders of the need for secrecy. Her letters were hardly more restrained, but once she put him in a frenzy by starting her letter 'Dear Sir' and ending it 'Your affectionate cousin'. When she told him it was a quiz, he

again found you what you are, what you ever must always be, my own dear *little woman.* You look a thousand times handsomer and better in my eyes as my *little woman* than as *my affectionate cousin.* The affectionate cousin is a saucy little baggage. I beg you will not keep her company.

It was one of the very few occasions, in hundreds of letters, when he praised her looks.

Not until 24th July 1802, after twenty months' 'secret engagement', were they married privately in the Dublin lodgings of Betsy's husband. Perhaps they thought this would be less likely to come to Hunting Cap's ears than a church marriage. Only three days later she seems to have returned to her mother at Tralee, and six days later he set off to Ennis on circuit. They did not meet again until the end of September, when business took

53

him to Tralee. Mary's grandmother was not in the secret, and as a cover he made a point of running down Mary.

'Madam, Mary would do very well, only she is so cross.'

'Cross, sir? My Mary cross? Sir, you must have provoked her very much. Sir, you must yourself be quite in fault. Sir, my little Mary was always the gentlest, sweetest creature born.'

They must have eluded her family's vigilance, for two months later Mary informed him that she was pregnant. He was over-joyed.

I insist on it that it must be a daughter. I *will* have it a daughter. I am the father and I cannot bear to have it anything but a daughter, a girl like her dear sweet mother, very fair and *cherry*-cheeked, *beautiful* fair hair, a saucy nose a little cocked, white teeth very even but a little advanced, thin lips, breath sweeter than all nature. Recollect, now, I bespeak such a one.

He was now writing every two or three days, and his concern for her health was redoubled.

You are so ill, so very ill that you even conceal your situation from your mother and Betsy. These cold perspirations, these shiverings fill my heart with apprehension and horror. Mary, dear Mary, sure you do not mean to leave your doating hus-band a prey to the tortures of knowing ... that my foolish wish for secrecy prevents you from taking that regular exercise, those medical assistants which would render your situation so comparatively easy and trifling.

I sat down to read a treatise on midwifery. I read it through, and every species of illness which accompanies pregnancy being mentioned in detail, I filled my head with them and trembled for every one of them.

Do you mean to forsake me so early? ... Do you mean to let me feel I was the death of the sweetest innocent? Spare, my darling, your distracted husband.

Fortunately he was not to suffer these torments during her many subsequent pregnancies.

Clearly the news must be broken to Hunting Cap before he heard of her condition through the family grape-vine. After Christmas at Carhen, O'Connell had to go on to Derrynane. 'I wish to God my story was told to the old gentleman. I shall feel devilish awkward. But I am full of hope and know no reason to be otherwise ... I will not quit my uncle until I tell him of our marriage.'

In the event he lost his nerve and broke the news in a letter written after his departure. Hunting Cap reacted with rage, tears and disinheritance. But Morgan professed himself delighted at the marriage, and would be happy to receive his daughter-in-law at Carhen. Dan returned to Dublin, Mary remained at Tralee, writing letters much calmer than his, urging him not to give way to unavailing grief at the loss of a fortune. Nor did he; his sanguine temperament persuaded him that his dear uncle's anger was a storm that would soon blow over:

If not, my love, things are very well as they are. We have ample means of support for the present and most flattering prospects for the future. And we have love enough to sweeten the cup of life. Darling, I do *so* doat on you.

It was a fairly optimistic assessment, for in 1803 his total income from fees was £465 4s 9d, not very much for a man with a wife, a child and another soon on the way.

It was a pity the General was in no position to intercede. The Irish Brigade he had raised for King George was decimated by West Indian fever, disbanded, and the survivors transferred to other units. He himself married, against Hunting Cap's wishes, a Creole widow with whom, after the Peace of Amiens in March 1802, he departed to France to visit the scenes of his youth. There, on the resumption of war the following year, they and many more foreigners were detained, not uncomfortably, with considerable freedom to move around but not to return home. He lived in Paris on parole and refused Napoleon's offers of employment.

Hunting Cap was wrong. Marrying Mary was the best day's work his nephew ever did. She was no intellectual and no great reader, but was full of common sense and must have been good company or he would soon have tired of her. Although apparently delicate, she must have been a tough little thing to bear ten children, of whom seven survived infancy. She was courageous in adversity, she was resilient (and needed to be, for she had a lot to put up with); in eighteenth-century terms, she 'had bottom'. In the first year of their marriage, including a difficult pregnancy, she spent very little time with her husband, though there seems to have been no particular reason for his not bringing her to Dublin; but she never moped, never complained – or not much. Her fervent Catholicism (stronger perhaps for her being the daughter of a mixed marriage, her father and brothers being Protestants) gradually brought him back into the fold. A pretentious Deist when they married, within six months he was

> running into a kind of sermon, for the fact is that since our marriage I have grown somewhat more serious on these subjects. I always had a kind of meditative piety, but it has grown alive in some measure. Be sure you pray for me. [1]

Two months later he wrote, 'If I were a religionist, I should spend every moment in praying for you – and this miserable philosophy which I have taken up and been proud of in the room of religion affords me now no consolation.' [2] The leaven worked, for after six years Mary expressed her happiness that he had for some time been saying his prayers, attending Mass regularly and observing the days of abstinence – but not always without prompting: 'I hope, darling, you did not eat meat on Friday and Saturday ... You can't be at loss for fish in Cork. And Good Friday the *judges* will go to prayers, and certainly you can *spare time* to go.' [3] If she had not converted him, he would never have been the Catholic Liberator.

She had very conventional reactions about, for instance, the 'common people' whom she distrusted and feared, and the gutter press: 'I have to beg you seriously, heart, to stop the *Southern Reporter*. We are really tormented with it. Besides, it is a nasty, *filthy* paper.' She detested 'that odious' Conway, editor of the Dublin *Freeman's Journal*, the *Messenger* and the *Dublin Evening Press*, which veered between pro- and anti-O'Connellism.

For all her nerves and hypochondria, she provided the stable home background for his turbulent career, and coped efficiently with her side of the partnership, never plaguing him unnecessarily with domestic troubles. The only serious threat to their marriage was to be his uncontrolled extravagance and multitudinous debts.

For over two years in all his letters he never mentioned his work or his political views. Then he realised she was interested in both and discretion itself, someone in whom he could safely confide. He first did so in a letter describing a row he had in Ennis, a town he loathed, with one of the circuit court judges, Baron Cusack Smith, who had ill-used him in court. Young O'Connell boldly bearded the formidable judge in his private room at the inn.

He is a singularly capricious animal. He received me with a strong threat to complain against me to the twelve judges, but concluded by paying me all manner of compliments and offering me any restitution in his power. I believe he will not try again to put me down ... The command over my temper fits me for scenes of this kind.

Indeed O'Connell's anger was always controlled and generally calculated.

Throughout his courtship and the early days of his marriage O'Connell was living in stirring times, though one would not think so from his letters. Although the back of the 1798 rebellion had been broken, the mountains of Dublin and Wicklow were infested with rebels turned highwaymen who robbed travellers even on the main roads and made Mary very anxious about his safety. The authorities feared a renewal of the rebellion and the Lawyers' Artillery Corps was constantly on duty patrolling the streets, guarding public buildings, searching houses for 'croppies', in all of which he did his bit.

It was against this background that the Younger Pitt viewed Anglo-Irish relations. It seemed to him most unsatisfactory that the British government was in fact responsible for the government of Ireland, the defence of which was vital to Britain, but had to work with and through the creaking, corrupt, bigoted Irish administration. Even before the rebellion was ended, the idea of a union between England and Ireland was being mooted. Fitzgibbon had been urging its advantages for years.

Irish opinion about union was divided. On the whole, Protestant gentry deplored the idea. Some, like Grattan, had a general feeling of Irish identity and hated the idea of it being submerged; others saw no further than the threat to their power and privileges when, instead of three hundred Irish M.P.s in Dublin, there would be only one hundred in Westminster. The Presbyterians of the north, recently so fiercely republican, were now becoming as fiercely royalist and unionist, even inventing indelicate embellishments to the historic toast of 'The Glorious, Pious and Immortal Memory of the Great and Good King William'. But some Orangemen felt that the British government would stop them dealing properly with Papists. Other Protestants, however, felt that union would be the best safeguard against another rebellion. Most Catholic gentry, including O'Connell's father and uncles, were in favour of union, considering (in Castlereagh's words) 'any transfer of power from their opponents as a boon'. They, too, felt they would be safer in a union, for the rebellion had worked violently on Protestant fears and it seemed as though fanatical Orange-ism was on the increase and might become entrenched in the Dublin parliament. They would rather trust in Westminster to remove their remaining grievances than in Irish Protestants whose vested interests would thereby be endangered. Catholics were never actually promised that union would be followed by complete emancipation, but by many a nod and a wink were given to understand this. It was certainly Pitt's intention. He also intended that provision should be made for the state to pay the Catholic clergy, thus compensating them for receiving no tithes. Archbishop Troy in Dublin and Bishop Moylan canvassed assiduously for union. But most Dubliners, Catholic and Protestants alike, opposed a measure which, by removing their legislature and legislators, would reduce the capital to a decaying provincial town; lower the value of house property; ruin hundreds of tradesmen and manufacturers dependent on the custom of the gentry and nobility who flocked into Dublin for every parliamentary session; and reduce calamitously the supply of loaves and fishes. Lawyers, of whom about four out of five were Protestants, were particularly indignant, since they stood to lose a great deal of litigation and all their fees for the drafting of parliamentary bills.

The common people probably did not care much one way or another. To them, the government meant Colonel Blennerhasset and the Knight of Kerry.

In January 1799, the Irish House of Commons by a majority of five refused to discuss union. This was no problem to eighteenth-century statesmen. Peerages, pensions, places and hard cash were distributed in well-calculated profusion. The Lord Lieutenant, the Marquis Cornwallis, 'despised and hated himself for engaging in such dirty work' – but continued to do so. Skilled 'management' bore fruit; by a majority of forty-six the Irish House of Commons committed ritual suicide by voting for union with Britain, to come into effect on 1st January 1801.

A spectator to these transactions, O'Connell had no doubt where he stood – with his fellow Dubliners. A quintessential Irishman, he resented any diminution of his country's status and authority, while as a lawyer he was threatened in career and pocket; furthermore he had, and retained all his life, a veneration for Grattan's parliament as the procurer and guarantor of Irish freedom. He believed that Irish M.P.s, living in Ireland (albeit Protestants), did not like meeting every hour neighbours who 'looked shame on them'; and that there was therefore more to be hoped from them than from M.P.s at Westminster. To people conditioned to regard Ascendancy Protestants as not really Irish at all, O'Connell's love of their parliament is puzzling and wrong-headed. But the O'Connells of Kerry were a Catholic family who had prospered, they had no inferiority complex about their Protestant neighbours and got on perfectly well with them; nearly all his colleagues and probably most of his friends at this time were Protestants; and though he was not infrequently at variance with resident Protestant landlords, attacking them with savage vituperation, he never thought of them as anything but Irish.

At an 'aggregate' (public) meeting of Dublin Catholics assembled at the Royal Exchange on 13th January 1800, O'Connell made his first political speech in support of Curran's motion protesting against the extinction of Irish liberties and the reduction of Ireland to the subject condition of a province. Before he spoke, Major Sirr arrived with a patrol of yeomanry, glanced through the resolution and tossed it contemptuously back on to the table. 'There's no harm in this,' he said. These talking shops!

O'Connell rose to his feet. He admitted afterwards that his face glowed and his ears tingled at the sound of his own voice, but he plucked up courage as he went on. It was very important, he said, that Catholics as a body should oppose union, because it had been industriously circulated that their support had been bought by the promise of emancipation.

> Can they remain silent under so horrible a calumny? ... Let every man who feels with me proclaim that if the alternative were offered him of Union, or the re-enactment of the Penal Code with all its pristine horrors, he would prefer without hesitation the latter ... that he would rather confide in the justice of his brethren, the Protestants of Ireland who have already liberated him, than lay his country at the feet of foreigners ... I know that the Catholics of Ireland still remember that they have a country, and that they will never accept any advantage as a *sect* which would debase and destroy them as a *people*.[4]

He sat down to a din which he was to hear hundreds of times in the next forty-five years, tumultuous, intoxicating applause; and an anti-union resolution was carried unanimously.

The success of his first speech was gratifying, but it produced an angry reaction from Hunting Cap. By thrusting themselves forward as a distinct body, the Dublin Catholics (he wrote) were depriving themselves 'of the only support and shelter they had – the countenance and kindness of the executive government'. These impotent resolutions would not strengthen their cause but would leave them friendless and hopeless,

> the dupes of designing and insidious men, slyly and treacherously urging them on to their ruin ... With respect to the part you took in that business, had I previously known or suspected it, I would by no means have consented. I know you have a facility of disposition which exposes you rather to an incautious compliance with those you live in habits of friendship with, and I am also aware that professional young men are in general disposed to accede to measures which place them in a conspicuous point of view. In some instances it may be useful, very often not. The little temporary attentions it produces soon expire. Popular applause is always short-lived but the inconveniences may be serious and lasting ... I earnestly recommend that you keep clear of all further interference ... you

should be particularly circumspect and correct with respect to your words and conduct.

Dan's reply, no doubt tactful and soothing, has not survived; but a year later, newly engaged and anxious to remain in his dear uncle's good books, he promised to 'take no further part whatsoever in the politics of the Catholics of the City'.
On 1st January 1801 O'Connell was

> maddened when I heard the bells of St Patrick's ring out a joyful peal for Ireland's degradation, as if it were a glorious national festival. My blood boiled and I vowed, on that morning, that the foul dishonour should not last if ever I could put an end to it.[5]

This statement, made over forty years later, needs examination. If O'Connell really felt as strongly at that time, his sense of outrage should have been reflected in his speeches and letters. Yet only four times in the next thirty years does he seem to have raised his voice in public for repeal of the union.[6] In 1,202 letters written by and to him between 1st January 1801 and 24th May 1825, the union and repeal are mentioned precisely three times, casually, in passing. Then, on 25th May 1825, he writes to Mary, 'Oh, if some noble spirit would take up the Repeal of the Union! *That, that* would be the cry!'[7] But he did not take the lead himself. The Catholic Emancipation Act was passed in April 1829; a year later he described himself as 'a thorough Repealer'.[8] O'Connell always got his priorities right. For him, Catholic emancipation was top priority: he hardly bothered with repeal until that had been achieved. Furthermore, there were many who supported emancipation but would oppose repeal (and very few who opposed emancipation but would support repeal.) It was therefore only prudent not to show himself as 'a thorough Repealer' until emancipation was in the statute book. That would account for his keeping quiet in public on that subject; but his ignoring the whole matter in his *private* correspondence surely indicates some lack of interest in this cause until about 1825. After 1830, his correspondence is full of it.
Dublin felt most of the dire consequences predicted of the union. Many a grand house in Merrion Square and Fitzwilliam

Square was closed, the furniture draped in dust-sheets or shipped over to London. Luxury trades wilted and failed. Dublin soon looked shabby and provincial. To George III's erratic understanding any concession to Papists seemed a breach of his Coronation Oath, so Pitt had to renege on his half-promises and resigned in disgust. The real problems of Ireland were concerned with land-ownership, usage and tenancy, and the union did nothing to solve these.

On 23rd June 1803, Mary's baby was born at Tralee, a boy, tactfully christened Maurice after Hunting Cap. She immediately took him to Dan's rooms in Dublin.

On 3rd July, just after her arrival, O'Connell came home from the Four Courts and told her, 'There is great bother at the Castle, and they are turning out the small guns at the entrance. I fear there is mischief in the wind.' A few minutes later came a messenger summoning him to parade with the Artillery Corps.[9]

The 'mischief' was a pathetic postscript to 1798, a rising in Dublin led by a young Protestant United Irelander, Robert Emmet. It was hopelessly planned and mismanaged, and the rebels' most notable feat was piking to death, in his coach, the Chief Justice, about the most humane man on the Bench. But it caused O'Connell a deal of trouble. Night after night the corps was out, searching houses for 'croppies'. He dreaded seeing some friend in the line-up of prisoners, but never did. A veteran of five years' service, he could act for himself and speak his mind, at some risk to life and limb. Defending a quite innocent bystander, he narrowly escaped being cut down by an infuriated yeoman; and when a terrified young lad was dragged away under arrest because a crude drawing of a pike had been found in his room, Private O'Connell insisted on his being released. These events left him with an abiding horror of arming civilians and of part-time soldiers. 'Everyone', he said, 'has a tendency to become a ruffian when he has arms in his hands.' Regular soldiers, under discipline, were less ruffianly than part-timers.

Emmet's rebellion occasioned the first political comment by O'Connell in a letter to Mary.

Young Emmett [*sic*] is, they say, certainly arrested in Dublin. If he has been concerned in the late insurrection of which, I fancy, there is no doubt ... he merits and will suffer the

severest punishment ... A man who could coolly prepare so
much bloodshed, so many murders and such horrors of every
kind has ceased to be an object of compassion.[10]

Mary was so agitated that she had to stop nourishing young
Maurice at nature's founts and hurry back to Carhen to engage
as wet-nurse the wife of Jack Darby Moran, Dan's own foster-
brother:

> for which reason I prefer her to any other nurse though she
> does not speak a word of English which to me, you know, is
> unpleasant ... You can't think what a nice room we have got
> inside the drawing-room, by far the snuggest in the house.[11]

Mary's attitude to the Irish language may have influenced
Dan's. He spoke it long before he spoke a word of English. His
grandparents had always spoken it at home, and his grandmother
was a noted Irish poet. But Morgan and Hunting Cap, though
fluent in Irish, usually spoke English. O'Connell, too, spoke Irish
fluently, but it was not an accomplishment he valued, merely a
patois useful for communicating with servants, tenants, witnesses
in court and occasionally with audiences at his public meetings.
Gaelic culture was in decay. The language had (for the time
being) almost ceased to be written. The few remaining bards
lived in a dream-world, singing of lords and ladies as remote as
the Court of King Arthur and flattering the 'Colonels' or anyone
else who could give them a meal and a dram as though they were
Cuchulain or Brian Boru. The eighteenth century produced one
famous Gaelic poem, Merriman's earthy and anti-clerical *Mid-
night Court*, but there is no evidence that O'Connell ever read it.
The Annals of the Four Masters he dismissed as a monotonous
recitation of battles and pedigrees. The culture and language was
to be rehabilitated by the devoted work of nineteenth-century
romanticists and scholars, but O'Connell played no part in this;
he was a man of the eighteenth century, the Age of Reason, not
of the Romantic Revival, and certainly did not regard a smattering of Irish as the hallmark of patriotism. He said:

> I am sufficiently utilitarian not to regret its gradual abandon-
> ment. A diversity of tongues is no benefit; it was first imposed

on mankind as a curse, at the building of Babel. It would be of vast advantage to mankind if all the inhabitants of the earth spoke the same language. Therefore, although the Irish language is connected with many recollections which twine round the hearts of Irishmen, yet the superior utility of the English tongue as a medium of all modern communication is so great that I can witness without a sigh the gradual disuse of Irish.[12]

Indeed his principal weapon in restoring Irish identity and national pride was his matchless command of the English language.

Nor does it seem that he took any interest in Gaelic folklore or legend. A distinguished biographer has stated that his indifference to Gaelic culture has been much exaggerated and that he was a patron of antiquarian organisations devoted to Irish history.[13] Well, a politician lends his patronage to organisations of all kinds if this brings in the votes. If O'Connell had any real interest in the language or the traditions, there would surely be some reference to these in the hundreds of letters he wrote, now collected into eight volumes. There are none. In 1824 an Irish-speaking priest wrote a long and urgent plea[14] for his support in promoting a Catholic Bible in the Gaelic language ('or such parts of it which they deem fit for the perusal of the unlearned') in order to frustrate the knavish tricks of Protestant missionaries whose Gaelic Bible (unexpurgated) had a surprisingly wide circulation. Any Catholic interested in the language would surely have jumped at this, and there would have followed a lively correspondence. If O'Connell sent a reply, it is not extant. Only in his life-style after inheriting Derrynane does he seem to have preserved old traditions, dispensing, like a clan chief, lavish hospitality even to complete strangers, and justice to everyone for miles around, never disputed, never questioned, though he had neither the solvency to support the one nor the magisterial status to give authority to the other.

Emmet's execution in September brought no respite to the Lawyers' Artillery Corps. There was a grand review in Phoenix Park with Private O'Connell under arms from ten in the morning until the late afternoon, and a week later he was 'tired as a dog ... having been out seven hours through the Park, firing, marching, running and counter-marching.' However in November he transferred to a yeomanry corps based in Kerry. Mary was delighted, though she would rather he was not in any:

> It is a great consolation to me, should the French land, not to have you obliged to remain in Dublin. Kerry will be the last place they come to, and the yeomanry, I trust in God, will be able to keep down the common people. They are the only [word missing] I dread in this part of the world.[15]

At the end of 1803, all being quiet in Dublin, he fetched her from Kerry and established her in more commodious lodgings at 7 Upper Ormond Quay, conveniently adjacent to the Four Courts. He gave her £30, with the warning that it was all he had in the world. When they were down to the last pound, he said he knew not where they could get more – but at that moment there arrived at the door a barrister with a brief for him worth £5, and more came in the same day. They were happy. When he came home from work, they dined quietly together and then, if it was fine, walked through the streets and in the park. They stayed in Dublin until early in March when he set off on circuit and she returned to Tralee. She was again in a delicate condition, but this time Dan was spared the tortures of pregnancy – indeed he wrote almost flippantly: 'Do, now, dearest, contrive to get rid of your burden as early in October as possible for indeed, indeed, I cannot possibly go to Dublin without you. The fact is, heart, we arranged the matter badly.' Their second son was born on 31st October 1804, and was christened Morgan. The pattern was repeated the following year, the baby, Ellen, being born on 12th November. It was a curious life for a young married couple, spending a couple of months together in Dublin after Christmas and then together only when he took a day or two off during his spring (March–April) and summer (July–August) circuits, and during his annual September holiday.

Accustomed to turning to Hunting Cap whenever he was under financial pressure, O'Connell ran into debt after their breach in 1803. Moreover he had an unfortunate propensity for borrowing from Peter to lend to Paul and could never give No for an answer. Thus he borrowed from the Knight of Kerry to accommodate the egregious Splinter O'Connell, and borrowed from Ralph Marshal, the High Sheriff, to lend to one of the

Mahonys money which, Mary told him, he was very lucky to see again: 'I wish all who owed you money would surprise you as he has done.' She begged him to hand straight over to her any money he made on circuit, for he had only to show his nose in Kerry for his importunate friends and relations to descend upon him, 'Splinter first of all'. In July 1805 he said farewell to solvency when he bought a house in Dublin, 1 Westland Row, together with all its massive furniture including several handsome Indian cabinets. The deal had all the hallmarks of Dan's financial transactions. He had to borrow, 'for a year', £200 (nearly a quarter of his annual income) from a friend:

> but it is still much more necessary for me that no third person should know that I wanted or got the money. If it were your convenience to accommodate me, I should be sure of *discretion*. This is the first serious favour I have *ever* asked of any person.

However, relief of a sort was at hand. He had been corresponding with Hunting Cap since the breach coldly and formally on business matters, including a windfall of forty barrels of brandy washed up from a wreck, on which the old gentleman 'cleared £1,000 ... but not a word about that'. But Hunting Cap had met Mary and little Maurice at Carhen, and they must have made a good impression. In March 1806 he and Dan were reconciled; Dan was assured of the hereditary part of the Derrynane estate and much more as well. There was nothing in hard cash, but as the old gentleman was now seventy-eight, it should not be difficult to raise reversionary loans on the property. Perhaps, indeed, it would be all too easy.

Mary, too, had her problems. Little Morgan was sent to foster-parents on Valentia Island, half a mile from the mainland. But as she could not 'conquer the dread I have on me of getting into a boat', she hardly ever saw him, even when he was ill. Maurice – dear, chubby, saucy little fellow – at eighteen months was a great talker, but only in Irish. 'Nothing', declared his father, 'can give such delight to the heart of a parent as watching the first faint glimmerings of rational ideas as they fall from the lips of little *beginning babblers*.' But when he had mastered a few words of English, he took to calling his Mama Mary a bitch. Mary's mother contracted a secret marriage to Harry Blennerhassett. Of course the secret was soon out and Tralee tongues wagged. 'Why', asked Dan, 'should you be angry because the folks of Tralee have made verses about your mother and Harry? ... Harry certainly is a subject for comic verse. Do not be angry, darling, but laugh. One certainly lives the longer for laughing.' But there was worse than comic verses. The mature bride was actually caricatured visiting her bridegroom in his sickroom and 'he seated on a certain chair. Only think of their wickedness!'

At the Bar O'Connell made steady progress, his income rising from £346 18s in 1802 to £840 12s in 1805. In 1803 he was briefed in a case arising out of the Popery laws.

My argument lasted about an hour ... I had handsome things said of it particularly by the Chief Baron and by Baron Smith. You need not say anything on this subject further than just mentioning it as you know my father exaggerates every matter of this kind ... The thing has made some noise here.

A few days later he told Mary 'there is not a single individual of the Irish Bar with whom I would consent to change professional expectations'. In 1804 he was *'very, very* busy – not one idle moment and though I am up before eight every morning yet I cannot get through half my business.' At the end of the year his business was increasing daily: 'I do fondly hope that the time is not distant when you shall have all the luxuries of life, now I cannot bestow on you much more than *endearments.*' It would amuse Mary to take a peep at his fee-book. In the 1805 summer assizes he made twice as much in fees as anyone else.

Only think of the fatigue which another would feel in being kept in Court until ten at night without eating a single morsel. This has occurred to me more than once during these assizes and yet I was never in better health or spirits. You know how I love the bustle of the Courts.

He would be seeing her soon in his September holiday.

And now, you villain, I shall when we meet put you in mind of all your fair promises of compliance with every request of mine. In your letters you are the best of all possible wives and the most obedient. But in point of fact you are the sauciest and sturdiest little Vixen that I ever met with ... Seriously, darling, I do *so* doat of you.

It was particularly gratifying, he told his dear uncle after their reconciliation, that those who employed him once generally did so again. Among these satisfied clients was one who, having threatened to horsewhip a lawyer in court for being abusive, was about to be punished by the judge.

I took up the question in that state and made a discourse of about an hour before the most thronged audience you ever saw or that even I ever witnessed. The consequence was that my client, on whom a fine of at least £500 and an imprisonment of three months was about to be inflicted, was discharged with a fine of thirteen shillings and four pence. You cannot conceive of anything so much spoken of as my exhibition was.

Mary might be assured that there was not the least danger 'of any want of complete success in this trade of mine'. At a splendid assize in Limerick,

All my prisoners have been acquitted. The dock alone has produced me a small fortune [i.e. from dock briefs]. I had the County Court House this day for near an hour in a roar of laughter at a witness whom I examined, the judge, jury and all the spectators. I have always remarked that nothing advances an Irish barrister more than the talent of ridicule. At present, darling, I am a little proud of my success in that line.

He was almost as successful, or at least as prominent, in politics, the Dublin Catholic politics in which he had promised Hunting Cap to take no further part. These were conducted by the Catholic Committee under the cautious, conservative aegis of John Keogh, a Dublin tradesman somewhat past his prime, and the Earl of Fingall, who with his yeomanry had been active in suppressing the rebellion but was markedly less valorous in the council chamber than in the field. Under such leadership the Committee was unlikely to set the Liffey on fire.

The prevailing opinion in the Committee was that emancipation could be achieved only by dutiful obedience to His Majesty's government. On 17th November 1804, a sub-committee of twenty-five was elected to draw up a petition for the complete abolition of the Penal Laws which Pitt would be asked to present to parliament. O'Connell was a member, along with (he noted complacently) four peers and three baronets. He took a lead in drafting a 'most *beautiful* Petition' with which Lord Fingall and a deputation of Catholic aristocrats waited on Mr Pitt in March 1805. But Pitt, fearing to precipitate another attack of the royal malady, had promised George III never again to plague him with such Jacobinical measures as Catholic relief; so it was presented to the Upper House by Lord Grenville and to the Lower by Charles James Fox, and thrown out by both.

The Committee was not downhearted, or not much. The king's health was such that at any moment the Prince of Wales might become Regent and they were enthusiastic for Prinny and his friends. He had often made noises favourable to Ireland and Irish Catholics, and Mrs Fitzherbert, indubitably his wife though not Princess of Wales, was herself a Catholic. His great friend, Charles Fox, had always, from a position of relaxed Anglican agnosticism, supported religious liberty, and Fox's star was surely in the ascendant as he joined the 'Ministry of All Talents' as Foreign Secretary and Leader of the House in February 1806. But Fox died in September, and when in 1808 the Committee had another go, O'Connell (with no hope of success) supported the petition only when 'urged on by several of the gentlemen who have been active in its preparation' – the implication being that he hadn't.

On 18th September 1810 he made a speech attracting much attention.[16] It was not on Catholic emancipation, but on a subject in which he had not hitherto shown great interest, the repeal of the union. It was delivered at an aggregate meeting of the freeholders of Dublin (which had been hard hit by the union) assembled to petition parliament for repeal. In the course of a very long, vigorous speech, addressed to a mainly Protestant audience, O'Connell said:

> The Union was a manifest injustice, and it continues to be unjust to this day; it was a crime, and must be still criminal, unless it shall be pretended that crime, like wine, improves by

old age ... We have been robbed, my countrymen, most foully
robbed of our birthright, of our independence ... We have not
forfeited our country by any crimes, neither did we lose it in
any domestic insurrection. No, the rebellion was completely
put down before the Union was accomplished: the Irish militia
and the Irish yeomanry put it down ... England, whom we
have loved and fought and bled for – England whom we protected and still do protect – England, at a period when out of
100,000 seamen in her service 70,000 were Irish – England
stole upon us like a thief in the night and robbed us of this
precious gem of our liberty: she stole from us 'that which
nought enriched her, but made us poor indeed.' ... The Protestant alone could not hope to liberate his country, the Roman
Catholic alone could not do it – neither could the Presbyterian
– but amalgamate the three into the Irishman, and the Union
was repealed ... I trample under foot the Catholic claims if
they can interfere with the Repeal; I abandon all wish for
Emancipation if it delays that Repeal. Nay, were Mr Perceval
tomorrow to offer me the Repeal of the Union upon the terms
of re-enacting the entire penal code, I declare it from my heart
and in the presence of God that I would most cheerfully
embrace his offer. Let us, then, my beloved countrymen, sacrifice our wicked and groundless animosities on the altar of our
country – let us rally round the standard of Old Ireland, and
we shall easily procure that greatest of all political blessings,
an Irish King, an Irish House of Lords and an Irish House of
Commons.

Thereafter, for at least seventeen years, O'Connell hardly mentioned the union or its repeal in public. All his political energies
were concentrated on securing emancipation.

It is, in fact, useless to look for consistency in O'Connell. He
was then aged thirty-three; his character was formed, and would
not greatly change in the next forty years. He was a strange blend
of impetuosity and cool – some would say cold-blooded – calculation. He was, for instance, impetuous in rushing to join up in
1798 and in his marriage, but crafty in his handling of Hunting
Cap on both occasions. He could denounce the Saxon in terms
of unmeasured vituperation, but he never lost sight of the practical advantages of some political connection with a powerful

neighbour. He was often economical of the truth, telling different versions of it to different people; antagonists had to be very careful to mark *exactly* what he said, not what he seemed to imply. He was vain and could joke about it. His letters to Mary are naively full of his triumphs, and when asked who was the greatest living Irishman, he replied without hesitation, 'After myself, I suppose old Harry Grattan.' Complimented on his modesty in an after-dinner speech, he replied that he had indeed a good stock of that quality, never having had occasion to use any.

He was jovial, witty, convivial, boundlessly (and imprudently) hospitable in the pattern of a Gaelic chieftain, an enchanting conversationalist and an entertaining raconteur.

Various incidents in his career, his avoidance of several duels and confrontations, gave the ill-disposed the opportunity to question his physical courage. Since this could be ruinous to an Irish politician, it is indeed fortunate that the only duel he did fight was against a dead shot. Thereafter jibes that he was frightened of powder and ball could not really be made to stick.

His over-sanguine temperament, afterwards to distort his political judgment, was at this time applied disastrously to his personal finances. His income from the Bar was rising year by year, amounting in 1809 to £2,736, a very handsome sum. But every penny was spent long before it was earned. His letters to Mary are full of complicated instructions to pay off one creditor, give another enough to keep him quiet and put off a third. He never really knew how much he owed, and certainly never understood how much she must spend to support his household and family. He wrote:

I am really getting a load of money. At this rate you will soon have not only carriages but a country house. It is an infinite pleasure to me to suceed thus as it enables me to give my sweetest little woman all the luxuries of life. We loved each other, darling, when we were poor, and as we were really so, it was almost our only consolation to love each other. And now that we are becoming rich it is the chief sweetener of life.

But two years later she had to write:

I want money, love ... How are you darling, after all your wrangling? I suppose by this time on your way to Cork where

I expect you will make another small fortune ... I paid McKenna's bill ... and yesterday I paid the Fire Insurance £3 3s 11d for you. So you see, heart, if you are sending me the money how fast I *am disposing* of it again, and how incumbent it is on you to be *prudent* with so large a family to support in Dublin where every article at present is as dear as dear can be.

Nothing could have been more imprudent than his sale in the autumn of 1809 of the modest house in Westland Row (not yet paid for) and the purchase of a much larger, more expensive house in the fashionable Merrion Square. 'My dearest love,' wrote Mary in despair,

I wish to God you could get the house in the Square off your hands. Where on earth will you be able to get a thousand guineas for Ruxton? I can't tell you, love, how unhappy I am about this business ... For God's sake, darling love, let me entreat you to give up this house in the Square if it is in your power, as I see no other way for you to get out of difficulties. If you borrow this money for Ruxton, how will you pay it back? In short, love, I scarce know what I write I am so unhappy about this business.

He paid not the smallest attention, but pressed ahead with the purchase as though she had never written a word.

In 1808, two years after their reconciliation, Hunting Cap actually gave him £100, and promised the same for every assizes. During the next two years he gave Dan about £2,750 for the purchase of land in Kerry: 'He was never half so fond of me as he is at present.' With his father's death in May 1809, O'Connell came into the property at Carhen. In 1811 his gross rental amounted to £2,400. Even though he had to pay a jointure to his mother of £227 and mortgage interest amounting to £224 a year, with his income from the Bar (about £3,000 in that year), it should have been more than enough. It was, however, a mere drop in the ocean of his expenditure.

And not merely in his expenditure. Hunting Cap had something to say about his fatal propensity for obliging a friend.

I can scarcely express to you the uneasiness I feel ... well knowing, as I before mentioned, the softness and facility of your disposition and with what ease designing men may draw you into their measures ... I therefore again and again most earnestly caution you against it and further add that no feeble or temporising excuses will have any sort of weight with me and your neglecting to comply with what I not only so urgently beseech and request but what I decidedly command will cause a breach between us never to be healed.

This was a warning which he would be imprudent to ignore, and no doubt he paid much more attention, for a few months, to his uncle's views than to his wife's. Indeed in these matters he treated her abominably, especially in view of her nervous disposition.

Yet he passionately loved his 'sweet bedfellow ... and what a saucy wretch I am to talk to her in this way'; for fear of a scolding, he still wrote to her almost every day they were separated, 'see what it is to be too indulgent to a saucy cocknosed woman'. As for the children – six – by the end of 1810* – he doted on them, and sent them with nearly every letter 'a thousand thousand kisses'. But it was Mary who had to discipline them.

Maurice, in his father's somewhat over-sanguine view, was the very mirror of himself when young – lively, affectionate, 'never without a book' (including Gibbon's *Decline and Fall of the Roman Empire* at the tender age of seven), longing for the day when he could be given a gun. When Mary reported that he was sometimes ill-mannered, sheepish and careless, she was instructed to 'reduce him to perpetual obedience' by confining him to the nursery or excluding him from the dinner-table. 'As to my darling Morgan, you *must* control him'; but Morgan was a difficult child, due perhaps to his infancy on Valentia Island when his mother, unable to overcome her dread of setting foot in a boat, hardly ever saw him. He was inclined to sulk, did not display affection as the others did, and was so averse to learning that he often had to be put in 'the black hole' before he would say a

*Maurice, b. 27th June 1803; Morgan, b. 31st October 1804; Ellen, b. 12th November 1805; Catherine, b. 18th March 1807; Betsey, b. 21st February 1810; and John, b. 20th December 1810. Edward, born in July 1808, died only six months later.

word of his lesson. Nevertheless, 'poor neglected Morgan' got a full share of his father's epistolary kisses.

To her fond father Nell was good as gold, 'sweetest temper and disposition'. In Kate's view she was a tomboy who preferred playing with whips, tops and balls to playing with dolls. To the teacher of her day-school, a sister of the feminist Mrs Wollstone-craft Godwin, she was a thoroughly objectionable child, a bully, and idle about learning her hymns, for which she was beaten. This brought about a scene with her mother next day: 'you may suppose how bold she must have been when I was obliged to beat her with a rod, all occasioned by fear and terror of going to school.' Dan congratulated Mary on her firmness: 'if you had given up the point, she would have conquered you for life' and been a 'torment to herself and to us'. Kate was a saucy little baggage, growing more impudent every day but a little darling and her father's treasure. Even Kate, however, 'should not be allowed to be so *decided* in her opinions' (at the age of three). 'Consider of it, my love, and see whether it be better to begin with an early and gentle control.' Betsey, at four weeks old, caused no problem, clinging to her father's heart like a 'sweet little fly of a babe'. Should not little John be inoculated for the cow pock? Mary must see to it.

6

The Counsellor

In the Four Courts in Dublin and the assize courts of Ennis, Limerick, Tralee and Cork, Counsellor O'Connell's reputation grew year by year. Men charged with every crime from murder to common assault clamoured to be defended by him. Unable as a Catholic to take silk, he made up his income by a multitude of small fees from poor men involved in petty cases. Even petty cases could be complicated and time-consuming, but he quickly mastered the essentials of each and, striding from court to court with a huge, bulging brief-case, often conducted several cases a day like a grand master playing several games of chess at once. His *forte* was the cross-examination of hostile witnesses, his technique that of a man tapping away at a masonry wall to find a weak spot wherein to drive home a peg. With the utmost good humour, in a coaxing, confidential voice, from time to time rolling his large, blue-grey eyes at judge and jury as he made a point, he would ask question after question, many quite irrelevant, until he trapped the witness into a lie or a contradiction. Dwelling on this only long enough to ensure that the court appreciated it, he would tap away somewhere else, and reveal another flaw in the prosecution case.

Of course he knew the law backwards; there was no one so quick to take advantage of an opponent's technical error. One of his regular clients was acquitted in successive years of highway robbery, burglary and attempted murder; then he seized a brig and set up as a pirate. He was caught red-handed, and again

O'Connell defended him, getting him off, against all the odds, because his offence, if any, had taken place on the high seas, over which only the Admiralty, not the assize court, had jurisdiction. The ruffian, surprised and delighted, exclaimed as he left the dock, 'May the Lord spare you, Counsellor, *to me!*'

He had often to cross-examine in Irish. There was no regular court interpreter, but one would be co-opted and sworn in for a particular case. The delay caused by the interpretation of question and answer must have handicapped him because the witness (who might understand a little English though he preferred to speak Irish) would be given time to consider his next answer. But it was to his advantage that he could often spot the meaning of an English-speaking witness who had translated in his mind direct from the Irish, as his meaning might not be quite what a native English speaker would understand from the words. In one probate case the issue was whether the testator had been alive when he 'signed' the will (by making his mark), or whether his hand had been held and moved after death. Witness after witness deposed, in the same words, that 'life was in him' (*Bhi beatha ann*) when he made his mark. O'Connell was struck by the constant repetition of the unusual phrase 'life was in him', and asked, 'By virtue of your oath, witness, was the man alive?'

'By virtue of my oath, life was in him.'

'Aye, so I suspect. Now, by the solemn oath you have taken, and as you shall one day answer for it, was there not *a live fly in the dead man's mouth* when his hand was put to the will?'

The unnerved witness confessed that it was so.

Singularly enough (for a man whose own finances were in such chaos) he was particularly skilful at unravelling complex financial cases, and on one occasion proved that a client being sued for a debt of £1,100 was actually owed £700 by the plaintiff.

He was adept, however weak his case, at winning the jury's sympathy by a well-timed joke. In one case concerning the diversion of a client's stream, the opposing attorney was a stout man with a very expensive face named Fogarty. O'Connell related how his client's stream, once copious, had been reduced to a miserable trickle until 'there is not now, gentlemen, as much water remaining as would make grog for Fogarty!' The Solicitor General, Doherty, affected an upper-crust English accent, in which on one occasion he told a witness, 'You may go down, sir.'

At once O'Connell, a gifted mimic, was on his feet: 'Naw, naw, daunt go down, sir!' and the court collapsed in laughter.

He was not above discrediting a witness by blatant trickery. In a murder case (O'Connell for the defence) the strongest evidence for the prosecution was the accused's hat, left at the scene of the crime and positively identified by a prosecution witness. O'Connell examined the inside of the hat with care, slowly spelling out the accused's name, 'J, A, M, E, S, ... Were these words in the hat when you found it?'

'They were.'

'Did you see them there?'

'I did.'

'This is the same hat?'

'It is.'

'Now, my lord,' – O'Connell held up the hat to the Bench – 'there is an end to the case – there is no name whatever inscribed in the hat.'

No one knew better when to browbeat, when to coax and when to flatter a witness – and a judge, too. Baron M'Clennand tried it on with him: 'When I was at the Bar, Mr O'Connell, it was not my habit to anticipate briefs.'

'When you were at the Bar, my lord, I never chose you for my model, and now that you are on the Bench, I shall not submit to your dictation.'

But when he undertook a hopeless defence in a murder case, and found that the young, inexperienced Judge Lefroy was presiding (his senior being ill), O'Connell deliberately put to the witness a number of leading questions, which the judge disallowed. 'As you refuse me permission to defend my client, my lord,' said O'Connell, 'I leave his fate in your hands, his blood be upon your head if he is condemned.' He then swept out of the court and Lefroy, unsure of himself, instructed the jury to acquit.

The weaker his case, the more perfect his act of indignation. He

> caught up his brief-bag in a seeming fury and dashed it against the witness-table, frowned, muttered fearfully to himself, sat down in a rage with a horrid scowl on his face, bounced up again in a fit of boiling passion and solemnly protested in the

face of Heaven against such injustice, threw his brief away, swaggered out of the Court House – then swaggered back again, and wound up by brow-beating and abusing half-a-dozen more witnesses and, without any real grounds whatever, finally succeeded in making half the jury refuse to bring in a verdict of 'Guilty'.[1]

No one could play the buffoon with more effect. A client named Boyle was a thorn in the flesh of the Cork Corporation, mocking them, defying them, lampooning them in the press and generally causing trouble but keeping just to windward of the law. At last they thought they had him, for assaulting a Sheriff in a minor brawl. O'Connell knew it was useless to conduct a normal defence against a prejudiced judge and a packed Cork Protestant jury so, instead, he told them a story. A man, he said, was charged with murder, following a faction-fight at a fair. The evidence against him was strong – until he called as his first witness his supposed victim, not merely alive but hale and hearty. The judge charged the jury to bring in a verdict of Not Guilty, but after a long absence they returned and to everyone's astonishment declared the accused Guilty. 'Good God!' exclaimed the judge. 'Of what is he guilty? Not of murder, surely.' 'No, my lord,' said the foreman, 'but if he didn't murder that man, sure he stole my grey mare three years ago.'

O'Connell turned to the jurymen. 'So, gentlemen, if Mr Boyle did not wilfully assault the Sheriff, sure he has libelled the Corporation. Find him Guilty, if you dare!'

They dared not.

He would not allow his own witnesses to be bullied. One prosecuting counsel who tried it on was silenced by a roar from O'Connell, 'Sit down, you audacious, snarling, pugnacious ram-cat!' As the Ram-Cat he was known for the rest of his days.

O'Connell also had compassion. It upset him when even the worst of his clients was hanged. But he had no qualms about securing the acquittal of the most unmitigated rogue. When reproached for his successful defence of a blackguard who 'was not fit to live', he replied solemnly, 'Well, my friend, he is still more unfit to die.'

He was remarkably successful at defending those accused of terrorist offences – murder, arson and so on. He attributed this to the fact that he never, in addressing the court or in examining witnesses, mitigated or excused atrocious crimes; indeed he constantly expressed his abhorrence of them, which inclined judge and jury to view favourably his argument that his own client was totally innocent of the horrid deed.

His lifelong political and personal foe, Robert Peel, paid a remarkable tribute to his forensic genius. If ever, he said, he had a really difficult case, he would 'readily give up all the other orators of whom we have been talking, provided I had with me this same broguish Irish fellow'. One of O'Connell's many Orange clients took a friend to hear him cross-examine a witness. 'Now,' he said, 'you see why I give my money to that Papist rascal.'

Indeed a high proportion of his clients in civil cases were Protestants, because Catholics, never quite confident of obtaining justice in courts where all the judges and most of the jurymen were Protestants, felt it more prudent to hire a Protestant lawyer than a Catholic who had, moreover, a reputation for intemperance of speech.

He did not always have things his own way. Defending a boy charged with stealing a calf, he was cross-examining the wife of the complainant, who was not going to be browbeaten or shaken by the famous counsellor.

'How did you come by this calf, my good woman?'

'What's that to you?'

'Oh, I have a reason for asking.'

'Honestly, then, which is more than the boy who took it can say.'

'Oh, of course you wouldn't have it any other way, but how did you get the calf?'

'To buy it, I did.'

'Where did you get the money?'

She would not give a plain answer, and when he asked the question for the tenth time, she suddenly shouted, 'Ah, you knows all the *roguery* of it, but you don't know the *honesty* of it!' The court was convulsed with laughter at the counsellor's discomfiture.

The laugh was also against him when he appeared in court in an unaccustomed role, complainant in a lawsuit against a pugilistic Dublin attorney named Toby Glasscock who had threatened to send a servant to horsewhip him. Since Glasscock was both violent and deficient in intellect, O'Connell judged it prudent to have him bound over to keep the peace. Glasscock declared in court that his small size should have saved a big fellow like O'Connell from any apprehension, and offered to produce the servant. He dived under the table, hauled out a large bag, untied the string and shook from it a diminutive black boy, clothed in green livery and grinning from ear to ear.

For a young barrister so successful, and so popular with his colleagues, the Munster circuit was a delight – the long rides or coach drives through magnificent country from inn to inn with O'Connell, as was his habit, jovially roaring out some Latin hymn:

> *Lauda Sion Salvatorem,*
> *Lauda Ducem et Pastorem* ...

– the bustle and excitement of the courts, the clink of the guineas paid to him by grateful clients. In the evening the Bar forgathered round a long table in the best inn under the genial presidency of Gerry Keller or Con Lyne ('Con of the Hundred Bottles'). The jugs of claret and the decanters of port circulated while men who a couple of hours earlier had been in bitter conflict of word and wit exchanged Bar (and doubtless other) stories and called for more wine and song, a sentimental ballad, perhaps, or some less sentimental ditty such as 'The Night that Larry Was Stretched'.

Only the town of Ennis was still hateful to him, with its mean cabins and narrow, squalid, disorderly streets. The inhabitants were mean, too, with

> a strange want of hospitality. Only think that I am obliged to trudge off to a solitary dinner at a tavern every day, and that too when without vanity I may be allowed to say I have made an impression on *the natives*. After all, darling, I am more pleased by myself than in any of their companies.

Indeed Ennis's only virtue was 'a most laudable spirit of litigation'. It is ironical that he should have thought so badly of the place destined to be the scene of his greatest triumph.

The politics of Catholic emancipation were roused from torpor by an issue as old as the differences between Church and state – the Crown's claim to disallow, on political grounds, the Pope's choice of a bishop, known in political jargon as the 'Veto'.

In preliminary soundings before the union was enacted the government had canvassed the idea that Catholic emancipation (not actually promised but implied if the union went through) should be accompanied by two safeguards or 'wings': firstly the Veto, and secondly the endowment by the state of a fund from which Catholic bishops and clergy should be paid.

This was considered by the trustees of Maynooth College, which had been set up by the government to provide reliable Catholic clergy rather than foreign-trained priests who might be contaminated by Jacobinism. In 1799 the trustees (including four archbishops and six bishops) informed Castlereagh in a confidential memorandum that in the appointment of bishops 'such interference of the government as may enable it to be satisfied with the loyalty of the person appointed is just and ought to be agreed to.' This was not made public, and on the failure of Pitt to deliver his side of the bargain in 1801 the issue lapsed.

In May 1808, however, during a Commons debate on an unsuccessful motion by Grattan for Catholic emancipation accompanied by safeguards, the contents of the Maynooth memorandum were disclosed and aroused much indignation in Dublin. In September the Catholic bishops in synod rejected the Veto as inexpedient, but not as wrong in principle. Again, the matter lapsed.

It was revived early in 1810 by an inaccurate press report. On 16th January the *Dublin Evening Post* stated that the English Catholic Board intended to offer the Crown the Veto. What had, in fact, happened was that Lord Grenville, who supported emancipation, had written to the Earl of Fingall suggesting that Irish Catholics should offer the Veto in order to expedite emancipation. Edward Jerningham, Secretary of the English Catholic Board, wrote on 9th February to O'Connell, who was acting as secretary to the Irish Catholic Committee in the absence of the permanent secretary, denying categorically that the English Catholic Board had even considered the Veto. However he admitted that, after consultation with Grenville and Lord Grey (also a supporter of emancipation), and solely to oblige their lordships, the Board had voted that 'they are firmly persuaded that adequate provision for the maintenance of the civil and religious establishments of this kingdom may be made ... and that any arrangement founded on this basis ... will meet with their grateful concurrence.' This could mean almost anything, and seems to relate mainly to the endowment of the clergy; but Jerningham assured O'Connell that it had nothing to do with the Veto and nothing to do with Grenville's approach to Lord Fingall.

It was, in short, a right cock-up. John Keogh, doyen of Dublin Catholics, wrote to O'Connell, 'It seems that Lords Grenville and Grey have yielded the important point of not calling the Veto *by that name*. These statesmen and candidates for power are content with the *substance* under any other *title*.' The ensuing differences between English and Irish Catholics were to delay emancipation for a generation.

Catholics like Fingall generally supported the Veto because it would hasten emancipation and provide by endowment a source of income for the clergy more reliable, and less resented in times of depression, than voluntary contributions. Conservative and loyalist to the core, they saw nothing wrong in the Crown being able to reject a politically suspect prelate.

O'Connell, however, took the lead in passionate agitation against the Veto. His objections were:

1 It would increase the Crown's patronage.
2 In breaching O'Connell's cherished principle of the separation of Church and state, it would give an English Protestant government considerable power in the affairs of the Irish Catholic Church.
3 The people would lose all confidence in bishops chosen and priests endowed by the Crown. As he wrote to the Knight of Kerry (the M.P. for the county) who supported emancipation, 'The *Crown Priests* will be despised and deserted by the people, who will be amply supplied with enthusiastic anti-Anglican friars from the continent.'[2]

It should have been a time peculiarly favourable to emancipation. Since 1810 the Prince of Wales had been Regent. After the assassination of Spencer Perceval in 1812, Lord Liverpool became Prime Minister, and his Cabinet included a minister,

George Canning, who supported the Catholic claims. In 1812
Canning brought in a bill for emancipation, with 'wings', which
was passed by the Commons but thrown out by the Lords. In
1813 Grattan tried again; his bill was passed by the Commons in
February and hopes ran high. But Canning then proposed two
commissions, one in England and one in Ireland, composed of
Catholic landowners who would exercise the power of Veto in
the name of the Crown. The English Catholic Board favoured
this idea, but O'Connell violently attacked it and abused Grattan
for supporting it; the Irish hierarchy took the same line and,
because of divisions among Catholics, the bill was thrown out.

Meanwhile the English Catholic Board, having third thoughts
on the matter, had appealed to Rome for a decision on whether
the Veto was schismatic or harmful to the Church. The Pope
being Napoleon's prisoner in Fontainebleau, the decision had to
be made by the aged (and, according to many biographers, face-
less) Vice-Prefect of Propaganda, Monsignor Quarantotti. In a
rescript sent in February 1814 to the Vicar Apostolic in London,
he laid down that English and Irish Catholics (he clearly had
difficulty in distinguishing between them) should accept the Veto.
The rescript was not published in Dublin until May, and since
Napoleon had abdicated on 3rd April it was widely and erroneously assumed that the rescript had been issued by the Pope
himself as his first act on being liberated. This caused great
consternation, and a rumour that His Holiness had turned Or-
angeman, but rumour had exaggerated. The fury of O'Connell
and the anti-Vetoists then turned against Quarantotti, 'a mischievous understrapper'. O'Connell, never an ultramontane, declared that he would as soon receive his politics from Constanti-
nople as from Rome. The rescript was then recalled by the Pope
and submitted to the mature deliberations of the Cardinals of the
College of the Propagation of the Faith, but significantly the
mischievous understrapper was made a cardinal.[3]

During the summer of 1814 the Catholic Board (formerly the
Catholic Committee) was declared by the government to be an
unlawful body because, in claiming to represent Irish Catholics,
it breached the Convention Act. O'Connell, perusing the banning
order, exclaimed, 'It's illegal, every word of it! ... We are not an
elected or delegated body.' It was decided, however, to drop the
name 'Catholic Board' while continuing its functions as a body

organising the agitation for emancipation, principally through aggregate meetings. Most of the Veto-ists, headed by Lord Fingall, left it, and leadership passed into the hands of O'Connell and a group of young, middle-class Dublin activists, mainly lawyers. But he had little hope of achieving emancipation in the near future and wrote to Mary, 'Every *thing* seems to be against it and surely, while the Catholics continue to disagree among themselves, what can they expect?' Moreover the Regent, in whom high hopes had been placed, harboured in his obese carcase, beneath those layers of perfumed blubber and royal affability, a stone core of anti-Catholic bigotry.

In January 1815 there was a rumour that the Pope favoured the Veto. At an aggregate meeting in a Catholic chapel, speaking from the very altar, O'Connell made an angry speech which in former days might have attracted the unfavourable notice of the Inquisition.

> Let our determination never to consent reach Rome ... I am sincerely a Catholic, but I am not a Papist. I deny that the Pope has any temporal authority, directly or indirectly, in Ireland. We have all denied that authority on oath, and we would die to resist it ... If the present clergy shall descend ... to become the vile slaves of the clerks of the Castle ... I warn them to look to their masters for support, for the people will despise them too much to contribute ... and the Castle clergy will preach to still thinner numbers than attend in Munster or in Connaught the reverend gentlemen of the present Established Church.[4]

In March he heard that the Pope was positively backing the Veto: 'God grant that it may not be true.' A few days later he heard that the Pope wasn't. But he was. In April came a formal communication from the Vatican that the Pope agreed to submit to the Crown for approval the names of candidates for vacant dioceses.

O'Connell was furious, and the Irish hierarchy much perturbed. The better to continue the agitation, he suggested that the defunct Catholic Board be resurrected as the Catholic Association. Keogh warned that this also might fall foul of the Convention Act, so O'Connell, who boasted that he could drive a coach-and-four through any law, took paper and pen and drafted the article which would frustrate any Crown lawyer on that score: the Association 'were not representatives of the Catholic Body nor of any portion thereof, nor shall they assume or pretend to be representatives of the Catholic Body or any portion thereof.'

In August the bishops met in synod and came out, in respectful defiance of the Pontiff, unequivocally against the Veto.

O'Connell was delighted, although emancipation was indefinitely postponed. But he was hurt by the breach the Veto controversy made with so many friends, particularly Grattan whom he loved and respected although Grattan had 'watched Irish independence in the cradle and followed it to the tomb'. When Grattan supported the Veto, O'Connell attacked even his old hero: 'Since he has inhaled the foul and corrupt atmosphere that fills some of the corridors to Westminster, there have not been the same health and vigour in him.' Grattan, who had himself a nice line in invective, savaged O'Connell as a vain, swaggering and shallow opportunist who, when insulted, would not fight. Another friend, Stephen Woulfe, made a strong pro-Veto speech at an aggregate meeting in Limerick. O'Connell then told them the story of the sheep who were fattening under the protection of their dogs, 'when an address to get rid of the dogs was presented to them by the wolves. The leading Woulfe came forward and persuaded them to give up their dogs – they obeyed him and were instantly devoured.' Said Woulfe afterwards, 'How useless it is to contend with O'Connell. Here I have made an oration which I have been elaborating for three weeks – and he demolishes the effect of my rhetoric by a flash of humour!'

Another friend and emancipation activist who differed from O'Connell on the Veto was a much younger man, Richard Lalor Sheil, a well-to-do lawyer and dramatist with a French and Trinity College background. He was a turgid orator, spouting out a torrent of words several lengths ahead of his thoughts, but became one of O'Connell's most valued lieutenants when the Veto controversy was disposed of and all good Catholics could unite in the campaign for emancipation.

Most of his group, however, stood by him on the Veto. There was Keogh, old but respected for his past services and still valuable to the cause. Edward Hay was for many years the indispensable secretary to the Catholic Committee/Board/Association – diligent, reliable and accurate. He was to be succeeded as secretary by Nicholas Purcell O'Gorman, a bulky, whimsical but earnest barrister and O'Connell's 'friend' in a duel. Peter Bodkin Hussey was another of the group, a barrister and a Kerryman, an old flame of Mary's who would have liked to have married her but who remained a good friend to her and Dan after their marriage – so good as to lend him £500.

Less of an asset to a responsible political organisation was Jack Lawless – amusing, slapdash, a troublemaker at meetings and thoroughly unreliable. Another liability was Dr Thomas Dromgoole, beetle-browed and belligerent, who would gladly have reactivated the Holy Inquisition, rack, stake and all. He was bad-mannered, bad-tempered, and made (said O'Connell, perhaps with some exaggeration) the only really bigoted speeches on the Catholic side during the whole emancipation campaign. Mary, Hay and O'Connell himself all thought Dromgoole odious.

These were to form the inner circle of O'Connell's Catholic Association. Allied to them were some Protestant liberals whose support he prized very highly – his old friend Bennett; Maurice FitzGerald, Knight of Kerry, their indispensable representative in the House of Commons; George Lidwill, a County Tipperary landowner; and Major William Nugent MacNamara from County Clare.

Perhaps the most important result of the Veto controversy was that it brought O'Connell, in the prime of his intellect and vigour, to the forefront of Catholic politics. The Veto was hardly an issue to stiffen the sinews and summon up the blood of the man in the street or the potato-patch, and O'Connell, who could have made a fortune on the stage, used to give a hilarious impersonation of a parish priest instructing his flock on the subject:

Now, *ma boughali*, you haven't got gumption and should therefore be guided by them that have. As none of you know what the Veto is, I'll just make it all as clear as a whistle to yez. The Veto, you see, is a Latin word, *ma boughali*, and none of yez understands Latin. But *I* will let you know all the ins and outs of it, boys, if you'll only just listen to me now. The Veto is a thing that – you see, boys, the Veto is a thing that – that the meeting on Monday is to be held about! (Cheers, cries of Hear! Hear!) The Veto is a thing that – in short, boys, it's a thing that has puzzled wiser people than any of yez! In short, boys, as none of yez is able to comprehend the Veto, I needn't take up any more of your time about it now; but I'll give you this piece of advice, boys; just go to the meeting, and listen to Counsellor O'Connell, and just do whatever he bids yez, boys![5]

It set a pattern; more and more the Catholic Irish people were to go to 'the meeting', listen to Counsellor O'Connell, and just do whatever he bid them.

The Veto was not O'Connell's only problem. In 1812 there arrived as Chief Secretary a 24-year-old Tory politician with whom he was destined to be linked in enmity for over thirty years. Robert Peel was the kind of Englishman that the Irish most detest. Arrogant, cocksure and supercilious, he had a habit of closing his eyes while arguing, as though the very sight of someone who disagreed with him were too painful to be borne. He was determined to have no truck with emancipation and to stand no nonsense from Papists. O'Connell promptly named him Orange Peel; and, ascertaining that he was the son of a self-made manufacturer, opened the round with a smart punch below the belt by describing him as 'this youth squeezed out of the workings of I know not what factory in England ... sent here before he got over the foppery of perfumed handkerchiefs and thin shoes – a lad ready to vindicate anything or everything.'

Peel's opportunity came in 1813 with the retirement of the Viceroy, the Duke of Richmond. There were dozens of Dublin newspapers, all owned by Protestants, most of them subsidised directly or indirectly by the Castle. But the *Dublin Evening Post*, although owned and edited by Protestants, supported the Catholic cause. The editor, John Magee, attacked the Duke of Richmond as no better than the worst of the viceroys.

They insulted, they oppressed, they murdered and they deceived ... The profligate, unprincipled Westmorland, the cold-hearted and cruel Camden, the treacherous Cornwallis left Ireland more divided and oppressed than they found her

87

... increased coercion and corruption and uniformly employed them against the liberties of the people.

Proceedings were instituted against Magee for criminal libel of the Duke of Richmond. The case was heard in the King's Bench on 26th July 1813 before the Chief Justice, William Downes, the prosecution being led by the Attorney General, William Saurin, and the defence by O'Connell. The jury was packed, Protestants to a man, including several known Orangemen.

Black-eyed, lank-haired, with a lean and hungry look, Saurin resembled a Gilray cartoon of a Frenchman. He was, in fact, the grandson of a Huguenot refugee and, like many such, bitterly anti-Catholic. Although he had opposed the union, and had once struck an Artillery Corps drummer for wearing an Orange sash, he now seemed to regard the law courts as a political battlefield, and politics as the Saurins' opportunity to avenge the *dragonnades*. He really believed that 'the tremendous licentiousness of the Press calls for the intervention of the law', and in his closing address violently abused not only Magee but the Catholic Board which had nothing to do with the case.

O'Connell knew that, before this judge and jury, he could not hope to extricate Magee from the morass into which his unguarded words had led him. Probably with his client's agreement, he more or less abandoned the defence of Magee and used the court as a sounding board for the most audacious attack on judge, jury, Attorney General and the whole Ascendancy system.[6]

He professed pure and unmixed compassion for the Attorney General and his discourse:

a farrago of helpless absurdity ... violent and virulent, it was a confused and disjointed tissue of bigotry, amalgamated with congenital vulgarity ... He called my client a malefactor, a Jacobin and a ruffian ... he called him a brothel-keeper, a pander, a kind of bawd in breeches ... I cannot repress my astonishment that the Attorney General could have preserved this diet in its native purity; he has for some years mixed among the highest orders in the State; he has the honour to belong for thirty years to the first profession in the world – to the only profession with the single exception perhaps of the military, to which a high-minded gentleman would condescend

to belong – the Irish Bar ... With this galaxy of glory flinging
their light around him, how can he alone have remained in
darkness? How has it happened that the twilight murkiness of
his soul has not been illuminated with a single ray shot from
their lustre? ... How can he have memory enough to preserve
his original vulgarity? ... from my inmost soul I bestow upon
him my compassion and my boundless pity ... As to his attack
on the Catholic Board, I do here brand him as an infamous
and profligate liar.

The Chief Justice here intervened, 'What, Mr O'Connell, can
this have to do with the question the jury has to try?'
'You heard the Attorney General traduce and calumniate us,
you heard him with patience and with temper. Listen, now, to
our vindication.'
All Catholics asked was to share in the advantages of the
excellent constitution. Why on earth, then, should they seek to
destroy it? The Attorney General had boasted that he had put
down the Catholic Committee, and that he would, in his own
good time, put down the Catholic Board. His venting of unmeasured and malignantly expressed hatred of Catholics had, to be
sure, no connection with the case –

but, gentlemen of the jury, it had a direct and natural connection with you ... Gentlemen, he thinks he knows his men, he
thinks he knows you. Many of you signed the No Popery
petition ... He knows you would not have been summoned
upon this jury if you had entertained liberal sentiments ...
Therefore he endeavours to win your confidence and command
your affections by the display of his congenital illiberality and
bigotry. You are, of course, all Protestants. See what a compliment he pays to your religion and his own when he endeavours thus to procure a verdict by the violation of your oaths!
... Will you allow him to draw you into perjury out of zeal for
your religion?

O'Connell now turned to the Chief Justice who was noted for
his wealth, Bible reading and godliness:

No judge ought to dictate to a jury, no jury ought to allow

itself to be dictated to ... At some future period some man may attain the first place on the Bench by the reputation of churchwarden piety, added to a great gravity and a maidenly decorum of manners – I am putting a purely imaginary case – he may be a man without passions and therefore without vices. He may be a man, my lord, superfluously rich and therefore not to be bribed by money but rendered partial by his prejudices. Such a man, inflated by flattery and bloated in his dignity, may hereafter use his character for sanctity, which has served to promote him, as a sword for hewing down the struggling liberties of his country. Such a judge may intervene before trial and at the trial be a partisan. Gentlemen, should an honest jury – if an honest jury were to be found – obey with safety the dictates of such a judge? ... Is there among you any one friend of freedom? Is there among you one man who esteems equal and impartial justice? ... If there be, Mr Magee appeals to his kindred mind and confidently expects an acquittal ... But if there be none, if you be slaves and hypocrites, he will await your verdict – and despise it.

The jury was neither amused nor impressed, and found Magee guilty. But O'Connell was not addressing the jury, his words were addressed to a wider audience. His speech was reported in every Irish newspaper, so that something like 100,000 copies of it were sold in Ireland. It was translated into French and sold in France and a copy was sent to every member of the Spanish Cortes. O'Connell, a star turn in Ireland, had stepped on to the European stage.

Peel wrote to Lord Whitworth, the new Viceroy:

O'Connell spoke for four hours completely, but intentionally, abandoning the cause of his client – I have no doubt with his client's consent – taking the opportunity of uttering a libel even more atrocious than that which he proposed to defend upon the Government and administration of justice in Ireland. His abuse of the Attorney General was more scurrilous and vulgar than was ever permitted within the walls of a court of justice. He insulted the jury individually and collectively, accused the Chief Justice of corruption and prejudice, and avowed himself a traitor, if not to Ireland, at least to the British Empire.

There was much indignation in the Castle at the Chief Justice's weakness in letting O'Connell get away with it, and Peel hoped that the Chief Justice would not 'again allow the Court to be insulted and made a vehicle of treason'.

Peel was no lawyer, and O'Connell was far too wily ever to expose himself to a charge of treason throughout his career he had the warmest admiration for the British Empire and an understanding of the advantages for Ireland of belonging to it, for in Australia and Canada Irishmen would find opportunities denied them at home.

When Magee came up for sentence, Saurin complained of this wanton and malignant attack on an officer of the Crown. O'Connell replied:

I yield in nothing to the Attorney General. I deny, in the strongest terms, his unfounded and absurd claim to superiority. I am at least his equal in birth, his equal in fortune, his equal certainly in education; and as to talent I should not add that, for there is little vanity in claiming equality with him. Only my profound respect for this temple of the law enables me to overcome the infirmities of my nature and listen with patience to an attack which, had it been made elsewhere, would have met merited chastisement.

Judge Day was horrified. 'What's that you say? Chastise the Attorney General?'

O'Connell repeated that, had he been thus assailed elsewhere, he would have gone beyond the law 'to inflict corporal punishment for that offence which I am ready, out of consideration for the Court, to pardon'.

How crafty he was, like a skilful guerilla fighter, hitting hard but always leaving himself with a way of escape!

All this did Magee no good. He was sentenced to a £500 fine and two years' imprisonment, and compelled to give security for good behaviour for seven years. He resented being sacrificed to O'Connell's fame and thereafter was more circumspect in his editorials. To that extent Peel won the round, but O'Connell came out of it vastly enhanced in repute, particularly among those who set little value on good manners or, indeed, on a pedantic adherence to accuracy.

Lidwill sat through the trial in case O'Connell should require the services of a second. Later he passed it round the Dublin clubs that the Attorney General had disgraced himself first by his vulgar attack on a gentleman and then by failing to issue a challenge.

A peasant wishing to dispose of his landlord might shoot him from behind a hedge. The Establishment sometimes achieved the same result by arranging an affair of honour. They tried it twice on Wilkes, and it is very likely – but this is mere surmise – that they tried it on O'Connell. The trick was to have him challenged by a noted duellist and dead shot. If the challenge was accepted there was a good chance that the troublemaker would be killed or put out of circulation for a long time, and if it was refused or if an apology was made he would be politically damned as a poltroon. O'Connell had avoided duels with Thompson and Segerson; more recently he had gone out with a colleague named Magrath and, when they were about to be given the signal to fire, had said, 'I am about to fight a man against whom I entertain no enmity,' at which they were reconciled. Purcell O'Gorman wrote, 'My dear Dan ... there's no fair man can think ill of the matter, but you know the host of enemies you have and the consequent misinterpretation.' Even O'Connell's brother-in-law, Rickard O'Connell, confessed to 'an unfavourable impression on his mind ... the most serious uneasiness', and a good many people felt that O'Connell had not shown that eagerness for the fray that became an Irish gentleman. If he had backed down once, indeed more than once, might he not do so again?

The Establishment's champion was John D'Esterre, a Limerick Protestant and a member of the Dublin Corporation, who had displayed spectacular courage as an officer of Marines and was known to be 'one of the surest shots that ever fired a pistol'.

On 22nd January 1815 O'Connell referred in a speech to 'the beggarly Corporation of Dublin'. It was one of the mildest epithets ever applied to that body, and no doubt he was greatly surprised to receive a few days later a letter from D'Esterre asking if he had indeed used that expression as reported in the press. He duly replied:

Without either admitting or disclaiming the expression ... I deem it right to inform you ... that no terms attributed to me, however reproachful, can exceed the contemptuous feelings I entertain for that body in its corporate capacity, although doubtless it contains many valuable persons ...

The correct move was now for D'Esterre to 'send a friend' to O'Connell. Instead he sent another letter, which was returned by O'Connell's brother, James. Point to O'Connell.

O'Connell asked George Lidwill to be his second, but by 30th January no challenge had come. Since neither protagonist was noted for his reticence, Dublin was humming with rumour. Lidwill, puzzled at D'Esterre's inaction, passed word to him that O'Connell was ready to meet him without a moment's delay; there being no reply from D'Esterre, Lidwill was inclined to think that 'this aggression, originating in folly and perhaps urged on by party, had been abandoned.'

D'Esterre's next move was most ungentlemanly, and was described by O'Connell in a letter to Bennett.

The ruffian appeared in the Hall [of the Four Courts] with a whip. The instant I heard of it I left the King's Bench and he disappeared. He paraded the quay with his whip. Richard O'Gorman met him and asked him did he want me, for that I told him I would fight him [D'Esterre] in three minutes whenever he chose; that he had but to send me a message and that he should instantly be met.

D'Esterre then said, 'The challenge should come from O'Connell, but the man is a poltroon and will not fight.' At which O'Gorman merely laughed. D'Esterre then took post with his friends and his horsewhip in College Green; O'Connell hastened there with *his* friend, Major MacNamara, 'but the delinquent had fled. The crowd accumulated so fast that I took refuge in Exchequer Street, where Judge Day followed me and bound me to keep the peace on *my honour*. Was there ever such a scene?'

Although bound over, O'Connell could still *accept* a challenge, which was brought next day by Sir Edward Stanley, D'Esterre's second. Lidwill having had to leave Dublin on urgent business, it was dealt with by MacNamara, an authority in these matters, who agreed with Stanley on the time and place – three-thirty the next day, at Bishop's Court, just outside Dublin. MacNamara suggested one shot each, but Stanley said, 'No sir, that will not do. If they fired five-and-twenty shots each, Mr D'Esterre will never leave the ground until Mr O'Connell makes an apology.'

'Well then, if blood be your object, blood you will have, by God!'

Hundreds of spectators, gigs, horses and carriages were waiting on the snow-covered ground at Bishop's Court. O'Connell arrived punctually. The Church forbade duelling, but a suspended priest waited nearby in case his services should be required.

O'Connell spotted his tailor in the crowd. 'Ah, Jerry,' he called, 'I never missed you from an aggregate meeting!'

At half past four MacNamara made O'Connell take off his white cravat, which would make a good aiming-mark, and remove a large bunch of seals from his fob which would make a hideous wound should the ball hit him there. These somewhat grisly preparations must have shaken O'Connell who said, 'I have one last request to make of you.'

'What is it, my dear fellow?' asked MacNamara.

'Let me beg you not to say another word until the affair is over.'

D'Esterre arrived when it was nearly dark. He seemed quite calm as he stood nonchalantly twirling a cane while the seconds measured out the ground. Bennett loaded O'Connell's pistols, measuring the charge and ramming down ball and wad with care. They took post at ten yards. At the fall of a handkerchief, D'Esterre took a pace to the left and a pace forward, then fired. His shot, an astonishingly bad one, hit the ground at O'Connell's foot. O'Connell fired almost simultaneously. Wishing only to wound his man, not kill, he aimed low, at the thigh, and the ball struck exactly where he aimed. D'Esterre fell.

After ascertaining that D'Esterre did not appear to be dangerously wounded, O'Connell drove back to Dublin. But D'Esterre died the next day.

In law O'Connell had committed murder, but if a duel was fair and the duellists of a class permitted by public opinion to shoot at each other, it was almost unheard of for the law to take its course. Nevertheless, politics being what they were, it must have been with some relief that O'Connell received a letter from

Stanley assuring him that there was not 'the most distant intention of any prosecution'. In return he assured Stanley of his 'deep and lasting sorrow' at the 'loss society had sustained by the death of Mr D'Esterre' – the proper conclusion to the business.

Within six months he was involved in another affair of honour, this time with the brash young Chief Secretary, Robert Peel. In the Commons, in the course of some observations unfavourable to the Catholic Board, Peel had described O'Connell as 'a very leading man among the Catholics, not simply to be considered as an individual, but as an individual who enjoys the greatest share of the confidence of the Catholics'. These seem hardly to be fighting words, but the mutual antipathy between the two men was such that O'Connell chose to take exception to them, and said in the course of a speech against the Veto:

> I said at the last meeting, in the presence of the note-takers of the police who are paid by him, that he was too prudent to attack me in my presence. I see the same police informers here now, and I authorize them carefully to report my words – that Mr Peel would not dare, in my presence or in any place where he was liable to a personal account, to use a single expression derogatory to my interest or honour.

Next day, 31st August, Sir Charles Saxton, Under-Secretary at the Castle, called to demand an explanation. O'Connell said the newspaper reports were accurate. Saxton said that Peel stood by everything he had said. 'In that case,' replied O'Connell, 'I consider it incumbent on me to send a friend to Mr Peel.'

He asked Lidwill to carry the challenge, but Lidwill thought it was up to Peel to issue one. There followed much to-ing and fro-ing, each party wishing to manoeuvre the other into being the aggressor. Saxton, thinking O'Connell was backing out, published their correspondence in the newspapers. O'Connell described this as a paltry trick: 'I have disavowed nothing; I have refused the gentleman nothing: I have only to regret that they have ultimately preferred a paper war.' This goaded Peel into sending a formal challenge by Colonel Browne (the Deputy Quartermaster General). Since Lidwill had got himself involved in a duel with Saxton, O'Connell asked Bennett and the Knight of Kerry to second him.

His uncle, the General, was on a visit to Dublin, staying at Merrion Square. Mary's suspicions were aroused by the newspapers, which were full of the affair, and by O'Connell's long talks with his uncle in French, which she could not understand; in the presence of a French-speaker, they switched to Irish. She tipped the Sheriff off, and as O'Connell stepped out of his bedroom he was arrested by two constables. Meanwhile Lidwill, through the intervention of his daughter, suffered a similar fate. In reply to a note from Colonel Browne asking about the delay, O'Connell was forced to reply that the delay had been caused

> by a circumstance of the most painful nature – his having been put under arrest by the Sheriff – which is still aggravated, in his feelings, from having been done at the instance of Mrs O'Connell who, agitated by the publications in the newspapers, sent privately, after he had gone to bed, to the Sheriff for that purpose.

Said the General to Mary, 'This is the only time in my life I ever was angry with you, and you have made me very angry.'

O'Connell and Lidwill (but not Peel and Saxton) were bound over in terms which precluded them from fighting even when challenged, so it was arranged by the seconds that both duels should take place outside the kingdom, with O'Connell and Peel meeting at Ostend and Lidwill and Saxton at Calais. The Dublin newspapers blew it up as though the nation's honour was at stake: 'The four champions of the Castle, all English, all placemen, all feeding upon Irish salaries, all lodged in Irish mansions, emerged from humble conditions at home to wealth and rank in Ireland' – nonsense, of course, but good polemics. Saurin was distressed by the 'unhappy situation in which two excellent fellows, Peel and Saxton, have been provoked by the two very worst miscreants in the country', and the Lord Chancellor described it as an affair of honour between a gentleman and a blackguard.

There was no attempt to stop Peel, who on 15th September took ship from Dublin to Ostend. But O'Connell, unable to book a passage direct, had to go via England. Peel's father offered a reward for O'Connell's arrest; he was duly arrested and again bound over, and warned that if a fatal duel took place the survivor would be hanged. So he returned to Dublin, 'lying on the cabin-floor as sick as a dog, with three gentlemen's legs on my breast and stomach'.

His and Lidwill's enemies naturally made the most of their discomfiture, and the wits had a field-day. Among them was Charles Bushe, the Solicitor General, who commented:

Two heroes of Erin, abhorrent of slaughter,
Improved on the Hebrew command;
One honoured his wife and the other his daughter,
That their days might be long in the land.

O'Connell's enemy Lord Norbury, the hanging judge, was even able to score off him in court. 'Pardon me, my lord,' said O'Connell, 'I fear your lordship does not apprehend me.' To which Norbury replied, 'Pardon me also, no one is more easily apprehended than Mr O'Connell, *whenever he wishes to be apprehended.*'

Nothing was more fortunate for O'Connell in his whole career than his duel with D'Esterre. Having stood up to 'one of the surest shots that ever fired a pistol', he could brush off allegations of cowardice in other affairs. He could even forswear all duels in future and refuse all challenges. No doubt he did this for conscientious and religious reasons, but it was a prudent move by a man who was sure to make many enemies in a class which was notoriously quick on the trigger. With duelling just beginning to go out of fashion, no serious criticism of his attitude could be made. He would have been beyond reproach if he had also refrained from invective to which gentlemen less polemically gifted could retort only by 'sending a friend'. So his abuse, often very scurrilous, was restrained only by the law, and no one knew better than he just how far the law would let him go.

His remorse for killing D'Esterre was genuine. With more generosity than prudence, he offered to 'share his income' with the widow who, perhaps fortunately, declined. Years later, hearing that D'Esterre's daughter was involved in a troublesome lawsuit, he represented her free of charge and won her case. There is probably no truth in the legend that he always wore a black glove on his right hand at Mass in mourning for the man he had slain.

7

The Counsellor in Trouble

Hunting Cap was proud, in a way, of his nephew's fame, but disapproved of almost everything he did. Dan's conduct in the Magee case was, he thought, really shocking:

> However averse and hostile the Attorney General may be to the Catholics ... the high situation he enjoys as first law officer of the Crown demands a degree of respect and consideration from the Bar which should not be lightly forgot or neglected ... I have therefore most earnestly to request, and will even add to insist, that you will in future conduct yourself with calmness, temperance and moderation towards him.

Dan's 'political avocations occupied too much of his time and thoughts and might possibly have the effect of taking him off from his professional pursuits ... on which the support of his family and credit depend.'

O'Connell was far from forgetting his duties to his family, with six children and a seventh on the way. The seventh, alas, died within two years, and was followed by a little girl who also died in infancy.* On 22nd August 1816 was born another boy, also christened Daniel, who survived. He was the last of their children. O'Connell wanted more, writing to Mary three years after Dan's birth:

---

*Daniel, born in December 1812; and Ricarda, born in 1815.

My darling Dan's nurse was here yesterday ... greatly mortified you would not give her another chance of a nursing. I
assured her all the blame ought to be attributed to me. *Is it
not so, darling?* ... Oh, how I wish you were preparing another
nursing for her!

These words could be taken as an arch reference to unremitting
exertions to that end – or as indicating exactly the opposite.
There is no way we can tell.

O'Connell was 'good with children'; he liked taking them for
walks, chatting with them, reading aloud to them. Moore's *Lalla
Rookh* and the *Fireworshipper* were favourites for family reading,
as was Dickens – he was furious when the author, bored with
Little Nell, did away with her. Ellen responded best to this
literary diet and grew up extremely well-read, able to hold her
own in discussions on Burns, Scott and even Carlyle who was
hardly the young lady's favourite author. Travelling *en famille*,
for instance from Dublin to Tralee where he used to leave Mary
and the children for the sea-bathing while he went on circuit,
there was strong competition among the young to sit with him
outside on the box where he would entertain them with stories.
He was a wonderful raconteur; a visitor to Derrynane who had
recently been at Abbotsford judged him to be better even than
Sir Walter Scott, reputedly the best story-teller in Europe. His
forte was the sort of story – recounted with a knowing twinkle of
the eye and often against himself – that illustrates the Irish
countryman's sly dexterity.

When Maurice was eleven and a half and Morgan ten he sent
them to Clongowes Wood College, a boarding-school run by
Jesuits, noted for high academic standards and fees which were
certainly not low. Maurice, he instructed the rector, Father
Kenny, should be prepared for the Bar, for which he would begin
to read after five and a half years at Clongowes. Of Morgan his
expectations were not so strong. Both should acquire a solid
foundation in the classics, especially Greek, and should learn
French and as much simple mathematics, modern chemistry and
experimental philosophy as was compatible with the school cur-
riculum. 'Of course I am most anxious that they should both be
strongly imbued with the principles of the Catholic faith and
national feeling.'

In Maurice, his firstborn, O'Connell saw his own image. But Maurice was no swan, merely an easy-going goose who resembled his father in nothing but his love of country life and field sports, being happy only with gun, fly-rod or horse. He had scholastic talent, but his loving father gradually came to the painful conclusion that he was bone idle, 'with a loose and rambling turn of mind':

My Maurice, my noble boy. Oh, how triumphant he would make me if he would but exert himself ... He *can* do it if he *will*, but what does that signify if *he won't*? ... How little does he think of all the miseries which his unhappy listlessness inflicts on his fond father! The fact is that he intends and resolves to be diligent, but then his diligence is to commence tomorrow and, of course, tomorrow never comes. Would to God he would once resolve to be diligent *this day*.

Poor red-headed Morgan was a problem. He was not as affectionate as the other children, and idler even than Maurice. Father Kenny, while giving Maurice rather more praise than was his due, added, 'Of good Morgan I cannot say so much. Less talented, he wants application, which alone could supply the deficiency.' Mary concluded that 'Morgan's great objection to apply himself will, I fear, be the means of rendering him unfit for any profession except the army which is the *last* I should wish for him.'

Both parents had a high opinion of Father Kenny, but about the school Mary, always so conventional, had her reservations: 'What nice mannered boys Maurice and Morgan were when they went to Clongowes ... It is almost impossible to get them to divest themselves of the vulgarity they acquired at *that* college.' At least they became proper little sportsmen. At fifteen and fourteen they each had a gun, and they had acquired ponies four years earlier. Maurice's was well schooled, 'but Morgan gets his at once in a gallop and that is all he cares about'.

O'Connell's best-loved child was saucy little Kate, though on one occasion her breath 'smelt most terribly of worms. Darling, see what can be done for her.' Nell (Ellen), although given to saying silly things which she knew were silly, was the best letter writer of all the children, and a great help to her mother in looking after Betsey and Dan. Of Dan, the baby, Nell (then aged fifteen) wrote to her father:

Little Dan is as bold as ever. Mama *says* she whipped him the other day, but I don't think either you or I would attach much credit to that assertion ... To say the truth, he is a most bewitching little darling, and I don't wonder he should be a *little* spoilt.

A small cloud over the O'Connells' marriage was that neither Mary nor the girls ever accompanied O'Connell on holiday to Derrynane. Mary was a thoroughly urban type, never happy save in Dublin or in some civilised watering place. She *abominated* Kerry, and above all she abominated Derrynane and had to be coaxed into taking the children on the briefest of visits to Hunting Cap. But it was the place O'Connell loved best in all the world, and his autumn holiday of trout-fishing, grouse-shooting and hare-hunting was the greatest treat of his year. Maurice and Morgan loved it too, especially when they had been given guns. The Patterns* were the greatest fun. At one of these, in Waterville, where the country is rideable, the boys and their father had a great fox-hunt, Morgan boasting that he fell off only twice. There were faction-fights, with many a broken head, and horse-races on the strand: 'I spent the rest of the day in deciding wrangles, preventing riots, throwing boys into the trenches and flinging hats among the crowd etc.' Pure heaven! Why could not Mary and the girls enjoy it too? 'It is to me the only unpleasant sensation I know that my sweet Mary cannot enjoy the pleasures of Kerry with me.' Besides, with Hunting Cap in his late eighties, it would have been the height of folly to offend the old gentleman by omitting the annual visit. So every autumn there was a tussle, with O'Connell seeking reasons for spinning out his holiday by a few more days while Mary tried to reduce it to a minimum, stooping even to appealing to his love of the girls: 'My poor Nell and Kate wept and wished Iveragh was out of the world, "every

*Patterns or Patrons: annual holidays in honour of the patron saint of a parish.

barrister returnes to stay with his family (but our father) when circuit ends." '

Among the excuses he gave for prolonging his holiday was that he was 'getting so abominably fat that I hate and detest myself'. Grouse-shooting and beagling were the best means of keeping his figure under control. His Lenten fasts, generally during the spring circuit, were undertaken not merely as religious duties but to combat increasing avoirdupois. Mary, who four years ago had hoped he would be strict in his Lenten observances, now hoped he wouldn't.

I fear you are observing this Lent too strictly. At all events, while on circuit, I think you ought to relax in some degree ... To be from nine o'clock in the morning to perhaps ten at night without eating a morsel in a cold court-house is more than any constitution (however good) will be able to bear.

He replied, 'It fatigues me sometimes a little but it agrees perfectly with me and I eat on abstinence days an enormous dinner of fish.'

The greatest threat to their marriage was the chaos of his finances. In 1814 his income from the Bar was £3,808, a very large sum; but the post-war agricultural depression reduced this. 'Think what a Tralee Assizes,' he wrote in August 1816, 'when I received but thirty-four guineas.' Mary lamented, 'In truth, I believe the people have not money *even* for law.' In addition there was a large rent-roll, £2,400 gross in 1811. While the war was on, agriculture flourished and rents were easily collected because he would not allow tenants competing for land to pay more than the land was really worth. But with the depression, almost every country gentleman was on the brink of ruin. 'What is to become of us', wrote his brother James, who managed the family estates, in 1816, 'if the times do not improve? I have had recourse to the harshest methods to try and extort some payments from your tenants for the last week, all the pounds in the county filled with their cows but all to no purpose.'

But if the tenants were often behind with their rents, O'Connell, alas, was forever in advance with his expenditure. He bought a barouche and embellished it with his coat of arms on each panel – and then had to sell a hogshead of claret given him by the General because he could not pay (cash) for freight and customs.

His letters to Mary abound in instructions about who is to be paid, how much, and what is the latest possible date for the payment, in order to maintain his precarious and complex system of credit. One passage[1] out of many shows the intricacy of his obligations, the variety of his indebtedness, and the diplomacy, resource and attention to detail expected of her.

I perceive by a letter I got last night from James Sugrue that Dr Wilson's bill lies over unpaid. Let it be so, darling, for a few days longer. You have therefore got from me in half-notes* between you and James Sugrue £200 and he has got £100 from Roger so that, as you gave him the other £50, you will only have to add £12 10s to it. Then, giving your mother £15, you will still have £172 10s in hand. Take out of that £42 10s for house expenses, it will leave you £130 out of which you will, before this reaches you, pay tomorrow £40, Eyre's bill, and the day you get this £50, Higgins's bill, and you will have £40 towards meeting the bills due on Thursday. I believe my letter of today was erroneous in supposing that Eyre's bill would not be due until Wednesday. I hope this error will not occasion a protest, as in the list I sent I marked down a £40 bill as due on the 9th. I will, please God, send you a banker's bill for at least £200. The bills which are to be paid are 9th, £40 to Eyre, 10th, £50 to Higgins, 11th, £58 *with interest* to Mr Mahon – same day, 11th – £138 10s to Dr Wilson, a *fresh* bill not the one already due, 15th, £69 19s to Roose, 25th, Clongowes Wood College payable, I think, to Elliott, 28th, £50 to Cooper.

If she slipped up and paid anybody too much, too soon or too late, he was extremely cross – and afterwards humbly, tearfully repentant.

He promised her faithfully not to lend money or go surety for anyone else's debts, but in March 1815 she was appalled to learn from his brother James that he had become involved, to the

*The safest way to send money by post was to tear a note in half and send the halves separately.

extent of £8,000, in the bankruptcy of a Killarney merchant, James O'Leary, who decamped to London where, on O'Connell's money, he set up as the greatest buck in Bond Street. To satisfy O'Leary's creditors he had to ask help from James (not for the first or last time) and then borrow a further £3,600 at a rate of interest and on terms which perhaps reflected the creditors' estimate of their chances of repayment. Mary was beside herself with anger; her letter is not extant, for he destroyed it, but its general tone may be judged from his abject reply:

> I never in my life was so exquisitely miserable as your last letter made me. I wept over it for two hours this morning in bed and am ready to weep over it again. When once suspicion enters the human mind, there is an end to all comfort and security ... Indeed, indeed, indeed you have no cause of uneasiness, but my heart is too full and I cannot write more ... Darling believe me, do believe me, you have no cause for your misery. Did I ever deceive you? Ever, sweetest Mary, your most tenderly and faithfully doating Daniel O'Connell.

He borrowed money from the General, he borrowed money from his brothers James and John, he borrowed money from Bennett, he borrowed money from half his friends and relations in Kerry, he borrowed money to be repaid after Hunting Cap's death. In an exasperated letter written in March 1817, James calculated that Dan's debts which he personally knew of amounted to £19,199, and that there must have been many more:

> the bare interest ... will absorb the entire of your landed property and scarce leave a guinea to the paying of the principal. My dearest fellow, what do you mean by stating that in two years the far greater part of your debts will be discharged? Surely, when you speak this way, you are not aware of the magnitude of them.

And still, month after month, Mary had to write, 'I *want* money, love,' and 'You say nothing, heart, of *how* or where I am to get money.'

James's prudent character and life-style, modelled on those of Hunting Cap, contrasted strongly with the tendencies of

O'Connell's second brother, John, who, without the means to support it, lived the life of a country magnate out of a Charles Lever novel, near Killarney. He kept a famous pack of staghounds, fought eighteen duels, and staved off bankruptcy until a ripe old age. O'Connell found him an easier touch than brother James, and not so free with good advice and reproaches.

Although Mary was often cross with him, and with reason, no shadow of sexual jealousy marred their marriage. She knew something about his pre-marital wild oats. Referring to letters which she received from an anonymous female who demanded money, she wrote:

I am quite displeased that you should for a moment suffer the slightest uneasiness on *this* subject. Believe me, my *own* Dan, when I assure you that the machinations of our anonymous friend have not lessened my confidence in you ... When I got the first letter ... I really thought it might have come from one of your female *acquaintances before I knew you,* and recollecting you had contributed to the support of Mrs Y, I considered you might think it incumbent upon you to contribute to the support of *this person* ... On this subject I will say no more until we meet and then I will scold you well.

In his long absences from home, in Cork and Limerick where women of easy virtue were not hard to find, in Iveragh where many a peasant girl would have been gratified by the attentions of the famous Counsellor O'Connell, heir of Derrynane, he had ample temptation and ample opportunity to philander. If he occasionally strayed into the wrong bed – and there is nothing but folk-legend to say that he did – Mary's suspicions were not aroused nor were his emotions involved.

The only woman of whom she showed any jealousy was the girls' governess, Mary Jane Gaghran. When first engaged in 1815, Miss Gaghran seemed a treasure, so much so that O'Connell, on circuit, was 'half in love with her on your description'. She spoke excellent French, of which Mary was ignorant; she was a good teacher. But she was too interfering, even dictating the children's letters to their parents: 'Beg of Miss Gaghran to allow the girls to compose altogether their own letters.' Because she was so good at her job, Mary had to

105

pass over many little unpleasant traits in her manners to me
for my children's sake ... She is naturally haughty and, having
authority from the early age of sixteen to this day, is the only
way I can account for the very great opinion she has of herself.
She has it to a fault.

Miss Gaghran, in short, was too big for her boots, the sort of
governess that any spirited wife might have to put up with but
would naturally resent. Eventually she departed, and Mary's indignation was unbounded when she (in France) discovered that
her husband (in Dublin) had been visiting the ex-governess.
Again her letter is not extant, but its tenor may be judged from
his reply:

I never in my life showed the slightest tinge of preference to
any being above you, and why *now*, when I would not look at
any other woman for a moment, you should thus persevere in
an angry correspondence on a subject so trivial – at least in
my estimation – is to me quite unintelligible ... Can you for
one moment doubt that, if I thought it would have given you
the slightest pain, I ever would have paid her a visit? If you
think I would, you do indeed wrong me. I have no shred of
gratification in her visit.

From an involved sentence later in the letter it is clear that
Mary's objection to Miss Gaghran was that she was insufferably
bossy, and she thought Dan disloyal, but not it seems unfaithful,
in visiting her.

In 1819 O'Connell thought he had found poor Morgan's me-
tier. John Devereux, a Wexford gentleman who had been out in
1798 but had got away to America, returned to Ireland twenty
years later in order to raise an Irish Legion to help Bolivar
liberate Venezuela from Spanish rule. It was a cause of which
O'Connell approved, and he offered Devereux the services of
Morgan who had attained the ripe age of fifteen. The offer was
accepted, and in June 1819 Morgan was commissioned as a captain in the Legion and A.D.C. to General Devereux. He had his
portrait painted in a magnificent huzzar uniform and settled
down to await the General's departure for the field of glory.
Devereux, alas (though O'Connell could never see it), was the
worst kind of mercenary – vain, flamboyant, incompetent and far

keener on feathering his own nest than on furthering the cause of Venezuelan freedom. Having launched his Legion to the Spanish Main in the autumn of 1819, he lingered on in England and Ireland, lionised by the friends of liberty, until the summer of 1820. Not until mid-June did he, and his A.D.C., arrive at the scene of action. They then discovered that the Legion, without its General, without proper administration and without, it seems, much in the way of regular pay and rations, had mutinied, and the greater part of it had been packed off to Jamaica. The remainder had suffered a few battle casualties and many deaths through sickness. In September 1821 Morgan was on his way home without hearing a shot fired, his dreams of glory disappointed. But he had seen a bit of the world, learned to write long, lively, interesting letters and (said his father) had developed some prudence with money.

But the problem of Morgan's career remained. He could not just hang around Dublin doing nothing and earning nothing. His heart was set on a military career, preferably in the British army. O'Connell had nothing much against the British army, particularly as (he used to boast) three-quarters of the soldiers were Irish. But the army at home was too often involved in unpopular operations in aid of the civil power; it was the age of Peterloo and the Bristol riots. It would not do at all for Counsellor O'Connell's son to be reported in the press as firing on a Dublin mob or assisting at an eviction. O'Connell did not really want him to be a soldier in any army, but if he insisted, it had better be the French army. But in the French army after Waterloo there was unlikely to be a very warm welcome or very promising career prospects for any subject of King George, and since France was Britain's most likely enemy, Morgan in the French army might well find himself fighting against British (indeed Irish) troops. The General's opinion was that the French service was neither practical nor desirable for Morgan, and that the Austrian service would be far better. Although the Emperor was not exactly in the vanguard of liberalism, it was his policy to employ promising young foreigners, especially Irishmen, in his polyglot armies, and it was most unlikely that Austria would ever be Britain's enemy. But O'Connell could not bear the idea of 'poor Morgan' going into 'that rascally Austrian service', and wanted him to be an attorney. In the end it was Mary who settled the matter:

107

Now, love, to answer you on the subject of Morgan's becoming
an attorney. I totally and entirely disapprove of it ... You
don't know Morgan as I do. Believe me, he is too fond of
liberty to submit to the control of any person for a period of
five years, much less consent to be bound to a *desk* ... The
enclosed letter [from the General] will show you what he still
will do for Morgan. Can you, Dan, in justice to your other
children, refuse this commission to Morgan? Why should not
Morgan get on as well as other young men in the Austrian
service? ... Believe me, it would be lost money to give him
any other profession but the army.

So the General and his friend Baron O'Brady (Freiherr von
Brady in the Austrian army) pulled strings, and in June 1823
Morgan set off for Vicenza in northern Italy to join the 4th Light
Cavalry as a cadet.

A year earlier the painful decision had been taken that, until
O'Connell could achieve solvency, Mary and the five younger
children would reside in France, where the cost of living was
(erroneously) supposed to be lower than in Ireland. O'Connell
and either Maurice or Morgan (taking it in turn) would live very
quietly in Dublin, having sold the horses and carriage, let (if
possible) the grand house in Merrion Square and discharged all
the servants save those absolutely essential to their existence. It
was Maurice's turn first. He read lethargically for the Bar under
the guidance of a tutor and maddened his father by his fidgeting.
'I do all I can but, I fear, in vain. He has now got a trick of
gapping and, as it were, slapping with his mouth that has a very
silly effect. Poor fellow.' The idea was that he would continue his
studies in London, but his father was beginning to despair of
him.

The move of Mary and the children to France was a very bad
plan. O'Connell was desperately unhappy without them, and
Maurice's company was small consolation. He complained constantly of the paucity of news from them.

What shall I say? What shall I do? Oh, Mary, what is the
meaning of all this? How could you all use me so ill? How
could you be so cruel to me? ... I cannot forgive Morgan. He,

however, cares nothing for me. What I say or do is quite a matter of indifference to him ... I stamp and rave and know not what to do. It is so cruel, so malignant not to write. Oh, it would be troublesome to Mr Morgan, would it?

And in another letter:

I now want, my sweetest Kate, details of your travelling, not stiff letters telling me you are well and send me your love and have no more to say. You have all plenty to say ... In short, darling Kate, it will be quite a treat to chat as it were with you all by letter and hear you talk among yourselves.

His own letters were far longer, and written almost every day. All he enjoyed was his continued success at the Bar. Of a case against the evangelist Kildare Street Bible Education Society (more properly, Kildare Place Society) he gloated:

I was greatly delighted in beating those scoundrels. They failed by reason of the inaccuracy with which they keep their accounts, and it appears that for three years they never accounted with the public for their stock of books, paper, slates, quills etc etc of the value of from £6,000 to £10,000, so that they are covered with disgrace and ridicule. You know how I dislike the canting hypocrites that belong to that association, and you can easily form an idea of how cheerful you would have found me at dinner had I my family about me but, alas, I came home to a miserable solitary table, for even Maurice dined out, and I had to spend my wretched evening as well as I could.

Moreover O'Connell had taken against the French – 'the nasty French' as little Dan called them. He began, in the spring of 1823, to consider moving his family to Devonshire, where he would be in closer contact with them, and they could live as cheaply as in 'rascally France. Oh, how I hate France. I hate it in all moods and tenses, past, present and to come.' If they should have soldiers or officers quartered on them, Mary should take care to divide the house 'so that you or my girls should not be at all in their presence or company ... They are a kind of people not to be associated with.' He had even turned again against Napoleon whose 'colossal power was wielded to enslave the Church'. How delighted they would all be to get out of France! It had been a bad plan.

It did not even relieve his finances. As brother James did not fail to point out, in reply to a desperate appeal for another loan:

> In the course of a few months they move from Dublin to Pau, from that to Tours [where, James added in another letter, a barouche was sent from Dublin to them], now they are in the most expensive part of Paris and will wind up by fixing their residence in England, the dearest country in Europe to live in. In fact I must think of *my* wife and family ... You must wait until the death of that dear and venerated uncle at Derrynane, a period not very remote, I fear ... I have on my knees bound myself on oath, during the rest of my life never again to join you in bill, bond or note or in any other security, either verbal or otherwise, for one guinea, and further I have solemnly sworn on my knees never to give you in any one year any sum of money exceeding twenty pounds ... Now where you are to get my remaining £500 I really do not know ... It is an insult to common sense to have you talk of the *security* you can offer for money.

O'Connell, of course, was waiting on Hunting Cap's death and borrowing on that expectation: 'God forgive me if ever I was so criminal as to wish for that death.' In 1823 the old gentleman was ninety-five, and still going strong.

In the early 1820s O'Connell's Bar income was enormous, well over £5,000 a year. But his rents had again dropped catastrophically, for the Whiteboys were out in Kerry, and their No Rent campaign hit the O'Connells just as hard as it did any English absentee landlord. In January 1822 James warned him that there would be very few rents coming in, '*every peasant in the barony of Iveragh is a Whiteboy* and, as such, are determined to pay neither *rent, tithes nor taxes.*' James had put himself in peril by hitting back at the Whiteboys, lodging seven of their ringleaders in Tralee jail. This quietened the barony, but did not bring in rents.

Your tenants as well as those of every other gentleman in Iveragh ate the pigs and beeves and laid out any money they received [since the Whiteboys first appeared] in buying clothes and whiskey. There is no use distraining their stock as they really have *now no money to pay*.

There was, however, one advantage (though O'Connell did not see it) in his family's absence: he could devote the evenings to politics. The man who in 1812 had been a promising barrister with political leanings had by 1823 become a rising politician whose income and fame were derived from the Bar. The change of emphasis was accompanied by a strengthening, but no change, in his political ideas. He became more liberal, in the sense of being devoted to individual liberty. When Napoleon had been at the height of his power no one in Ireland had been keener than O'Connell to see his downfall, but after Waterloo O'Connell lamented the triumph of legitimacy and reaction in Europe. Presumably he still resented the union, but of this there is no hint in his political or private correspondence; his sole political aim seems to have been religious freedom. In Ireland this naturally meant Catholic emancipation, though in Spain and Portugal it would be Protestant emancipation, and everywhere Jewish emancipation. There should be a complete separation of Church and state – well, almost complete, for he was not in all circumstances opposed to safeguards such as the Veto; but these should never be part of a package deal on emancipation. The government should first revoke all the Penal Laws and bring to an end all the jerrymandering and sectarian patronage which buttressed them; then Catholics would gladly concede to the Crown such safeguards as were necessary in the choice of bishops. (It is a question which bedevils Anglo-Irish politics today: should concessions be made on trust, or on conditions?)

His hatred of violence for political ends was, if anything, strengthened. The Catholic cause, he told Hunting Cap, would prevail only if pursued openly and legally. 'I have more than once been alarmed lest a spirit of insubordination or secret conspiracy should be resorted to'; but he was sure his fears were groundless.

He could not have been too sure, for law and order seemed to be, in Ireland as well as in England, on very insecure foundations.

The post-war agricultural depression, the potato-crop failures in 1817 and 1821, and above all the land hunger of a rapidly increasing population* were producing all the evils of the nineteenth-century 'Irish Problem'. Rents which had been perfectly fair in 1814 simply could not be paid five years later. More competition for leases, and the fact that there was more profit for landlords and large farmers in pasture than in tillage, raised rents and reduced the size of holdings. The number of evictions increased rapidly. The small farmers, cottiers and landless labourers reacted with their traditional weapons – secret societies such as Ribbonmen, Whiteboys, Terry Alts and Carders (who tortured their victims by raking their bodies with the wire combs used for carding wool). There was an alarming increase in rural outrages, whole families being butchered and the women raped because one of the family had co-operated with authority, raised rents, evicted a tenant, or taken a farm from which the previous tenant had been evicted. In their murders, arson, cattle-houghing and illegal oathing, the Whiteboys were not nationalist – they were not even anti-Protestant except in so far as most landlords were Protestants. They were anti-landlord, and especially hostile to the 'improving' landlord who turned out tenants when their leases expired in order to have farms of a more viable size or to increase his profitable grazing land at the expense of tillage. In fact, the successful middle-class Catholic who bought land as part of his new status was very likely to be an 'improving' landlord, determined to make his investment pay. He was also likely to be the backbone of O'Connellism. O'Connell's friends suffered as much as anyone from Whiteboys, Terry Alts and their ilk: a son of Denys Scully was murdered. Despite the efforts of James and other landlords, Kerry was plagued with robberies and rickburnings. As a lawyer, O'Connell felt it his duty to defend some of the worst terrorists, never mitigating their crimes but simply arguing that they were not the criminals; he defended, unsuccessfully, eleven of the 'finest looking young fellows' for the appalling butchery of the Dillon family. But as a law-abiding citizen he had no hesitation in informing the authorities about the most dangerous terrorists in the county: 'the plan of getting

*In 1791, 4,753,000; in 1821, 6,802,000; in 1831, 7,767,000. But these figures are mere estimates, not based on any proper census.

these scoundrels arrested and enforcing evidence from others would be the very best.'[2]

As for Orangemen, the way to deal with them was to go to law, not to war – even though juries in political cases were habitually packed, and the Bench included judges like that 'sanguinary buffoon' Lord Norbury, well into his eighties and so deaf that even O'Connell had to bellow to make him hear a single word; Judge Day, also in his eighties but in full possession of his faculties, 'such as they are'; and Judge Lefroy, who knew no more of the law than he had known when O'Connell bamboozled him fifteen years earlier.

Though convinced of the errors of Protestantism, he had no animus against Protestants and pointed out on innumerable occasions that it was to Grattan's Protestant parliament and to their own Protestant brethren that Catholics owed any freedoms they now enjoyed. There could be no greater proof of friendship and confidence than asking a man to second one in a duel, and in his affairs with D'Esterre and Peel three out of his four seconds had been Protestants. He loathed sectarian divisions. Of a proposed Catholic dinner to collect funds for the cause he wrote, 'The dinner should be given by Catholics and Protestants (Oh, how I hate these distinctions!) that is, by Irishmen.' He tried to promote a society for the furtherance of non-sectarian schools.[3] In forming a Society for Parliamentary Education he asked Lord Cloncurry to nominate half a dozen good Protestants and promised 'to get you a batch of Papists of the first water'.

In 1820 Grattan died. He had been a great man for Ireland, but his stage was the Irish House of Commons where he had been a power. For the last fifteen years of his life he had been playing on the Westminster stage, where he was merely a character, his wit, charm and polished eighteenth-century oratory making many friends but few converts. He was essentially an Establishment do-gooder – and he did a great deal of good – but quite unable to communicate with the multitude: it is impossible to imagine him holding spellbound a mass meeting. His death, by which time the futility of his methods was obvious, left vacant the leadership in parliament of those M.P.s sponsoring Irish freedom. O'Connell, debarred from the Commons by his faith, could not fill the vacancy, though he was in every other respect well equipped for it.

Of the Catholic Association, which in 1817 reverted to the name of the Catholic Board, he was undisputed master. 'Honest Ned' Hay, whom he had once thought so efficient and reliable, proved a broken reed, incompetent and (oh, horror!) financially inept, perpetually insolvent: 'that scoundrel can never again show his ugly nose and dirty person in Catholic affairs'. As for Lord Fingall, 'I am sincerely sorry for it because he is an excellent gentleman and personally as pure as gold but unhappily subject to some influence from less clean quarters. No matter, we must do without him.' So O'Connell *was* the Catholic Board. And why not? On a visit to England he studied the English Bar: 'they are just *nothing* to the Irish Bar' – of which he was the acknowledged star. 'I felt it would not be difficult to excel in intellect and sound views men of high names.' Always sanguine, he confidently expected emancipation in 1823. He would then be able to take silk and be spared a vast amount of drudgery, concentrating on the more lucrative cases.

The trouble was that no one could think of a better *modus operandi* in the campaign for emancipation than petitioning parliament or the Crown, which for thirty years had proven useless. This was especially true since George IV, in whom as Regent they had placed their hopes, could no longer be counted as a friend. Perhaps this was not surprising when the Board passed the so-called 'Witchery Resolution' which more than hinted that, after ridding himself of his Catholic wife, Mrs Fitzherbert, he had been bewitched by the ample charms of the Papist-hater, Lady Hertford. When he tried to divorce his queen for adultery, Irish Catholics were 'wild' for her. O'Connell even tried to have himself made Attorney General for the queen in Ireland, a post which carried neither duties nor emoluments but would have been a fine tease for her husband.

So it was no use Catholics hoping for anything from the king, though they continued to do so. In 1821 he visited Dublin, elated at the providential death of his queen, Caroline of Brunswick, slightly drunk and sporting in his hat an enormous bunch of shamrock to which he continually drew the attention of the cheering crowds. Catholics vied with one another in their expressions of fidelity. O'Connell, always sensitive to charges of disloyalty to the Crown, was ecstatic in his account of Catholic prelates being received by His Majesty in their robes, wearing their crosses and chains; of Lord Fingall, invested with the blue ribbon of the Order of St Patrick; and of the Catholic laity 'received and cherished precisely as Protestants were.' At the royal departure from Dunleary (renamed Kingstown), on bended knee he presented the king with a laurel wreath. It was a gesture which he later found hard to explain away, though to the calumny that he had abased himself by grovelling in the sea he replied that actually the place where he had knelt was a good twenty paces from the edge of the ocean. While Irishmen fawned on 'the gluttonous despot', the English Lord Byron expressed other views:

> Ere the daughter of Brunswick is cold in her grave
>   And her ashes still float to her home on the tide,
> Lo! George the Triumphant speeds o'er the wave
>   To the long-cherished isle which he loved – like his bride.

> Will thy yard of blue ribbon, poor Fingall, recall
>   The fetters from millions of Catholic limbs?
> Or has it not bound thee, the fastest of all
>   The slaves who now hail their betrayer with hymns?

> Wear, Fingall, thy trappings! O'Connell proclaim
>   His accomplishments – His!!! – and thy country convince
> Half an age's contempt was an error of fame
>   And that Hal is the rascallest, sweetest *young* prince.

However it was not long before O'Connell realised he had made a fool of himself, and that emancipation was not to be won either by loyalty to the Crown or by the methods of Grattan. On 8th February 1823, at a small dinner party at Glencullen House in the Dublin mountains, O'Connell and Sheil, who had quarrelled over the Veto, were reconciled. Those present then decided to revive the campaign for emancipation and found a new body for that purpose.

8

The Agitator

In his late forties O'Connell was still a fine figure of a man. He was chested like a bull, and not without a magisterial protuberance lower down, about which he was very sensitive: 'I am growing daily more and more corpulent ... I rise early, keep on my legs and walk very fast through the streets. Yet I get fat. I ought not, I believe, to eat so much.' His clothes, every stitch of Irish cloth, seemed to make him larger than life – a high, wide-brimmed top hat, or a fur hat in cold weather, a coat with padded shoulders and over it a long, sweeping cloak. His face was like a Roman Emperor's – one of the strong Emperors – square, heavy-jowled, with a broad nose and big eyes, rather pale from much work indoors. His hair was blacker, thicker, curlier and glossier than ever, being, in fact, a wig. This, when quizzed, he turned to his advantage, boasting that he had gone bald in the service of his country. His orator's voice was wonderfully flexible, changing from an angry or challenging roar to a confidential near-whisper which in some extraordinary way he projected effortlessly to the most distant man in a crowd.

As a polemicist he was equally adept with the bludgeon, the rapier and the slim poniard driven between a troublesome colleague's shoulder-blades. With all the expertise of a private in the Lawyers' Artillery Corps, he dismissed the victor of the Peninsular War and Waterloo as 'a stunted corporal'. Barbers used to make their apprentices practise on beggars, so a somewhat inexperienced Chief Secretary was 'the shave-beggar of Ireland'.

He likened Peel's smile to 'the silver plate on a coffin', and Judge Day, crouching under Castle influence, to 'a goose trying to get under a gate' – just the sort of homely simile to set a rural audience into a roar of delighted laughter. He spoke extempore, without even notes, and long practice at the Bar enabled him to deliver a lengthy speech lucidly and logically, giving every point its due weight. But he was pugnacious by nature, and his language was often exaggerated, abusive, coarse, scurrilous and truculent. 'If I did not use the sledgehammer,' he said, 'we would never crush our enemies.' Fingall finally understood this, and on his death-bed sent word to O'Connell that the Catholic aristocracy, including himself, had been 'criminally cowardly'. 'We never understood that we had a nation behind us,' he said. 'O'Connell alone comprehended that.... We owe everything to his rough work, and to effect further services to Ireland, there must be more of it.' Naturally it enraged his opponents but, as Henry Brougham said, verbal assaults on him were like paper pellets thrown at the hide of a rhinoceros. His model as an orator was the Elder Pitt, 'that terrible Cornet of Horse' whose 'tongue dripped venom'.

To what extent the repeal of the union was his prime object is difficult to say; it was probably not so before 1827. But despite his leanings towards Grattan's parliament, it must have been borne upon him that there was really no point in agitating for its restoration in the 1820s, when Protestants had become more or less reconciled to the union, when the forty-shilling freeholders generally voted according to their landlords' instructions, the City Corporations were Protestant closed shops, and Protestant Sheriffs habitually appointed Orange juries in any political case. The priorities must therefore be:

1 Catholic emancipation, which would place in parliament a solid block of reliable Catholic repealers.
2 Franchise reform, to break the Protestant grip on the Corporations and help the freeholders to stand up to landlords in the shires.
3 Repeal of the union.

To the task of achieving these aims he brought very sensitive political antennae, though he was inclined to over-optimism; a lawyer's grasp of the possibilities and limitations of agitation; the ability to concentrate on essentials in their due order of priority; a mastery of emotive popular oratory; and an instinctive understanding of the mental processes of Catholic Irishmen. Charles Greville, a fervent non-admirer of O'Connell, wrote, 'He operates on their passions with the precision of a dexterous anatomist who knows the direction of every muscle and fibre of the human frame.'

His energy was phenomenal. Ellen itemised a typical day's work in Dublin:

4.00 a.m.	Rise. Prayers. Light fire.
5.00	Sit to work.
8.30	Breakfast.
10.30	Walk to the Four Courts – 2 miles in 25 minutes.
11.00–3.00 p.m.	In Court.
3.30	Call to the offices of the Catholic Association.
4.00	Dinner.
4.00–6.30	Sit with family.
6.30	Sit to work.
10.00 p.m.	Bed.

When his family was away, every evening was given up to political work – discussions, committee meetings, private meetings, aggregate meetings – the endless drudgery of political activism.

I had to arrange the meetings, to prepare the resolutions, to furnish replies to the correspondence, to examine the case of each person complaining of practical grievances, to rouse the torpid, to animate the lukewarm, to control the violent and inflammatory, to avoid the shoals and breakers of the law, to guard against multiplied treachery and at all time to oppose, at every peril, the powerful and multitudinous enemies of the cause.

Always he must steer clear of the Convention Act of 1793 which banned all bodies – except parliament itself and Corporations – claiming to represent a wider public.

Essentially he planned to make emancipation, hitherto the con-

118

cern of a few Catholic aristocrats and Dublin lawyers, the object of a nationwide mass agitation. Several factors made the time ripe for this.

The ground had been well prepared by two members of the Catholic hierarchy. In the past Irish bishops had been very chary of committing themselves in politics – unless, like Archbishop Troy (O'Connell's 'pliant Trojan'), they were committed to the Castle line. But in January 1820 there appeared the first of a series of public letters signed Heirophilos. The writer was John MacHale, a lecturer in theology at Maynooth* where he had studied and taught for eighteen years. Armed with logic and satire, most of his letters attacked Protestantism and particularly the proselytising Bible Societies. Politically he was inspired mainly by Burke (a Protestant), arguing that the admirable British civil liberties should be extended to Ireland by a total repeal of the Penal Laws; that the Act of Union too should be repealed and the only constitutional link between Britain and Ireland should be the Crown. To the Crown he was conspicuously loyal: indeed one of his objections to Protestantism was that disloyalty was inherent in it.[1] Otherwise, why had they thrown out their lawful king, James II?

Two years later there appeared the first Address to the People over the pen-name 'J.K.L.' (James Kildare and Leighlin). The writer was Bishop Doyle, a product of continental Catholic education (Coimbra University in Portugal). His *Vindication of the Religious and Political Principles of Catholics*, which insisted that all the ills of Ireland were due to unjust laws and which was published throughout the English language press, had as much effect in Ireland as Tom Paine's writings had in America on the eve of the revolution. The two prelates differed in many matters: MacHale was anti-Protestant, Doyle was ecumenical; MacHale was for repealing the union, Doyle was for maintaining it as the best guarantee for Catholic rights. But at a time when on the continent Catholicism was everywhere synonymous with reaction, Dr MacHale and Bishop Doyle, with all their ecclesiastical authority, firmly associated the Irish Catholic Church with liberalism. Foreign visitors were astonished at the phenomenon of the Catholic Church in the van of social and political progress, not to say

* Later Bishop of Killala and Archbishop of Tuam.

protest. If it was ever true, as O'Connell asserted, that you could spot a Catholic walking down the street by his humble, crouching demeanour, these two must have raised many a head and straightened many a back.

On a less intellectual plane, Thomas Moore's *Irish Melodies* and *Captain Rock*, although too sentimental and over-romanticised for the sophisticated, made very good propaganda for O'Connell. He himself greatly admired the *Melodies*.

The spread of English literacy was of great value to O'Connell's agitation. In 1808 there had been about 4,000 schools educating about 200,000 children; by 1824 there were 18,000 schools educating 560,000 children, nearly three out of four being Catholics.[2] (This was a higher proportion of pupils to population than in England, though lower than in Scotland.) Many Catholic girls were educated by nuns, many Catholic boys by the Christian Brothers, founded in 1802. There were also schools run by the Kildare Place Society, founded in 1811, which were government-subsidised and supposed to be non-sectarian, but were suspected of Protestant proselytising. O'Connell had at first supported but later detested the Society. By 1841 70.6 per cent of the adult male population in towns and 50.8 per cent in rural areas were literate, able to absorb Catholic Association pamphlets and read O'Connell's and Sheil's speeches in the newspapers.

English language newspapers were increasing rapidly. In 1800 there were only twenty-five newspapers in the whole country, mainly in Dublin; in 1830 there were sixty-six, including thirty-two in Leinster and sixteen in Munster. They nearly all reported O'Connell's speeches, and when he complained that one report was inadequate the exasperated editor retorted that as he spoke for three hours at 200 words a minute, full coverage was difficult. The postal service was improving, as was public transport by road, canal and, latterly, rail. By 1841 only a very small part of the country was more than ten miles from some public transport service.

During the war-time agricultural boom, O'Connell had remarked that agitation was impossible when butter was selling at one shilling and sixpence a pound. In the 1820s the farmer was getting far less for it. In the depression landlords, rents, tithes and all the interrelated ills of Irish agriculture were more than usually resented, and provided ideal opportunities for the grievance-mongering which was the Catholic Association's most potent form of propaganda.

The growth of towns facilitated agitation. During the 1820s there were half a million people living in towns in Leinster, a quarter of a million in Munster. All these were accessible to written propaganda, and mass meetings could easily be called for the illiterate. O'Connellism was strongest in towns. Finally, there was sufficient oppression (and folk memories of more) to make authority odious, and at the same time sufficient liberty to make agitation safe and effective, especially for an agitator well versed in the law and agile at getting round it.

The arrival in 1822 of the Marquis Wellesley, the Duke of Wellington's brother, the first Irish Lord Lieutenant since James II's reign, was also helpful to the cause. He shook hands twice with O'Connell and said civil things: 'he is a very nice old gentleman, full of fire and spirit and with all the appearance of a decided character.' Wellesley was also vain, pompous and so uninhibited in his amours that his brother, no puritan, wished he could be castrated. But he was nevertheless a firm and competent administrator, willing to be fair to Catholics if this could be done without endangering the Ascendancy. His policy was to smother discontent with kindness, and his first act was to remove Saurin, who had been Attorney General for fifteen years. Soon after his removal a discovery was made which proved most embarrassing to Saurin. A letter was found in the lining of a chair sent for repair, and delivered by the upholsterer to O'Connell. In it Saurin, as Attorney General, advised Lord Norbury, the Chief Justice, to warn Protestant gentlemen of the dire consequences of emancipation which would surely lead to Catholics being nominated Sheriffs and even judges: 'if you will judiciously administer a little of this medicine to the King's County ... you will deserve well.' O'Connell published with glee a document which completely vindicated everything he had ever said about the administration of justice under the Ascendancy, and even the Castle was embarrassed.[3]

He expected an Orange rising to discredit the new administration, and suggested the raising of a volunteer force of a thousand or twelve hundred brave, honest Dubliners to combat it. It would be armed and officered (half-Catholic, half-Protestant) by the government, and he would find the rank and file within forty-eight hours. There seems to have been no reply to this public-spirited offer.

The revived Catholic Association made a slow start. The Glencullen House dinner was on 8th February, but it was not until 12th May, after several abortive meetings, that the Association was actually formed, with forty-seven members. O'Connell laboured hard to work up enthusiasm. Most people were just not interested in emancipation, to them a vague and remote issue. What mattered to them were local grievances – tithes, high rents, evictions by tyrannical or (even worse) 'improving' landlords, rigged trials, packed Orange juries and the persecution of those who voted against the landlord's wishes. O'Connell argued that the people must be (a) involved in agitation by concentrating on and remedying their grievances; and (b) *educated* into seeing a cure for injustice not in burnt ricks, houghed cattle and a landlord shot from behind a hedge, but in lawful, peaceful political agitation leading to an Act of parliament. Only when they were involved and educated could they be guided towards emancipation. Moreover he insisted from the first that right-thinking Protestants must be allowed, nay welcomed, into the Catholic Association: 'I wish we may find Protestants liberal enough to join us, that is all.'[4] They did. It is estimated that between a quarter and a third of the members, paying one guinea a year, were Protestants.[5]

During the early months of the Association there was much opposition to his views. The 'lousy' Catholic aristocrats thought that agitation was the greatest mistake and politics were no concern of the common people. Even his trusted colleague, Denys Scully, believed that Catholic unionism and loyalty to Britain would bring emancipation as its reward, and moreover he had no use for Protestants or for Grattan's parliament, which he thought was the club-house of the Ascendancy. It was, perhaps, as well that Mary was in Southampton, not in Dublin joining her voice to theirs; for she thought that Dan should 'wait patiently for a few years and what is now refused you as a boon will be given to conciliate and secure your assistance for strengthening the *throne*.' She did not believe there was 'one *real* Protestant anxious for the emancipation of the Catholics. They are a horrid, bigoted set.' As for the Catholic Association, she was 'cross as a cat, and wished it at the bottom of the sea'.

But neither she nor his colleagues could change O'Connell's mind. In all that mattered he had his way, especially in the vital matter of the 'Catholic Rent'.

Late in 1823 he suggested that, besides the more affluent members of the Association who paid a guinea a year, every single Catholic should be urged to join as an associate member, paying only a farthing a week which even the poorest could afford. There were probably six million Catholics in the country; even if only one million paid the 'Catholic Rent', this would produce a fighting fund for the Association of £50,000 a year, an enormous sum.

After a committee chaired by O'Connell had studied and reported on the idea, a full meeting was called for 4th February 1824 to vote on it. There was no quorum until O'Connell went into the street and hauled in two reluctant clerical students (*ex officio* members of the Association) to make up numbers. O'Connell then read out the recommendation of his committee, that the objects of the Catholic Association should be:

1 To petition parliament on Catholic emancipation and all Irish grievances.
2 To obtain legal redress for Catholics injured by Orange violence and oppression who were unable to obtain redress themselves. To prevent, legally, Orange processions, violence, etc., and to bring the perpetrators to court. To prosecute Orange murderers. To procure for Catholics all rights to which they were entitled by law but which for thirty years had been denied them. (Cost of above, £15,000 p.a.).
3 To encourage and support a liberal and enlightened press (£15,000 p.a.).
4 To promote Catholic education (£5,000 p.a.).
5 To help Catholics in North America by supplying them with priests (£5,000 p.a.) and to supply priests to their neighbours in England.

O'Connell laid great stress on buying newspaper support both in Ireland and in England, but at first had little success in this.

The meeting then passed a series of resolutions relating to the Catholic Rent, its collection parish by parish, its returns and accounts, and the Committee of Accounts which was responsible for expenditure. Members would pay a minimum entrance fee of one guinea; associate members would pay not less than a penny a month and not more than two shillings. O'Connell was elected secretary of the Association and James Sugrue, another Kerryman, assistant secretary.

It is a measure of O'Connell's genius that he turned upside down the normal eighteenth-century political practices. It was universally assumed that the only way to win people's support was to give them money in one form or another. He saw that far more devoted support could be won by taking their money – not enough to cause them hardship, but enough to make them feel committed to his cause. He kept associate members' subscriptions low (the sky was the limit for full members) because of the snowball effect of large numbers of people each contributing a tiny sum: 'There is nothing encourages our friends so much as the readiness to contribute in money exhibited universally'; 'If one million persons each contribute one farthing a week we shall have £50,000. Let this never be forgotten.'

Another enormous advantage of the Catholic Rent was that it kept control of the Association in the hands of O'Connell and his close associates, the Dublin activists. To the Treasurer in Dublin went every farthing collected; every farthing expended had to be authorised by the Committee of Accounts in Dublin. O'Connell insisted that the accounts of the Association (unlike his own) be kept and audited 'with mercantile precision', and published regularly in the press.

The inspiration for the Catholic Rent has always been credited to O'Connell though he admitted himself that Lord Kenmare had the same idea in 1785. Only recently has there been discovered a letter[6] dated 3rd December 1811, addressed to Denys Scully, a Catholic barrister and landowner from Tipperary, two years younger than O'Connell. Scully had compiled a scathing summary of the remaining Penal Laws and of the ways Catholics were being deprived of rights granted to them by law. He seldom made a mistake because he seldom made a decision, and he had kept the Catholic Association just afloat during the interregnum between Keogh and O'Connell. He had an astute mind and was an invaluable backroom adviser and subordinate; but his person, squat and clumsy with a very large nose and a very small chin, was unprepossessing, and his extreme diffidence made him a poor public speaker. In 1815 his customary prudence had deserted him when he lent O'Connell £2,274 for six months only. He was still trying to get it back nine years later.

The letter to Scully was written by William Parnell, grandfather of Charles Stewart Parnell. In it he wrote:

> I think nothing would give more unity to the Catholic body than to raise generally and annually a very small voluntary subscription, if only a penny from each labourer, a shilling from each farmer and five shillings from each gentleman. Your Parish Collectors and your Treasury would be the connecting medium between you and the people – so small a donation could hardly become an object of great obloquy. It might be raised for the ostensible purpose of paying the law expenses where poor Catholics were oppressed; and for the necessary expenses of your petitions; but your Executive in Dublin might be allowed a sum for secret service money accountable to a Select Committee, for contesting the elections of members inimical to your cause, and for remunerating the newspapers and employing the Press ... The direction of affairs would soon rest, where it ought, in the hands of the residents of Dublin who were most zealous in the cause.

Parnell also suggested that the collection of the money and the whole organisation of the Catholic Association should be on a parish basis, 'nearer to men's hearts and interests'. His letter is almost a blueprint for the emancipation campaign twelve years later. It is inconceivable that Scully should not have discussed its contents with O'Connell. There is a pleasing irony in O'Connell's campaign for Catholic emancipation having been devised by a Protestant Ascendancy landowner.

The collection of the Rent and the running of a mass campaign required a regular organising machine. O'Connell saw one ready to hand in the Catholic Church. As soon as the details of the Rent were decided, O'Connell wrote to the Archbishop of Cashel (and presumably also to all the bishops) giving details of the scheme and asking His Lordship, if he approved, to give it a fair wind and provide him with an accurate list of the parishes and their incumbents. In each parish there would be a secretary and committee to collect the Rent, sometimes house-to-house, sometimes at the church door after Mass. The active co-operation of the Church, which at first held aloof, was obtained by the Association interesting itself in Catholic education, providing money for Catholic schools, and opposing Protestant proselytisers. When 'J.K.L.' had been won over, many followed. O'Connell found the Church, thanks to MacHale and Doyle, open to liberal ideas, and by enlisting it in his cause actually made it much more liberal.[7]

The part played by priests in the emancipation agitation has been exaggerated. On the whole the leaders were middle-class laymen. In a few elections – Waterford in 1826, Clare in 1828, and Kerry in 1831 are conspicuous examples – priests took a lead and marshalled the freeholders behind O'Connell. But this was not the general rule. A lot depends on individual personalities; a priest might have been the sort of man to whom people naturally looked for advice, but one can hardly see intelligent, middle-aged, newspaper-reading men seeking political guidance from a young fellow just out of Maynooth. Irishmen are not like that. Priests, and by no means all of them, played a part similar to that of modern election agents: they helped collect the Rent, organised public meetings which were probably chaired by some local land-owner, and made a chapel available for political purposes as though it were a modern village hall; but they did not as a rule give a lead. On the contrary, they followed the flock and if they failed to do so, Mass attendance and collections dropped sharply.[8]

The political militancy, low social status and poor education of Maynooth-trained priests has undoubtedly been overstressed, even by Catholic gentry such as Wyse and Sheil. By 1827 about half the priesthood were Maynooth-trained, and according to Protestant polemicists they carried to their parishes the rancour of partisans and the gross habits of peasants. This is untrue. In 1827 Dr Bartholemew Crotty, President of Maynooth, giving evidence before a parliamentary commission, said,

> Our students are generally the sons of farmers who must be comfortable to meet the expenses;* of tradesmen, shopkeepers; not a very small proportion are the sons of opulent merchants,

---

* Variously estimated from £20 to £69 a year.

and rich farmers and graziers ... A good many gentry from time to time.

The Commissioners accepted this view:

> An opinion has prevailed that the free education ... has both induced and enabled persons of a much lower class to enter the Roman Catholic priesthood than those who formerly filled the ministerial office ... We collect, however, from the evidence that this effect has not been produced; and that the costs of previous education, the expenses of admission and the charges which still attend the course of instruction at Maynooth, accompanied by other regulations adopted by the Roman Catholic bishops, have prevented this result.

Six years earlier Dr MacHale, then a lecturer at Maynooth, had written:

> It is not true that the clergy are taken from those low classes with which low vices are generally associated ... Twenty or thirty pounds a year, the average of the money expended on their education, is proof that they belong to the more decent class of farmer.

A detailed breakdown of Maynooth students' fathers' occupations in 1807 gives the same picture of an overwhelmingly middle-class priesthood, tending towards upper rather than lower middle class.[9] So the average Maynooth priest's father was a well-to-do farmer or grazier who probably kept a hunter; his brothers might be doctors or lawyers, his sisters would be genteelly educated and expected not to marry beneath them.[10] Maynooth provided, besides theological training, a good general education in the classics, English and natural sciences, with much stress on loyalty to the Crown and obedience to the law. Quite high academic standards were required for admission: Charles Connor, Mary's nephew, with all O'Connell's influence behind him, was sent home after his first interview to polish up his Greek and Latin before trying again. The surpliced peasant ruffian, preaching murder and mayhem from the pulpit, was a product of fevered Tory imaginations. A more valid generalisation is that friars of the religious orders, all trained on the continent, were more militant than lay priests.

127

Father L'Estrange, for example, O'Connell's confessor and a very zealous politician, was a Carmelite, and his church in Clarendon Square was a centre for the Catholic Association. Bishop Doyle ('J.K.L.') had been an Augustinian, and Bishop Egan of Kerry a Jesuit. Another valid generalisation is that young priests were more politically aware, and more radical in their politics, than the middle-aged. But the young men were not all Maynooth trainees, nor were the middle-aged all products of continental seminaries: Maynooth had been turning out priests for thirty years, and there were still in 1827 one hundred and forty Irish clerical students in France, Spain and Portugal.[11]

(In parenthesis it is interesting that Catholics saw, or thought they saw, a similar change for the worse in parsons of the established Church. The old-fashioned parson, fond of his hunting, shooting, fishing and card-playing with the local gentry, marrying a landlord's younger daughter and not markedly enthusiastic about propagating the faith, had been quite harmless, so long as he got in his tithes, and not unpopular. The new-style bustling, zealous, evangelical parson, sour, rancorous and pharisaical, busy proselytising and luring Catholics to his church with tracts and nourishing soup, was a menace.[12])

It is not true that O'Connellism was a movement of the poor and 'under-privileged'. In so far as he was 'King of the Beggars', a term of opprobrium invented by the English press, his humbler subjects, like those of other kings, had only to cheer, obey and, as always, pay. The movement was run, the Rent was collected, the meetings were called, the petitions were drafted, cases of oppression were exposed, by middle-class activists – merchants, millers, journalists, 'strong farmers' and, most notably, lawyers. The large farmers and graziers had a particular grievance: pasture for dry cattle had in the past been exempted from tithes, but the Tithe Composition Act of 1824 made them liable for tithes on all their wide acres, and they did not like it.

In 1822 the Catholics had been lethargic, Sheil said, 'like galley-slaves in a calm'.* By 1824 they were militant and eager for action. 'When I took the helm,' said O'Connell,

---

* Not the best of metaphors, when one comes to think of it, since a calm is when galley-slaves must most exert themselves. But Sheil's oratory was noted for colour rather than exactitude.

I found all the Catholics full of mutual jealousies, one man trying to out-rival another, one meeting rivalling another, the leaders watching to sell themselves at the highest penny ... You have no idea what carrion finds a ready sale in the market of corruption.

Well, they were not in 1824 free of quarrels and schisms – that would be too much to expect of any collection of Irishmen – but at least they were, most of them, going in the same direction and, more or less, acknowledging the same leader.

Early meetings of the Association were in Capel Street, where Trinity College students threatened to break them up. O'Connell changed the venue to the Corn Exchange, conveniently adjacent to the Liffey, into which, he informed the College lads, his Praetorian Guard of 'coalies' would be delighted to heave them if they caused any trouble.

While the Catholic Association was girding itself for action, O'Connell was separated from his family. Maurice was in London, reading for the Bar with a diligence that was as gratifying as it was unexpected. Morgan was still in Vicenza, enjoying the life of a cadet in a smart regiment of light cavalry, but not, his father thought, studying his profession as he must if he were to make a success of it. Mary and the younger children were established, not happily, at Southampton. The trouble was that they did not get on with the English whom they found cold and unfriendly, 'a nasty, selfish lot'. Danny could hardly forbear abusing them in the street, 'such a little patriot as he is'. The girls were miserable because at a ball they were asked to dance only twice, and pined for Dublin where they would have no shortage of beaux. Betsey was extremely difficult – defiant, foul-tempered, hard-hearted and too old to be whipped: 'our other children have their faults, but none equal to Betsey's'. The only future Mary could see for her was as a nun – why, oh why, could she not feel a vocation?

After much long-range discussion and many changes of plan and misunderstandings, it was agreed that they might as well all economise together in happiness rather than separately in misery. The Merrion Square house was redecorated (with even gas-lighting installed), the servants were re-engaged (including John the coachman, hardly an emblem of economy), and 'Fado' (the younger children's name for their father) bought two spanking horses for the barouche. In May 1824 they were back in dear old Dublin again. Soon Nell, to general satisfaction, became engaged to the highly suitable Christopher Fitz-Simon of Glencullen House, where the famous dinner party had been held. In September Morgan arrived on sick leave, suffering from a rupture probably due to riding with the exaggeratedly straight-legged 'sugar-tongs seat', which was perfectly useless, indeed dangerous, for any form of equitation except jogging slowly about on ceremonial parades, but which was considered smart and fashionable in peace-time cavalry. He intended, when he arrived, to leave the Austrian service, but changed his mind and went back after a few months' furlough. He was promoted, strutted about Vienna as 'a bold lieutenant', and joined his new regiment, hussars, in Hungary. Maurice, a newly qualified barrister and turning out better than had been thought likely, also came back to Ireland to be initiated by his father into the tricks of the trade on the Munster circuit and to give a hand with the Catholic Association.

In December 1824, O'Connell made one of his rare slips and exposed himself to a charge of uttering seditious language. His words as reported in *Saunder's News-Letter* were:

I hope Ireland will be restored to her rights – but, if that day should arrive – if she were driven mad by persecution, I wish that a new Bolivar may be found – may arise – that the spirit of the Greeks and of the South Americans may animate the people of Ireland.

It was hardly compatible with his policy, announced time and time again, of using *only* peaceful means to secure his ends, and the government pounced. But the preliminary hearing by the Grand Jury turned out to be one of those occasions in which the gentlemen of the press joined together to obstruct what they regarded as interference with free speech and free reporting. Although dozens of reporters had been present, none of them seemed able to recollect O'Connell's exact words; and as for the reporter of *Saunder's News-Letter* he had, he said, been asleep during Mr O'Connell's speech, and had asked someone else, he could not remember whom, what Mr O'Connell had said. The Grand Jury threw out the bill of indictment. In a speech a few

days later O'Connell swore that when England and Ireland were
two free and independent countries, he would shed the last drop
of his blood to preserve the connection between them, the 'golden
link of the Crown'.

Hunting Cap had not long to live. Aged ninety-six, he was
physically frail and needed the constant attention of a physician,
but was mentally full of life. Many years earlier he had felled an
oak which had since been seasoning to provide planks for his
coffin, and now he had a vigorous argument on the subject with
the estate carpenter, who had cut the planks seven foot long, a
wicked extravagance. 'You idiot! I was never more than six foot
and an inch in my vamps, the best day ever I saw!' 'But Your
Honour will stretch after death!' 'Not eleven inches, you blockhead! Well, make it six foot and six inches and I'll warrant that
will give me room enough.'

Within a few days the matter was put to the test. To each of
his nephews – Dan, James and John – he left a third of his
personal property and a third of his land, of which Dan's share
included the Derrynane estate. The personal property included
some £8,000 arrears of rent, most of which the brothers remitted.
The Derrynane rents brought O'Connell's total income from land
up to about £4,000 a year, and the £15,000 which was, in the
end, his share of the personal property sufficed to pay off the
more pressing of his creditors and to renegotiate a lower rate of
interest with the remainder. For a short time he was free from
financial pressure.

Meanwhile the campaign for emancipation was getting under
way, albeit rather jerkily and experimentally. It can be divided
into four parts:

1 Measures taken to educate the people, such as the formation
  of Liberal Clubs and of reading rooms stocked with suitable
  newspapers and pamphlets.
2 Measures taken to ensure the support of the Church, such as
  providing funds for church-building and Catholic schools.
  O'Connell took a particular delight in attending and disrupting
  with argument 'Bible meetings' held by Protestant proselytisers. 'We discovered by accident that there was to be a Bible
  meeting in the Court House. We accordingly broke in upon
  them. Bric, Sheil and I spoke. Sheil made an admirable

address. I spoke for about an hour with some effect, and we prevented them passing one single resolution and made them adjourn to the next day.'

3 Measures taken to stimulate the people, including especially the defence of tenants harassed for voting against their landlords' directions or prosecuted for politically motivated offences, and loans to tenants who were in arrears with their rent.

4 Measures directly connected with parliamentary elections (but these came a little later) such as the scrutiny of electoral rolls to remove the names of opponents who were improperly included, and identifying candidates (Protestants, of course) who were worthy of Catholic support.

All these activities, in addition to the unending collection of the Catholic Rent, gave activists something practical to do.

Most efficacious, serving all four purposes, were public meetings at the parish, county or provincial level. Here the speeches of Sheil and O'Connell could work audiences up into the wildest excitement – yet always impressing upon them that they must be loyal to the Crown and entirely peaceful in their behaviour. It was the essence of the campaign that the government should be kept in constant apprehension of a rebellion which O'Connell would never actually allow to take place. He had to be able to say, 'Give us emancipation – or I will not be answerable for the consequences.' Public meetings were also the occasion for grievance-mongering which formed a great part of the Association's propaganda, and for petitions to parliament to remedy grievances great and small, from the Penal Laws and packed juries to the distraint for tithes of the Widow McCarthy's geese. Any petition, properly handled by friends in parliament (though this took practice) could be debated four times, on motions that it be brought up, received, lie on the table and be printed.

Although the campaign had not yet really got into its stride, and Rent collections for 1824 totalled only £7,573, the government was alarmed by its unexpected, indeed unprecedented nature. Wellington wrote to Peel, Home Secretary in George Canning's Ministry, in November 1824, 'If we cannot get rid of the Catholic Association we must look to civil war in Ireland sooner or later.' The king, forgetting all about his huge bunch of shamrock, also wrote to Peel:

> The King is apprehensive that a notion has gone abroad that the King himself is not unfavourable to the Catholic claims ... The sentiments of the King upon Catholic Emancipation are those of his revered and excellent father; from those sentiments the King never can and never will deviate.

So it was decided to bring in a bill to suppress the Association. In February 1825, O'Connell set off with a delegation of Catholics to prepare the ground for yet another Grand Petition to parliament for emancipation by means of a Catholic Relief Bill. Preparation of the ground meant, for him, cultivating the best people, Catholic and liberal aristocrats and influential radicals like Brougham and William Cobbett. After all, English Catholics, from the Duke of Norfolk to the humblest labourer, were equally debarred from the most important offices in the land: they could not become Privy Counsellors, ministers of the Crown, members of parliament, Generals, Admirals, judges, Sheriffs, Lords Lieutenant; however distinguished at the Bar, they could not take silk. They could not even vote. So he, Sheil and the rest were lionised in London, dining on one occasion with four dukes, four earls and four barons, O'Connell sitting between the Duke of Devonshire and Earl Grey. But when it came down to business, he found the English Catholics not as zealous as one might expect. 'There is an English coldness; and, after all, what is it to them if we are crushed?' The Whigs were apathetic.

However, he was examined at the Bar of the House of Lords and was so pleased with his own performance that he was sure of emancipation that very session. 'Lord Stourton said that neither Pitt nor Fox was my equal. Charles Butler said that since the days of Lord Chatham* he had heard nothing like me.' 'Darling, darling,' he wrote four days later, 'Call my children together ... Tell Danny to fling up his cap for Old Ireland. I have now no doubt that we shall be emancipated. May I thank heaven that it was your husband, sweetest, that won it.'

So elated was he that he could even brush off a mutiny in his

---

* The Elder Pitt, 'that terrible Cornet of Horse'.

own ranks. Under examination before a committee of the House he had conceded that, as the price for emancipation, Catholic priests might be paid by the Crown – the 'wing' to the Veto that he had denounced ten years ago – and that the qualification for the franchise in Irish counties might be raised from forty shillings to £10 a year from freehold property. The case for disenfranchising the forty-shilling freeholders, thus reducing the electorate from about 100,000 to about 16,000,* was that they were too many and too unruly. Also, paradoxically, they were notoriously venal and subservient to landlord pressure.[13] In general a forty-shilling freeholder did not *own* property worth forty shillings a year, but was tenant for one or more lives – perhaps his own, his son's and his grandson's, or the landlord's, or even the king's. When a 'life' expired he paid the landlord a 'fine' to renew the lease; when the lease expired it was often, but by no means always, renewed for more lives, so that it became almost hereditary. A freeholder could not be evicted for any reason other than a failure to pay rent. But pressure could be put on him by demanding a large 'fine' when his lease came up for renewal, or by insisting that he pay his rent on the dot, to the uttermost farthing. In the fifteenth century property worth forty shillings a year in rent conferred a modest independence, but inflation had reduced its economic value to virtually nothing. Its political value, however, could be high if the freeholder's landlord was not politically minded and the tenant could put his vote up for sale. Moreover politically ambitious landlords conferred the freehold on very poor men who would often be in arrears with their rent or who were dependent on the landlord for a job. So it could be argued that disenfranchising the forty-shilling freeholder would actually reduce landlord power.

Nevertheless the concession got O'Connell into trouble with English radicals, occasioning a bitter open letter from Cobbett to the Catholics of Ireland. The erratic Jack Lawless attacked

---

*There are wide variations in estimates of the number disenfranchised and the number remaining on the voters' rolls. These figures are taken from J. Reynolds, *The Catholic Emancipation Crisis*, p. 168. The M.P. for Kilkenny stated in the Commons that 191,000 forty-shilling freeholders out of a county electorate of 216,000 lost their votes. C. Dod in *Electoral Facts, 1832-52*, says that in 1832 there were 92,152 electors, nearly two-thirds of them in the counties.

O'Connell in the Dublin *Freeman's Journal*. But O'Connell in his hour of triumph was unmoved by attacks from 'that miserable maniac Lawless ... Darling, do not be a bit uneasy. *The game is won.*'[14]

Alas, it wasn't. The Catholic Relief Bill passed its third reading in the Commons by a comfortable majority. All was going well in the Lords until the Duke of York, the king's brother and heir presumptive – than whom it would be hard to find a man less moved by religious scruples – with tears pouring down his cheeks pledged himself to defend Protestant principles, 'So help me, God!' The Lords threw out the bill, and the 'wings' accompanying it were dropped. O'Connell had 'nothing to say or sing but defeat. We must begin again.'

Moreover the government had, by Act of parliament, banned the Catholic Association. But on his return to Dublin O'Connell, ever resourceful, reacted promptly, forming the New Catholic Association 'for the purpose of public or private charity, and such other purposes as are not prohibited by the statute of 6 George IV, cap. 4' (the banning Act). At its first meeting on 16th July 1825, it was resolved to carry on collecting the Catholic Rent 'for all purposes allowable by law'. The Crown lawyers would have difficulty in finding a chink in that armour, and almost every disbursement from the Rent (which included £10,000 inherited from the defunct Association) could, by a competent defence counsel, be shown to be 'public or private charity'. Furthermore O'Connell devised (and this delighted him) a uniform for the New Catholic Association, of buff and blue, the colours which Charles Fox had chosen half a century ago for the Whigs in compliment to George Washington's army.

They were in business again.

With Hunting Cap's death O'Connell was master of Derrynane at last and revelled in it. To his delight Mary was every day more pleased with the place. She even persuaded herself that she had always liked Iveragh. (Perhaps it was really Hunting Cap she had not liked.) 'A *home* endears the most solitary place to those who have everything in this world to make them happy.' She took an interest in the estate, the sale of butter, the calving of the house cows, the price of bullocks, the killing of the pigs. Only in her first winter the terrific gales and endless rain were depressing;

she simply must have some covered conveyance in which to take the air on the strand, as no horse-drawn carriage could reach within a mile of the house. O'Connell instructed his agent, John Primrose, to build two outdoor privies, the lack of which was a cruel grievance. 'Let everything be very snug and warm. Mrs O'Connell will send down some parlour chairs and tables ... I should delight to spend my Christmas in the old Iveragh festivity.' The girls, however, wouldn't. Derrynane, Mary pointed out, was a dreary place in winter for young people, and it would be cruel not to take Kate to Dublin before the end of the season's gaiety there. If they were obliged to give a dinner and ball in Merrion Square to great folks, 'let us not ask as many *folks* of the other description as we have been in the habit of asking.'

O'Connell threw himself with zest into the running of the place. He was, perforce, generally an absentee landlord, but kept a finger in every pie. The Earl of Cork gave a long extension of the Derrynane lease, but more than doubled the (very modest) rent, so the estate must make more money. Primrose must arrange for a great deal more tillage in the demesne, and extend it to take in more of the fertile land towards Derrynanebeg without dispossessing anyone but one old man who would be given a pension in compensation; there must be a solid bounds ditch to keep out the *casual* entry of the tenants' cattle. 'What have you done about the digging of my potatoes? Do not let John O'Connell neglect *that*. If you do not yourself go to Derrynane and remain there until the potatoes are all housed, they will be lost to me.' The tenants must be made to understand that their rents, which he had reduced, must be paid or they would be evicted: 'they may depend upon it that I will get new tenants ... but the fact is that they do not believe me.' (The picture given is of an easy-going landlord exhorting his agent to be tough.) The bullocks must be sold at Killarney fair for any price they would fetch, unless in the meanwhile there was a calamitous fall in livestock prices. And were the sheep still suffering from the rot? If so, 'let them be *rubbed* and *rubbed* and *rubbed* while any appearance of the disease remains.' If they could not be cured, they had better be slaughtered, for he must not propagate the disease by selling them and could not buy more while the disease continued. The Cork butter merchant was complaining that he had not received a single cask of butter from Derrynane:

'you know I ought not to treat him badly. I implore you to be rigid with my tenants on this point. I am quite content to make it worth their while to do what I ask.'

He ordered extensions and alterations to make the old house suitable for a family in the 1820s, but Mary stopped him at the third storey since their family was bound in future to diminish rather than increase. He even bought a capital twenty-five-ton hooker to bring Derrynane produce and fresh fish to Dublin, an enterprise which failed owing to the incompetence of the skipper. In fact the novel sensation of solvency rather went to his head and Mary had to reprimand him: '*Pray* what was the necessity to order six dozen of bottled cider and six of bottled ale, love, just at this time? I perceive I must exert *my authority* and *try* and keep you in *proper* order.'

Whenever he could spare a few weeks for Derrynane there were the trout, the grouse and the hares. He had a free hand now with the hounds and was able by scientific breeding to build up a pack few in numbers, but able to hunt up and down the steep, rough mountains and famous for nose and cry. He enjoyed a fox-hunt if one came his way, as it sometimes did on circuit, but (like many a hound expert) believed hare-hunting to be the better sport because it was more of a test for the hounds' scenting powers. Some Orange fox-hunting squireens, he said, despised hare-hunting as a sport fit only for Papists, but the English foxhound was bred merely for speed, like a greyhound – that was not true hunting: 'I am the only fellow who knows how to hunt rationally.'

Alas, he had far too little time at Derrynane. Mary might stay for months, but he had to post back to the daily grind at the Four Courts and the endless drudgery of the Catholic Association. He took to having a cold shower first thing in the morning, even in the depths of winter, and found it envigorated him for the rest of the day.

He might put a bold face upon it, but as he would certainly have taken the credit for success he could not escape the blame for failure in London after raising everyone's hopes so high. Moreover he had ditched the forty-shillingers and agreed to the payment of priests and got nothing in return. Later he admitted his error. Jack Lawless, the cantankerous Belfast man, returned to the charge, and even repeated Cobbett's monstrous canard that O'Connell had been bought by the promise of being made King's Counsel. Lawless was aided and abetted by O'Connell's fat friend, Purcell O'Gorman, and an earnest busybody from Cork, Stephen Coppinger. O'Connell was in trouble and losing popularity. There was, he told Mary, 'a most violent party raised against me ... Their object, probably, is to drive me off the stage of Catholic politics ... It would be a great triumph to them.' Mary was outraged, for her own brother-in-law was involved in the mutiny and '*Master* Sheil, I think, is wheeling round again.' Were she in her darling Dan's place, she would 'give up Catholic politics and leave the nasty ungrateful set to sink into insignificance' and 'make a fortune [at the Bar] without sacrificing your health and your strength'.

How cruelly and ungratefully the Catholics are acting by you! Is it not enough to make you retire with disgust from their service? It seems in vain to serve Ireland ... They deserve to be slaves and as such they should be left ... It is foul ingratitude and base duplicity.[15]

But O'Connell got out of the scrape by an adroit retreat, admitting the possibility of human error; by cruelly deriding Coppinger's sepulchral and funereal gait, he set the Dublin mob hooting with laughter; and finally at a provincial Catholic meeting in Carlow he beat the enemy out of the field. 'O'Gorman was most heartily hissed and all but pelted to pieces ... The good sense, the good feeling of *my* poor people, may the great God bless them. They would not listen to the Wingers [the mutineers] and their fantasies.'

With the mutiny suppressed, O'Connell goaded the parish committees into ever more activity. Public meetings multiplied in number, held usually outside a chapel (or inside in wet weather), presided over by some Catholic or liberal Protestant bigwig, worked up into a frenzy of excitement by Lawless's harsh, Belfast-accented diatribes or by Sheil's even more inflammatory oratory. Barely five foot tall, nervous, with a shambling gait and a shrill rasping voice, he orated in grandiloquent, flamboyant phrases (long prepared and learned off by heart), with uncoordinated gestures and a flow of classical allusions incomprehensible to nine-tenths of his audience. He was more ambivalent than

O'Connell on violence, and sailed much closer to the wind in skirting round sedition.

O'Connell in private meetings of the Association was very much the man of business, opening, directing and summing up the discussion, keeping strictly to the point and making others do likewise – no easy matter in Ireland. At public meetings he was another man. Speaking always impromptu, his face and gestures in two minutes expressing twenty different passions, moving his audience to laughter at some luckless opponent, to tears at the Emerald Isle's ancient glories and to roars of rage against the Saxon oppressors, he ranged far from the point at issue and seldom with any consistency. In him there were, it was observed, eight or nine men who were not always of the same opinion but who combined to curse the Penal Laws and denounce the misrulers of Ireland. 'Known personally to the Irish peasantry, and living with them for a great portion of the year, he has something about him of their manners, their language and even of their accent.' O'Connell suited his accent to his company and, in direct contrast to the immortal 'Flurry Knox' (of the *Irish R.M.* stories), spoke like a gentleman among gentlemen and a stable-boy among stable-boys.

> You should see him with his cravat loose, his waistcoat un-buttoned, in a chapel in Munster. He boasts of the beauty of Ireland ... and above all of the incontestable superiority of her inhabitants above those of every other quarter of the globe; you instantly see tears of joy sparkle in every eye. He lends an eloquent voice to the sentiments, the passions and even the prejudices of six millions of men. Hence his extreme popularity ... Of what consequence is it to the people that he does not say the same things to them today that he did yesterday, pro-vided they always hear what pleases them most?

So wrote a very percipient French traveller, Duvergier, in 1826. In one point he was unfair: O'Connell did not always say what the people wanted to hear, for on many and many occasions they were hoping for a blaring trumpet-call to arms, and he never gave it. He always told them that they must stick to lawful, non-violent agitation, and often told them to be loyal to the Crown.

The first provincial Meeting was held at Limerick, attended by numerous Protestants who 'contributed rather too visibly their patronage ... They condescended, they advised, they encouraged, they approved.' At subsequent meetings they were less obtrusive, but the general attitude of many, even liberal, Protestants was illustrated by one who, having taken drink before a meeting, mislaid his hat during it. 'Damnation to you all!' he roared. 'I come to emancipate you and you steal my hat!'

Besides keeping people on the boil, meetings stimulated the flow of parliamentary petitions. A mere parish meeting might produce two or three. Edward Dwyer, Secretary to the Association, issued to every parish detailed instructions on what form petitions should take, how they should be worded and the most effective mode of obtaining signatures (a table with pen and ink outside the chapel door or ruled sheets of paper taken house to house). 'Care should always be taken to have some signatures on the paper containing the words of the petition.' Petitions should be submitted from every parish in Ireland: 'every person who can write should be called upon to sign his name.' Parliament was deluged with them, 11,700 in 1827-8. Night after night M.P.s and peers were invited to contemplate and debate the iniquities of the Penal Laws, breaches of the Treaty of Limerick, the denial to Catholics of the appointments and rights which they were allowed by law, Irish loyalty to the Crown, the valour of Irish soldiers in the late war, the virtues and harassment of the forty-shilling freeholders, excessive rents, and the injustice of making Catholics pay tithes to a Protestant pastor. The sheer wasting of parliamentary time was a weapon invented by Wilkes, developed by O'Connell and perfected by Parnell. Just as in the 1760s the tribulations of Mr Wilkes had almost monopolised M.P.s' time, so in the late 1820s the Mother of Parliaments seemed, to weary members, to have not a moment to spare from Irish troubles. 'There is', said O'Connell, 'a moral electricity in the continuous expression of public opinion concentrated on a single point, perfectly irresistible in its efficacy.' It was by politicising every issue, every grievance, relating it to emancipation and making it the subject of petitions with which he bombarded parliament, that he gave point to this aphorism. He believed that:

Incessant repetition is required to impress political truths* on the public mind. You must repeat the same lesson over and over again if you wish to make a permanent impression ... Men then find the facts at last quietly reposing in a corner of their minds, and no more think of doubting them than if they formed part of their religious belief.

O'Connell, remarked O'Neill Daunt, '*wears out* one speech before he gives another.' Sheil, less uncritically admiring, said, 'He flung a sturdy brood of ideas upon the world without a rag to cover them.'[16]

The Association depended greatly on a postal system which seems to have been a great deal more efficient than it is today. Four thousand receipt books had to be distributed to collectors of the Catholic Rent; 6,000 copies of pro-emancipation newspapers were posted every week, to be read aloud in pubs and outside chapels after Mass. In one month, March 1827, 30,000 copies of O'Connell's Address to the People were distributed. An educational survey organised by Frederick Conway (Mary's *bête noire*), the rather troublesome editor of the *Dublin Evening Post*, and a national census organised by Sheil (neither possible without a good postal system) threw light on Catholic-Protestant population figures on the extent to which Protestant proselytising societies were subsidised from public funds.

Support for emancipation was stronger in the towns (though not in Dublin itself) than in the country, and in Leinster and Munster than in Ulster and Connaught. In 1824, for instance, Leinster produced £3,254 in Catholic Rent, Munster £3,364, Ulster £446 and Connaught £509. The paucity of support in Ulster was, of course, due to its large and aggressive Protestant element. What is surprising is that the western, largely Gaelic-speaking counties, which include Donegal in Ulster and Kerry in Munster, should have been so lukewarm; one would expect them to be more militant than the semi-anglicised midlands, east and south. This was due partly to the Association's indifference to the Irish language, press reports all being in English, partly to poor mass attendance in counties with bad roads and scattered populations, and partly to sheer poverty.

* Or, for that matter, political lies. Repetition is the secret of any propaganda.

However ambivalent some of his lieutenants, O'Connell never hedged on political violence. 'The great Catholic cause of Ireland is the cause of virtue and honesty ... There must be no drunkenness, no debauchery, no riots, no secret meetings, no illegal oaths, no Whiteboy outrages. Above all there must be no murders.'[17] There is some difference among contemporary informed opinion on the effect of his agitation on law and order. An Inspector General of police reported in 1824 that by raising expectations it encouraged violent crime, but a police magistrate reported that by increasing the influence of the priests it promoted tranquillity. The Knight of Kerry, a friend of O'Connell and a steady supporter of Catholic emancipation in the Commons, got cold feet, advising O'Connell more than once to tone down the stridency of his campaign and even to suspend the Association, which he was sure would have a good effect on parliament. But O'Connell would have none of this: 'We *never, never, never* got anything by conciliation ... speak out boldly, let it be called intemperately, and rouse in Ireland a spirit of *action*.'

The Catholic Rent was both the lifeblood of the campaign and the barometer by which its success could be measured. The enemy trembled when collections rose and rejoiced when they fell. To Edward Dwyer, full-time clerk and essential anchor-man of the Association in Dublin, O'Connell wrote, 'The new Catholic Rent, like the old, requires only persons to collect it. It is not the sending of large donations that I desire so much as the extension of the collection to various parishes.' Even in the best collection year, 1828, only about one Catholic in twelve, say one man in three, can have paid a regular farthing a week.

The first eight months' collection, May to December 1824, produced £7,573; the next three months', the phenomenal total of £9,263. Then the old Association was dissolved and for a long time Rent collections were in abeyance. In September 1826 O'Connell implored his son-in-law, Fitz-Simon, to 'set on foot the new Catholic Rent ... Small contributions are best, because their tendency is to multiply themselves.' So ever more effort was demanded from the collectors. Chapel-door collections after Mass on special Rent Sundays brought in the cash but were unpopular with the priests because they had a bad effect on collections for Church purposes, including the priests' dues, at Mass. So every parish was divided into 'walks' for house-to-house collection.

These measures brought in £5,680 during the second half of 1826.

Every penny was needed, for in the general election of 1826 the Association intervened openly for the first time in county elections, checking voters' rolls, watching out for (Orange) impersonations and fraud, advising freeholders which of the Protestant candidates were pledged to emancipation and worthy of their votes, encouraging them to vote in their own, not in their landlords' interests, and helping any who might be persecuted for doing so by lending them the money to pay their arrears of rent, thus safeguarding them from eviction. Against this and other forms of landlord pressure the Association provided free legal aid and cash if it were needed. Sometimes a little talk with the landlord sufficed.

These tactics had very gratifying success: pro-emancipation candidates (all, of course, Protestants) won in nine counties, besides those already represented by liberal Protestants such as the Knight of Kerry and William Vesey FitzGerald of Clare. The most dramatic success was in County Waterford, so long a stronghold of the Beresfords that O'Connell deemed it impregnable. But Thomas Wyse, a level-headed Catholic landowner and the Association's leading man in those parts, thought otherwise and persuaded O'Connell, rather late in the day, to throw all his weight in support of a liberal Protestant, Henry Villiers Stuart. So O'Connell stormed up and down the county haranguing against the 'bloody Beresfords', and the freeholders thronged to his meetings and cheered him to the echo: 'I could never form a notion of the great effect of popular declamation before yesterday.' He and his candidate were drawn in a coach by the freeholders for three miles into Lismore: 'I never had a notion of popular enthusiasm until I saw that scene.' Beresford supporters were to be conveyed to the polls by steamer, but O'Connell warned them that so unseaworthy was the 'Tea Kettle' that they were going straight to a watery grave, so none took the risk. He well earned his £600 as Villiers Stuart's election counsel. Urged on by their priests, the freeholders deserted Lord George Beresford, the sitting member, in shoals. The Marquess of Waterford said, more in sorrow than in anger, to his old huntsman, '*Et tu, Brute?*' (or words to that effect). His voice broken with emotion, the old man replied, 'Long life to yer honour, I'd go to the world's end with yer honour, but sure, please your lordship, I cannot go agin my country and my religion.' Villiers Stuart used persuasions of another kind and, rather than be humiliated by a meagre vote, Lord George withdrew and left the field to Stuart, who was reputedly £30,000 the poorer for this exercise in popular democracy.

It was a famous victory, but was followed by a reaction, partly due to complacency – the feeling that the game was won and that Canning and the Marquess of Lansdowne, soon to be made Home Secretary, were emancipationists at heart though they did not seem to do much about it. Rent collections dropped to a miserable £2,900 for the whole year. O'Connell then made two churchwardens in every parish, one chosen by the priests and the other by the Vestry, and supervised by county inspectors, responsible for Rent collection. They had also to report every month, on a pro forma devised by himself, about collections, tithes, Anglican church cess, cases of proselytising, harassment of freeholders and any other petition fodder. Another pro forma was devised and circulated to churchwardens to show them exactly how petitions should be presented – legibly, in plain, not ornamental, writing, on one side of the paper only, with as many signatures or marks as possible on the same sheet as the text of the petition. The churchwardens circulated the *Weekly Register* of important speeches and other propaganda and read it aloud at the chapel door. Their activities were co-ordinated by Maurice, appointed by his father as Secretary of Churchwardens.

The collection of the Rent was all-important. Careful and detailed accounts[18] show expenditure on a wide variety of items: £400 for the relief of freeholders evicted by the Beresfords after the Waterford election; £10 and a new set of pipes for 'poor Drohan the piper' of Dungarvan, who had led three processions for Lord George Beresford but then voted for Villiers Stuart; £40 for a Catholic school at Youghal; £20 to help parents who refused to send their children to Kildare Place schools; a barrister's fee for defending a man charged with murder; the cost of printing handbills; an advertisement in the press for premises in which to house a seminary for young Catholic ladies; hundreds of pounds to Dublin and provincial papers for publishing advertisements of meetings, accounts of the Rent, details of petitions, important speeches, etc.

The liberal clubs were a particularly fruitful idea of Thomas Wyse. A whole network of clubs at town and county level was gradually built up to bring emancipationists together, stimulate their ardour, reconcile patriots who were at variance and co-ordinate their work. They served at the same time as social centres, political offices and reading rooms stocked with news-papers and pamphlets. The Orangemen, alarmed by the progress of the liberal clubs, started a network of Brunswick clubs; but these, except in the north-east, never really thrived because their roots were not in the people, and Ascendancy gentry really could not be bothered to ride twenty miles to attend a political meeting, read the Tory newspapers and hobnob with Protestant tradesmen.

A less happy inspiration was the 'Order of Liberators' founded by O'Connell in 1826, the membership of which, at an appropri-ate rank (Knights of the Grand Cross, Knights Companion and plain Liberators) would be conferred by him on those who had done signal service to the cause. An embarrassingly gaudy uni-form was designed which O'Connell wore on every possible oc-casion despite a good deal of derision, but there seemed to be a strange reluctance to follow his example and the Order wilted and eventually faded quietly away.

O'Connell was in a great tizzy at the prospect of the Duke of Wellington becoming Prime Minister: 'all the horrors of actual massacre threaten us'.[19] Canning died in August 1827, and after an interregnum presided over by the ineffective Lord Goderich the Duke formed a ministry in January 1828, with Peel as his Home Secretary. The Catholic Association then resolved to oppose any parliamentary candidate who supported the Duke's ministry.

O'Connell, however, had overestimated the hostility of that man of blood. Having no particular religious opinions, the Duke was no bigot. He had refused to join the Orange Order because it was founded on the assumption that Catholicism was synony-mous with disloyalty and his experience led him to no such assumption. He held a poor opinion of the sagacity of the lower orders and a worse one of religious 'enthusiasts', be they Hindu, Methodist or Catholic, and was therefore basically against Cath-olic emancipation which was bound to undermine the Ascen-dancy of which so many of his friends and relations were both buttress and beneficiary. But as an Irishman – albeit not conspicuously devoted to the land of his birth – he knew that Irish Catholics were not the moronic sub-humans depicted in *Punch*. Indeed in the House of Lords he paid what was, for a man notoriously sparing of praise, a generous tribute to their good feeling. In his Peninsular army, he said, there had been many thousands of Irish soldiers who fought with the utmost courage and loyalty. He supposed most of them were Catholics. But never, in all those years, did he see a single one perform any act of devotion other than making the sign of the Cross to persuade the people of the country to give them wine. Anyway, however deplorable Catholic emancipation, there was something far worse – civil war, of which he had seen a great deal and of which he had a real horror. Presumably the disciplined forces of the Crown would defeat any peasant revolt, though 'all concerns of that kind are matters of risk and doubt ... But', he put it to Peel,

> should we be better situated afterwards? I think not. We should find the same enemies blasting the prosperity of the country and ready to take advantage of the weakness of the country at any moment to do us all the harm in their power.

He once said that the most difficult thing in war was to know when to retreat and to have the courage to do it. He would hold out against Catholic emancipation as long as he thought proper, but when he judged the position untenable he would retreat, carrying Peel and the king with him. He would not, of course, disclose his intentions beforehand, either to his own troops or to the enemy commander. That, in a rearguard action, was always unwise.

For this operation it was vital to know what was going on 'the other side of the hill'. The Duke had excellent information and advice, some of it unpalatable, from three sources. One was none other than Dr James Doyle, Bishop of Kildare and Leighlin ('J.K.L.'); another was Dr Patrick Curtis, Archbishop of Armagh and Primate of All Ireland. Both had given invaluable help during the Peninsular War, the former as a student at Coimbra and the latter as Rector of the Irish College at Salamanca, in organising a band of spirited young Irish theological students into a sort of irregular intelligence corps for Wellington's army. They were ardent emancipationists, and although their continued friendship with the Duke was sometimes stormy it remained friendship. The third major source of information was the Marquis of Anglesey who as Lord Paget had run away with Wellington's sister-in-law and as the Earl of Uxbridge had commanded Wellington's cavalry at Waterloo. ('I'll take damn good care he doesn't run away with me,' was the Duke's comment on hearing of his appointment.) The loss of a leg in the last minutes of the battle had not inhibited his gallantry or his fox-hunting. Canning, just before his death, had appointed him Viceroy. He was a phenomenon more common than is generally realised – the dashing, aristocratic officer with advanced political views. He thought Catholic emancipation was not only inevitable but right. He had (like most cavalry officers, in the Duke's opinion) an unfortunate tendency to gallop too fast and too far, albeit in the right direction – a quality which might make him a liability for the closely controlled rearguard action in which the Duke excelled.

Other Irish contacts were with Wellington's (and O'Connell's) friend, the Knight of Kerry; and, on the other side, with all the Pakenham family headed by Wellington's brother-in-law, the ultra-conservative Earl of Longford.

In May 1828, the Wellington government repealed the Test Act in so far as it banned Dissenters from certain high offices of state. It was a discreet signal that the ministry was not wholly averse to change, and it strengthened the tendency of English Catholics, never conspicuously warm towards their Irish brethren in the Faith, to view Irish complaints with a certain detachment. A few months later, to his chagrin, they blackballed O'Connell when he was put up for a London Catholic club. 'It was a comical "testimonial" for my services in emancipating them. It would be well, perhaps, if I could *unemancipate* some of them.'

In the midst of all this excitement he could still find time to write to his Mary, 'I loved you when you were young and the prettiest little girl that ever picked a clean spot for a sweet little foot to tread on amidst the mud of a dirty pavement ... We, your son and I, are just going to O'Gorman's to dine ... He is perfectly well and so is your husband, love, only old and bold but not cold.'

9

The Liberator

In the summer of 1828 the M.P. for County Clare, Vesey Fitz-Gerald, accepted a place in Wellington's ministry and was obliged, by the rules of the day, to stand for re-election.

A few months earlier the Catholic Association had resolved to oppose *any* candidate who supported Wellington and Peel; but FitzGerald – popular, a good constituency M.P. who had always supported Catholic emancipation and whose father had voted against the union – was about the last man they would choose to oppose, and his constituency the last county they would choose for a trial of strength. The cause thrived in counties such as Kildare, Waterford, Limerick and Tipperary, with busy towns and large, prosperous farms. Most of Clare is rocky and shallow-soiled. The northern part of it consists of the Burren, some two hundred square miles composed largely of bare limestone rock where (complained one of Cromwell's Major-Generals) there was neither a tree to hang a man, water to drown him nor soil to bury him. Containing a wonderful variety of wild flowers, it is of more interest to botanists than to farmers. There were few towns in Clare, none prosperous; and to its county town, Ennis, and its inhabitants O'Connell had a strong aversion dating back to his early days on the Munster circuit. Many of the local landowning families, both Gaelic and Norman in origin – O'Briens, O'Callaghans, MacNamaras, McLysaghts and Fitz-Geralds – had 'turned' to preserve their estates. It was largely Irish-speaking, and few of the Association's star orators had a word of Irish. However the Association could hardly, at its first test, back down from its resolution and be derided as all bark and no bite. On 16th June it was decided, reluctantly, that Vesey FitzGerald must be opposed, and two emissaries, Clare men, landowners who had already put in some groundwork with the liberal club, were sent to take local soundings – Thomas Steele and Charles James Patrick O'Gorman Mahon. They were a very odd pair.

Tom Steele was one of O'Connell's strangest adherents. He was a Protestant whose liberalism and combative spirit had led him to take a vigorous part in a recent rebellion in Spain. Apparently solid, stolid and baldish, he was a paladin of reckless language and wild excitability with a total lack of reasoning power and common prudence, the slave of a succession of wild ideas each of which, for the time, completely absorbed him. His eccentricity was redeemed by single-hearted devotion to O'Connell with whom (a singular distinction) he never quarrelled. O'Connell was the only person who could manage him: when Steele was in one of his wilder flights, O'Connell had only to say quietly, 'Tom, don't do that,' or 'Tom, don't say that,' and he would instantly comply.[1] O'Connell made adroit, if improbable, use of his energy and devotion by giving him the title of 'Head Pacificator of Ireland' and the duties of reconciling squabbling patriots and preaching peace in counties plagued by Whiteboy outrages. His first act on arriving in Clare was to offer to fight any landlord who might feel aggrieved by the Catholic Association canvassing his tenants.

O'Gorman Mahon resembled more an Algerian corsair than a graduate of Trinity College. Noisy, rumbustious, swashbuckling, with a wild mop of black curls and luxuriant whiskers, he would have been happier leading a cavalry charge against the Saxons than engaging them in a war of words. He was not *all* piss and wind; from time to time he did good work for the cause, and from time to time work was very bad.

After a few days in Clare, he and Steele decided that FitzGerald was vulnerable. The question was, whom to put up against him? Their first thought was O'Connell's old duelling second, Major MacNamara. This elderly buck, still a veritable Lucius O'Trigger in his expertise in affairs of honour, spent most of his time while in Dublin lounging between the Kildare Street Club and a score of tailors, and affected the dress and deportment of his sovereign (though he had not 'let his belly down'); but in the County Clare, among his fighting MacNamaras, he was every inch a king himself. Protestant in religion, Catholic in politics, of an ancient Gaelic family, he was the obvious candidate except for his shortcomings as an orator. (He had once apologised to a bemused audience for 'forgetting to omit' an important point.) He was, however, a personal friend of Vesey FitzGerald and would not stand against him. Nor, it seemed, would anyone else in Clare. Steele suggested putting up a Protestant gravedigger, who could be provided from Association funds with a property in the county to qualify him, in order to make a monkey out of the Duke and the law. Rejecting this spirited proposal, O'Gorman Mahon posted to Dublin to persuade Lord William Paget, Anglesey's son, to stand, a course almost as heroic. In Dublin, however, Sir David Roose, a Protestant and a Tory under a personal obligation to O'Connell, suggested to their mutual friend, Patrick FitzPatrick, that the counsellor himself should stand.*

Even before it was suggested that O'Connell throw his hat into the ring, the Clare gentry had become suddenly aware of the unexpected danger and at a meeting in Ennis passed a resolution expressing surprise and indignation

> at the attempts which have been made through strange and unconstitutional channels to dissolve the connection and good feeling which has subsisted (*sic*) in this county between the Proprietors of the soil and the tenantry under their protection. .... We are determined ... to counteract such attempts as subversive of good order and tranquillity, and to use the most effective means of securing the peace and upholding the Independence of the County of Clare.[2]

Their strongest objection was to an influx of outsiders, Dubliners and suchlike, interfering in what was a matter purely for the people of Clare.

---

*Denis Gwynn states (*The O'Gorman Mahon*, pp. 48-9) that Roose had first obtained the approval of the Lord Lieutenant, Lord Anglesey. I can find no authority for this.

The suggestion that a Catholic stand for parliament was an extraordinary one, because he would be prohibited from taking his seat – or rather, to be exact, could not in conscience take the oath required of all M.P.s (except Quakers who had recently been exempted). But it was not illegal for a Catholic to be elected to parliament, and at the novelty and daring of the plan FitzPatrick exclaimed, 'Good Heaven, the Catholics are emancipated!'

O'Connell took a good deal of persuading, partly because of the expense of fighting a county election, but Fitzpatrick undertook to raise the money and in ten days produced £14,000. O'Connell then agreed to have a go, and hurried to the office of the *Dublin Evening Post* with whose editor, Frederick Conway, he had long been at variance. 'Let us be friends,' he said, offering his hand. Conway shook it, and O'Connell sat down then and there to write his election address.

TO THE ELECTORS OF THE COUNTY OF CLARE
FELLOW-COUNTRYMEN – Your county wants a representative. I respectfully solicit your suffrages to raise me to that station.

... The habits of public speaking and many, many years of public business render me, perhaps, equally suited with most men to attend to the interests of Ireland in Parliament.

You will be told I am not qualified to be elected. The assertion, my friends, is untrue. I am qualified to be elected, and to be your representative. It is true that, as a Catholic, I cannot and of course never will take the oaths at present prescribed to Members of Parliament; but ... I entertain a confident hope that, if you elect me, the most bigoted of our enemies will see the necessity of removing from the chosen representative of the people an obstacle which would prevent him from doing his duty to his King and to his country.

The oath at present required by law is, 'that the sacrifice of the mass, and the invocation of the blessed Virgin Mary, and other saints, as now practised in the Church of Rome, are impious and idolatrous.' Of course I will never stain my soul with such an oath. I leave that to my honourable opponent, Mr Vesey FitzGerald. He has often taken that horrible oath. He is ready to take it again and asks your votes to enable him so to swear. I would rather be torn limb from limb ...

151

Electors of the County of Clare! Mr Vesey FitzGerald claims, as his only merit, that he is a friend to the Catholics. Why, I am a Catholic myself; and if he be sincerely our friend, let him vote for me ...

He took office under Perceval – under that Perceval who obtained power by raising the base, bloody and unchristian cry of 'No Popery' in England ... He voted for a measure that would put two virulent enemies of the Catholics into Parliament ... He voted for the suppression of the Catholic Association of Ireland!

And after this, sacred Heaven, he calls himself a friend to the Catholics.

He is the ally and colleague of the Duke of Wellington and Mr Peel ... the most bitter persevering and unmitigated enemies of the Catholics; and ... he calls himself the friend of the Catholics of Ireland ...

If you return me to Parliament I pledge myself to vote for every measure favourable to Radical REFORM in the representative system ...

To vote for the diminution and more equal distribution of the overgrown wealth of the Established Church in Ireland ... and to bring the question of the REPEAL OF THE UNION at the earliest possible period before the consideration of the Legislature.

Electors of the County of Clare! Choose between me and Mr Vesey FitzGerald; choose between him who has so long cultivated his own interest, and one who seeks only to advance yours; choose between the sworn libeller of the Catholic faith, and one who has devoted his early life to your cause, who has consumed his manhood in a struggle for your liberties, and who has ever lived, and is ready to die, for the integrity, the honour, the purity of the Catholic faith, and the promotion of Irish freedom and happiness. Your faithful servant, Daniel O'Connell.

The full address was published in the press. An abbreviated version, in leaflet form, was distributed by the thousand. The main difference between the two is that the latter makes no mention of repeal of the union. Can O'Connell have doubted if this was, without much more preparation, an election winner?

A curiosity of both addresses is that Protestant voters are completely ignored: the appeal is purely sectarian. This is in striking contrast to his usual speeches and addresses in which he constantly appeals for Protestants' support, treating them as no less Irish than Catholics. One result of this omission was that a Protestant declaration in favour of Catholic emancipation, circulated soon after the election, was signed by nearly two thousand Protestants from all over Ireland – but not more than half a dozen from County Clare. O'Connell seems to have realised his mistake, for his second address to the same electors, seeking re-election a year later, contains no less than eleven complimentary references to Protestants and concludes, 'Protestants and Catholics, friends and brothers, I am your devoted servant, D. O'Connell.'

Having issued his address, he went to Clare where the ground was being prepared by many helpers besides Steele and O'Gorman Mahon. 'Honest Jack Lawless', friends again with O'Connell, had come down from Belfast: eagle-beaked, eyes glowing under shaggy brows, making great play with a quizzing-glass, he was almost as effective an orator as Sheil. Two Irish-speakers were of great value – Dominick Ronayne, a barrister from Cork, and the celebrated 'Father Tom' Maguire who brought all the way from his parish in Leitrim one of the most powerful voices in Ireland and a sharp scholastic logic which he elaborated or simplified to suit his audience. There was little scholastic logic in his pastoral address to FitzGerald's tenants:

> You have heard the tones of the temper and the charmer, whose confederates have through all ages joined the descendants of the Dane, the Norman and the Saxon in burning your churches, in levelling your altars, in slaughtering your priests and in stamping out your religion. Let every renegade to God and his country follow Vesey FitzGerald, and let every true Catholic Irishman follow me.[3]

Most, though not all, of the local priests preached for O'Connell, particularly the aged Father Murphy from the picturesque but far from prosperous parish of Corofin. Gaunt and lank of hair, 'with a voice like subterranean thunder', he had the air of one subsisting on locusts and wild honey, and indeed much of his parish was not unlike the wilderness beyond Jordan. By his formidable personality and the burning stare of his deep-sunk eyes, he persuaded his flock that it would be far, far better to defy their landlord, Sir Edward O'Brien, than to defy Father Murphy, the Church and the Catholic Association. From an open-air altar where he served Mass – while O'Brien waited frustrated and deserted by the door of the Protestant church nearby – he called upon them to be true to their country, their God and their counsellor, Daniel O'Connell.

'Are the freeholders slaves of their landlords?' asked O'Connell when he arrived – as did Sheil, and Jack Lawless, and O'Gorman Mahon, and Father Maguire, up and down the county – 'Are they poor negroes to be lashed by their torturers to the slave mart, there to be sold to the highest bidder?' If anyone asked himself, 'What slaves? What lashes? What torturers? What mart?', none was so brave as to ask it aloud. When a priest told of a man so debased as to vote against his country, the mob howled with rage – and then sank to their knees in prayer while he told them in hushed tones how the miserable sinner had then and there been struck dead of apoplexy.

The election opened at the Court House. On the edge of the balcony, long legs swinging, sat a bizarre figure, wild of hair and beard, wearing a green coat and breeches, an open-necked blue shirt and an enormous green sash bearing the badge of the Order of Liberators. It was O'Gorman Mahon, never one to hide his light under a bushel. The Sheriff unwisely attempted to extinguish him. 'I tell that gentleman to take off his badge.'

But O'Gorman Mahon would not be put down by a vulgar East Indian Nabob who had made a quick fortune in tea. 'This gentleman', he replied with insolent courtesy, laying one hand on his breast, 'tells that gentleman' – pointing with the other to the Sheriff – 'that if that gentleman presumes to touch this gentleman, this gentleman will defend himself against that gentleman, or any other gentleman, while he has the arm of a gentleman to protect him.'

Like Steele, he had already made known his perfect readiness to fight anybody in Clare who objected to his activities. The Sheriff prudently sat down.

Sir Edward O'Brien then proposed Vesey FitzGerald, followed by other landlords including a Mr Gore, a gentleman of very large estate but reputed to be descended from a nail-maker in

Cromwell's army. O'Gorman Mahon and Steele proposed O'Connell. Vesey FitzGerald then rose to his feet; about forty-five with hair beginning to grey and a round red face which suggested too great a fondness for good food and drink, he had a remarkably agreeable air and an expression of earnest frankness. He made a very good speech, reminding his audience of all his past services to the Catholic Association which had now turned to savage him, of his help to Maynooth and of his father's steady opposition, against all the arguments of self-interest, to the union. The old man was now ill, perhaps dying, and tears trickled down FitzGerald's face as he spoke of the grief his father would feel if he heard his tenants and fellow Clare men had turned against him. The well-timed, but perfectly genuine, touch of pathos roused the whole audience to sympathy and many to loud cheers.

O'Connell had many weapons in his armoury – wit, sarcasm, invective, sentiment, appeals to the spirit of the Faith and of Old Ireland. To counter FitzGerald's extremely effective peroration he resorted to sheer brutality. 'I never shed tears in public,' he growled, and with those six words turned the audience's sympathy to cruel derision.

Gore he demolished by a few references to 'hitting the nail on the head' and 'hammering nails into coffins' which made everyone laugh. As for FitzGerald, 'the Catholics' friend', why, so he should be. He was the friend of the bloody Perceval, the manly and candied Orange Peel, 'He is our friend, he is everybody's friend!'

The poll began next day. It was in the interests of the land-owners, with their greater financial resources, to spin it out over as many days as possible so that the O'Connellites, hungry and bored with waiting, drifted off home without voting, while their own freeholders, well fed and content, patiently awaited their turn. They therefore insisted on a requirement of the law which was generally, by mutual consent of the rival candidates, waived to save time – that every Catholic voter make a formal declaration of loyalty and obtain from a magistrate a certificate that he had done so. As there was no rush of magistrates to witness the declarations and issue the certificates, on the first day things seemed to be going badly for O'Connell. On the second day, however, he came up not merely with the answer but with an accommodating magistrate who was prepared to hear the freeholders in batches of twenty-five simultaneously repeating the oath, and then deal out signed certificates like a pack of cards. Soon O'Connell's lead was obvious. 'It's not fair,' complained FitzGerald, the brutal jibe still rankling. But to O'Connell politics were not a game, to be played by the rules and may the best man win.

Day after day the freeholders poured into Ennis. From Corofin they came marching as to war, waving green branches like banners, led by their Father Murphy, a piper piping away beside him. But most were led in by their landlords – O'Brien, MacNamara, O'Callaghan, Singleton, Vandeleur. They came in to vote as directed, but defected in shoals to the cheers and slogans of the O'Connellites who thronged the streets and alleys. Not merely the voters but all their friends and relations poured in, nearly 30,000 men, women and children bivouacking in Ennis every night, queueing up in orderly fashion for the priests and O'Connell's lay helpers to issue them with vouchers for bread, milk, beef and beer provided by the shopkeepers and taverners. (That disposed of most of the money collected by FitzPatrick.)

The turbulent priest from Corofin was charged with intimidation. Gaunt and haggard, he stared unblinking at FitzGerald's agent. 'But I said nothing. I suppose I may look at my own parishioners?' 'Not with *that* face!' exclaimed the startled functionary, and the charge was dropped.

The landowners watched, helpless and appalled, their world turned upside-down.

Fearing trouble, the Castle had reinforced Ennis with regular troops, but the election was conducted with such good order that they were kept discreetly in the background. As O'Connell was chaired past their barracks he called out, 'Take off your hats, my friends, to the officers of the bravest army in the world!' When soldiers and O'Connellite processions happened to pass one another, they cheered lustily, and a smart young sergeant left the ranks to wring the famous counsellor's hand – an ominous development for the Establishment when Irish Catholics formed a large proportion even of regiments which were nominally English and Scottish.

O'Connell and his principal lay helpers gathered for late supper at Mrs Carmody's tavern, worn out by their exertions but exhilarated by the smell of victory and the comfortable knowledge that they would not personally have to foot the bill for the huge dishes of roast beef, pork, mutton, tongue, turkeys and fowl which loaded the deal tables, and the claret which circulated freely. When they were full they called for whiskey, lemons, sugar and hot water and Jack Lawless presided over the making of a noble punch. He had barely downed the first sample glass when a sepulchral figure, like the ghost in *Hamlet*, stalked in, and the deep churchyard voice of Father Murphy raised its awful peal. 'The wolf! The wolf is on the walk! Shepherds of the people, what do you here?' Lawless, just about to enjoy the fruits of patriotic endeavour, turned a look of piteous despair on this relentless foe of conviviality. But out they all had to go, to combat the wolf on the walk – in other words, the demon drink which the good Father feared would be ravening in the streets of Ennis.

In fact, the good order of the election was attributed mainly to the unusual sobriety with which is was conducted. By order of the Catholic Association, no whiff of whiskey or poteen polluted the Ennis air (except, of course, in Mrs Carmody's tavern). Nothing harder than beer and cider was distributed to the vulgar, for which a wine-merchant was dunning O'Connell a year later. Indeed it was said – a typical O'Connell legend – that the only person in the least intoxicated was his English coachman, whom he personally committed to jail for breach of the peace. This might well have been true if O'Connell had been a magistrate, if he employed an English coachman while so many Irish coachmen were going begging, and if that coachman had managed to get at the hard stuff.

The only doubt was about the size of O'Connell's majority. At the final count he got 2,057 votes, FitzGerald 982.

It was a triumph remarkable for its scale, stupendous in its implications; but beneath the conquering hero's elation was a nagging conscience which troubled him all the more as FitzGerald continued to show his support for emancipation. Some months later he wrote to the Knight of Kerry:

Mr FitzGerald ought to be seen without delay by some friend of mine who would pledge himself to my willingness and that of the Catholics to atone to him for our conduct and to express our sense of the magnanimity of his ... The sin of ingratitude is heavy on us.

The journey from Ennis to Merrion Square was one long triumphal procession with addresses of welcome, bonfires, green boughs waving and his horses unharnessed at Kildare so that his admirers could draw his carriage across the Curragh. But the manner and the size of his victory aggravated an existing problem, the problem of the liberal Protestants to which the sagacious Wyse now addressed himself.

A Protestant who conspicuously supported Catholic emancipation was in a difficult position.[4] Most of his friends regarded him as, at best, a woolly-minded idealist, and at worst a traitor to his religion and his class. He regarded emancipation as a once-for-all concession (and a very generous one) which would put an end to interminable Catholic complaints; but Catholics regarded it as merely the first step in the transfer of power. He was constantly having to make excuses for inflammatory speeches and outrageous deeds by Papists which, however understandable against the historical background, seemed abominable when regarded in isolation in the 1820s. Intellectually he could see the justice of Catholic claims and complaints, but the habits and outlook of generations are not easily changed: even the most liberal Protestant instinctively saw Catholics not as 'us' but as 'them'. It was difficult, with his own background, to support their cause without seeming to patronise, to which they responded either with indignation or with a servile flattery equally degrading to both parties. Many Catholics – though never O'Connell – could not refrain from sneers and from crowing: they were the masters now, or soon would be. Carried away by the exuberance of their own oratory, they rubbed it in, and even O'Connell complained privately of the half-heartedness and paucity of Protestant support. Some Catholics could not resist the temptation, after a hundred and fifty years of snubs and worse, to spit on the hand held out diffidently and belatedly in friendship. Nor were Protestants favourably impressed by demonstrations of Catholic economic power such as an Association-sponsored run on the banks, checked only by the prompt import of £1,500,000 in gold. It was only because of some characteristically adroit manoeuvring by O'Connell – a tough speech followed by a resolution which effectively shelved the matter – that the Association was prevented from launching a campaign of 'exclusive dealing' which could have become an economic boycott of Protestants.

So in the years 1825–8 liberal Protestants tended to withdraw into their shells, into the *Morning Chronicle* and the *Edinburgh Review*, wishing the Catholic Association well but doing nothing to help it.

The blatantly sectarian nature of the Clare election and the feeling that it could be repeated almost anywhere made matters much worse, and some of the more active liberal Protestants decided that something must be done about it. The result was a Protestant declaration in favour of immediate Catholic emancipation signed by an array of Irish Protestants which was more impressive then than it would be now – two dukes, sixty-nine other peers, twenty-two baronets, fifty-two M.P.s and nearly two thousand ordinary, untitled gentry and men of position. O'Connell, in an ungenerous mood, dismissed this as a mere excuse for doing nothing: 'I want to see something *done*'; but Wyse thought that the government, and especially the Duke, would be impressed by the views of so many gentlemen of property and standing.

Counties Limerick and Tipperary seemed very close to rebellion. They were notorious for 'faction fights', with no political motive, between rival families. In September the Association sent Steele and O'Gorman Mahon to try to make peace between the Longs and the Macnires, which they did by investing the slightly bemused faction-chiefs with the Order of Liberators and calling upon them to shake hands over the chapel altar. Encouraged by their success, they continued their peace-making progress. But there was a spirit of rebellion far more dangerous than faction-fighting, with pikes and pistols hidden in the thatch of many a cottage. When O'Connell himself arrived, his supporters marched into Clonmel in military formation, wearing green uniforms, carrying banners and preceded by pipe, fife and drum bands. There were cries of 'When will he call us out?', 'answered with a finger on the mouth and a significant smile and a wink from the bystanders'. Nor was tension eased by reports of Orangemen and Brunswickers talking of a second 1798. At Clonmel O'Connell took full advantage of this. 'Oh,' he bawled,

Would to God that our excellent Viceroy Lord Anglesey would but give me a commission, and *if* those men of blood should attempt to attack the property and persons of His Majesty's loyal subjects, with a hundred thousand of my brave Tipperary boys I would soon drive them into the sea!

Wyse wrote this off as mere rhetoric. More probably every word and gesture was calculated, for nothing illustrates better than these words, and the savage shout of exultation which greeted them, O'Connell's methods of agitation. There was not a word there of sedition, nothing the Crown lawyers could pick upon; yet they served to keep the government in apprehension of a rebellion which only he could, with difficulty, restrain.[5]

Whether or not Wellington was impressed by the Protestant declaration in favour of emancipation, he was alive to the danger of civil war and aware of the uncomfortable fact that the regular army (35,000 strong) and police in Ireland were composed very largely of Irish Catholics. Modern and contemporary estimates of the proportion of Irish Catholics in the rank and file of the British army vary from one-third to three-quarters: there were also many Irish Catholic officers, some of distinction. The police consisted of some 600 men in Peace Preservation Forces raised specifically for service in ten disturbed counties and about 7,000 men in four provincial forces, formed in 1822. Most of these, outside Ulster, were Catholics. Peel noted that most of the military and police in Clare in 1829 were Catholics. A soldier of a fusilier regiment, nominally Scottish but fully half Irish in composition, was heard to say, 'There are two ways of firing, *at* a man and *over* a man, and if we were called out against O'Connell and our country, I think we should know the difference.'[6] In Limerick there was a riot between two regiments, one for and one against O'Connell. Nothing horrified the Duke so much as the army being involved in politics. A withdrawal was obviously necessary, but, as was his custom, he would go in his own time without announcing his intention.

His letters and orders were usually so clear that the greatest fool could not fail to comprehend them; but in reply to advice from his old friend, Archbishop Curtis, to press on with emancipation, he wrote a letter which was a model of obscurity.

I am sincerely anxious to witness a settlement of the Roman
Catholic question ... but I confess I see no prospect of such
a settlement ... If we could bury it in oblivion for a short
time, and employ that time diligently in the consideration of
its difficulties on all sides (for they are very great) I should not
despair of seeing a satisfactory remedy.

On Sheil's suggestion the letter was shown to Anglesey, who
'thought it looked very well for the cause' but was displeased at
the Prime Minister corresponding with the Archbishop behind
his back. Leaked to *The Times*, it could be interpreted according
to the wishes of the interpreter; but it seemed to indicate that
the Iron Duke was not inflexible.[7]

Then there was the problem of Anglesey. Nothing irritated the
Duke so much – and he was an irritable man – as a gallant officer
acting without orders. That was what Anglesey was doing. He
wrote to Leveson Gower, Chief Secretary designate, that the only
sensible course was to deprive 'the demagogues of the power of
directing the people. And by taking O'Connell, Sheil and the rest
of them from the Association and placing them in the House of
Commons this desirable object would be at once accomplished.'[8]
He was the sort of Englishman who, on landing at Dunleary,
immediately takes a euphoric view of the Irish and is convinced
that only a little goodwill is needed to solve all their problems.
Light-hearted and sociable, he entertained in style, mixing Catholics with Protestants at all viceregal social occasions which he
thoroughly enjoyed. 'Let every exertion be made', he wrote in a
memorandum on the Catholic Association, 'to obtain emancipation with full securities – this done, disenfranchise at once the
40-shilling freeholders – show partiality to neither party and two
years will see Ireland a happy country.' He was 'more than
ever convinced that there would be no difficulty whatever in
adjusting the question'. He seemed almost to set himself up
as Catholic Ireland's political consultant, assuring Dr Murray,
Archbishop of Dublin, of his devotion to the cause so long as it
was pursued without violence, and advising the Archbishop
to keep in with the Association in order to exercise such
control as was possible – not much, he feared – over the political
priests.[9]

Anglesey even gave O'Connell, at his request, a long interview[10] three weeks after the Clare election. Lord Forbes, Whig M.P. for County Longford, was present. O'Connell repeatedly stressed that no one was more anxious than he for the maintenance of law and order, and he thought a rebellion extremely unlikely. The sole object of the Catholic Association was to secure the return to parliament of men devoted to their cause who would compel the ministry to grant emancipation. For his good intentions Anglesey gave him full credit, but

> observed that when a very sensitive and half barbarous people were brought into great excitement, no one ought to presume that he had the power of controlling them ... If it were attempted to carry on future elections in the spirit of that of Clare, he might depend upon a great reaction in England, that it would become a No Popery question and that many of the present supporters of the Catholics would lose their seats.

Anglesey warned O'Connell that many Catholics were behaving extremely irresponsibly, for example a priest

> who in haranguing in his Chapel called upon the soldiers present to contribute to the Rent, using much inflammatory language and telling the congregation that, *in the event of insurrection*, not a Catholic soldier would obey his officer but that all would lay down their arms.

To this O'Connell replied:

> I hope and believe that Your Excellency will find that this is a mere fabrication or at all events a great exaggeration of facts, but I do most humbly and most energetically call upon Your Excellency if the fact can be made out, to prosecute the priest and to punish him with the utmost severity of the law.

Anglesey said he was determined to keep order, for which he had ample resources, but he could not close his eyes to the possibility of the worst imaginable case:

> that of my being compelled, in aid of the King's troops, to

162

arm the Orange population. What must be the dreadful consequences of such a measure? War to extermination and the total extinction of all hope to the Catholics! For how could any Government which had called for the energy of Protestants to put down Catholic rebellion, ever propose to the former to receive into the Constitution upon an equality of rights those whom they had been called upon to assist in subduing from open rebellion?

Anglesey commented:

This appeared to strike Mr O'C very forcibly. He quite acquiesced and said not only would such an event put off to an unmeasurable term the adjustment of the question, but in the event of insurrection (which again he assured me was not to be apprehended) even the power I possessed (and he thought it great) would not enable me to suppress the rising of the Orangemen.

Anglesey gave O'Connell 'a pretty strong lecture' on his abuse of the Duke of Wellington, who was placed in a most difficult situation in having to manage both his ultra-Tory supporters and the king, and that whatever the Duke's feelings about emancipation, he could not be expected to carry it out at once and by force.

I told him I had not a particle of authority to announce the Duke's conversion, but that my belief was, he would willingly set it at rest by fair concession. At all events, I said, the Duke is the only man who can carry this question, and I do not despair of his attempting it.

Anglesey made it quite clear that he himself was in favour of emancipation, but he spoke for himself, and had no authority to negotiate on the matter. 'I said I was in this unusual situation, that I had no instructions on the general course to be pursued in Ireland.'*

* In this Anglesey was being treated by the Duke exactly as he had been treated at Waterloo. Although the command of the army would pass to him if Wellington was killed or wounded, he was given no idea beforehand of how the Duke intended to fight the battle.

As for the methods which the Association should use, His Excellency assured the agitator that, 'so far from discouraging the agitation, the presenting of petitions, its frequent discussion, I would advise a continuance of the same course.' He did not even object to public meetings to further these ends, but suggested that it might be good tactics to discontinue these for a while, which would favourably impress English opinion. When he hinted that emancipation might have to be accompanied by safeguards, notably the disenfranchisement of the venal and unruly forty-shilling freeholders, O'Connell raised no objection. Indeed his last words, according to Anglesey, spoken to Forbes after leaving the room, were, 'I see but one difficulty. It is the forty-shilling freeholders. We cannot *all at once* give them up. We must have time.'

Both had agreed that the content of their talk should go no further, and both kept their word. Anglesey made a memorandum of the meeting but does not seem to have sent it even to the Duke, and O'Connell let not a word of it leak out.

Anglesey wrote of O'Connell:

He is the vainest of men, and easily taken by a good bait ... I told him he would, of course, be in Parliament, but this, he said, he did not wish. I observed that he must by his talent command that, or anything else he ambitioned ... My firm belief is that O'Connell is perfectly sincere. I should be laughed at for my gullibility, but I repeat that I believe him sincere. That he has a good heart and means well and means indeed always what he says, but that he is volatile and unsteady and so vain that he cannot resist momentary applause.

O'Connell had behaved throughout, naturally, as one gentleman talking to another. Both men believed that the interview had gone very well.

Continuing to take his own line, Anglesey stayed with Lord Cloncurry the night before Cloncurry attended a Catholic Association meeting. His son and his A.D.C. were seen at Association meetings. When Moloney, High Sheriff of Clare, demanded that O'Gorman Mahon and Steele be dismissed from the Magistrates' Bench in consequence of remarks the former had made (not in his magisterial capacity) which were derogatory to Moloney's dignity, Anglesey, in consultation with the Attorney General, decided that as they had committed no crime, there was no case for dismissing them. This was too much for the Duke, and the Cabinet decided that Anglesey must go as soon as a replacement could be found. Two days before receiving his notice of dismissal, Anglesey wrote to Dr Curtis that, while observing the law and avoiding offensive language, the Catholic Association should keep up its agitation for emancipation. Worse still, he sent a copy of his letter to the press. This cooked his goose. 'I differ from the opinion of the Prime Minister,' he had written. By God, it was like the commander of a division announcing that he differed from the opinion of the Commander-in-Chief! Anglesey was soon on his way home.

His departure was universally lamented by Catholics, and by none more than O'Connell. 'The people are heartsore for the loss of the brave and gay and good Anglesey ... One ounce of common sense would govern Ireland as though by a magic charm.'[11]

But the omens were good for emancipation. Its greatest enemy was 'his most sacred Majesty', but for this O'Connell blamed the 'pimps and parasites around the throne.' Wellington was 'about to lower the flag of intolerance ... because we annoy his Irish friends and are likely to cause them more annoyance.' (He could never credit Wellington with any but the basest motives.) The Duke would no doubt speak to the king (a chastening experience, even for a king, being spoken to by the Duke of Wellington); and the king's brother, the Duke of Clarence – not, to be sure, very bright, but important because he was heir presumptive to the throne – was actually canvassing the peers and made a speech strongly supporting Catholic emancipation. The Commons were no obstacle, and the Lords would surely be wheeled into line. Catholic emancipation was almost won. Any doubts were set at rest on 6th February by the King's Speech on opening the parliamentary session. Nothing, now, could prevent it.

But there was a fly in the ointment, as O'Connell knew very well, having been warned by Anglesey. The government intended to attach 'wings' to the Catholic Emancipation Bill. Two were on trumpery issues: restrictions on the Jesuits and other monastic orders, and on the titles taken by Catholic bishops; O'Connell could drive a coach-and-six through them.[12] In addition the government intended to bring in a bill banning (not for the first time) the Catholic Association. Well, that did not matter either; its work was done and it might as well dissolve itself (which it did) rather than be dissolved forcibly. The trouble was the third 'wing': to emasculate peasant power, the government would revive its 1825 plan of disenfranchising the 85,000 turbulent forty-shilling freeholders and raise the county franchise qualification to £10 a year from freehold property. This put O'Connell in an awkward position, though he had received plenty of warning. In 1825 he had, as everyone knew, agreed to that 'wing', got into trouble over it and wriggled out of trouble by admitting his mistake and promising never to err again. In September 1828, two months after his interview with Anglesey, he wrote to Pierce Mahony:

> I totally deny that any man is a fool or a knave who thinks the Catholics can expect Emancipation without securities ... This position I am thoroughly convinced of, namely, that an Emancipation bill *cannot* pass accompanied with *securities* ... I have at my side the experiment of 1825, at which time I am convinced we should have had Lord Liverpool compelled to grant Emancipation if I had not foolishly acceded to the securities called 'the wings' ... I was deceived once, but I should indeed be more than insane were I to be deceived in the same way again.[13]

In December he declaimed at a public meeting:

> If any man dares bring in a bill for the disenfranchisement of the forty-shilling freeholders, the people ought to rebel if they cannot otherwise succeed. Sooner than give up the forty-shilling freeholders, I would rather go back to the Penal Code ... I would consider it just to resist that by force, and in any such resistance I would be ready to perish in the field or on the scaffold.[14]

In March 1829, urged even by Brougham to give way on this issue, he assured Mary:

> I need not tell you that he totally failed. They *trapped* me before. They cannot possibly succeed in that way a second

time. Besides, darling, I really am too much indebted to the
40s freeholders. You do not think I could ever turn my back
on the poor fellows in Clare.

Was he deceiving himself, or trying to deceive others? One never
knows, with O'Connell. On the same day he pledged Dwyer his
'perpetual and unconquerable hostility' to the measure, and six
days later he assured Mary, 'I have not and will not now abandon
the forty-shilling freeholders.'[15] But he would. He did. He had
no choice, and even while he was promising Mary, Mahony,
Dwyer, Dr Doyle and anyone else who would listen that he
would never do anything of the kind, he was beginning to hedge,
writing – and Wyse emphatically agreed – 'In my opinion the
£10 will really give more power to the Catholics.'[16] Politics for
him was seldom a matter of hard and fast principle, but rather
of compromise and bargains, a concession here for a greater gain
there. He had not liked dropping the forty-shilling freeholders
for Catholic emancipation in 1825, but it was unthinkable now to
drop Catholic emancipation for the forty-shillingers. He would
hear more of this; indeed he would never hear the end of it; the
'wing' was that of an albatross hung round his neck.

Otherwise the Catholic Emancipation Bill at its first reading
was

a great and glorious triumph ... Whoever thought we should
get such a bill from Peel and Wellington? Catholics can be
judges, mayors, sheriffs, aldermen, common counselmen, peers
of parliament, members of parliament, everything, in short,
everything ... Darling, may I say that I contributed to this?

On 10th April the bill passed its third reading in the Lords. 'Thus
the ascendancy and proud superiority which your neighbours had
over you will be at an end the day you receive this letter. And it
was your husband who contributed most to this measure. Was it
not, sweetest?' The royal assent was given on 13th April. According
to legend His Majesty threw to the ground and stamped on the
pen with which he signed the bill. Alas for legend! The royal
assent is given verbally, not in writing. What he may have said
was, 'Wellington is King of England, O'Connell is King of Ireland, and I am Dean of Windsor.' To the faithful Dwyer,
O'Connell wrote a passage which is very revealing.

It is one of the greatest triumphs recorded in history – a bloodless revolution more extensive in operation than any other political change that could have taken place. I say *political* to contrast it with *social* changes which might break to pieces the framework of society ... This is a good beginning and now, if I can get Catholics and Protestants to join, something solid and substantial may be done for all.[17]

Already something solid and substantial was being done for the Liberator. A committee of Catholic magnates set on foot a collection of money to be known as 'The O'Connell Testimonial'.

With mixed feelings he attended the first levée after emancipation. Approaching the king, he saw the royal lips move in what he took to be a few gracious words of welcome – perhaps even of congratulation. Gratified at this pleasing instance of royal magnanimity, he took the pudgy paw held out to him and reverently kissed it. Afterwards he asked the Duke of Norfolk what His Majesty had actually said. The Duke obliged: 'He said, "There's O'Connell, God damn the scoundrel." '

He still had to take his seat, and hoped he would be allowed to do so by swearing the new oath, not objectionable to Catholics, which had been laid down by the Catholic Emancipation Act. But at the time he was elected for Clare, the old oath had still been required. There are obvious drawbacks to retrospective legislation – it sets a bad precedent – but if the ministry had wished to conciliate Ireland by a generous gesture which cost them nothing, they could have done so. Typically of British governments dealing with Ireland, they chose rather to stand firm on principle – and perhaps indulge their abhorrence for the man who had so signally defeated them. When he advanced to the Bar of the House he was presented with the old oath, refused it, withdrew and three days later was given leave to argue his case for taking the new oath. He lost the argument and, coming to the Bar of the House for the third time, was again presented with the old oath.

He perused it carefully and said with great dignity, 'This oath contains one proposition which I know to be false, another proposition which I believe to be untrue. I cannot, therefore, take it.' He then bowed to the Speaker and withdrew.

This meant that he had to be re-elected for Clare with all the trouble and expense. (He tried, and failed, to purchase a pocket borough instead.[18]) In his 'Address of a Hundred Promises' (addressed, perhaps, more to English radicals than to the free-holders of Clare) he committed his support to every nostrum dear to the radical reformer, from abolition of the East India Company's monopoly to one man one vote, including of course, the restoration of the forty-shilling franchise. He was returned almost unopposed, a greater triumph even than that of the previous year: 'How wise of Master Peel & Co to send me back!' At the opening of the new session he duly took his seat.

He had won his greatest victory, stupendous in its effects on Catholic morale and its implications for the future, and was about to embark on the next campaign, over ground unfamiliar to him, towards an objective of which many of his closest colleagues did not approve.

10

The Member of Parliament

Many a rabble-rouser has failed to impress the Mother of Parliaments, where the style is ceremonious and urbane, where one's bitterest enemy is 'The Honourable Member' or 'The Right Honourable Gentleman opposite', where speeches are addressed only to the Speaker, and where the rapier of polished irony inflicts deadlier wounds than the bludgeon of coarse invective. But just as O'Connell never addressed an aggregate meeting as though it were a court of law, and seldom addressed a court of law as though it were an aggregate meeting, so he struck exactly the right note in the House of Commons. His maiden speech, as the first elected Catholic M.P. since the Reformation,* consisted mainly of some low-key observations on the King's Speech.

What did it [the King's Speech] contain? The first point was that foreign nations continued to speak in terms of peace, but did they ever do otherwise when a war was on the point of breaking out? The next information was that the Russian war was at an end. That was an important discovery indeed ... They were next told of the partial distress of the country. But was that a fact? He thought that the expressions which had fallen from the three Honourable Members on the other side

---

* The Duke of Norfolk had rushed his son in for a pocket borough just ahead of O'Connell.

who had supported the Speech were – the one that the distress was general; the second that the distress was extraordinary; and the third that the distress was overwhelming. The Chancellor of the Exchequer, however, had made one happy discovery: he had found an oasis in the desert – a country where no distress at all existed. And that country – who would have thought it? – that country was Ireland.

It was no great performance, but this was no occasion for a great performance. It made a good impression on the House, even on George Villiers, one of his steadiest non-admirers, who wrote:

I have no hesitation in saying that it was successful. He made three or four exceedingly good hits and his speech would have been excellent if he had not rambled from the subject before the House into legal and radical reform ... He spoke of course with great fluency and brogue but with tact and temperance and firmness. His speech was not a great display, but a pretty specimen, and the gentlemen [illegible] on the other side of the House that before Parliament is up they may have an opportunity to curse the *unpaid suffrage* which sent them such a customer. He was listened to with respect and attention.

A few weeks later Villiers described him as 'temperate and discreet, not effective ... but people feel he will have greatly added to his power on any future occasion by the good will his tact is now earning him.'[1]

It had been predicted that his inflammatory agitator's style would not go down well in the Commons, but Thomas Wyse observed that there were two O'Connells, one for Ireland, the other for England. A radical member, Leslie Grove Jones, made the same point: 'Forgive me when I say you are much nearer perfection here than when in Ireland. There is something there which intoxicates you. Pray come over and sober yourself.'[2] In England O'Connell always emphasised that only by repeal of the union could Ireland be made the Empire's stoutest defender and the Crown's sturdiest buttress. He probably believed this, but it was not an argument to set 50,000 Cork men halloo-ing and throwing their hats in the air. Nor was it politic in England to call for the expulsion of the Saxon despot and betrayer. Like a chameleon, he changed his colour to suit his environment.

Mary was ecstatic at his performance and pictured him on St Patrick's Day 'going out to Mass with the largest shamrock that could be had in London looking as independent as if you were already Prime Minister of England.' As, indeed, she expected he would be: 'they will see they cannot do without you and you will have everything your own way.'

This was too good to last. By the autumn he complained:

> There never was yet any man so beset as I was when I went into the House and, during the first speeches, every allusion to me of an unkind nature was cheered. Although Peel attacked me directly, he sat down amid rapturous applause. I got up at once ... I rebuked them with indignation and certainly took my wicked will of them.

Deciding that he had rated too highly the fairness and intelligence of the Mother of Parliaments, he 'threw out in his old Association style' and in a debate on the King's Speech enlarged on all Ireland's grievances. This produced an improvement in the attitude of honourable members and sometimes he routed his enemies, but it did not last.

On 16th November 1830, Wellington resigned and a Whig ministry was formed by Lord Grey. O'Connell's first intention was to earn its gratitude by giving it selective support. It was to no avail. Two months later Grove Jones warned him, 'A *great horror* is entertained of you and more so with the Whigs than the Tories.' Soon he was completely disillusioned with the Whigs: 'There is a fatuity in this Administration.' Even the 'rascally Speaker' (who was a Tory, but supposed as Speaker to be neutral) seemed set against him and would not give him a chance.

Although he did as much as any man to whip up anglophobia in Ireland to show that his heart was in the right place, he was surprised and mortified by the discovery of a fundamental anti-Irish prejudice in England, even among Catholics, whipped up by Establishment (but by no means Tory) papers such as *The Times* and *Punch*. It was like the anti-Scots mania in the England of Wilkes and Dr Johnson, and, similarly, was stronger in peace-time when the services of 'Pat' were not required for the defence of Britain and the Empire. Anti-Popery in England, said O'Connell, meant in fact anti-Irishry, and he deluded himself into thinking that it would be a stimulus to repeal.[3]

O'Connell was at the peak of his career. Thereafter a graph of his influence and his fortunes would show an irregular decline. At meetings attended by scores of thousands of excited Irishmen his oratory was more inflammatory than ever, but less effective. His propaganda had lost the essential element of *concentration*. He knew quite well that 'you must repeat the same lesson over and over again if you wish to make a permanent impression.' For six years, with brilliant success, he had related every Irish grievance, every Irish issue, to emancipation. Thereafter his main object was, probably, repeal of the union, but as a Westminster M.P. he involved himself in cause after cause dear to English radicals but of little relevance to Ireland or to repeal. His 'Address of a Hundred Promises' was a foretaste of that fatal dispersal of effort. He was in favour of a codification of the law, reform of the House of Lords, the Tolpuddle Martyrs, three-year parliaments, the secret ballot, Lord Shaftesbury's Factory Acts (in principle), universal male suffrage (sometimes) and the Chartists (briefly). He was against slavery, military flogging, and the Corn Laws. He immersed himself in radical causes partly in the hope that English radicals would, in gratitude, support repeal. They didn't. They wanted nothing to do with Ireland and regarded him personally as alien, dangerous and unreliable. His dodging from one issue to another gave an impression of deviousness which put people off. George Villiers, a liberal Protestant to whose sagacity and knowledge of Ireland O'Connell gave high praise, wrote in December 1830, 'People think he is a little frightened of [Repeal of] the Union and is backing out of it, but one never knows where one is with such a soaped-tailed pig.'[4]

His inconsistency helped to give O'Connell a reputation for shiftiness. It was surely un-radical to inveigh against the introduction to Ireland of the English Poor Laws, on the grounds that the relief of poverty should be a matter for private charity; and, while agitating for the Tolpuddle Martyrs in England, to denounce the trade unions in Dublin. There was nothing necessarily incompatible between a flamboyant - perhaps even genuine - devotion to the Crown, especially when it was worn by the 'darling little Queen', a proprietorial pride in the British Empire

173

where so many Irishmen found opportunities denied them at home, and the most uninhibited, pugnacious and violent abuse of the Saxon, the stranger, the taskmaster polluting the soil of Old Ireland. But many people thought these attitudes must be incompatible, and that anyone expressing all of them must be a shameless and mendacious hypocrite.

Distrust of his motives was enhanced by his converting to his own use the machinery set up to collect the Catholic Rent. The relief afforded by Hunting Cap's death did not last long. By the summer of 1830 he was back at his old tricks of running up new debts to pay off old ones, promising to pay by monthly instalments, begging this creditor or that for a little more time. In order to devote his whole time to politics – an extremely expensive pursuit – he gave up his Bar practice. He was obliged to maintain three establishments (in Derrynane, Dublin and London), and there was the enormous cost (but cheaper than hiring) of sending his coach and horses from Dublin to London and back again for every parliamentary session. In London he kept open house for all Irish repeal M.P.s, and at Derrynane for anyone who happened to drop in. Dan was still being educated at Clongowes, and Morgan in Hungary was quite unable, on his pay and allowances, to support a life-style suitable for a Kerry gentleman and officer of light cavalry. So after the dissolution of the Catholic Association in 1829 the churchwardens and their helpers, kept up to the mark by FitzPatrick's unflagging exertions, were employed in keeping the Liberator himself beyond reach of want by collecting what was at first supposed to be a once-for-all O'Connell Testimonial and became an annual O'Connell Tribute.

Really it was fair enough. He had virtually abandoned his Bar practice, which earned him £5,178 in the last full year, to give his whole time to politics. M.P.s had no salaries, no City directorships or trade union sponsorships to sustain them. Unless they had ample private means they had to find a place on the government payroll in the ministry, in the Palace or elsewhere, with emoluments as large and duties as few as possible. Since the acceptance of office – which was more than once offered him – would emasculate O'Connell as an agitator, he must look to his followers to support him and his creditors. They did not fail him, but the annual collections, parish by parish with the priests acting as local treasurers, varied according to the Liberator's popularity and the exertions of the collectors. In 1829 about £20,000 came in, but in 1830 only about £4,500. Then came two good years, totalling £38,307, an enormous sum. But even FitzPatrick sometimes needed jogging: 'This is the time to do something about the Fund. This, of course, is confidential; that is, it must not be known to come from me.'[5]

Naturally this was picked on by his critics, and every *Punch* cartoon of O'Connell shows him sitting on, or pocketing, or grasping a fat bag labelled 'Rint'. It seems that the poor did not grudge him their farthings a week, but some of the more affluent loathed his 'mendicant patriot touch'. 'We have had a *great day* here,' wrote George Wyse to his brother Tom, 'for Dan, the patriotic cormorant ... Close on £600 collected. To avoid observations *here* and *elsewhere* I agreed in your name for £20 – my own for £10.' O'Connell's relations with Sheil had always been patchy: they had been at variance over the Veto and then reconciled in 1823. Sheil had been of the utmost value in the campaign for emancipation. But in November 1829:

> a *tremendous* quarrel took place at the Finance Committee between Sheil and O'Connell. The abuse dealt out exceeded any witnessed for a long time. The Rent etc the subject. It ended for the present by a partial reconciliation, O'C being obliged by Purcell O'Gorman to make a most abject apology to Sheil. The case has not closed. The subdued hostility will soon rekindle and end in a fatal explosion to Dan's fame ... Dan is *quaking*.[6]

Eighteen months later Lord Melbourne, the Home Secretary, was informed:

> Sheil, who knows O'Connell better than anyone, says that his present outrageous conduct has reference chiefly to the Tribute, and the amount of the contributions will be directly in proportion to the violence with which he assails the government and the extravagance of his promises.[7]

His credibility, and the support for repeal, was also damaged by the ferocity and frequency of his quarrels with many an old comrade of the emancipation struggle. They were not all his fault, but they occurred too often to have been caused solely by chance and circumstance. In the years 1829 to 1831 O'Connell was constantly embroiled in rows with MacNamara and O'Gorman Mahon, occasioned not merely by the former's vanity and the latter's intransigent pugnacity but by O'Connell's devious, and ultimately unsuccessful, manoeuvres to consolidate his position in County Clare.

Generally the two members for the county were chosen by agreement or competition between the O'Briens, FitzGeralds and MacNamaras, but O'Connell's intervention in 1828 had broken the cosy pattern, and now O'Gorman Mahon's political ambition stirred up the pieces. O'Connell's manoeuvres began even before his re-election in July 1829. In June at an election meeting he had disparaged in wounding terms[8] the contribution to the Catholic cause of the mildly liberal, Protestant head of the O'Briens in Clare, Sir Lucius, and advised voters in any future election to support Major MacNamara instead. He added that Sir Lucius and his brother, William Smith O'Brien, believing that 'the House of Dromoland might yet want a prop', had promised to support O'Connell's admission to the Commons in May but had reneged on their undertaking by walking out before the vote was taken. These observations brought a challenge from Sir Lucius's son, Donough, which O'Connell treated as he treated all challenges.

> There is blood, human blood, on my hand and nothing can tempt me to commit that crime again. May God forgive me. The knowledge of my resolution on this subject has made many men exceedingly valiant to me who are as shrinking from others as it is possible to be.[9]

That put him on worse terms than ever with the most powerful family in Clare, including the future Young Irelander, William Smith O'Brien.

O'Connell realised – indeed it needed little percipience – that he was bound to have trouble with O'Gorman Mahon, and tried to persuade his bellicose co-agitator to stay in reserve, well away from the scene of action.

If there is to be a *battle*, we cannot go to *battle* without you and if there is to be a storm, why you must once again *ride on the whirlwind and direct the storm*. For the present everything is going on most smoothly ... Attend to what I say and I will see you representing this county and that soon.[10]

He won the seat comfortably, without O'Gorman Mahon's help, but – having encouraged his ambition – was extremely vexed to find him, only twelve days later, conducting 'a most foolish canvas' on his own account, with a view to fighting the next election. 'It is strange that a man in his circumstances should dream of such a thing but he is so eaten up with inordinate vanity! I am sincerely sorry for him.'[11]

In the spring of 1830 O'Gorman Mahon's circumstances were much improved by his engagement to the affluent Christine O'Brien, whom O'Connell had selected as Maurice's bride. With George IV obviously dying and a general election therefore in prospect, all potential candidates, including O'Gorman Mahon, redoubled their efforts – all, that is, except O'Connell who was tied to Westminster. Mary wrote reassuringly:

If he had a hundred thousand pounds to contest Clare with you, the general opinion is that he would not stand two days, he is so fallen in the estimation of the people and of the aristocracy of that country. I think, darling, you may feel quite secure on that subject.

But it was worrying, all the same, and O'Connell asked for a report on his prospects from one of his clerical supporters, the parish priest of Kilrush.

Father Kenny replied[12] that there would probably be four candidates, all more or less liberal, for the two county seats – Sir Lucius O'Brien, Major MacNamara, O'Gorman Mahon and O'Connell:

O'Brien is by no means a favourite. MacNamara is very generally disliked by the aristocracy on account of his liberal principles, and O'Gorman Mahon is fully as great an object of aversion to your greatest enemy in Clare as you yourself could be. From the pecuniary embarrassment of every one of the

177

three, I do not think bribery would be resorted to, so that if no other candidate appears, your election may in my mind be considered certain.

But if the landlords put up a Tory candidate, such was their influence that he would surely win one of the seats, leaving the other to be competed for by three or four liberals. 'I candidly confess I have no doubt of your return. I should be sorry, however, that anything should lead you into a false security. No time should be lost in setting on foot an active canvas.' It was rather disquieting that Richard Scott, who had been O'Connell's election agent in 1828, was now MacNamara's.

This did not prevent Scott from warning O'Connell[13] that his stock was rather low in Clare as he had not been able to obtain from parliament all the goodies he had promised the freeholders. If O'Gorman Mahon 'were out of the way, you and the major would walk over the course'; but if O'Gorman Mahon insisted on standing, the major would certainly get one seat, and it would be a close-run thing for the other.

In this difficult situation O'Connell reverted to the politics of Old Sarum – or anticipated those of Tammany Hall. An ally he must have, more pliable than MacNamara, who would take one of the seats and help him fight O'Gorman Mahon for the other. He must be a local man with lots of pull, both with the aristocracy and with the freeholders. Why not Vesey FitzGerald, if MacNamara could be induced to withdraw? The FitzGeralds had recently made indirect overtures, suggesting that they let bygones be bygones. In the strictest confidence O'Connell wrote to Bennett,[14] who was financially in low water and avid for a government job:

As to Vesey FitzGerald. You are the only man living to do what is *doable* in that respect. Mark me, my excellent friend, everything you do is to be done *by yourself, from yourself and without authority* ... I have reason to believe that the friends of Vesey FitzGerald desire to coalesce with me, that we may both come in without contest. The thing is *perfectly practicable*, that is, no declared coalition but an arrangement made *in the county by* his friends having the same effect. You are just the only person living to make that arrangement as from yourself so as at the same time to make FitzGerald your sincere and useful friend. You imagine Major MacNamara is a stumbling block. No such thing. He is perhaps the very means of insuring [*sic*] that result. Of course FitzGerald should manage him. A *baronetage* for himself and a step of promotion in the army for his son *might* do all. Surely FitzGerald could not have the least difficulty in getting these things and something else also for one or two of his brothers, especially for his brother John. Surely the Ministry must *owe* so much to FitzGerald. Now you could *first* see FitzG's friends – some discreet one or two. Suggest the idea by degrees as your own, as exclusively your own. Act under the seal of secrecy. If the thing is rejected by the Veseys, there is an end to it. If they think it plausible, bring it to a point with them. Then, *from yourself*, sound Major MacNamara under the strictest seal of secrecy. Do not commit yourself to one word except under that seal. This hint is enough for you ... Consult O'Loghlen without giving even to him the slightest hint that you heard from me. If you succeed in making an arrangement between the Major and Vesey, why then the gentry might all call on their tenants to give one vote for them, leaving them at liberty to give me the other ... As to O'GM, he would be rapidly put *hors de combat* ... When you have read this letter you may as well to prevent accidents put it into the fire ... Recollect what pleasure it would give me if anything connected with me were to place you fairly and honourably as an object of patronage to such a man as VF. He could *easily* accomplish everything for you and for the major.

O'Connell oscillated between eighteenth- and nineteenth-century politics. He had first won Clare on a straight – well, almost straight – fight about principles and personalities. Now he was reverting to the old-fashioned politics based on 'interest', a long way from his first fine democratic rapture. But O'Connell, not for the first or last time, was being too clever by half. He must have forgotten that before the 1928 Clare election he had promised in writing to support MacNamara for Clare in future, and even to resign Clare to MacNamara if ever the major should require this of him.[15] O'Connell, when reminded of this awkward promise, claimed that it had been invalidated by a later conversation, which the major denied; but as a lawyer he must have realised the weakness of a case based on a conversation without witnesses when set against a written undertaking. If he did not realise it MacNamara's present (and O'Connell's former) agent, Richard Scott, rubbed it in. 'You bound yourself to the major. He did not bind himself to you ... I advise you to steer clear of obliging him to act adversely to you.'[16]

The king died at the end of June and the protagonists got into full swing for a general election in August. Early in July O'Connell, still in London, heard from Steele[17] of the arrival in Ennis of a squad of O'Connellites including

> a certain Austrian Irishman called Morgan O'Connell whom I brought with me from the Kingdom of Kerry for some rather important purposes which I shall hereafter explain ... I brought Morgan to Ennis to challenge Major MacNamara for his daring to accuse his father of fabricating a conversation for the purposes of evading the performance of a written pledge.

Morgan wrote MacNamara such a letter, Steele said, 'as became a son, a soldier and a gentleman'. But the major, secure in his reputation as a duellist, brushed off the whippersnapper's challenge and informed Steele that he would make use of O'Connell's written engagement at any time when he should find it necessary for his purposes. Scott informed O'Connell,[18] somewhat gratuitously:

> You have been *outgeneralled and ill advised* as to your conduct towards Major MacNamara and ... I fear it will be my painful duty to advise Major MacNamara to apply to the Court of King's Bench for a criminal information, even though it should have the unpleasant result of making public all your correspondence and transactions with regard to Clare politics.

Clearly Clare, when O'Connell arrived there, would be a very uncomfortable place, and he was in imminent danger of a humiliating defeat on the very scene of his recent triumph. Tom Steele strongly advised him to stand down, using as his excuse the letter to MacNamara which he had repudiated. Fortunately he had invitations to stand for eight other constituencies, including Waterford where Villiers Stuart, to the annoyance of those who had put him in four years ago, had resigned for financial reasons. Back in Dublin on 13th July, O'Connell issued an address to the electors of County Waterford declaring that he was standing down for Clare 'because of a pledge I am incapable of violating'.[19]

But for his reputation he must put in one more appearance in 'that vile Clare, corrupted by that bad man, Mahon,' and head a triumphal procession – though it is not clear what triumph they were celebrating – from Limerick to Ennis. It was met by a procession of O'Gorman Mahon who does not seem to have quite made up his mind whether to welcome the Liberator, to oppose him or to usurp the head of his procession. At any rate he boarded O'Connell's lofty chariot and actually grappled with him. 'I'm as prepared to meet death as yourself!' roared O'Connell and, seizing his antagonist by the collar – a bruiser strong, athletic and thirty years younger than himself – hurled him down on the heads of the mob.[20]

To continue the unedifying tale of Clare, O'Gorman Mahon was returned in the general election in August, but in November a petition was lodged, possibly by the 'Dannites', against his election on the grounds that he had resorted to wholesale bribery. A committee of the House of Commons found these allegations to be true, and he was unseated. To Mary, O'Connell wrote more in sorrow than in anger:

> There is no doubt of the bribery and you know, love, he had no chance of being returned unless he bribed high ... Darling, O'Gorman Mahon is *not* to be relied on and his absence from the House is *not* a subject for regret. This is entirely between you and me.

He thought the miscreant would be forced, unless his wife's family came to his aid, to seek refuge from his creditors on the continent, but when a writ was issued for a new election O'Gorman Mahon, debarred by the findings of the committee from standing himself, put up his brother William, 'though he has no more chance of succeeding than he would have of turning the Shannon.'

Nevertheless O'Connell did not approve of Maurice displaying the feuds between patriots by standing against him. Maurice, however, persisted, and was proved right by winning the second seat (the first going to MacNamara) actually with O'Gorman Mahon's erratic support. But the Prime Minister, Lord Grey, called for another general election to rally support for his Reform Bill, so in May 1831 there was a replay in County Clare, with O'Gorman Mahon himself now standing in such fierce opposition to Maurice that the latter's life was in danger, both from an intemperate attempt by William Mahon to fight him, and from the distinct possibility of assassination by terrorists whose electoral support O'Gorman Mahon sought by claiming himself to be a Terry Alt. Two coachloads of gentlemen arrived in Ennis, heavily armed, to act as Maurice's bodyguard, and he eventually prevailed, again taking second place to MacNamara.

O'Gorman Mahon's outrageous behaviour at this election drove O'Connell to the ultimate abomination in Irish politics of passing secret information to the Castle. On 8th May[21] he wrote to the new Chief Secretary, a tough patrician politician named Edward Stanley:

I believe I can form a tolerably accurate estimate of the state of the Co. Clare. I have my information from sources of the *safest* kind. I have seen much and heard more ... The spirit of rebellion is extensive, the combination formidable from numbers and more so from the 'terror' that keeps it together ... All the farmers are most anxious to put an end to the dominion of miscreants. If they could be *protected*, they would join in putting down the *Whiteboys*, but it is impossible for Government to afford individual protection to a sufficient extent. The home of an Irish small farmer is anything but his 'castle' save in the theory of law. In practice it is worse than no defence. It makes him and his family liable to be burnt to death altogether in disturbed times ... I can get the oaths, passwords etc but they vary often ... This unhappy man, O'Gorman Mahon, has uniformly canvassed only by and through the Whiteboys. He has publicly read threatening notices which he says were sent to freeholders to vote for him ... He has given people directly to understand that he is a Terry Alt ... His exertions have given a strength, a permanency and a consistency to *this organisation* which no other within my memory ever had. Only think of a man canvassing for Parliament through the medium of actual felony if not treason ... You have *all* the Catholic clergy with the Government most heartily desirous [*sic*] ... This person O'Gorman Mahon has been before his last election for more than 12 months countenancing the progress of the combination, the oaths, the meetings etc. ... I have the heads of a clue to some at least of the murderers and if we had a return towards tranquillity I make little doubt that I would be able to put the magistrates in the confidence of the Crown in the track which would enable them to bring the miscreants to punishment ... Accept any little assistance I can give. My assistance is and must be *unnoticeable*.

O'Gorman Mahon was not prosecuted, for no one – least of all O'Connell – would go into the witness-box to testify against him.[22] His defeat had, for the time being, sickened him of politics, but the evil that he did lived after him, and in May O'Connell found the state of Clare 'very, very bad. The poorest class have got the mastery and even the small farmers are now enduring an atrocious tyranny.'[23]

Three years later, to the Liberator's great embarrassment, the *Observer* and the Cork *Southern Reporter* got wind of the letter to Stanley. He assured FitzPatrick, 'The story in the *Observer* is a perfect lie' (which it wasn't) but admitted, 'Mahon was named in my correspondence with Stanley. Let nobody deny that.'[24] He warned the editor of the O'Connellite *Pilot*, Richard Barrett, that the *Observer* editor was 'an *élève* of Stanley, with whom I was in correspondence about the Clare election and the conduct of the arch-miscreant.' Since his letter was doubtless in the Castle archives, the denial must be managed with caution.[25]

I have, then, with professional tact – or call it artifice – made a violent attack on the *Courier* for another lie and thrown off as much as possible the public attention to the other scent. Your plan is to assail the *Courier* also, just discreetly talking of the falsehood of my accusing Mahon ... But be discreet in *that*.

In County Waterford for the general election of August 1830 he found a haven of peace (compared to Clare), a cosy arrange-

ment with the Beresfords and the end of his alliance with the
Wyses.[26] He was, personally and professionally, on good terms
with the Beresfords who a year earlier had invited him to be
Lord George Beresford's election counsel. He had refused
because, as M.P. for Clare, he might find himself sitting in judgment upon an election petition against his own client. To his
annoyance, Sheil had secured this lucrative retainer. Now it was
arranged that the Beresfords and the Duke of Devonshire, the
largest landowners in the county, would instruct their tenants to
give their first votes to Lord George and their votes for the
second county seat to O'Connell. This greatly annoyed Thomas
Wyse who was already canvassing for the popular vote. There
were also two outsiders who scratched before the start. *All* candidates, including Lord George, declared in favour of repeal.
George Wyse was confident that Dan would not this time succeed
in 'agitating the county' against his brother, but Dan's magic still
worked, as did Dan's tactics: he said he would resign rather than
split the popular vote – not, of course, with any intention of
doing so, but to force Wyse's hand. It worked. Wyse felt obliged
to resign, very reluctantly, lest the Liberator be thwarted, and
O'Connell and Lord George shook hands most cordially on being
declared elected. By in-and-out running O'Connell had won an
election, almost free of expense, but had made two powerful
Catholic enemies, both to himself and to repeal. Soon after this
Thomas Wyse flatly refused to sign a repeal petition and George
Wyse wrote, 'The Dannites ... what a *vile* race! A Repeal of the
Union, forsooth! Good as it might be in principle, under the
guidance of such a junta it could not fail to disgust every rational
man.'

A year earlier, in October 1829, the counsellor had given almost the last, and certainly the most dramatic of his performances
in court.[27] A number of farmers in the neighbourhood of Doneraile in County Cork had assembled in a drinking booth at a
fair – a curious venue for secret plotting – and conspired to
murder three landlords. One of these, George Bond Low, an
'active' magistrate and therefore particularly odious, was assassi-
nated by four men who were duly arrested and charged with the
crime. Others, who did not actually take part in killing Low,
were charged with conspiracy to murder; the four ringleaders had
allegedly formed a 'committee of direction' which included an

elderly farmer, John Daniel Leary, to select and brief the actual assassins.

On 23rd October three of the killers and Leary were found guilty in Cork and sentenced to death. The trial of the other three 'directors' was set for 26th October and a messenger was sent galloping up the road to Derrynane to summon O'Connell to their rescue. He arrived on the 25th at breakfast-time, and the Liberator did not fail him. There was not a moment to lose. The best horse was saddled for the first twenty miles and a messenger was sent ahead to have a carriage ready and waiting for him at Kenmare. While the carriage rocked and jolted over the rough mountain roads and down into the valley of the Lee, O'Connell managed to read the evidence on which Leary had been sentenced and found it was mainly that of accomplices, of spies who took part in the conspiracy in order to expose it and probably, O'Connell surmised, acted as *agents provocateurs*. In English and Irish courts accomplice evidence is regarded with extreme suspicion: it is not unacceptable, but is seldom accepted unless confirmed by non-accomplice evidence.

At the end of his ninety-mile dash, O'Connell's carriage clattered up the road to the Court House just as the case was about to open. Leaving his horses with sweating, heaving sides, himself almost as tired, he pushed his way through the crowd into the court-room, his arrival in the nick of time producing a tremendous sensation. Wolfing a couple of sandwiches and gulping down a bowl of milk, he studied the witnesses' original depositions.* The sworn evidence given by the witnesses in the box differed significantly from their earlier depositions, and O'Connell tore their evidence to pieces. On the very evidence on which Leary had been convicted and sentenced to death three days earlier, the jury could not now agree on a verdict, and the other three 'directors' were discharged. Two days later fifteen more accused, charged with conspiracy on the same evidence, were found Not Guilty. Furthermore the death sentences of the four men tried before O'Connell's arrival were commuted to transportation for

---

* Statements made, not on oath, to the police during the investigation of the case. According to the romantic legend, repeated by some biographers, these depositions were stolen. Not so. They were made available to the defence by the judge, Baron Pennefather, whose conduct of the case, wrote O'Connell, was 'marked by intelligent and judicious humanity'.

life. It was a great swan-song for the counsellor – who did not for one moment deny that the actual assassins, caught in the act, deserved hanging – and he was eventually able, by representations to the Castle, to obtain a pardon for old Leary.

When in Dublin he was accompanied on his walks between Merrion Square, the Four Courts and the Corn Exchange, by a ragged bodyguard of 'coalies' (coalheavers) known as 'the O'Connell Police', who insisted on all passers-by paying homage to the Liberator. Most citizens meekly complied with the raucous shouts of 'Hats off!', but with Trinity College lads it was a point of honour to refuse. One evening Steuart Trench, scion of a minor Ascendancy family, and a Trinity friend were walking peaceably about their business when they heard the menacing cries of 'Hats off! Hats off!' from the coalies who preceded the Liberator. They affected not to hear and kept their hats on. Immediately they were assailed and attempts were made to knock off their hats, but they struck out and walked steadily on past O'Connell. 'I remember', wrote Trench, 'his smile as he nodded good-humouredly to us as we passed him, and I must say it was of approval rather than otherwise.' But as soon as he was well away – he never allowed his 'police' to commit serious violence in his presence – a gang of ragged coalies turned and followed them, pressing closer and closer, repeating their cry of 'Hats off!' louder and louder. Whenever they turned, fists clenched, the 'police' fell back, but pressed closer when they retreated. At length they felt they would never get home safely, and ran up the steps of a substantial house. They knocked on the door, which opened a few inches, and a nervous face looked out.

'Let us in,' cried Trench, 'or the mob will murder us!'

'Sir, I hate these rascals ten times as much as you can ever do, but this is Lord Norbury's house ... and the villains will pull it down about his ears if I let you in.' The door was then slammed in their faces, and they turned at bay.

A brisk battle ended in one of the students getting a bloody nose and the other a split ear, and their hats being carried off in triumph, held high on broomsticks, with the victorious 'police' shouting and halloo-ing. 'Whether they laid the hats at O'Connell's feet or not I never heard: probably not, as we never saw them after.'

Electioneering in County Waterford O'Connell received a letter from his wife of which any 55-year-old husband might be proud.

My darling love, this is the eight-and-twentieth anniversary of our wedding-day – the day of the week too – which to me was the commencement of a happiness that through your fault was and never will be decreased. I have been the happiest of women since I first knew you and feel that if you don't love me more, you do not now, in my old age, love me less. And oh darling how dear, how very dear are you to my fond and grateful heart!

Mary continued that she

cared little for your *increasing* size, the more particularly as you always exaggerate your size. It can't at all events be un wholesome. It does not proceed from inactive or sedentary habits. You are neither an epicure nor a hard drinker. Indeed if you were like [Purcell] O'Gorman who is [illegible] large and a gormandizer, I should then be very unhappy about you.

Her admiration, like her love, was unabated, and she positively expected that he would one day be Prime Minister of England. She was 'anxious to make a good appearance in London for the sake of the girls. It might be of great advantage to them.'

Nell's Kit Fitz-Simon was everything a son-in-law should be (even accepting Nell's dowry, £5,000, in instalments), and a reliable political ally. But Kate at twenty-three and Betsey at twenty were still unmarried. They moved, however, in the best circles in Dublin:

Tell my girls how sorry I am that I did not see them in their Court dresses. I wish I had been present when my Betsey was kissed by the Duke [of Northumberland, Lord Lieutenant]. She must have blushed pretty deeply as much from indignation as anything else.

Actually O'Connell rather approved of the Duke, who arrived in Dublin in March 1829, though not of some of his understrappers. His Chief Secretary was the Peninsular and Waterloo veteran, Major General Sir Henry Hardinge, who on 18th October 1830, in the absence of the Lord Lieutenant, issued a proclamation for the suppression of dangerous societies – the sort of societies, in fact, which O'Connell had offered to help suppress in County Clare. But among the societies suppressed was the Liberator's perfectly peaceful, law-abiding Anti-Union Society, and he retorted with a most scurrilous attack on the Chief Secretary. Hardinge sent a challenge which O'Connell treated like all other challenges:

> Mr O'Connell will not receive any kind of communication with reference to a duel ... He spoke of Sir Henry Hardinge in his *public* capacity as an instrument of despotism. He did not say one word of him in his private capacity ... and he must say that fighting a duel would be a bad way of proving Sir Henry was right or Mr O'Connell wrong.

He had, in fact, described Hardinge as 'that paltry, contemptible little English soldier' and 'a chance child of fortune and war', which by any standards was an outrageous personal insult for which he refused either to apologise or to give satisfaction.

He was mortified to be cut in the London clubs, where the general attitude was expressed by Charles Greville apropos another unedifying quarrel between politicians:

> Formerly, when a man made use of offensive expressions and was called to account, he thought it right to go out and stand a shot before he eat up his words, but nowadays that piece of chivalry is dispensed with, and politicians make nothing of being scurrilous one day and humble the next.

O'Connell, however, never apologised and was never humble. George Villiers, whom he admired and who had praised his maiden speech in the Commons, gloated:

> It would have done anyone's heart good to see O'Connell cut in the House of Commons last night. He came out of his ordeal as foul and begrimed as a man from the pillory. Littleton and Althorp positively hooted him and there is such a feeling of

execration at his audacious baseness that people did not easily refrain from kicking him in the House.

Later Villiers enlarged with relish on this theme.

> I am sure that if a man was proved beyond all shadow of cavil to be a wilful liar and a stinking coward that an English mob would no more idolise him than they would be slow to see through his shallow-hearted selfishness. It does put the standard of honesty and intellect so low in Ireland that such a man should be such a god ... that I am vexed to the quick by it. It is all mighty well to say that nobody that is respectable, nobody that is honourable, is on terms with him – there he stands, omnipotent through moral influence, and can break down and deride every tie that is held binding upon the better portions of society. Honour and principles are valueless in fight with him.[28]

In the general election of May 1831, O'Connell was urged by his brother John to stand for his native county, Kerry. He gave no reason for leaving Waterford and the *Pilot*, his mouthpiece, refused to comment on it; no doubt the hostility of the Wyses had a bearing on his decision. 'My dear, dear John,' he wrote to his brother,

> you will never repent what you have done, come good, come evil ... I had an Address to the County of Waterford actually in print when your letter and the Tralee paper arrived. You must now instantly begin to work. You must ransack the county. Speak to the bishop. Engage every voter. Write every priest. Send Maurice and [cousin] Charles Brenan in every direction where a vote may be had. Write to James to come home at once and assist us ... If proper arrangements are made, the expense will be as nothing.

The Knight of Kerry, no repealer and a Liberal Protestant, was his main opponent, but withdrew from the contest, taking it very hard.

The priesthood were marshalled under a Jesuit bishop, and I

was depicted as a traitor at once to King and country – described as never having supported Catholic claims!! and that my vote on Reform was an attack on the people and their religion, and all this was piously and sincerely believed – the effect was a general fury equal to that raised against Vesey in Clare and with much more personal rancour. I should have polled little more than the Protestants, giving Dan a universal triumph and committing the County to religious and agrarian warfare.[29]

It was the end of a long friendship with a man to whom O'Connell owed much more than money.

One writes of 'friendship', but had O'Connell any real friends? He had colleagues, admirers, satellites, acquaintances, visitors, patrons in youth and protégés in middle and old age; but, for all his conviviality and charm (when he chose to exert it), who were his friends? In the eight volumes of his correspondence I cannot find a single letter (apart from those to and from his immediate family) dealing with gossip, anecdote, family affairs, day-to-day life, such as a man might write to a friend. All the non-family correspondence is about business, 90 per cent politics, 10 per cent his estate, debts, etc. The only real records we have of his day-to-day conversation and interests come from visitors to Derrynane and from O'Neill Daunt, whose *Personal Recollections of Daniel O'Connell* are full of non-political anecdote. But Daunt was thirty-two years younger than the Liberator, his secretary and protégé rather than his friend. He had enjoyed a real friendship with Bennett when they were both young, even to the remarkable degree of moving into Bennett's house to look after Mrs Bennett when she was having her first baby while her husband was on circuit. FitzPatrick, too, was more than a valued colleague and collector of the Tribute. But after 1831 O'Connell seems to have dropped Bennett (whose conduct was 'most awkward'); and there is hardly a word in his letters to and from both of them which does not relate strictly to politics or business. At least he never dropped FitzPatrick: he could not afford to. It is possible that he had no time to cultivate friendship, which does not flourish untended; possible, also, that he was too domineering; and possible that as the Liberator he was (except by those who detested him) lifted on to too high a pedestal. His tendency to equate criticism with disloyalty was not conducive to friendship with the sort of person one wants for a friend.

In the years 1830-1 O'Connell was at his worst. He was up against it. Emancipation, for all its immense implications for the future, had not as yet brought any great improvement in the status and prospects of Catholics. The Ascendancy still dispensed patronage, almost entirely to Protestants. With emancipation achieved, the Catholic hierarchy, guided by 'J.K.L.', ordered priests to lay off politics and in Leinster not even to make churches available for political meetings. It was not the first or last time in Ireland that such instructions have been issued from on high, or that many priests and bishops have turned a blind eye to them: some argued that the collection of the Tribute was not politics but charity. But undoubtedly during the early 1830s clerical support for repeal was much weaker than it had been for emancipation.[30] O'Connell was driven to unbecoming transactions in order to find a succession of parliamentary seats, in the course of which he lashed out right and left at many old comrades. His activities are here described in some detail because the antipathy they aroused in the upper and middle classes, and not merely among Protestants, nourished opposition on both sides of the water to the repeal of the union.

11

The Repealer

O'Connell saw repeal from three points of view. As a lawyer he believed that the Irish parliament had no right to commit suicide in 1800. As a radical he believed that proper parliamentary reform, including the secret ballot which he saw as the *sine qua non* of democracy,[1] could never be given to Ireland save by an Irish parliament; English M.P.s regarded the Irish as a lesser breed, not yet capable of self-government. Nor would a parliament predominantly Anglican ever tackle the obvious injustice of making Catholics (and Presbyterians) pay tithes to the Anglican Church, or reduce the overblown wealth and privileges of the Church of Ireland, or end the scandal of Protestant monopoly of power in the Corporations, or cut government subsidies to proselytising educational societies, or disarm the Orange yeomanry in the north, or repeal the well-meaning but unpopular Sub-letting Act which sought to prevent the fragmentation of holdings by prohibiting sub-letting save with the landlord's consent.[2] Finally, as a Catholic and a Gael, he had developed over the years something which he had certainly not acquired from his father and his uncles – a strong resentment against the Saxon and the Protestant Ascendancy.

He saw – or said he saw – repeal as nothing more revolutionary than a return to the conditions of 1800 but with Catholics now sitting in the Dublin parliament and occupying any offices in the state to which their talents and connections entitled them: 'in short, salutary restoration without revolution, an Irish Parliament, British connection, one King, two legislatures'. It must be achieved entirely by lawful methods and with the full consent of Protestants. It implied no social revolution, no social change: *'the full preservation of all vested interests* would be an indispensable preliminary stipulation'; 'the nobility to possess lands, titles and legislative privileges as before the Union'; there was no question of Catholic supremacy; Protestants would enjoy full equality of rights, franchise, laws and privileges; 'no living man would be made worse off than he is.'³

But if that was how *he* saw repeal, he was almost unique in this view. To the vast majority of those who thronged his mass meetings, repeal meant driving the Saxon into the sea and taking back the lands the Saxon had usurped. If he was to retain their support (and collect their money) he must in some degree appeal to their instincts and gut reactions, and at the same time strain every nerve to prevent rebellion breaking out while keeping the government in constant apprehension of it. 'The Irish people', he wrote in December 1831⁴ to the radical M.P. Leslie Grove Jones,

> are making up their minds to go to war with England ...
> There is no conspiracy, there is no regular organization, there
> is an opinion daily gaining ground from man to man that
> Ireland will obtain independence through a bloody struggle
> ... There is only one man who can prevent the coming fight
> ... I will prevent the war and preserve the connection in a
> state highly advantageous to both countries.

Grove Jones was a radical but an anti-repealer. He was also a Peninsular veteran who had commanded a battalion of Foot Guards. He replied that if it came to war, the Catholics had not the ghost of a chance. So thought Anglesey when he returned as Lord Lieutenant: 'If we once begin, it will be a war of extermination. A pleasant prospect! Yet I hope still to avoid it.'⁵

The case for repeal was strong in principle. Why on earth should gentlemen in Westminster legislate for a country about which most knew nothing and cared less, the economic interests of which often clashed with those of England, most of the people of which followed a religion which was odious to most English people, and which had suffered much from English rule in the past?

The anti-repeal case, though, was more arguable in detail. At the lowest level it was based on self-interest. Irish Protestants, who had supported emancipation because it was so obviously fair and because a few Catholic M.P.s could do them little harm in Westminster, saw their whole life-style threatened by a mainly Catholic parliament in College Green. The Liberal Protestants such as Lord Cloncurry, Bennett, the Knight of Kerry and O'Connell's friend, solicitor and parliamentary agent, Pierce Mahony, and Catholics such as Sheil, Wyse, 'J.K.L.' and Edward Dwyer feared that the repeal of the union would be followed by wholesale attacks on private property, and felt that Catholics could obtain a perfectly fair deal without repeal. The intangible sentiments of loyalty to the Crown and pride in the Empire – although frequently and publicly professed by O'Connell – ranged many men against a Dublin parliament which would surely become a focus of agitation for complete independence, after which Ireland might well side with England's enemies in war and exclude England's manufactures in peace-time. There was, and is, in England a basic distrust of Ireland, which O'Connell hoped would bring Irish Protestants into seeing the merits of repeal, though here he deluded himself. Nothing could have been further from O'Connell's wish than to widen sectarian divisions: he constantly and publicly appealed for Protestant support and praised Protestants who supported him. Nevertheless to most Protestants the thrust of his agitation and, even more, of the agitation of his colleagues and of the scores of militant clerics who appeared at the Waterford 1826, Clare 1828 and Kerry 1831 elections seemed to be intolerantly and fanatically Papist. As the astute de Tocqueville remarked, most Catholic priests hated Protestantism and, in particular, the Protestant clergy. The other side of the coin was the hatred and fear of so many Irish Protestants for Popery. Early in 1833 O'Connell and Dr Boyton of Trinity College, doyen of Dublin conservatives, had tentative, indirect talks through FitzPatrick on the possibility of an informal pact between Tories and repealers. Boyton declared anti-Popery was the insuperable obstacle.[6]

In January 1831, Philip Crampton, the Solicitor General for Ireland, put the Ascendancy point of view:

Catholics of property with scarcely any exception and the whole of the gentry are still untouched, but they stand aloof not so much from disinclination to the thing as from fear that it could not be effected without a disturbance that would endanger their property.[7]

Repeal would lead to full separation: 'this is the argument to which all O'Connell's arguments tend.' A deep-rooted hatred to the English connection 'or, as they are taught to understand, to English subjugation, is the predominant feeling in every Catholic's heart.' They long for the expulsion of the Invader, the Tyrant. 'This is the feeling to which O'Connell appeals when he talks of the Saxon, the Stranger and the Taskmaster.' Various people including Lord Anglesey 'prophesied that the Tribute would be a failure and that O'Connell would get on very well and be very popular until he put his hand into the people's pockets, but Sheil told us that it would succeed'. The advantages promised by O'Connell from repeal were only possible with complete separation.

Tithes, taxes, the Protestant Church, the tyrannical aristocracy, £8 million per annum of absentees' property which is to be expropriated for the uses of the poor – But the Protestants have taken alarm ... The north is up: they consider themselves a superior race ... Not one of [the conspirators] with the exception of O'Connell is possessed of talents, courage, wealth, station, character or any of those qualities which qualify a man for the station of a dangerous demagogue ... But all who know O'Connell are convinced that this boldness is fictitious and that he is this moment trembling in his skin lest a premature explosion should take place and this affords a key to his letter of supplication to the [illegible] of Kilkenny not to break the peace accompanied by the convenient threat that 'if they got themselves into a scrape he would quit them and leave the Union unrepealed ... Sheil told me that he saw O'Connell when he was suffering under the terrors of the warrant which was issued against him for the Bolivar speech and so deplorable an object of grief and terror he never beheld.

George Villiers, writing to Philip Crampton in the same month,[8] referred to 'the two rulers of Ireland', O'Connell and the Lord Lieutenant.

O'Connell's disgusting insolence to Lord Cloncurry, his threatened destruction of the monied interests by a run upon the banks and his proposed bankruptcy of merchants and retail dealers by the non-consumption of exciseable articles must surely rouse everybody who has anything to lose or who happens not to like being being trampled to death by the most iron despotism that ever sacrificed the happiness of the many to the vicious interests of the one. It is impossible to deny the extreme ingenuity of his speeches and writings and the more than Protean variety of his resources – surely though he will be caught at last. He cannot create mad excitement and then, for long, make it act with sanity and composure, and if he can't, he must either be hanged by the government or damned by his party. I am of course delighted that the Orangemen see through the shallow charlatanism of this man.

The attitude of the Orange, largely Presbyterian, north was something which O'Connell never comprehended. The north was *terra incognita* to him: he hardly set foot there, and on one spectacularly unsuccessful visit narrowly escaped ambush by booking coach-horses for one day and arriving, under a false name, in a coach bristling with blunderbusses, two days earlier. Ulster Presbyterian attitudes were compounded of radicalism and a dislike of the Ascendancy, anti-Popery and, increasingly, unionism, based both on anti-Popery and on the real economic advantages which the union had brought to Belfast. From time to time O'Connell, with the wishful thinking that was one of his weaknesses, deluded himself that Presbyterian radicalism would prevail; Presbyterians were refusing to pay tithes and rents; Presbyterians were for reform; Presbyterians would surely revert to their liberty-loving past, to the spirit of 1798 (but not its methods) and rally to repeal. But they wouldn't. In 1830 O'Connell had high hopes of Henry Montgomery, an extremely influential, liberal, Presbyterian minister who had supported emancipation. But Montgomery organised an address to Lord Anglesey pledging support for the union, and thereby became 'a fauning, cringeing sycophant'. Montgomery's dignified reply, published in the press, did much to alienate liberals from repeal.[9]

The union, wrote O'Connell in October 1830,

196

should now be agitated in every possible shape ... A permanent society is absolutely necessary in order to collect funds *in primo loco*, to collect funds *in secundo loco* and to collect funds, thirdly and lastly, because we have both mind and body within us and all we want is the means of keeping both in regular and supple motion.[10]

In eight days, he wrote, he had attended four public dinners and four meetings for petitioning and the redress of grievances. 'AGITATE! AGITATE! AGITATE!'

The anti-repeal feeling of all classes in Britain and of the upper classes in Ireland was strengthened by the wave of agrarian terrorism which swept the country (not only in County Clare) in the years 1830–2. In 1832 there were reported 242 murders, over three hundred attempted murders and 568 cases of arson.[11] There was an anti-tithe campaign which brought about frequent and bloody clashes between police, process-servers, soldiers and the peasantry. There were campaigns for rent-reductions and even for the total abolition of rent. Secret societies – Whiteboys, Terry Alts, Ribbonmen – killed, burnt, houghed cattle and ransacked houses for money and arms. In no way were the crimes desired or countenanced by O'Connell. He denounced them at every opportunity; he despatched Tom Steele and other 'Pacificators' to do their best in troubled areas; he warned the Castle of what was happening but had no remedy to suggest save 'the increase of the King's troops in Ireland. The exhibition of such force may alone do good. The yeomanry are worse than useless.'[12] But undoubtedly his agitation and inflammatory oratory aroused the feelings which stimulated terrorism.

One of the first decisions of the Grey ministry, in November 1830, was to send Anglesey back to Ireland as Lord Lieutenant. He was to restore law and order and exploit his popularity with Catholics by every conciliatory measure short of repeal. O'Connell was wary of Anglesey's return, advised him not to come and warned him that if he opposed repeal he would lose all his popularity. Anglesey, less naive than in 1828, acted with circumspection. He cultivated a friendship with Cloncurry of whose acumen he had a high opinion. In a long talk which touched even on the Liberator's finances, he tried to buy O'Connell with the office of Attorney General, which was refused to Mary's great relief: 'Thank God you acted like yourself, and your wife and children have more reason to be proud of you now than they ever were. Had you acted differently ... it would have broken my heart.'[13] With Sheil, who had recently married both beauty and money, Anglesey had better luck, establishing him in parliament as member for an English rotten borough. Sheil promptly declared war on his old chief. 'He does not speak to me,' wrote O'Connell.

> Indeed I believe ... he was sent into the House for the very purpose of abusing me ... If he attacks me, I promise you he will have his answer. I will not spare him of all men, for a renegade is the worst species of traitor.[14]

Indeed Sheil had already, in January 1831, passed to the Home Secretary, Lord Melbourne, advice on dealing with O'Connell which was very similar to O'Connell's on dealing with O'Gorman Mahon.

> Sheil would send over from London three reporters of the best class to take down O'Connell's words at any of the Repeal meetings, he could not help speaking sedition for he has grown careless with impunity ... He would then set the Attorney General at him.[15]

Soon the 'brave and gay and good Lord Anglesey' was metamorphosed into 'the hare-brained and vain Anglesey', 'the most mischievous thing that could possibly have happened' and

> one of the very worst enemies Ireland can have. I know he is *not to be relied on*, but at the same time I do not believe he is our enemy from hatred or malignity. No, he merely desires to preserve the superiority of England. Anything consistent with that superiority he would do for the good of Ireland, but when the good of Ireland clashes with English domination he would with the coldest disdain sacrifice everything dear and sacred to Irishmen.[16]

Anglesey's current opinion of the Liberator was no higher. In 1828 in a public speech he had praised O'Connell's peace-making efforts; in 1829 he had positively encouraged his campaign for Catholic emancipation. Now, opposed to repeal and having failed to buy the arch-repealer, he rolled up his sleeves to deal with him – albeit with good humour. His first move was to ban a procession which O'Connell had organised in Dublin, arranging that his proclamation was laid on the Liberator's breakfast table 'at which anticipation he chuckled mightily'. But O'Connell got the better of this exchange by promptly issuing handbills desiring the people to obey, 'as if the order of the Lord Lieutenant was to derive its authority from his permission'.

'*You* talk of conciliating,' wrote Anglesey to Lord Holland, Chancellor of the Duchy of Lancaster, in January 1831,

> but how is that now possible? *I* cannot do it, and I told you, after the last conversation I had with him, I was quite certain nothing would tame him ... It is true he is a coward, and may be more practicable whilst he is in a difficulty than when he is kicking the world before him ... I told him what would be the result of this continued agitation, that I was sure he would force me to take very strong measures ... I told him I trembled at the thoughts of what he might force upon me ... and having exhausted all my efforts of kindness, and forgiveness, and of consideration, I endeavoured to work upon his fears by representing myself as a furious Dog with a sword in my hand. Now tame him if you can. He is worth having, at any price; and if by sacrificing me, by disavowing my act, by recalling me, even by disgracing me, you can save this wretched people by removing from them their *Evil Spirit* (removing him, I mean, from the country by weight of gold or by place) believe me I shall submit with the utmost cheerfulness ... On the other hand, if you all concur in the necessity of fighting it out with him, then I do believe that I am the *Man*, for I know the rogue to a turn.[17]

As successive Lords Lieutenant and Chief Secretaries harried the repeal movement, O'Connell had little difficulty in keeping a length ahead of them. Although the Catholic Association had been dissolved after achieving emancipation, its machinery for propaganda, meetings, petitioning and the collection of funds remained in being under a variety of names – the Irish Volunteers for the Repeal of the Union, the Anti-Union Society, the National Political Union, the Society of Friends of Ireland of All Religious Persuasions, the General Association of Ireland for the Prevention of Unlawful Meetings and for the Protection and Exercise of the Sacred Right of Petitioning for the Redress of Grievances. As fast as it was banned, or dissolved in anticipation of being banned, under one name, it was resuscitated under another. To evade the ban, 'repeal breakfasts' were held, attended by hundreds, and if these were to be banned, O'Connell promised to organise repeal dinners and teas.

In January 1831 he went too far: in a public letter he called for a run on the banks. This was intolerable: 'The question is, whether he or I govern Ireland?' The Attorney General pounced. In the Liberator's indignant words, 'Common thief-takers were sent into my house to drag me from the bosom of my family.' O'Connell and five others were arrested on some thirty-one charges of conspiring to evade the Act for the Suppression of Dangerous Associations or Assemblies in Ireland and proclamations made under it. 'I have got O'Connell in the net,' wrote Anglesey on 29th January. 'He cannot get out ... He will be committed, and very likely for a year.' O'Connell having been released on bail, would probably suspend his agitation and even give some support to the government to get his neck out of the noose. 'Protestant, Catholic, Banker, Merchant, Bar, Church – all have rallied to me,' wrote Anglesey. '*Entre nous*, Dr Doyle ["J.K.L."] is at my feet.' ... 'He [Dr Doyle] is a clever man, full of information, full of prejudice and full of condemnation of that in others.' ... 'You must see the importance of having a counter-poise to the Arch-Fiend, O'Connell. This Prelate, in his heart, hates him.' The country, Anglesey was convinced, was turning his way; all that was now needed were a few popular measures and money to create work for the people, without a moment's loss of time. 'And finally pay the Priests – and I promise you will never hear more of O'Connell.' The Attorney General said to Stanley, 'I now give him bound hand and foot into your custody – don't let him go.' And Stanley positively gloated to Melbourne, 'I think he may be dealt with – *and transported* – and if he were, I really hope Ireland would be tranquil.'

But O'Connell was a match for them. By adroit use of procedural tactics, and not without some sympathetic handling of the case by Chief Justice Charles Kendal Bushe, O'Connell contrived to drag out the pre-trial procedures until the ministry realised, to its chagrin, that they needed his help in the Commons to push through the Reform Bill. In exchange for his plea of Guilty, the ministry (while vigorously denying that there was any bargain) postponed the trial until the Crown lawyers discovered that the miscreant could be prosecuted only under a statute which had just expired.[18]

O'Connell repaid them on 8th March 1831 with a magnificent speech on the Reform Bill. 'The knife', he said, 'has been applied unsparingly, but with no unskilful hand, to the rotten and corrupt part of the constitution.' When people complained to him that a new constitution was being surreptitiously introduced, 'I ask then, "What is the old?" - that the mound of Old Sarum or the park of Gatton should be represented?'

Tories claimed that peers and other borough-owners enjoyed 'a wonderful facility of discovering young men of genius and rewarding them by a seat in Parliament'. But what was the constitution? At the beginning of every session, even before the King's Speech, the Commons formally declared that it was a gross infringement of their privileges for any peer or prelate to concern himself with the election of an M.P. 'I accuse them of infringement of the liberty of the Commons.'

Tories often argued that a rotten borough was the owner's private property, of which parliament had no right to deprive him.

They have stolen the right of the people to vote, and now the spoliators cry, 'Stop thief!' ... The people out of doors are in the habit of talking common sense, and this is the language which they hold to the borough-proprietors, 'You have taken away our rights; you have usurped our franchises; you have robbed us of our property; and, do what you will, you shall disgorge.' ... No man in the House is so little connected with England as I am. Yet have the agents [of the borough-proprietors] been at me, offering to return me at the smallest possible expense ... Are not the prices of [the nomination boroughs] known as well as the price of stocks? ... They are sold like stalls in Smithfield Market.

Granted that the rotten borough system had introduced some able and useful men to parliament,

Is there some fairy touch which opens that door only to men of talent and intelligence? Are there no dull, stupid, drowsy members returned for boroughs? – Members without talent to join in debate but with sufficient perseverance to attend at a division? Members without any regard for the interests of the country, but only the most devoted regard for their own interests? Men who have raised themselves as the country has fallen, and become high and mighty on the spoils of the people?

Tories had the effrontery to claim that the system, with its fundamental defects in principle, nevertheless worked well in practice. Had they ever heard of the Walcheren expedition? Of a national debt approaching £1,000 million, or of the misery and starvation in Ireland? And they claimed that the system worked well!

I entertain no ungenerous jealousy at advantages conferred on England and Scotland. All I ask is that Ireland should not be excluded from a share in these advantages ... But where the political rights of Ireland are concerned, I have not observed the same liberality here. [Nevertheless] I am prepared to vote for the Bill, even in its present state.

It was a triumph. The ministers, including Stanley, applauded loud and long; even *The Times* could scarce forbear to cheer. Everyone seemed to be crowding round to congratulate him – except Sheil.[19]

Anglesey could only hope that the Arch-Fiend, seeing there was a government not afraid to grapple with him, would now behave himself. Indeed the Arch-Fiend could sometimes make himself useful. In May Clare and Tipperary were in a shocking state. (O'Connell thought so too.) Anglesey was 'nearly at his wits' end about those Terry Alts'. So was O'Connell. 'O'Connell is gone to try his hand. If he don't succeed, I must act.' The Liberator's impassioned denunciation of secret societies in Ennis had no effect at all, but already the government had acted. On 2nd June, partly no doubt as a result of O'Connell's secret correspondence with Stanley, a special commission of two judges sat in Ennis to try 290 men charged with terrorist offences. O'Connell, in one of his last professional appearances in court, defended most of them but with little success, and Anglesey could rejoice, 'Our success in Clare surpasses all expectations. Fourteen Terry Alts convicted there the first day were in the Transport in Cork in three days. This has done more [good] than hanging.'[20]

In October 1831 the ministry made another attempt to buy O'Connell, this time using 'J.K.L.' as their emissary. It failed, partly because they would not specify exactly what was on offer in terms of a job and of a more liberal policy towards Ireland. The bishop warned them that they *must* come to terms with O'Connell 'for without him you cannot in his lifetime govern the country' but 'I can no longer serve you in any negotiation with him.'[21]

Again and again Anglesey warned the government:

You could not please me more than by disposing of O'Connell in England ... but I caution you against him. Depend upon it, he is not to be trusted in any way whatsoever. I do not know how he can be had. If you can effect it, you will do a world of good ... Try him, but do not put it in his power to boast of having resisted a temptation, for he would inevitably throw you over. Should you not succeed, of course they must make the best fight they can against him in the House of Commons.[22]

Was he saying that O'Connell would not be bought, or would not stay bought? A bit of both, perhaps.

The only thing O'Connell ever accepted from the government was the silk gown of the Inner Bar, making him King's Counsel with precedence 'next after His Majesty's second serjeant', on 4th November 1831. It was by then an empty honour, for he had given up his Bar practice. Sheil, a far less distinguished lawyer, had been thus honoured two years earlier. But O'Connell was nevertheless gratified by this belated recognition, which Anglesey thought was no more than was due to his professional eminence.

In O'Connell's view Stanley, the Chief Secretary, was even more abhorrent than Anglesey. He had

rendered himself more odious than any other man who ever

assisted in the mis-government of Ireland – Mr Stanley, the snappish, impertinent, overbearing, High Church Mr Stanley, who spoke of the 'tried loyalty' of the Orange Yeomanry ... It is idle to conceal it. Mr Stanley *must* be put out of the government of Ireland.

No one much liked Stanley, not even Anglesey – he was altogether too bossy. But at least, like Peel and Anglesey, he was not afraid of O'Connell.

Much of the disorder stemmed from an agrarian revolt against the payment of tithes.[23] There was a manifest injustice in Catholics and Presbyterians having to support a parson who might minister to a mere handful of Anglican parishioners, and moreover the establishment of the Church of Ireland was grossly overendowed. An annual income of £800,000 to £1 million, about half of it collected in tithes, maintained four archbishops, eighteen bishops and some 2,000 parish clergy to serve the needs of 800,000 Anglicans. (Catholics numbered six million.) Over one-third of the parishes in 1833 contained less than fifty Anglican parishioners; a third of the benefices were held by absentees.

In addition, Catholics and Dissenters could be charged cess (unless they succeeded in packing a parish Vestry meeting) 'not only to build, repair, ornament and warm the Protestant churches, but' (O'Connell complained) 'to pay for the very spitting-boxes of the clerical functionaries.'

The burden was heaviest when a parson had his tithes collected by a 'tithe proctor' or leased to a 'tithe farmer' whose object was to extract as much as possible from those who must pay and pass on as little as possible to the parson. O'Connell in 1825 told the Lords' Select Committee on the State of Ireland:

> The peasants are infinitely better treated when the tithes are in the hands of the clergyman himself; where he leases them they are always very badly treated; and it is quite immaterial whether he leases to a Protestant or a Catholic, the Catholic treats them as badly as the Protestant.

The Whiteboys made the same point, posting up such warning notices as, 'I do strictly caution you and all of you to surrender, give up and deliver unto your respective rector your tithes for this harvest' (i.e. not to any middleman). They were not really against tithes (particularly after Goulburn's Tithe Composition Act of 1823), provided these were, in their view, not excessive, any more than they were against fees paid to Catholic priests – provided these were, in their view, not excessive. Their enemy was the landlord, not the parson. The principal objectors to tithes were the sort of farmers who would not engage in terrorism, so the anti-tithe agitation spread the area of protest, often violent protest, wider than Whiteboy terrorism.

Tithe assessments were often unfair, and before Goulburn's Act they were not levied on grazing land, so the large farmer and grazier got off comparatively lightly. They were paid, only on tillage, in one of three ways: (a) a fixed annual payment per acre; (b) according to an annual 'view' of the crops to see what tithe-payers could afford that year; or (c) one-tenth of the crops in kind. The last two methods were reasonably fair, but clumsy and hard to operate. Goulburn's Act, besides making pastures liable to tithes, allowed individual parish Vestries to appoint a commissioner to bargain with the tithe-owner's commissioner for an assessment of landholders in the parish for twenty-one years. The intention was that tithes should be paid only by the larger landholders, who would recoup some of the money from the smaller farmers by higher rents; so collection would be comparatively easy and the burden fairly spread. By 1830 about half the parishes in the country had 'compounded', but the results were not as happy as the framers of the act had expected. Because voting in parish Vestries was 'weighted' according to the voter's acreage, the larger farmers were able to impose their choice of Vestry commissioner who, in making assessments, looked after their interests. Assessments were based on average grain prices for the years 1814 to 1821, but prices had subsequently dropped sharply, so what had at first been a fair assessment became excessive. Tithes had priority over rent, so a farmer who had paid his tithes might find himself faced with eviction because he had no money for his rent. This, and the recouping by tithe-payers through increased rents, inflated an anti-tithe campaign into a campaign against the payment of rents as well, and brought the Whiteboys into association with it.

An anti-tithe campaign was an obvious tactic for agitators, since those who paid tithes, directly and indirectly, were many, while those who received them were few and vulnerable. The tithe-owner's usual remedy for non-payment was the distraint and sale of the defaulter's livestock; but this was easier said than done, for by law animals could be seized only between sunrise and sunset, while they were scattered, grazing; they could not be taken when they were concentrated in byres or other enclosures at night. Moreover the role of police and troops was merely to keep order, not actually to assist in the seizures.

In 1830 at Graiguenemanagh in County Kilkenny an unpopular parson was so foolish as to seize for tithes the cattle of the parish priest, thus setting off a campaign which soon spread over most of the country. Lookouts and signals warned farmers to move their cattle before the tithe-proctor's party arrived; only a very brave man would buy distrained stock; arson and murder made their point. Troops, police and yeomanry were constantly employed in protecting tithe-proctors and keeping order at auctions of distrained stock, which resulted in fourteen deaths at Newtownbarry, seventeen in a similar massacre in Westmeath and the killing of a dozen policemen in Kilkenny. The Church of Ireland by 1833 was in financial trouble, with £818,518 (more than half the tithes since 1831) still unpaid.

In 1832 the Grey ministry, meaning well, passed another Tithe Composition Act, enabling the government to compensate tithe-owners in distress. But an ill-judged clause in the Act required the government to collect arrears, that is to say to distrain and sell livestock instead of merely holding the ring while tithe-proctors did so. Catholics and Presbyterians were equally outraged, and O'Connell was hardly less angry than Anglesey who wrote in June 1832 in something like despair:

The grant for the parsons is fair enough, although not many of them *deserve* aid. Still, they have lost their dues. But how am *I* to collect this rent for the State? To distrain and sell their cattle is utterly impossible. There will not be a buyer in all Ireland ... But the new law enables me to seize the persons of defaulters. A pleasant power, this! And I am advised to act upon it with promptitude and vigour! ... There will be no open resistance, but those arrested will allow themselves to be incarcerated. But how am I to find room for all the delinquents? ... Thousands will go to jail, but no one will pay tithe

... The parsons are plaguing my heart out. They call for aid – which the law requires me to give. Seizures are made – auctions take place. No buyer dare present himself: and thus the troops are harassed, the Government loses character. It even incurs ridicule.

Anglesey was proved right. In the year following the passing of the Act 43,000 decrees were issued, resulting in the collection of only £12,316, at a cost to the government of £26,000.

O'Connell the Agitator was not wholly opposed to tithes, for to abolish them *in toto* in the face of violence would obviously endanger rents, to the detriment of O'Connell the landlord. What he disliked was the landlords being made, in effect, tithe-proctors (since they paid and collected tithes), the two issues of tithes and rents being thereby confused.

In January 1833 Anglesey was still fulminating against

the most pernicious, unhappy measure that ever was adopted ... I would defy the ingenuity of human invention to produce any other measure which would so effectively strengthen the power of the agitators ... Let us not again commit the folly of *proceeding to coercion* and *declining to conciliate.*

But the government was coming round to Anglesey's view. In June 1833 the Church Million Act set aside £1 million for the compensation of tithe-owners and virtually wrote off arrears for 1831–3. Magistrates could order the police to attend distress proceedings only on the authority of the Lord Lieutenant, which Anglesey's liberal successors very seldom gave. Thus the bomb was defused.

It was not, however, a solution to the problem. The Grey ministry were still seeking one, and during the winter of 1832–3 the ministry worked out the details of the Irish Church Temporalities Bill, which would provide for the abolition of ten bishoprics and for a mixed lay and ecclesiastical commission empowered to suspend appointments to parishes where no service had been held for three years. Church cess, paid by all parishioners, Anglican and non-Anglican, would be replaced by a graduated tax on clerical incomes over £200 a year, the proceeds going to the Church. The guts of the bill were contained in the 147th clause under which tenants of the bishops' large estates would be enabled to buy their land outright, thus creating a fund of £2–3 million from which the state would pay bishops their former rent incomes; any surplus would be at parliament's disposal for unspecified 'religious and charitable purposes', which were taken to include the payment of Catholic clergy and some help to Catholic education. O'Connell thoroughly approved, especially of the procedure outlined in clause 147 which was known as 'appropriation'. But for fear of defeat in the House of Lords, the Appropriation Clause, the essence of the bill from the Catholic point of view, was dropped from it. So tithes remained a grievance, though not so burning a grievance as they had been before June 1833.

O'Connell did not at first appreciate the breadth and depth of the opposition to repeal and so was grotesquely sanguine about achieving it. In November 1830 (with Wellington still in power) he was convinced that repeal was 'not only practicable but certain if we persevere'. They must 'add *business* to *speechifying* and give the boat a shove'. But a month later, writing to Bishop MacHale, he seemed to be hedging his bets and treating repeal less as an end in itself than as a lever to extort other concessions from the government. It troubled him that he could not convert his oldest friend, Bennett, to repeal, but insisted that though his speeches might be rough, it was only his influence that kept his followers from violence: 'they all know that it is my decided conviction that they should not resort to force and that I would forsake them if they had recourse to violence.'[24]

He still hankered after the alliance achieved by Grattan in his youth when Catholic and Presbyterian joined to agitate for Irish freedom, and even for the spirit of 1798 without the consequences. He thought this not wholly impossible, and so, significantly, did Anglesey. In January 1831, O'Connell received a letter from Derry inviting support for a petition for reform, triennial parliaments and secret ballots: 'It was, I confess, rather a singular exhibition to see 1,000 Protestants, many of them Orangemen, picking you out ... as the only member worthy to be applied to on a Reform petition.' Presbyterians, like Catholics, were refusing to pay rents and tithes. Then there was the problem of the yeomanry, mainly Protestant, largely Orange, poorly armed and worse disciplined by regular standards, but still formidable against a peasant revolt. O'Connell constantly agitated for disarming them, especially after the government's Arms Bill made the possession of unregistered arms a transportable offence: this, he said, would be used unfairly against Catholics while the Orange yeomanry were armed to the teeth. Anglesey was almost as vexed by the Arms Bill, on which he had not been consulted: 'I was annoyed and, *entre nous*, disgusted that the very first bill brought in *for* Ireland [by the Grey ministry] was a *penal* one.' Furthermore he was just as keen as O'Connell to disarm the yeomanry who would be useless against a real enemy but were always liable to perpetrate massacres such as the one at Newtownbarry in June, when they opened fire on a very mild riot at an auction of cattle distrained for tithes and killed fourteen people. But he could not disarm them unless reinforced by 10,000 regular troops, both to supervise the disarming, 'a very ticklish job', and to take charge of internal security in the northern counties: 'I cannot afford to quarrel with them outright although I dislike them at least as much as you.'[25] There was another and very surprising reason for his concern:

The Orangemen were upon the balance. A feather would have turned the scale against us. An unnatural connexion was arising which, had it been allowed time to cement, would have led to the separation of the two countries. The rage for Repeal of the Union was at its height. The Orange and Green flags were about to be united. It was necessary to reclaim and enlist the high Protestant party ... I had nothing to trust to but the Yeomanry, and I had to save these from fraternizing with O'Connell.

Anglesey's solution to the problem was ingenious. The yeomanry were 'enregimented', i.e. embodied, provided with proper uniforms and arms suitable for a real war – but the arms were then withdrawn from them and stored in armouries from which they could only be issued under proper authority.

The case is this. O'Connell called them out, not I. One of us must have them and he was bidding so high for them that I was obliged to oppose him vigorously. If I had not won them, he would, in very short time, have had them as Repealers. I offered arms and red coats and saved them from him. Having got them, I now want to keep them out of harm's way by *forming* corps and taking away arms.[26]

Divide and rule – the classic imperial tactic.

It was a tragedy for Ireland that O'Connell and Anglesey were separated by an unbridgeable gulf of mutual distrust, for their ideas were very similar. Anglesey, indeed, might well have been a repealer, if repeal had not meant O'Connell. He told Lord Holland:

> The inconvenience or, I might say, the impossibility of legislating for Ireland from Downing Street is so obvious to me, that if it were not that no Parliament in Dublin would be free to do its duty, as Ireland now is, I should be against the Union ... The mischief in Ireland is not in the people. It lies with the Absentees and with the demoralized gentry. The lower orders are, for the most part, vilely oppressed and wickedly misled, imposed on by the priests and ground down by excessive exactions.

He could even, from time to time, make excuses for O'Connell:

> He has, in truth, a most intricate game to play. If he is to be useful, it is important that his character should not wholly break down with his Co-Agitators. I incline to think that he is riding the race well, and I am not disposed to jostle him.

> But, alas, he is the slave of vanity and of momentary impulse. He could not stand the taunts of a few worthless friends who suspected him. He feared that his mob popularity might be seized by other hands ... and has now irrevocably committed himself to violent agitation and mischief.

> Hard-pressed, His Excellency permitted himself to indulge in a pipe-dream: 'If I could but hang a dozen of each party, or perhaps two dozen of the Orangemen (exclusive of parsons), Ireland would do well enough.'[27]

Although neither trusted the other an inch and each wrote savage things about the other, there seems to have been an unspoken and unwritten understanding between Lord Lieutenant and Agitator. Young Henry Grattan, the great Grattan's son, sensed it, writing after O'Connell's death:

> What humbug is this they are going on with about O'Connell's principles? ... Why, O'Connell never had any *public principles at all*. He changed his opinion every session. We Protestants could never tell what he was driving at, and with the exception of Mad Steele and a few others, none of us could or would be led by him. *I myself* know that the Repeal *agitation* from the beginning was a delusion and was intended to be such. It was not my business to proclaim this, and even if I had, who would have believed me? I should have been denounced as an Orangeman and a false witness ... You may take my word for it that O'Connell during the greater part of the Repeal agitation was in *close* and *confidential* communication with the *Castle authorities*! That he had ample licence to *speak treason* in Ireland so long as there should be no outbreak of the people and so long as he should maintain the *Whigs in office*. The people were beginning to suspect this, but the influence of the *Bishops* and of the clergy and curates under their control always satisfied them for the time that whatever O'Connell said or did was right, and that it was *their* duty to support him. I could tell you some curious things.[28]

One curious thing he told, or, at least, hinted, was that the link between O'Connell and the Castle was 'Billy Murphy of Smithfield', who had been a 1798 rebel, had subsequently made a huge fortune in the cattle trade and took a zealous part in Dublin Catholic affairs, especially the collection and handling of the O'Connell Tribute. Entirely self-taught, he was very astute and had an astounding memory: it was said that he could take a hundred bullocks to market and, without a single note, remember the markings and price of every one. According to young Grattan, Anglesey took a liking to him: 'He had unbounded influence over Lord Anglesey, to the desperate annoyance of the Orange Order, Church and Castle corruptioners.' He was

> far superior to O'Connell in natural ability and, I believe, accommodated O'Connell with money occasionally. At all events he was of use to him, for though an *anti-Repealer*

211

O'Connell never ventured to quarrel with him as he did with Cloncurry, Peter Purcell and others.

Clearly young Grattan had a strong prejudice, perhaps inherited from his father, against O'Connell. His opinions are quoted at length not as gospel truth, but to illustrate the distrust O'Connell aroused even in those who were in agreement with his politics. Whether he had more confidential communication with the Castle than the single exchange of letters with Stanley about O'Gorman Mahon and the one interview with Anglesey, we do not know. But if Grattan believed this, no doubt others did too.

The interlocking issues of repeal and reform produced, for the Liberator, a chicken-and-egg dilemma. Which should come first, reform without which repeal might be impossible, or repeal without which reform would have no value for Ireland? In March 1831, when the details of the first Reform Bill were known, Thomas Wyse wrote:

> O'C is delighted, it will get him out of a scrape. He calls it an 'honest, substantial measure' and says he will now 'stop all agitation for the Union'. That in private, in public he says he will not bring on the question in the House if the measure be granted. He means not at all ... Some men may do anything with impunity.[29]

O'Connell was then reproached in Dublin for dropping repeal in favour of reform; and in November he was praised by English radicals for doing that very thing. A month later he positively boasted in a private letter, 'I turned the attention of the rest of the country [Ireland] from the overpowering question of the Repeal to the suitable one of Reform.' This he did to gain credit with the radicals in Westminster, but as soon as the English Reform Act was on the statute books he wrote:

> Repeal will be our cry; it will serve every purpose. In the first place it will compel a better Reform Bill for Ireland in order to disarm those who would otherwise join in the Repeal. Secondly, it will prepare the English mind for the more direct and constant agitation of the Repeal measure.[30]

His electoral machinery – the Catholic Association revived under one name after another – would support any candidate, even a Tory, who would pledge himself to repeal, and none who would not. Even Sheil was not beyond redemption, but

> unless Sheil gives the most explicit and unequivocal pledge to the Repeal, such a pledge as could not be explained away, I would not support him. I know him well and it would require a stout rope to keep him steady. He is a clever fellow ... but it costs him a great deal of trouble by not going straight-forward.

Sheil was a typical Angleseyite, and

> A whig or an Angleseyite is as bad for Ireland, indeed much worse, than a Conservative. A Conservative has but one fault, which is indeed a *thumper*: he wants Ascendancy – a thing impossible to be revived. But he is, after that, Irish, often very very Irish, and whilst in opposition may be made more Irish than the Irish themselves. An *Angleseyite*, on the contrary, is a suffocating scoundrel who would crush every Irish effort lest it disturb the repose of our English masters.[31]

The Irish Reform Bill was 'as bad as bad can be'. Only five extra seats were allotted to Ireland, though on a population basis there should have been many more; and two of these, Belfast and Trinity College, were of little use to him. The forty-shilling freeholders did not regain their vote, but the £10 freeholders were joined on the county voters' roll by holders of twenty-year leases worth £10 p.a. The best feature of the bill was the £10 leasehold franchise in boroughs, which broke the Protestant monopoly of power in Dublin and elsewhere.[32]

The Reform Acts cleared the ground. In the next general election, held in December 1832 and January 1833, he could concentrate, more than ever before, on repeal of the union.

For this election he revived the old Catholic Association in the guise of the National Political Union – same machinery, same methods and same personnel, less those who defected on the repeal issue. It was run in theory by a standing committee but actually by O'Connell himself who chose the candidates, the

213

election slogans and the essential policies to which sponsored candidates must subscribe – secret ballots, triennial parliaments, the abolition of tithes and church cesses, and, of course, repeal. FitzPatrick was his chief assistant, advising on constituency matters and personalities, keeping in touch with Richard Barrett, editor of the *Pilot*, and collecting the Tribute, of which he kept a percentage as his fee. The Union's headquarters in Dublin served as a clearing house for political information from all over the country. The Union was most active in the Dublin area where the two extremes of repeal and Orangeism were in stern conflict. From the first O'Connell realised the vital importance, with new franchise qualifications, of registering as voters as many as possible of his potential supporters and opposing the registration of potential opponents. It was efficient registration which gave him a decided advantage. There were an unusually large number of contested elections, in forty-five out of sixty-six Irish constituencies. Repealers contested nineteen counties and eighteen boroughs with their main efforts in the Dublin area, the south-east and south, and a few north midland constituencies: they did not waste resources on any forlorn hopes in the north-east.

O'Connell himself needed a firm and geographically convenient base. Eighteen months earlier he had declared in his election address, 'It is the height of my worldly ambition to be the representative of Kerrymen,' and from the hustings, 'While I live I will never ask a vote from any man but a Kerryman.' But in fact Dublin would suit him much better, so in August 1832 he had asked FitzPatrick to 'try how the ice will bear' there. In December he heard that Dublin had returned him 'unsolicited, even unavowed by me, perhaps the greatest triumph my countrymen have ever given me'. He longed to accept the seat if only he could find an understudy for Kerry. On Christmas Eve he wrote in triumph to FitzPatrick, 'I have cut the Gordian knot ... I succeeded in getting the patriotic people of Kerry to elect my son-in-law, Charles O'Connell, with Mr Mullins, and I BELONG TO DUBLIN.'

The general election of 1832–3 was on the same pattern as the Clare 1828 election, a class revolt of peasants against landlords. Some landlords took reprisals. Their power was still great. A freeholder could not be evicted simply for voting against his landlord's wishes, but he could be faced with a demand for immediate payment of rent and evicted if he could not find the money. It happened most notoriously in County Waterford after the Beresfords' defeat in 1826, and later in County Longford. But in some counties – Kerry, Kilkenny, Roscommon and King's County, for instance – the biggest landlords were Whigs and repealers, and O'Connell certainly expected them to tell their tenants how to vote.[33] He himself ordered the eviction of only one tenant for political reasons: the rascal had helped drive cattle distrained for tithes. The effect on the community of political evictions should not be exaggerated, however, for they were much less common than evictions for non-payment of rent or those perpetrated by 'improving' landlords intent on better estate management. After all, only one person in a hundred and fifty had the vote so only a small proportion of the rural population were at this particular risk. Much was made of O'Connell's fund for compensating victims in 1826 and 1832, but very little thereafter.

The Liberator's sons – Maurice for Tralee, Morgan (out of the Austrian army) for County Meath, and John for Youghal – and his sons-in-law – Charles O'Connell (Kate's husband, a distant cousin) for Kerry and Fitz-Simon for County Dublin – formed the core of his support in the House of Commons. His group in the first reformed parliament numbered thirty-nine, all pledged repealers. There were also from Ireland thirty-six anti-repeal Liberals and twenty-nine Conservatives (as the Whigs and Tories were respectively becoming known).

Greville remarked on how changed was the House of Commons since the Reform Act – all those new faces, and the swagger of O'Connell in his new role of party leader, walking about incessantly making signs to and talking with his followers. Thirty years earlier Henry Grattan had prophesied that with the union Ireland would take revenge for all her wrongs, 'she will send into England, and into the bosom of her parliament, and the very heart of her constitution, a hundred of the greatest rascals that can be found anywhere.' English M.P.s saw the election of O'Connell and his 'Tail' as the fulfilment of that bitter prophecy. Repeal M.P.s were constantly pictured and caricatured as ruffians of vulgar manners and low social status, Papists to a man. In fact they nearly all came from the same social class as most Liberal and Conservative Irish M.P.s. Of the thirty-nine 'joints in O'Connell's tail', thirty-one were landed gentry, the remainder lawyers and prosperous merchants; twenty-eight came from old landed families; and thirteen were Protestants. They did not as a rule own such large estates as Liberals and Tories, but they were of the same class. Nevertheless in London they suffered wounding social ostracism. Lady Salisbury was astonished the first time she met O'Connell in a gentleman's house, and Lord Melbourne remarked, 'Well, you know, after one has had O'Connell, one may have anybody.' Their only regular social entrée was to the house of the Liberal Irish peer Lord Duncannon, who acted as their link-man with the English Whigs. Meeting O'Connell there, Lady Holland liked him and would have been glad to see him at Holland House, but never actually invited him. He does not seem to have been at his best in English high society, for his manner was a mixture of embarrassment and arrogance. It must have been very trying to be regarded as a half-wild beast, imperfectly house-trained.[34]

The animus against O'Connell shown by *The Times* knew no bounds save those of actionable libel.

> Scum condensed of Irish bog,
> Ruffian, coward, demagogue!

'The worst being in human form that ever disgraced the floor of an English Senate' – such epithets flowed freely from the pens of the Thunderer's leader-writers. Goaded by such attacks, O'Connell hit back, not infrequently below the belt; constantly charged with Yahoo-ism, he sometimes behaved like a Yahoo, as when in a 'blackguard' speech he alluded 'with wretched ribaldry' to a bereavement in Stanley's family. It was, wrote Greville, one of those wretched and stupid brutalities which would obliterate (if possible) the great things he had done, but to recommend moderate language to O'Connell was about as reasonable as recommending him to drop his brogue.

It was held against repealers that (like modern trade union militants) they were too zealous, speaking at every opportunity, attending every debate and staying until the bitter end – all, by English standards, rather ungentlemanly. They suffered both from the odium in which poor Irish immigrants in the city slums were held, and from the disrepute attached in liberal circles to Irish landlords who were blamed for everything that went wrong in Ireland. English M.P.s resented the (much exaggerated) discipline of O'Connell's party, and also their pledges, quoting Burke's dictum that an M.P. should not be a mere delegate of his constituency. It was a time when behaviour in the Commons was as bad as it has ever been, before or since. Irish members were noisy and obstreperous, but no worse than the young Tories who drowned every speech of which they disapproved, especially from a repealer, with animal bellowings.

Nevertheless O'Connell continued to believe, or pretended to believe, that repeal was just around the corner. Surely he and his thirty-nine good men and true could force parliament to see its advantages for both countries. In April 1833 he exulted to FitzPatrick, 'It is here, it is here that the Repeal is to be carried. You have no notion of the state of the public mind.' In September he was sure that:

Without taking office I will be able to get, first, a number of bad magistrates removed; second, the yeomanry disarmed; third, the tithes abolished; fourth, the establishment of the Protestant Church reduced in every parish the overwhelming majority of whom are Catholics or dissenters; fifth, to have offices filled with Liberals to the exclusion of Orangeists ... Then, lastly but first in order of magnitude, there is the Repeal of the Union ... Believe me if God is pleased to spare my life but a few, very very few years longer (perhaps *months would* do, and I believe *months will do*) I will certainly have multitudes of Protestants of my party for the Repeal.

Again he said, 'I will not take office and I will not abandon the Repeal ... I want the Government to throw the Protestants into the ranks of the Repealers.' 'We must have Irish rents spent in Ireland. We must have no foreign landlords. Let those who will not live in Ireland sell their Irish estates ... Irish affairs must be managed by Irishmen.' 'Repeal', he assured FitzPatrick, 'is my first, my immediate, my constant duty.' But not too soon. When Feargus O'Connor, the future Chartist leader, M.P. for County Cork where he owned a small estate, pressed for immediate action on repeal at a meeting of repeal M.P.s, O'Connell opposed and narrowly defeated him.³⁵ The time was not ripe. The English were not in the mood to grant repeal. He was in an awkward dilemma, for if he brought forward the question too soon he would suffer an ignominious defeat in the Commons and expose the true weakness of his hand, while if he seemed to drag his feet his popularity in Ireland (to say nothing of the Tribute) would dwindle.

Whatever the frustrations of his public life, his family life was happy in the early 1830s. In 1831 Betsey had married (with her dowry paid in instalments) Nicholas Ffrench, a landowner in County Roscommon, and in 1832 Kate had married Charles O'Connell. Morgan came home to help his father in politics. Maurice and John were quite promising politicians, the former making a good debut in the Commons and, according to Anglesey, 'a match for most of our young combatants'. Danny was still at Clongowes, a dear, sweet fellow, abominably lazy over letter-writing. Early in 1832, while still at school, he was set up as partner in a new brewery (with FitzPatrick to keep an eye on him) – trading, without marked success, on the name Daniel O'Connell Jr & Co.

As for his Mary, 'My dearest love,' she wrote in December 1830,

> all our children quiz me not a little upon the regularity of your letters. I suppose they are surprised you should think so much of a little old woman as to write to her every post. It is a doubt to me, however, if even Sheil, who has got so much by his lovely wife, is as much attached to her as my darling old man is to his fond and grateful old woman.

Derrynane was his favourite place in all the world. With the additions he had made it was a comfortable family house rather than an imposing seat. It was of no particular style but rather the product of a series of afterthoughts. From the large first floor drawing-room, with windows on three sides, there were views to right and left over the gardens and plantations, and over the meadow and sand-dunes to the sea. Matching the drawing-room and directly below it was the dining-room. One wing contained O'Connell's private study below and the library above; the other, household offices and chapel. The bedrooms were on the second floor, with a bathroom containing a lead-lined bath, water for which was heated by a Cobbett stove. To landward of the house was a woody valley which sheltered the shrub and flower garden, entered through a tunnel under the avenue. There were bee-hives, a spring covered with an artificial canopy of shell-work, an orchard and a tower (or summer-house) where the Liberator used to retreat to plan his speeches and campaigns, or merely to escape the visitors for whom he kept open house. The visitors prolifer-ated, for O'Connell was acquiring a European reputation, even obtaining some votes in the 1831 election to choose a King of the Belgians.

He was a conscientious landlord. When there was a threat of famine in 1830, O'Connell's land agent, Primrose, was instructed to

> get any site you choose for the hospital. The excise on leather being off, this would be the time [to buy?] a tan yard ... I am sorry you did not give more than £20 to the poor. If they are starving near Derrynane, kill some sheep or a cow and give them and the calves – as they are produced – I would not rear one while the people want the flesh and the milk. Feed the dogs with grains and such food as the people would not use. Have all the boats fishing for the people. Give them all the salt fish as well as the fresh.

When cholera came dangerously near Derrynane, Primrose had to

> get Cahirciveen cleansed, whitewashed and as far as possible purified. I will readily sacrifice ten pounds or if necessary twenty for this purpose. The back yards of several of the houses were exceedingly filthy. It is incumbent to have clean-liness everywhere. Should this pestilence reach that country convert the old bridewell at my expense into an hospital or, if the new be finished, use it for that purpose. Give Mr Fitz-Gerald [the parish priest] in the event of the malady reaching you forty pounds from me to be laid out in *nourishing* the most destitute, for nourishment is of all things the best preservative. Nourishment and cleanliness are the two great protectors under God from this malady.

He dispensed justice like a clan chieftain.

> I decide all controversies in the district. I never allow a witness to appear until the plaintiff and the defendant have both fully told their tales and agree their *points*. In nine cases out of ten other testimony is unnecessary. The tribunal is so cheap, it costs them nothing; and is so expeditious that they reserve for me all their disputes, and it appears to me that they are satisfied with the results.

Written to Jeremy Bentham, one of whose bees-in-the-bonnet was the need for simpler, quicker, cheaper justice, it throws an interesting light on how a lawyer up to all the tricks of the trade would have liked justice to be dispensed in an ideal world – without lawyers.

His pride and joy were still his pack of beagles 'of the very best and most sagacious quality'. During his annual autumn holiday, which he enjoyed 'with the most exquisite relish', he hunted three days a week, and the only rule for his innumerable visitors was that, whatever their views on field sports, they should hunt too. It was no joke for men of sedentary habits. They were up before dawn, hurrying through the stone-walled fields of the demesne and up the steep, rocky mountainside for the first draw. The Liberator, running and leaping and hallooing up and down and across the mountain, in imminent danger of a broken ankle, showed extraordinary activity for a man of his age and weight. Not before a brace of hares had been killed would he stop for breakfast, in some prearranged spot where a jutting rock gave shade and shelter. While the visitors admired the stupendous view – the wide plain of Waterville, the distant islands of the Skelligs, the bays of Ballinskelligs and Valentia Island – O'Connell and the experts discussed every detail of the hunt: how hounds lost the hare when she ran through a flock of sheep, how the huntsman cast forward and old Drummer picked up the scent again. The postman toiled up the hill with a bag full of letters and Irish, English and continental newspapers, which the Liberator perused until it was time to start hunting again. And in the evening, exhausted with hard exercise and drunk with fresh mountain air, they walked back to Derrynane for hot baths and an early dinner. On non-hunting days O'Connell used to describe to the visitors, pointing up at the mountainside, all the best hunts he remembered – and he remembered most of them. Sometimes the company adjourned to an inn in Cahirciveen, kept by a remote O'Connell relation, and the conversation was entirely on hunting, shooting, fishing and agriculture. Some of the pilgrims to the shrine of Irish democracy must have felt that this was not quite what they had come for.

Maurice, alas, was so unnatural as to prefer his yacht to the beagles. 'There is nothing', he wrote in later years, 'men are more intolerant in than in their ideas of matters of amusement, and they do not see why all men should not be pleased with their own peculiar recreations. It was the only weak point in the Liberator's character.' O'Connell duly resented the yacht and begged Primrose to prevent Maurice throwing away more money on it. But Maurice eventually put his yacht to good use (or bad, depending on one's point of view), eloping in it with Mary Frances Scott, daughter of a County Clare Protestant landowner of Cromwellian descent. O'Connell and Mary were much annoyed, but soon forgave their son and wrote a loving letter urging the young couple to join the rest of the family at Derrynane. When the bride offered to accompany them to Mass, O'Connell insisted on sending her to the nearest Protestant church twelve miles away. He managed to establish friendly relations with Mary's father, although they were poles apart in politics, and thanked him for forgiving her eloping although 'she did wrong, very wrong, to marry without your consent.' Fortunately he and his Mary liked '*our* darling little Mary' and were delighted when she was 'in a certain way to give another O'Connell to the tribe'. This she did in August 1833 – a daughter, 'Fanny Fan Fan'.

O'Connell's own religious observances were devout and meticulously orthodox; he never made a slip in doctrine. He took the precaution, for instance, of consulting Archbishop Murray on the propriety of a Catholic taking the new parliamentary oath. (It was pronounced to be acceptable.) Among his papers were found the following 'Rules of Life':[36]

1 To avoid any wilful occasion of temptation.
2 To appeal to God and to invoke the Blessed Virgin and the Saints in all real temptation.
3 To recite the Acts of Faith, Hope and Charity every day.

4 To repeat, as often as may be, a shorter form.

5 To recite daily at least, and as often as may be, a fervent Act of Contrition.

6 To begin every day with an unlimited offering of myself to my crucified Redeemer, and to conjure Him, by all His infinite merits and divine charity, to take me under His direction and control in all things.

7 To meditate for at least half an hour every day if possible – longer if God pleases.

8 'We fly to Thy patronage' and St Bernard's prayer to the Virgin as often as may be convenient – daily.

9 To pray daily to God and the Saints for a happy death.

10 To avoid carefully small faults and venial sins – even the smallest.

11 To aim at pleasing God in all my daily actions, and to be influenced by the love of God in all, rather than by hope or fear.

Signed, Daniel O'Connell, Liberator of Ireland.

He attended Mass regularly, in Dublin almost every morning. He fasted when a fast was prescribed. It is curious how, from about 1830 onwards, expressions like 'with the help of God whose holy name be glorified' figure more and more in his letters, particularly his letters to Mary. He promoted the establishment in Ireland of a community of Trappist monks driven from France, and spent at least one week's retreat among them, astonishing even the Trappists by his austerity.

He stood for complete religious toleration – toleration for Catholics, Anglicans, Presbyterians, Quakers and Jews, and doubtless for Moslems and Hindus had any come his way. He stood for the complete separation of Church and state which he hoped would result from the Orleanist revolution of 1830 in France. In this he was disappointed, but the revolution did break the disastrous link between the Catholic Church and the legitimate branch of the Bourbon monarchy.

With these views, it is perhaps a little strange that, immediately after his re-election for County Clare, he should have written to Archbishop Murray, 'I wish to receive the instructions and commands of the Catholic prelates. I desire to consider myself their

1 At the County Clare election, 1828. O'Connell kneels before the Bishop. His son Maurice is kneeling behind him. Behind Maurice, standing and wearing the Order of Liberation, is O'Gorman Mahon.

THE GIANT & THE DWARF.

"The Dwarf who entered into an alliance
With a Giant, but who found that his tall comrade
Got all the plunder while he himself got all the blows"
Extract of speech at Crown & Anchor Feb 21ˢᵗ 1838.

2 O'Connell and Lord John Russell, 1838.

IRELAND'S BIG BULL-BEGGARMAN

3 A characteristic English Conservative view of O'Connell.

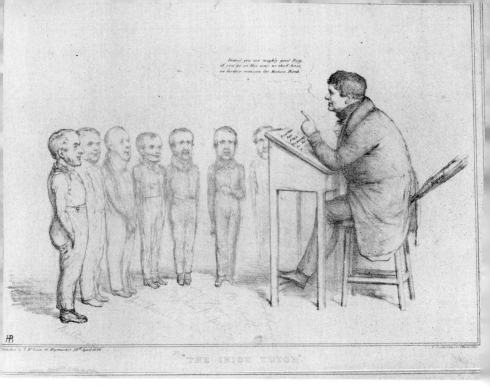

"THE IRISH TUTOR."

4, 5 and 6 *Above*, O'Connell and the Whig Cabinet, 1836: left, Melbourne; centre, Lord John Russell. *Below left*, O'Connell's problem with Young Ireland. *Below right*, *Punch* on the Irish potato famine.

"A GENTLEMAN IN DIFFICULTIES;" OR, DAN AND HIS "FORCES."

THE REAL POTATO BLIGHT OF IRELAND.

(FROM A SKETCH TAKEN IN CONCILIATION HALL.)

representative in some sort in Parliament.'[37] It is still stranger that four days earlier he should have written to Jeremy Bentham:

BENEFACTOR OF THE HUMAN RACE, I avowed myself this day on the hustings to be a Benthamite, and explained the leading principles of your disciples – the 'greatest happiness' principle – our sect *will* prosper. I begin my parliamentary career by tendering you my constant, zealous and active services in the promotion of that principle. You have now one Member of Parliament of *your own*.

The aged windbag's pet theory of 'utility' laid down: 'It is the greatest happiness of the greatest number that is the sole measure of Right and Wrong,' and said that 'Pain and Pleasure are the sovereign masters governing Man's conduct, it is for them alone to point out what we ought to do' – a strange doctrine for a devout and orthodox Catholic to embrace. It was Bentham's wish for a codified, simplified law that had the most practical appeal for Counsellor O'Connell, who treated his guru, his 'REVERED AND RESPECTED MASTER', with an admiration which was almost sycophantic.[38] Once again, one despairs of finding consistency in O'Connell.

Another celebrated political philosopher, Robert Owen the socialist, he treated with less respect. Owen sought his help in promoting 'a work of universal benevolence', and the Liberator replied blandly that he would always be happy to aid such a work.

'I expected no less from your character, Mr O'Connell. Would you not wish – I am sure you would – to elevate the conditions of the whole human race?'

'Certainly, Mr Owen.'

'Would you not wish to see a good hat on everybody?'

'Undoubtedly.'

'And good shoes?'

'Oh, certainly.'

'And good trousers?'

'Unquestionably.'

'And would you not desire to see the whole family of man well housed and fed?'

'Doubtless. But Mr Owen, as my time is much taken up, may

I beg that you will proceed at once to point out how all these desirable objects are to be worked out?'

Owen replied that the first necessity was to educate the population to atheism.

O'Connell rose and bowed him out. 'I wish you a very good morning, Mr Owen.'[39]

He was convinced that England would soon return to the Catholic faith: 'I hope I may yet live to see Mass offered up in Westminster Abbey. God has mercy yet in store for England.' Once, walking with Nell round Canterbury Cathedral, he remarked how strange it was that not a single Protestant prelate was buried there. The Cathedral guide heard him and asked, 'Are all these Archbishops Papists?'

'Every one of them, madam.'

'Bless me, I never knew that before!'

He described the High Altar as it would have been in olden times, ablaze with gold and jewels in the light of five hundred candles, and the great aisle, unimpeded then by organ-loft or other obstructions, thronged with kneeling worshippers. 'Oh!' cried the guide, clapping her hands, 'I should like to see that.' 'God grant you may yet,' he replied. Later he knelt to kiss the spot where Becket's blood was shed.

He used to say that Westminster Abbey, built and used for centuries by Catholics, had the atmosphere of a Christian church, but St Paul's, although a magnificent edifice, 'might as well be a temple to Neptune'.[40]

In nothing was O'Connell's instinctive social conservatism more clearly displayed than in his attitude to trade unionism.[41] He pleaded for mercy towards the Tolpuddle Martyrs because he was a compassionate man, but he thoroughly disapproved of labourers binding themselves by illegal, secret oaths to raise wages or improve working conditions. He understood perfectly the thoughts and grievances of small tenant farmers, cottiers and landless labourers, and sympathised with any measures they took, short of Whiteboyism, to improve their lot – indeed he devised various measures himself. He had no such understanding of the urban proletariat and no sympathy with their 'combinations'. Their leaders he denounced as ignorant, dishonest and incapable. It was in the main an English problem, but in Dublin too trade unionism was rearing its head. The Liberator was convinced that 'these combinations have had the most important and unhappy effect on wages and employment.'

Nor did the Dublin artisans give him the unquestioning adulation to which he was accustomed from his bucolic following. They gave him little credit for Catholic emancipation. 'What advantage is it', wrote the Dublin Trades Committee in an open letter to the Liberator, 'to the tradesmen of Ireland that 1,300 situations have been thrown open by Emancipation? Has it given a loaf of bread to any of the thousand starving families of the poor operatives in this city?' On the other hand they were very keen on repeal, contrasting ('with advantages') the glories and prosperity of Dublin when it was a capital city with its seedy provincialism in the 1830s. So their relations with O'Connell tended to be good when he was hot for repeal, and bad when he cooled towards it. They also varied with the price of bread in Dublin. When bread prices were high, in 1833 and from 1835 to 1837, trade unionism was militant and violent, with arson and the most savage assaults not only on blacklegs but on their families, who were knifed, bludgeoned, thrown into the freezing canals, and had vitriol thrown over them. O'Connell was appalled at the fate of a poor man who was

> going home peacefully in company with his wife. In her presence he was – Oh horrible! assassinated by two strangers employed for that purpose – men whom he had never offended – his only crime being having worked for the highest wages he could get but lower than some secret society or combination had fixed *for others*, as well as themselves.

(How very different from the conduct of his own bodyguard of honest Dublin coalies, or the cattle market butchers offering to take their cleavers to the peace officer who arrested him in 1831!)

In debates and peaceful confrontation between employers and unions he tried to avoid committing himself either way. But in fact he was opposed not merely to the unions' violence in pursuit of their ends but the ends themselves. He was, in modern terms, against the 'closed shop'; he was against a minimum wage; he was against restrictive practices such as the unions limiting the number of apprentices because these, used by employers as cheap labour, took jobs away from adults. All these union aims conflicted with the sacred theory of *laissez faire* and the no less sacred practice of monetarism. The workers, he explained to the Commons, 'were not entitled to wages out of capital; they were only entitled to them out of profits, and if their employers made no profits, then the wages must decrease.' It was in defence of the principles of *laissez faire* that in May 1836 he voted for an amendment to the Factory Bill which reduced from thirteen to twelve the age at which children ceased to be protected against long hours and gross exploitation. (When, however, it came to rural grievances, he was not nearly so dogmatic: he believed that the state should intervene to adjust the imbalance of economic power between landlord and tenant and, later, to prevent mass starvation.)

The Dublin artisans retorted with fury, warning him in the spring of 1833 that he would never again be returned for Dublin, and in 1837 that they 'would make daggers of their tongues and use them against him'.

With moral and political courage he faced – outfaced – them in two public meetings in January 1838. At the first, his three-and-a-half hour diatribe against combination malpractices was greeted with a furious uproar, he was in considerable personal danger and the meeting broke up in chaos. Three weeks later he confronted the same audience and confounded them by quotations from their own rule-books. Thereafter the price of bread fell, and with it the level of union violence. It was largely due to O'Connell that from 1838 until the advent of Jim Larkin the Dublin trade unions eschewed violence. In 1840 he started banging the repeal drum again, and from then until his death he was on good terms with the unions.

Nevertheless, if one accepts the premise that organised labour can do no wrong, the Liberator amply deserves the odium which has been heaped upon him by twentieth-century Irish socialists from James Connolly to Paddy Devlin.

Those sections of the English Poor Laws providing for the maintenance of illegitimate children he condemned as utterly destructive of female virtue. In many English counties

> not one woman in twenty is married amongst the working classes otherwise than in an advanced or at least very visible state of pregnancy. The moment a woman is pregnant she has

a choice of husbands. She can swear the child to any man she pleases and unless that man is capable of paying or securing a sum of about £40 he must either marry her or go to gaol. The consequences need not be described. A young woman is quite *safe* in a worldly sense to submit to illicit intercourse with unmarried men. If she be not pregnant she is not the worse in public estimation, that is she is not found out. If she becomes pregnant, the more men she has *a colour* of attributing the child to the better prospect she has of a husband to her choice ... One of the great temporal guardians of female chastity ... is thus done away, and a deluge of immorality opened upon the people ... If females be unchaste, there is but, alas, little prospect of restraining the passions of the male part of the community.

'An abandoned woman', he pointed out to 'J.K.L.', 'may easily and without the possibilty of detection impute the child to a totally innocent person. Nay, are the Catholic clergy quite safe from the vile perjury of any strumpet in the pay of an Orange or Biblical miscreant?'[42]

Holding (or at least expressing) these uncompromising views on chastity, O'Connell was particularly embarrassed when, in November 1831, a Cork-born former actress named Ellen Court enay[43] wrote to the English radical M.P. Henry Hunt (who detested O'Connell and enthusiastically took up her case), making a sensational accusation against the Liberator. In 1817, she alleged, when she was fifteen, she had consulted him about some property left her by her father. Eight months later, at their second meeting at his house in Merrion Square, he had raped her, as a result of which she had borne a son for whose maintenance he refused to pay. O'Connell fired back at Hunt a total denial, pointing out that the story, if true, would have been worth any money to his enemies in Ireland at any time in the past thirteen years. He hinted that 'H. Hunt' was trying to blackmail him. The painful affair dragged on, with Miss Courtenay publishing next year, while in a debtor's prison, a pamphlet describing his conduct. She alleged that Father L'Estrange, his confessor in Dublin, had given her £20 hush-money and begged her to destroy her seducer's letters; and that Major MacNamara had placed the boy in one of those 'charitable institutions which are favoured with many of Mr O'Connell's illegimate offspring'. The scandal rumbled on in the columns of *The Times* which was, as always, hostile to O'Connell. In 1836 John O'Connell was fined twenty shillings for striking the eighteen-year-old boy who claimed to be his half-brother, and the boy was warned by the court against further pestering.

In a court of law there would have been no case for O'Connell to answer, but in such matters it is innocence, not guilt, which must be proved, and he could not prove his innocence. According to Miss Courtenay the boy was born on 4th November 1818. His correspondence shows that he was in Dublin where the rape was alleged to have taken place, from early November 1817 to late February 1818, so he had no alibi. Nor was he really helped by his discovery that she had been on the stage in England 'during the years 1815, 1816 and 1817'. Hunt alleged that she had other children: 'I have ascertained that she has not one!!!' But if he announced his discovery the public would be likely to blame him for evading his responsibilities than to blame her for lying.

If there had been the child's birth certificate, a record of admission to a foundling home, a record of her teaching (as she claimed) at a 'boarding school of the first class' in Dublin before the alleged rape, or proof of any property in Cork which she had inherited from her father whom she described as a prominent man and owner of several elegant houses, one may be quite certain that *The Times* or other enemies of O'Connell would have disclosed it. But no confirmation of her story was ever discovered. It is simply her word against his, and she had an obvious motive, blackmail.

It is also possible that she was put up to it by O'Connell's political enemies. On 28th February 1831, nine months before approaching Hunt, she had tried to enlist the support of O'Gorman Mahon, M.P. for Clare before he was unseated. 'Many persons', she informed him, had urged her to publish the entire facts and 'make her fortune', but she was deterred by delicacy and patriotism. There is no record of O'Gorman Mahon taking any action, but someone must have paid for the printing and publication of the pamphlet, sold at half a crown, which she wrote in the debtors' prison. Why was there a nine months' gap before she wrote to Hunt? Did her political backers insist on her going to prison so as to gain the utmost sympathy? Her pamphlet was packed with denunciations of O'Connell's politics and praise for the 'worthy, intelligent and excellent Knight of Kerry'.

The strongest point against O'Connell is that neither Father L'Estrange nor MacNamara seems to have denied her story, though the priest remained the Liberator's confessor and political supporter until his death in 1833, and the major must have been reconciled to O'Connell, after their quarrel in Clare, by April 1832, when they shared a chaise from Holyhead to Liverpool only five months after Miss Courtenay's letter to Hunt.

She alleged that he had promised to let her have plenty of money on the death of his 'uncle, Mr Morgan O'Connell'. He could never have told her that his uncle's name was Morgan, so she must, before opening her campaign, have done her homework by investigating his background, and not done it very well.

Would a fifteen-year-old girl have consulted, unchaperoned, a lawyer about her property? Unlikely, but not impossible. From the family correspondence at that time, it seems that Mary and the children were in Merrion Square from November 1817 to the end of February 1818. Would he have taken the risk of assaulting her in his house full of family and secretaries who would have heard the screams and prayers for mercy which she said she had uttered? Again unlikely, but not impossible. Why did she then take no legal steps to obtain justice? She surely forfeits all credibility by the assertion that 'he has ten or twelve females whom he seduced compelled to visit him *at his own home*, in the midst of his grown-up family, or they would be deprived of the wretched pittance which he occasionally doles out to them.' At his own home, in the midst of his grown-up family – the very last place any man would choose for a pay-parade of his discarded mistresses!

O'Connell had his faults, but stinginess was not among them. Refusal to pay for his bastard in 1818, even though he was then very short of money, does not seem in character. And in 1831, when he had inherited Derrynane and was in ample funds from the Tribute, a refusal to take the easy course of buying the lady's silence is surely an indication of innocence.

The strongest point in O'Connell's favour is that in his correspondence with his wife during 1818 and again in 1831-2 there is not the slightest hint that she was suspicious or angry. On the contrary: on 25th March 1818, seven weeks after the alleged rape, she wrote that her brother

> says that I ought to lecture you well for being such a plague to young girls. He little knows how often I have *lectured* you on *that* subject to no purpose. Really, darling, it is a shame to annoy the poor girls so much. My poor Ellen often gets a complexion from you.

Unless one assumes that Mary was amazingly tolerant of infidelities – and there is no indication of this in eight volumes of correspondence – this teasing reproof surely means that she trusted him absolutely. It also suggests, however, that if Miss Courtenay had in fact consulted him on business, he might have behaved towards a very young and attractive girl in a jocularly flirtatious way that put ideas into her head. Two days later Mary ended another letter, 'I beg, my love, you will burn all my letters as you read them. I have a particular reason for making this request which I will tell when we meet.' She might have heard a whisper of scandal, and not believed it of her Dan.[44]

One cannot say with certainty 'Not Guilty', but one can say 'Not Proven'. Anyway, whatever M.P.s and *The Times* may have said of the matter, it probably did him no harm in Ireland. Indeed by embellishing his image of the Gaelic hero, which image does not perhaps exclude the possibility of a bit of harmless rape, it may have done him a power of good; for in this citadel of female chastity, a politician reputed to be 'a right boy-o' was, and is, held in high esteem provided only that he keeps out of the English divorce courts.

The Ellen Courtenay affair was an embarrassing distraction from more important events. Stanley, O'Connell wrote, had some success in suppressing lawful political activity, but 'the spirit which is curbed by day walks abroad at night. Whiteboyism is substituted for open meetings ... There never yet was so general a disposition for insurrectionary outrages.' The Agitator urged the authorities to reinforce the 'King's troops' in Ireland, otherwise the yeomanry would be called up and the consequences would be dreadful. Faced by 242 murders and 568 cases of arson in 1832, with wholesale intimidation of victims and witnesses, with the rural population refusing to give the authorities the smallest bit of information or assistance, the government decided, against Anglesey's advice, to bring in the harsh Coercive Measures (Ireland) Bill. It empowered the Lord Lieutenant to suspend Habeas Corpus, to replace ordinary courts by courts martial, to ban all meetings for petitioning parliament save those which had his prior consent, and to proclaim disturbed areas in which no public meeting of any kind could be held.

O'Connell was as strong as anyone for law and order, but thought that this 'Algerine Bill' provided powers which no government should have. In furious speeches he denounced the record in Ireland of English governments since Henry II, insisted that present disturbances were due to past oppression, and that if peaceful political activity were suppressed ('Do the Whiteboys hold public meetings?') there would be 'a revolution of the sword'.

He organised the presentation of hundreds of petitions against various aspects of the bill, particularly the substitution of trial by court martial for trial by jury in proclaimed areas. A Tory member interrupted, 'If it were deemed necessary, I am sure that petitions could be obtained from every town and village in England calling upon Parliament to defeat schemes of persons who agitate the country in order to promote their own selfish interests.'

O'Connell: 'I ask whether the Honourable Member alludes to me?'

Honourable Member: 'My observation applies to any person who desires to create a party in Ireland for the purpose of injuring His Majesty's peaceable and orderly subjects.'

O'Connell: 'I am answered. The Honourable Member does not allude to me.'

He resorted to the tactics of delay and obstruction that Parnell was to imitate – dividing the House on every pretext, prolonging proceedings until all but he (and his Tail, called up in relays) were almost dead with fatigue, diverting debates into interminable windy discussions of Irish grievances, and appealing to radical organisations outside parliament. He objected particularly to trial by court martial and to treating a refusal to pay tithes as though it were a criminal, almost a treasonable offence. Army officers, he insisted, were utterly unfit to be judges of the law of the land:

The whole course of education of military men, their want of discrimination and their habits of life unfit them for the office assigned them by this Bill. I cannot express in sufficiently strong terms my contempt for that species of tribunal which the Bill empowers to act to the extent of secret imprisonment and transportation.

Why, this iniquitous measure was nothing more than a Tithe Bill in disguise! It would permit the imprisonment, nay even the whipping, of a miscreant who had not paid his tithes!

It was claimed as a justification for the bill that witnesses did not come forward before ordinary courts of common law.

What power have the military tribunals to compel their attendance? It is said that courts of law are inoperative for want of sufficient evidence. Are these military tribunals to act with less? Are there no such things as informers, men who traffic in blood and for a paltry pittance will sell the lives of their fellow-subjects?

As a lawyer he explained to the House that informers were nearly always accomplices, and the admissibility of accomplice evidence, requiring corroboration, was one of the hardest questions for an experienced judge to determine: 'yet all this is to be settled by these military red-coated judges.'

It was argued that the bill would have a sedative effect. 'Yes: such a sedative effect as a blister has on a sore, or a scourge to a crying child: the scourge will make the child crouch, but it will scarce make it quiet.'

Gradually his support built up, as one English M.P. after another decided that the 'Algerine Bill' really did go too far. He obtained two important modifications to the original bill: a district would not be proclaimed as a disturbed area merely because of widespread refusal to pay tithes; and political offences, as distinct from criminal offences such as murder and arson, would not be tried by court martial. The 'emasculated Bill' as finally passed in April 1833 was, he thought, more foolish than infernal. 'I battled against it in despair but, blessed be God, not in vain. Its fangs were drawn.'

Several Irish Whigs voted for the bill. Even a repealer, Henry

Grattan, said in private, 'I wish to heaven you would hang or shoot O'Connell and pass some Algerine Act if you like, but not this one.' Sheil had, ostensibly, returned to the fold as repeal M.P. for Tipperary. (The cost, he said, was immense; but his wife could afford it.) He duly voted against the Coercion Bill, but was accused of privately urging ministers, 'Don't bate one single atom of the Bill, or it will be impossible for any man to live in Ireland.' He flatly denied these words, and O'Connell, with some magnanimity, supported him. Since the row had been aired in the press it was referred to the Committee of Privileges which exonerated Sheil. But some of the mud stuck and, in all probability, rightly stuck.[45]

In November 1833 the government prosecuted Richard Barrett, editor of the *Pilot* which was virtually O'Connell's house magazine, for seditious libel, in that he had published O'Connell's 'Letter to the People of Ireland'. The mere fact that the letter appeared over O'Connell's name was no evidence that he had written it – unless Barrett were to peach or O'Connell were to confess; and the government's obvious intention was to force O'Connell either to admit authorship and be prosecuted, or to experience the embarrassment of letting Barrett suffer on his behalf. O'Connell chose the latter alternative but not, apparently, without a twinge of conscience, for when Barrett hinted that the former might be more seemly, O'Connell in a long, self-exculpatory letter made it clear that this was a risk all editors took when the libel law was such that, with a properly chosen judge and jury, it could 'produce a conviction for the Lord's Prayer'. Editors could 'reject what they please, and publish what will increase their circulation'. He himself *could* not go to prison. 'There was never a moment in my political life when it was so essential for the interests of Ireland that I should be at large.' The court of the King's Bench, he pointed out, might send him down for *three years*.

I should be mad if I were to publish in Ireland without *considering* myself safe from personal detention . . . I always heard that you concur with me in these views. The pecuniary obligations are mine and mine alone. I think that the personal suffering, subject certainly to the right to the fullest compensation within my power, is yours.

It was more prudent than quixotic. Barrett, not very content, went down for six months; O'Connell paid his £50 fine and £556 in compensation, and attended a public dinner to celebrate his release.[46]

O'Connell's manipulation of the press became more effective and more crude in the mid-1830s. Barrett simply wrote what he was told to write. The *Freeman's Journal* and *Register* generally (but not always) followed O'Connell's party line, whatever that might be at the time, as did several radical provincial papers. In the days of the Catholic Association O'Connell had tried to buy newspapers by ordering large quantities every week which were distributed free. It had not worked because people did not value or believe what they were given free. It was better to 'Take care that our advertisements shall be a good thing for the honest papers ... See' (he instructed John) 'how you can augment the advertisements to compensate the papers that serve us.' Of course the Castle was up to the same game, more directly through the Secret Service Fund.[47]

O'Connell knew in his bones that any motion for repeal was, in the circumstances of 1833–4, a forlorn hope, but his followers kept jostling him from behind. 'Feargus O'Connor', he wrote in June 1833, 'has had his brains blown out by the trash in the *Freeman's Journal* and he has, without condescending to consult me, fixed his Union debate for the 16th of the next month.' O'Connell was convinced that 'this uncalculating and coarse-minded fellow' would do great mischief. Mary, whose political judgment he treated with increasing respect, advised him to have nothing to do with Feargus O'Connor's crazy initiative which was, in the event, not taken. But at last the pressure from behind became irresistible, and in April 1834 O'Connell moved in the House that a committee be appointed to examine the results of the union.

In a five-hour speech O'Connell was not at his best. He opened with his basic claim.

We are a separate nation. You have obtained no dominion here. This country owes allegiance to your King - he is ours, as he is yours. Ireland belongs to your King as England belongs to him: we belong to the same King, but we ought to have separate legislatures.

He proceeded with the familiar recital of Irish grievances over six hundred and fifty years, and passed on to the matter of inequitable taxation. Permitting an English parliament to tax the people of Ireland was like sending a hundred M.P.s over to the French Chamber of Deputies in order that that body might tax the people of England. 'It would be a suggestion that could only be considered as the act of a madman.' The Irish national debt at the time of the union was a mere £17 million: 'at present we owe, in conjunction with England, about £800 million and must bear an equal taxation with you until it is paid up.'

The emancipated convicts of Botany Bay have a parliament of their own, we have none, and we are eight million. The slave-drivers in the West Indies and the fishermen of Newfoundland have domestic legislatures, we are without one, and we are eight million. The United States of America threw off the British yoke and obtained freedom by the sword; they were three million, and we are eight million.

He then, unfortunately, proceeded to bore the House with interminable statistics purporting to show how prosperous Ireland had been before the union and how that prosperity had now vanished. But that was a game two could play, for statistics, suitably selected, can prove anything, and if he could bore the House with them (as he admitted he had done) then Thomas Spring-Rice, a County Limerick landlord, could argue at even greater statistical length that Ireland had benefited immeasurably from the union, particularly Irish agriculture from free access to the expanding English market. The division was humiliating to O'Connell, if not entirely unexpected – 523 to 38,[48] with only one English M.P. supporting his motion, and that because he thought it would strengthen the case for the union to have its results examined.

Thus ended in ignominy his first campaign for repeal. He was getting nowhere, and there was plenty to be done for Ireland by a Liberator willing to eat his own words and revert to the politics of the eighteenth century. To the faithful FitzPatrick he wrote:

You must not suppose there is the least relaxation of my opinions on the subject of the Repeal. My conviction on that subject is really unalterable, but I will get *what I can* and use the Repeal merely *in terrorem* until it is wise and necessary to recommence the agitation ... Take care this letter does not get into print.

Six weeks later he promised FitzPatrick to press on with repeal, but in fact did nothing about it.[49]

12

The Wheeler-Dealer

The government's character was changing. In 1833 Anglesey and Stanley had been replaced at the Castle by the Marquis Wellesley and Edward Littleton,* a change, in O'Connell's opinion, very much for the better. The Cabinet split on one of those bitter 'who-said-what' rows, arising out of the Coercion Bill. Littleton had given O'Connell the clear impression that the more liberal members of the Cabinet had defeated the more conservative, whereas in fact the opposite was true – Grey had overruled the liberals. O'Connell brought before the House his conversation with Littleton. The revelation that a member of the Cabinet had been dealing with the Agitator behind the Prime Minister's back led to the resignation, in a huff, of Lord Grey, described by O'Connell as 'a wretched old man with a childish hatred and a maniacal contempt for the people of Ireland'. O'Connell, never one to muffle his own trumpet, claimed, 'the dexterity with which the Ministry endeavoured to deceive me has been their own ruin. It was I, in fact, that turned out the Administration ... and if the next one be not better, I will turn that out also.' Grey was succeeded by Lord Melbourne, another change for the better. Better still, in May 1834 Lord John Russell, 'manly and determined', gave notice in the House that he favoured a Tithes Bill with *appropriation*, at which Stanley and three more of the

---

*There was a six weeks' gap between Stanley and Littleton, filled by Sir John Hobhouse.

conservative-minded ministers resigned. O'Connell rejoiced in, and took credit for, these changes: 'My victory is therefore admitted by everyone to be complete, and its ultimate results will, I think, be eminently useful to Ireland. We are on the way from a half-Whig, half-Tory government to one half-Radical, half-Whig.' He could work with such a government, perhaps even *in* such a government. Although in June 1834 he assured Fitzpatrick that he would not relax on repeal, other possibilities seemed to be opening to him. 'Have you a mind to be Lady O'Connell, my own heart's darling love?'[1]

In July O'Connell's friend (or patron), Lord Duncannon, became Home Secretary, an Ascendancy Protestant but of liberal views who knew well the Irish scene. O'Connell bombarded him with advice on Irish appointments, and in October seemed to be hinting that the 'Popular Party', i.e. the repealers, might still be conciliated if they had a fair share of the loaves and fishes and if the government acted generally in an enlightened manner in Ireland. The Whig dilemma was that only a more liberal policy would undermine O'Connell's influence, but the more liberal it was, the stronger the opposition from the Tories, and the more they would need O'Connell's support.

In November 1834 William IV, in a forlorn attempt to turn back the clock, dismissed the Whigs and called upon Peel to form a government. Peel could not do so, and there was a general election at the turn of the year. In this election O'Connell played down repeal and was uncharacteristically subdued. He must even have omitted to devote due care and attention to the registration of electors in his own Dublin constituency and left until far too late the vital task of ensuring that all his supporters had paid their rates, without which they were not qualified to vote. He even feared he might be beaten: 'I really think we have now no prospect of success.' In the event he did get in, but with a greatly reduced majority, and was promptly threatened with a petition for his unseating on the grounds that many of those who voted for him were not properly qualified. Overall in this election the Tories gained, but not enough to give them a clear majority in the Commons. The radicals gained also, and the Whigs lost ground. The final count of Irish seats was thirty-four repealers (five fewer than in 1831–3), thirty-three Whigs and thirty-eight Tories.[2]

With party membership less clear-cut than it is today, estimates of party strengths in the 1835 House of Commons vary. One calculation is that the Conservative government could count on 280–290 supporters against 218 Whigs, 116 radicals and O'Connell's 'Tail' of 33 repealers. Another calculation makes out that the government had 306 votes in the Commons against a combined Opposition of 316 Whigs, radicals and O'Connellites. However the calculations are made the Opposition was clearly in a strong position, but only so long as they could rely on the support of O'Connell. He was the only party leader who could command anything like a block vote – thirty-three repealers whom he controlled absolutely, and a number of Irish Whigs who generally voted with him. There was therefore an obvious case for a Whig-radical-O'Connellite alliance based (whatever their mutual aversion) on mutual benefits.

In February 1835 O'Connell wrote direct to Lord John Russell, the diminutive, blue-blooded, philanthropical Whig, offering from sixty to sixty-two Irish votes and a promise that 'the Irish members of the popular party will avoid all topics on which they may differ with you and your friends *until the Tories are routed*'. Russell was at first inclined to cold-shoulder him, but Duncannon persuaded him that he could not afford to be too squeamish, so he returned a civil reply, agreeing that they would work together to defeat the Tory ministry but adding warily, 'while I do not ask you to give up any of your opinions on public questions, you will of course understand that I cannot give up any of mine.'

At a series of talks there was hammered out what became known (from the venue of the negotiations) as the Lichfield House Compact. O'Connell guaranteed that his sixty good men and true would help turn out the Tories and then support the Whig government provided it followed a policy towards Ireland which was in patronage helpful to Catholics, and in general progressive. O'Connell's terms included a Tithes Bill with appropriations, unspecified amendments to the Irish Reform Act, and municipal reform. With O'Connell's help Peel was defeated in April and May 1835, specifically on an Opposition amendment to a government Tithes Bill which would have attached to it an appropriation clause. On 8th May Peel gave up and a Whig government under Lord Melbourne came in, with Russell in the key post of Home Secretary. O'Connell in jubilant mood wrote an open letter to the people of Ireland: 'A new day begins to shine upon us – a new era opens for Ireland – an Administration is formed pledged ... to justice for Ireland. I avow myself the devoted supporter of that Administration.'[3]

He certainly expected his reward, and on that there was a split in the Cabinet. The majority, who favoured giving him office, were overborne by two ministers, Irish landlords, who insisted on a longer period of probation. O'Connell half hoped to be offered either the Attorney Generalship or even the Chief Secretaryship of Ireland, but made no trouble when the half-offers were withdrawn. Later he refused the consolation prize of Mastership of the Irish Rolls, either because it was too trivial or because its acceptance would be seen in Ireland as a reward for good behaviour. Unimpeded by place, he prided himself that:

> I have been most highly flattered and thanked etc for my conduct, and yet it would be not only folly but guilt in me to accept any office until *I had seen* how the new Ministry works. My policy is obvious – to keep what control I have *over* the new government instead of being under *their* control. I will be more useful by influencing the appointments of others than by submitting to take an appointment myself.[4]

In the event he was often consulted on appointments and the Castle seldom in the next six years appointed anyone of whom he disapproved. As for repeal, he assured FitzPatrick that he was as much a repealer as ever, but wished to give the union a fair trial under a friendly ministry. He rationalised his decision as being designed to 'convince the most sceptical' that nothing but a domestic parliament will do Ireland justice'.[5]

So began a period of six years in which O'Connell operated not as an agitator in Ireland and a political pariah in Westminster, but as a pragmatic, not unsuccessful, wheeler-dealer politician, more concerned (like any eighteenth-century M.P.) with patronage than with causes.

In his family, 1834 was not a very happy year. Morgan, in no position to marry, trifled with a sweet and lovely girl; Mary was instructed, 'No, my heart, you must put an end to the idea ... Break the matter off, darling, in the kindest way you possibly can.' Later, however, he returned to his father's good books by

240

an unsuspected talent at after-dinner speech-making, short and to the point. Dan fell very ill and took a long time to recover. Also, the porter brewed by his brewery was of superlative quality but, his father feared, too expensive for anyone to buy – and his father was right, for no one did buy it. Nell's and Kate's babes were treasures, but by the autumn of 1834 he was beginning to realise that Maurice's Mary was not. She announced herself pregnant for the second time with a baby due in mid-November, and begged her mother-in-law to stay with her at Derrynane until the happy event. This was most inconvenient, as politics were in a flux and O'Connell up to his eyes in work; he wanted his Mary in Dublin. It was more than inconvenient when, by December, he was involved in a general election and the baby had still not arrived. 'Perhaps she is not with child after all ... What a prize my unfortunate Maurice drew for himself in the lottery of life. But he clearly has nobody to blame but himself which after all is but a poor consolation' ... 'Is it certain she is with child at all for I have my doubts? She fell into such a fatness, which is a symptom of ceasing to breed.' It was indeed cruel that, when he was so frantically busy with that plaguey election, 'Mary O'Connell should thus separate us. I believe the silly woman is not with child at all ... She could not mistake by so many months and her excessive corpulence and great appetite favour my opinion.' He positively believed she was playing a trick on them: 'I really have no patience with Maurice's wife. What, to mistake three months! It is impossible.' On 17th December he wrote in despair, 'What are we going to do with Mary O'Connell and her eternal pregnancy? I do not believe the foolish woman is with child at all.' But on the very next day he heard she had produced a daughter, little Mary, and all was forgiven – or nearly forgiven: 'I am glad, sincerely glad, to hear that Mary is so well.' But his daughter-in-law's fecklessness and lack of consideration still rankled, and for the next six years, until the break-up of the marriage in 1841, she is hardly mentioned in his correspondence. He had always been opposed to mixed marriages, and this confirmed his view.

The first-fruits of the Lichfield House Compact were bitter. Since the ministry was obviously kept in office only by O'Connell, the full wrath of the Tories turned against him as they made the most of two scrapes which would have embarrassed a more sen-

sitive soul. In April he had occasion, in the House, to call Lord
Alvanley a bloated buffoon, a liar, a disgrace to his species, and
heir-at-law to the thief on the cross. It was the kind of pleasantry
which came readily to his lips and which was hardly out of place
in the parliament of his day. But his lordship, who was indeed
robustly built, took exception to the remark and sent a friend
with the usual sort of message.

> I am aware that you assume to yourself a right to insult with
> impunity, and I can hardly hope that you will make an excep-
> tion in my favour by doing what any other gentleman would
> do, and giving satisfaction where you have offered insult. I,
> however, give you the option of doing so.

O'Connell replied to Alvanley's second:

> Lord Alvanley's letter is nothing less than a challenge to fight,
> to be delivered to me in London ... an inconvenient distance
> as the letter is dated at Clifden.* But this letter assumes an air
> of mere comicality when it turns out to be sent by one person
> in Clifden to another person in London, to be transmitted
> thence to a third person in Dublin, to fight a duel at a truly
> long shot. This, as we say in Ireland, 'bangs Banagher'. It is,
> after all, but an unvalorous – I believe I have coined the proper
> word – absurdity in Lord Alvanley to send me a challenge
> when my sentiments on that subject have been so publicly and
> so repeatedly proclaimed.

Alvanley's friends then set on foot a move to expel him from
Brook's Club for conduct unbecoming a gentleman. But this
came to nothing, and the matter was soon forgotten in a more
unseemly scandal.[6]

In May, the Tory members for County Carlow were unseated
on petition, and O'Connell invited an anglicised Armenian named
Raphael, a somewhat exotic candidate for an Irish constituency,
to contest the seat on paying him, O'Connell, £1,000 on nomination and a like sum on being returned. 'You will', Raphael was

---

* It was not so remarkable as it would be nowadays, since it then took only
two days for a letter from London to be delivered in Dublin.

assured, 'never again meet so safe a speculation,' as O'Connell additionally guaranteed him against any further expenses, including the cost of fighting any petitions. Raphael, with the help of the O'Connell machine, was duly elected, but was promptly threatened by a petition for his unseating. O'Connell undertook to fight the petition at his own expense on receipt of Raphael's second £1,000 instalment: 'it is necessary – *absolutely necessary* – that it should be paid *this* day.' He held to the letter of the agreement: Raphael had been returned and should pay up. To Raphael, however, suspecting that he had been conned, this interpretation did not commend itself, and he felt obliged to pay the second instalment only when his return was secured. In high dudgeon O'Connell wrote, 'I can hardly restrain my feelings on hearing that you shrink from performing your engagement with me. Rely on it, you are mistaken if you suppose that I will submit to any deviation from our engagement.' Raphael then, 'to prevent all possibility of doubt as to good faith on my part', paid the £1,000,* while expressing indignation at the tone of O'Connell's letter. O'Connell then proffered, somewhat clumsily, an olive branch: 'Tell me, in the strictest confidence, whether you have any wish to be a baronet.' In the end the unfortunate Raphael obtained neither the baronetcy nor the seat, and paid the costs of fighting the petition unsuccessfully. The Tories then moved for a parliamentary inquiry into whether O'Connell had sold a seat; the committee exonerated him of corruption, but declared – a meiosis, some might think – that his conduct had been intemperate.[7]

But there were, or seemed to be, better things in store. Besides claiming for Catholics a fair share of the loaves and fishes, O'Connell, in setting out his terms for the Lichfield House Compact, had stipulated that there should be reforms in municipal government and relief of tithes. The ministry tackled first the municipalities.[8] O'Connell was not particularly interested in local government for its own sake. (Who is, apart from those with a finger in the pie?) But he was interested in changing a system in which Protestant Corporations elected Protestant Sheriffs who chose Protestant jurymen in politically slanted cases. He was

---

* It should be added that O'Connell did not pocket the money, which went to pay the election expenses of Raphael's running-mate, Nicholas Vigors.

particularly concerned with Dublin where Catholics were in constant confrontation with a strong, well-entrenched and militant Protestant minority whom he had tried, without success, to convert to repeal.

In 1835 there were sixty Irish boroughs, most of which derived their privileges from charters issued by the Stuarts with the intention of increasing the royal power. The typical borough was governed, in a manner of speaking, by a Corporation consisting of a governing body and Freemen, fewer than twenty in number and exclusively Protestant. (Only four boroughs had any Catholic Corporation members.) Thirty had no annual income at all, and only seven had incomes over £1,000 a year. Two-thirds were in debt. There was no general right, not even by residence, of admission to the Corporations, and most recruited their members by 'grace especial', which is to say that they were self-elected. But they exercised great power in what was euphemistically known as 'justice'. They appointed, for life, corporate magistrates; they selected Sheriffs, and the Sheriffs selected the jurymen.

The Dublin Corporation, O'Connell's especial interest, consisted of a Common Council composed of two houses. The upper house was self-elected and had the useful privilege of admitting freemen, thereby conferring the parliamentary vote on those who might not qualify as £10 householders. The lower house was elected on a very narrow franchise, as were the Lord Mayor, Sheriffs and aldermen. In practice, though not in theory, the system excluded Catholics and liberal Protestants from admission as freemen and from the Corporation patronage. The Grand Jury, which voted municipal taxes amounting to about £30,000 a year, and the assize session juries, were notorious for partisan policies and verdicts. Despite a debt of allegedly over £30,000, the Lord Mayor and aldermen received salaries of £4,000 and £2,000 respectively.

In the summer of 1835 the ministry set to work at cleansing the Augean stables with an Irish Municipal Reform Bill proposed by the Irish Attorney General, Louis Perrin. In it, town councils would be elected in the larger towns on a £10, and in the smaller towns on a £5 household franchise. One-third of the council would come up for election annually, as would the Mayor. In those large towns and cities which were themselves legal counties,

Sheriffs would be elected by the council. The powers and proceedings of the borough courts were defined; their magistrates would be selected by the Lord Lieutenant from lists submitted by the councils. O'Connell expressed his 'infinite delight' at this bill, which passed the Commons without a division. Their lordships, however, owing to other preoccupations, never got down to debating it before the session ended and the bill automatically lapsed.

It had, however, provided the occasion for a Billingsgate duel between O'Connell and Disraeli who, endeavouring to overcome the heavy parliamentary handicaps of being a Jew, a dandy and an intellectual, resorted to the usual Tory convention of abusing the Irish Agitator. O'Connell, he wrote in *The Times*, was 'a systematic liar and a beggarly cheat, a swindler and a poltroon ... His public and private life are equally profligate; he has committed every crime that does not require courage.' He must, however, acquit O'Connell of religious hypocrisy in humbling himself in the mud before a simple priest:

the agent recognized his principle, the slave bowed before his Lord. When he pressed to his lips those robes, reeking with whiskey and incense, I doubt not that his soul was filled at the same time with unaffected awe and devout gratitude.

O'Connell, who had in the past befriended Disraeli, bided his time until in a Commons debate he could make a genial reference to the impenitent thief on the cross, 'whose name, I verily believe, was Disraeli'.

To continue, out of chronological sequence, the sad story of the Melbourne government's attempts at Irish municipal reform, in 1836 Michael O'Loghlen, Perrin's successor as Irish Attorney General and the first Catholic since the Reformation to hold that post, introduced a bill similar to Perrin's. It was passed by the Commons and thrown out by the Lords, as was a compromise bill proposed by Russell to placate the Upper House.

There followed three years of haggling between the ministry and the Opposition, and it was not until August 1840 that a much amended bill became law. The sixty Corporations were reduced to ten. Existing freemen's rights, as a sop to the Tories, were preserved. There was a general £10 household franchise for municipal elections which, together with high property qualifications for counsellors, kept power in responsible hands. As another sop to the Tories, Sheriffs were to be appointed by the Lord Lieutenant, without any recommendation from the Corporations. It was not exactly democracy in practice, and O'Connell protested formally at Ireland not being granted rights equal to those of English municipalities. But his protests were mild, for the ministry's compromise proposals, he admitted, would produce a decided improvement on the previous state of affairs. Given the power of the House of Lords and the impossibility, in present circumstances, of reducing that power, it was the best bill obtainable. It broke the Protestant monopoly – and was, incidentally, to make it possible for him to become Lord Mayor of Dublin. Purged of 'foul Orange leaven', juries would not automatically convict Catholics, liberals and repealers. When Protestants saw themselves politically emasculated even within the union, they might not be so adamant about maintaining it.[8] And if power rested in respectacle middle-class hands, he would be the last to complain.

But – to revert to the session of 1836 – O'Connell had plenty to complain of then. In May the lengthy proceedings of the committee considering the petition to unseat him for Dublin ended in his being unseated by one vote. It was a humiliation, and a very costly one, for he had poured out money, over £10,000, in fighting his case, plus £2,000 to help his son John in similar trouble with Youghal, mainly in counsels' fees of £75 a day and in bringing over witnesses from Ireland and maintaining them in London. And in the end O'Connell was unseated, 'principally by reason of the non-payment of a few shillings of piped-water and wide-street tax'. It was largely his own fault: he should have seen to it that his supporters' qualifications were checked, and that they were not in arrears with their municipal taxes. Of course the Tories made a dead set at him and his family, lodging petitions also (but without success) against Maurice for Tralee, Morgan for County Meath, Kate's Charles for Kerry and Nell's Kit for County Dublin. That they did not encompass his ruin was due to radical friends in England who raised between £8,000 and £9,000 on his behalf. Fortunately the repeal member for Kilkenny City vacated his seat so as to let the Liberator have it without a contest and at no cost.[9]

In his late fifties and early sixties O'Connell loved Derrynane 'for one thousand reasons'. He continued to nag Primrose, who earned every penny of his salary as agent. In February 1834 he was furious with Primrose for not giving him the latest information about cholera in Iveragh: 'it seems as if you took me for a mere dolt who was fit only to be deluded.' The parish priest must be given £50 for relief of the poorest tenants, and Primrose must have some cows killed and distribute the broth. The sale of whiskey must be stopped totally, and two or three gallons of the best brandy sent to Derrynane for medicinal purposes. 'May the great God be merciful, as He is all-powerful ... I would spend my last shilling rather than not have every possible precaution taken.' A doctor must be brought in, and the poor put on a meat diet so as to be able to resist the disease:

> two, three, four beeves I would think nothing of. Coarse blankets may also be very useful. Could you not get more coals from Dingle? ... Be *prodigal* of relief out of my means – beef, bread, mutton, medicines, physician, everything you can think of ... a Mass every possible day and getting the people to go to confession and communion, rosaries and other public prayers to avert the divine wrath.

The divine wrath was averted, or the meat diet was effective, for there was ultimately no great disaster. When he arrived for his autumn holiday the crisis was over, and Mary must not forget the custom of killing a cow *at least* every Christmas and distributing the meat to the poor. 'You cannot, sweetest, do too much for our poor people.' The hare-hunting was superb, but he had to tear himself away and go back to the turmoil of Westminster.

The health of his 'saucy little cocknosed woman', 'neat as a bride' for all her fifty-eight years, was giving him anxiety. In May 1836 she had to leave him in London to take the waters, for an unspecified complaint, at Tunbridge Wells. They did her good, but not for long. In July, when the session was over, his return to Dublin was delayed because she could not stand the journey. Two months later there burst upon him the appalling realisation that she was dying. 'God help me! My ever beloved is in a state of much suffering and daily losing ground. I do most potently fear she cannot recover. She may linger weeks. One week may - Oh God help me!' On 26th October he had to leave her at Derrynane and go back to Dublin, but 'she was in that state that she will not perceive that I am away.' Five days later she was dead.

He was desperate and inconsolable in his grief at the loss of a lover, a helpmeet and a friend. Moreover he had come to rely more and more on her political advice, and three years earlier had written that in 'almost all my political resolves she has been, I believe, uniformly right'. It is possible that without her steady common sense his judgment deteriorated. Certainly, after her death, he suffered occasionally from bouts of deep depression and despair which had never previously afflicted him. As an anodyne he plunged into more and more work for Ireland.

His most effective, and perhaps most satisfying work was in the field of patronage. To the Earl of Mulgrave, Lord Lieutenant from April 1835 to September 1839 (latterly under the title of Marquis of Normanby), to Lord Morpeth, Chief Secretary from April 1835 to September 1841, and to Thomas Drummond, Under-Secretary from April 1835 to April 1840, he directed a stream of letters advising whom to appoint - and, even more frequently, whom not to appoint - as High Sheriff, judge, stipendiary magistrate, Justice of the Peace, chairman (assistant barrister) of a county, or inspector of police (from 1836 organised on a national basis). He was plagued by people who believed that 'one word' from him would get them anything: 'How I hate that "one word"!' Most of his advice was to appoint Catholics and liberal or repeal Protestants and to reject anyone whom he accused of Orangeism. But one of his recommendations was for the son of a parson, 'a wicked anti-Repealer', and a Catholic priest once recommended to him a Protestant clergyman in low water, adding, 'An Irish *Catholic Priest* applying to a *Catholic gentleman* in favour of a clergyman of the Establishment is rather a novel feature in the history of the country. He is a truly worthy and much injured man.' Nor were his relatives starved of ministerial manna: brother John became High Sheriff of Kerry, cousin Brenan and Primrose became J.P.s, Morgan became Assistant Registrar of Deeds, and Kit Fitz-Simon became Clerk of the Hanaper (£600 a year for life and 'scarcely any trouble'.) Generally the Castle took his advice, but sometimes Lord Mulgrave or Lord Morpeth or Drummond were irritated by the constant flow and preferred to make up their own minds, even appointing those whom he had denounced as Orangemen.

All this was not only gratifying to the beneficiaries, but was of real benefit in giving Catholics a share of power and experience in public life. They had their foot inside the door and kept it there. No longer did Protestants enjoy a monopoly of the jobs which most affected everyday life. Some 25 per cent of the officer ranks in the new Irish constabulary went to Catholics, and as a result there were no more complaints that the police were anti-Papist. It was a psychological as well as a practical breakthrough important to Catholics rich and poor. Nevertheless it was hardly likely to arouse the enthusiasm of the ordinary freeholder, as O'Connell realised only too well, writing to FitzPatrick in September 1839:

I may be blamed by some for supporting the present Administration instead of looking for the Repeal; but in the first place the cry for the Repeal would only give increased strength to the vile Orange faction ... In the next place, I want to realise as much good for Ireland as I possibly can ... I stand exceedingly well with the present Ministry. They have but little patronage, but that little will be disposed of only to sincere friends of the country. I have, indeed, been of some service to the government.

His influence and popularity can be measured by the amount of money collected year by year on his behalf.[10] Whether the collection was termed the O'Connell Tribute, the National Rent, the Justice Rent or the Repeal Rent, the money was used both to maintain the Liberator in fitting style in London and Dublin and for all the purposes of whatever association he was running at that particular time. The amounts have been calculated as follows:

1831-2 £26,065
1832-3 £12,242
1833-4 £13,908
1835   £13,454
1836-9 No figures available; probably very low
1840   £2,688
1841   £8,685 - heavy defeat in general election due to shortage of funds

The cost of an election could amount to thousands of pounds, more in boroughs, less in counties. The official expenses, such as the salary of the returning officer and the cost of the polling booths, averaged only about £290, but the unofficial expenses included the salary of an agent, the setting up of a club, paying for addresses and advertisements in newspapers, and the costs of canvassing and of transporting freeholders for long distances to the polling booths and supplying them with food and drink. There were, besides, miscellaneous 'gratifications' such as the £1,500 which Pierce Mahony gave the Catholic Bishop of Limerick for charitable purposes before the 1832 election,* and the £3 each for 1,500 Dublin Freemen, the Tory 'Macedonian phalanx'. O'Connell took a lawyer's precautions never to expose himself to a charge of bribery, writing to Pierce Mahony before the 1837 election, '*We must not be bribers*,' and to a kinsman in Tralee:

As to the publicans, the £15 must be paid to them ... Take care not to have the amount so paid as to amount in *any way to bribery* ... Whoever they vote for – let them even vote against my son – the money shall be paid for them.

As to Diggan, who wanted a situation as waterguard, O'Connell could fix that: it must not be seen as a bribe, 'but, in point of fact, I authorise you to pledge yourself that, let him vote as he will, he shall get the situation as waterguard'. What about an honest man named Ash? What job did he want that he was fit for? And Hickman, who had lately turned very awkward politically – well, O'Connell would see that his fine was expunged: 'the thing *is done*.' Not bribery, of course, and not cheap either, when you consider the number of publicans in a town like Tralee.[11]

It must have been disappointing to the Liberator that only one of his sons, John, showed real aptitude for politics. He was becoming a useful understudy to his father and FitzPatrick, besides being M.P. for Youghal. Maurice was too idle even to exert himself for his own election: 'Tell him from me I shall be utterly offended if he leaves Tralee without my express permission.' His

---

* O'Connell had nothing to do with this, Pierce Mahony being at the time at variance with him.

father had to do half his electoral work for him. Morgan's ceiling was to sit in the back benches for County Meath and occasionally to fight someone who wanted satisfaction for being insulted by the Liberator. Dan was still brewing excellent porter at a prohibitive price.

In June 1837 King William IV died. O'Connell was sure that 'all will go right well with the new Queen' who was believed to be liberal in sympathy and was not surrounded by reactionary Tories. For the general election which followed her accession O'Connell made much use of the queen's name. His General Association – the latest vehicle for O'Connellism – named itself 'The Friends of the Queen', called upon the freeholders to secure the return of the queen's friends and set up an enormous placard outside their headquarters in Dublin's Corn Exchange, 'The Queen and Liberty, the Queen and the Constitution, the Queen and Reform'. During his election campaign O'Connell is recorded as making only one mention of repeal, 'Remember I am a RE-PEALER,' in his Address to the People. He had a personal triumph in Dublin, being returned with a safe majority, but his repeal party again shrank – to thirty-two, as against thirty-nine Liberals and thirty-four Conservatives. His policy of steady support for the Whig government was bringing in neither the votes nor the cash. The policies on which he fought the election – household suffrage, the secret ballot, three-year parliaments, free trade and the abolition of property qualifications for M.P.s – although admirable in Westminster, cut very little ice in Skibbereen. But as the government's majority in the Commons was reduced from over sixty to under forty, they were more than ever dependent on O'Connell's support: as Lady Holland observed, 'we have nothing to rely on but the Queen and Paddy.'[12]

From the government's point of view there were two items of unfinished Irish business – tithes and a Poor Law. Tithes were the more important but more difficult, so they tackled the Poor Law first.

In Ireland there was no relief for the poor from public funds, and instinctively O'Connell thought this was right.[13] The relief of poverty, he believed, was an act of grace; provision by the state would dry up the springs of charity, lay on the agricultural interest (including owners of impoverished estates in Kerry) a heavier burden than it could bear, and increase tensions between landlord and tenant as the former off-loaded, through higher rents, the cost of a poor rate. In particular he was opposed to the English system, based on the Elizabethan Poor Law and modified by the nineteenth-century 'Speenhamland' system under which, as the price of bread rose, agricultural wages were supplemented out of parish rates, thus pauperising labourers and encouraging farmers to pay the lowest possible wages.

English public opinion, well-informed about Irish poverty by a series of commissions' reports and inflamed against Irish landlords by the liberal press, was much in favour of a Poor Law for Ireland. 'It is', O'Connell observed, 'so easy to be benevolent and humane at the expense of others.' In 1833 the government appointed yet another commission, under the Protestant Archbishop Whateley of Dublin, to examine the problem. This recommended no direct relief to the poor, but assisted emigration and an expensive programme of public works. The government rejected this report and adopted instead that of a human dynamo named George Nicholls, a retired East India Company ship's captain of formidable application and mastery of detail, who recommended a system similar to that introduced in England by the Poor Law Act of 1834, based not (as hitherto) on outdoor relief but on workhouses, one for each union of several parishes supervised by a Board of Guardians. This was introduced by the Irish Poor Law Act of 1837.

O'Connell gave it grudging approval. 'A poor law we must have. We are come to it. We must have it as *the Repeal* slumbers ... We *must* have a poor law and *poorhouses*, and much of moral degradation and change in *the mode* of suffering.' In plain words, conditions in the workhouses must be so disagreeable that no one who was not really in need would resort to them. Very soon Nicholls's terrific energy achieved a workhouse system spread all over Ireland, giving O'Connell ample opportunity to inveigh against the application in practice of the law which he reluctantly approved. 'An English East India Company sea-skipper to regulate the Poor Laws of Ireland!' Nicholls had made his report after less than nine weeks in the country.

Was the like of this ever heard? ... They have erected in Cork a house for the accommodation of 2,000 persons, without a sewer ... They should be employed for the rest of their lives

in personally conveying away the filth of that workhouse ...
There is a hideous excess of the cost of the machinery of the
Poor Law over the actual amount of the relief administered
... In the Union of Dunkerrin £720 are charged upon the
ratepayers, and *four paupers* are relieved. To be sure, it is a
very good thing, and a very useful thing, to catch flies, but
what would you say to a wiseacre who gave £40 or £50 for a
most ingenious and admirable fly-trap, and lo! at the end of
three months the excellent fly-trap had actually caught a dozen
flies? The Poor Laws just show how a set of well-fattened
English Commissioners can get fat in minding the affairs of
the poor – and the *Irish* poor, too!

Not only English commissioners. At least the Poor Laws enriched the pastures of Irish patronage, and the Liberator took
advantage of them by securing for his cousin, Maurice Brenan,
the post of assistant commissioner for the Poor Laws. The Poor
Law Guardians, who controlled the dispensaries, fever hospitals
and workhouses, were elected rather than appointed, and Catholics soon gained control of the Poor Law machinery in most
counties outside Ulster, a further share of power.

The problem of tithes was a tougher nut to crack. Lord John
Russell had made, for the government, appropriation of surplus
Church of Ireland revenues the *sine qua non* of any tithe bill, and
the Conservatives, with their impregnable majority in the Upper
House, would not have that at any price. In 1835 and 1836 the
government, with O'Connell's support, put forward several Irish
Tithe Bills which incorporated appropriation clauses; regularly
these were passed by the Commons and thrown out by the Lords.
There seemed no way forward. O'Connell broke the deadlock.
Although furiously opposed by a minority of his party who would
accept nothing short of the complete abolition of tithes, in December 1836 he hinted to an English radical M.P., who passed
on the hint to Lord John Russell, that he would accept a compromise tithe bill. They must not, he said, be

swamped in the difficult details of an Irish Tithe Bill with its
troublesome 'Appropriation Clause'. I wish with all my heart
that the Ministry were decently freed from that *dilemma*. If

there were a proper deduction from the burden of tithes, there would for the present be no surplus; and it is really too bad to risk *on such* a point a ministry who are for the first time in history conquering the 'Anti-Saxon' spirit of Ireland and adding eight million to the King's subjects.[14]

Russell entered into negotiations with Peel, pending which he postponed his 1837 Tithes Bill after it had passed its second reading in the Commons. Melbourne was prepared to give up appropriation, though he could not say so publicly. In a package deal with the Conservatives, it was agreed that the Lords would pass the government's bills on Irish Poor Laws, municipal reform, and tithes, provided there was no appropriation. Finally, with much inter-party bargaining, there was thrashed out the details of the 1838 Irish Tithes Bill proposed by Russell and supported by Peel, Stanley and O'Connell with nearly all his 'Tail'. It sailed through both Commons and Lords. The former tithe composition was reduced by one-quarter and converted into a rent charge payable by head landlords, who could recover it from their immediate tenants, who in turn could recover it from subtenants; the liability, however, did not extend to tenants who held their land at the landlord's will or on a year's lease, the largest and poorest class of Irish peasantry. But to spread the burden between the landlords and the tenants who were obliged to pay the tithe-rent charge, 'rack rents', that is to say gross rents without fines or deductions of any kind, were reduced by a quarter of the old tithe composition. Rent charges were subject to variations with the average price of corn. Finally, all arrears from 1834 to 1837 were written off (a concession made to O'Connell) and tithe-owners were compensated with the residue, £260,000, of the 1833 Church Million Act.[15]

It was hardly a revolutionary, or even a radical change; it did nothing to alter the basic injustice of Catholics and Dissenters being taxed to support Anglican clergy. But it exempted the poorest, spread the burden among the less poor and made tithe collection administratively easy.

O'Connell's admiration for the queen never wavered, especially after February 1838 when he wrote in the strictest confidence to FitzPatrick: 'take care to keep it a secret – the Queen has expressed a wish to see me. She is determined to conciliate Ireland.

I will, of course, attend the next *levée* and perhaps some good to Ireland may be the consequence.' He, Maurice and Morgan were presented by Lord Morpeth to Her Majesty who, prepared for the squat, obese Yahoo of *Punch* cartoons, was astonished at the tall, handsome, courtly reality. 'Why,' she exclaimed afterwards, 'he's a *gentleman!*'[16]

But, laudable as the ministry's Irish legislation might be, and gratifying as its patronage was to those who benefited, there was nothing in it to set the people cheering and throwing their hats in the air – or putting their hands in their pockets. In January the Liberator wrote sadly to FitzPatrick, 'I see by the tone of your letters that my heyday of popularity is gone by, blessed be God!' There seemed to be nothing in politics but complaints by the Irish grocers at not being allowed to retail spirits. His mind turned again to a more inspiring, if hopeless cause: 'I am heartsore at many disappointments. Yet I *live for the Repeal.* The enmity to the Union was my first effort, it will be my last; and, idle as it may seem, I *do* hope for success.'[17]

So in August 1838 he formed the Precursor Society – forerunner to repeal. Its objects were to obtain from parliament full justice for Ireland, equality with Great Britain in all franchises, privileges and rights, and the total abolition of tithes, within the union. If these were not obtained within a year, the society would become a Repeal Association.

It did not catch on. Members came in very slowly. O'Connell was criticised for hoping for the impossible in a single parliamentary session. Moreover there were unworthy suggestions that he had misappropriated the Society's funds. These had indeed been credited to his private bank account instead of to the treasurers', but the latter exonerated O'Connell from blame and declared that the funds had been properly handled. However, some of the mud stuck.[18]

His alliance with the Whigs, although it had in the past brought to him and his country some modest advantages, had first deprived him of his freedom of action and then chained him to a Cabinet in a coma. For the ministry had no animation. Having achieved its quota of mildly beneficent Irish legislation, its Jamaica Act and its Penny Postage, for all of which O'Connell had dutifully voted, it had nothing more to offer. In May, after a bad division, Melbourne resigned and the queen, with evident distaste, asked Peel to form a ministry. Lord John Russell sent O'Connell a handsome letter of thanks for his steady support and hoped that he would tone down the repeal agitation so long as there was any hope of obtaining a fair deal for Ireland within the union. O'Connell resigned himself to a Tory government:

> Blessed be God, it is a sad infliction. Principally to be attributed to Joseph Hume. His conduct encouraged Smith O'Brien and others to revolt. O'Brien, though very ill-conditioned, would never have had the courage to behave so basely. We lost six Irish votes.[19]

Then there came a last-minute reprieve. Peel, while forming his ministry, insisted on the young queen dismissing two of her Whig ladies-in-waiting lest she be surrounded entirely by the government's enemies, and she indignantly refused. Peel then refused to take over, and *dear* Lord M. came to her rescue, taking office again although he had no policy, only the most precarious position in parliament and nothing but a twenty-year-old girl's adoration to sustain him.

O'Connell was ecstatic. 'Hurrah for the darling little Queen!' He proceeded in the next few weeks to express some startlingly undemocratic views. 'All is right, quite right, improving hourly. We owe all to the darling Queen.' ... 'As for the Queen ... she is *true*. But will she be able to resist *both* Houses of Parliament should the Tories get a majority in the Commons?' ... 'The Tories will NEVER again regain power. Blessed be God, the Queen is exceedingly angry with the Tories.' He was gratified by a smile from Her Majesty and civil bow from Prince Albert. He even – surely the *ne plus ultra* of loyalty – found the queen 'full of intellect'.[20]

The Chartists were now stirring up in England exactly the same sort of trouble that O'Connell had stirred up in Ireland, and was to do again. Having once supported them, even helping to write their Charter, he now took a great dislike to them because they refused to abjure violence, especially detesting their leader, the red-bearded, extrovert Feargus O'Connor who had once been one of the most insubordinate of his repealers. 'Let us see', he would say, perusing the Chartist newspaper, the *Labourer*,

what poor Balderdash has to say for himself this week ...
Upon my word, this paper of Feargus is a literary curiosity.
The first page is filled with praise of Feargus – second page,
praise of Feargus – third page, ditto – fourth page, ditto – and
so on all through till we come to the printer's name. What a
notion of the fellow to set up a newspaper to praise himself.[21]

(How very different from the honest, objective *Pilot!*)
Fortunately the queen's brave Irish soldiers were a match for
the rascals. 'Why', he asked More O'Ferrall, one of his 'Tail',

do you not boast to the English lubbers of Ireland and the
Irish? It was *we* beat the Chartists at Newport. Twenty-eight
poor raw Irish lads beat five thousand rebels, and then Captain
Stack is a Kerryman and I believe a Papist. At all events
Sergeant Daly and the privates are all Irish Papists.[22]

But loyalty to queen and Empire without policy or support
was not enough. He fell into a mood of deep despair, almost of
melancholia, such as Mary would never have permitted. His
debts were mounting again and the means to pay them were not.
He did not clear the account of Jerry McCarthy, his tailor (who
long ago had been a spectator at his duel), until Jerry was dead:
'He was an excellent friend, and I paid him some thousands.
God be merciful to him!' FitzPatrick, besides collecting the Tribute, did his best to sort out the Liberator's tangled finances and
prevent his cheques 'bouncing', but could never ascertain the full
amount of the debts; probably the Liberator did not know himself. FitzPatrick, too, bore the brunt of his despair. 'I am, I
confess,' wrote O'Connell in August 1839,

very unhappy. The country is plainly tired out of my claims.
I will write to you again on this *painful, painful* subject tomorrow ... I do not believe I shall long survive the blow I
apprehend from the desertion of me by the country at large
... At my time of life mental agony is poisonous.

The next day he wrote, 'It does mortify me but does not surprise
me to find that I have exhausted the bounty of the Irish people.
God help me! What shall I do?' He contemplated spending the

rest of his days in retreat at Clongowes, thinking of 'nothing but eternity ... If Ireland thought fit to support me, I might still be useful; but it is plain I have worn out my claim on the people ... I am, I believe, on the verge of illness – the illness of despondency.' Two days later he was more calm and resigned: 'I, of course, dislike the idea of terminating my political career and sinking into obscurity but, my excellent friend, it is inevitable.'²³

In April 1840 O'Connell launched his Repeal Association – or, to be more accurate, his National Association for Full and Prompt Justice or Repeal, a title which in itself betrayed the hesitation and ambivalence in his mind. In July he reconstituted it as the Loyal National Repeal Association, which at least clarified his object, except for those who saw a conflict between loyalty and repeal. It was planned as an improved version of the Catholic Association, with Repeal Wardens, Repeal Rents, clubs, badges and uniforms, geared to mass agitation rather than to electioneering. 'The Repeal will now spread like wildfire,' he told John in April 1840. But it didn't.²⁴

O'Connell was pleased that summer by Morgan's marriage with Kate Balfe, daughter of a County Roscommon landlord. Moreover Morgan achieved the summit of his modest ambition (and, indeed, modest capacity), as well as a regular salary sufficient to support a wife, in his appointment as Assistant Registrar of Deeds. Otherwise, O'Connell told FitzPatrick, he was very unhappy: 'but for you, I know not what would become of me.' To add to his misery, Betsey was suffering from 'moral scrupulosity', an emotional disturbance about morality, often referred to by laymen as religious mania. Her mother might have helped, but all her father could advise was that she place herself unreservedly in the hands of her confessor, doing whatever he told her, 'to pray or not to pray, to fast or not to fast, to confess or not to confess, and above all to go to communion whenever he advises or commands you.' But the good man must have had shortcomings as a psychiatrist, for ten years later the question arose of committing poor Betsey to an asylum. Dan's brewery was not prospering, and in 1841 he severed his connection with it. Nor was Maurice's marriage, and in the same year he severed his connection with Mary Frances. Kit Fitz-Simon, characteristically trying to tidy up the mess, had to report that a 'quiet arrangement' was not possible, for she was extremely grasping over the financial settlement.

Of all his children, only John, Nell and Kate gave him real satisfaction during that summer of his discontent. John was shaping very well, extremely businesslike.

But autumn in Derrynane worked its usual miracle. His hounds, which a while ago had contracted mange owing to the neglect of their 'scoundrel huntsman', were now at the top of their form, including drafts from England. At the age of sixty-five O'Connell followed brother John's staghounds at Killarney, beagled on the way to Derrynane, beagled again when he got there and found himself growing young again. On one September morning his beloved hounds 'ran down five hares in the best style and with long continued running'. In October Dublin claimed him, but he was back in Derrynane in November for a full six weeks and had '*great* hunting – only one blank day. Yesterday the most splendid hunting I ever saw.'

Derrynane was a regular hunters' lodge for Kerry sportsmen, including a somewhat unpolished gentleman nicknamed *Theig-a-wattha** who might not have been Mary's favourite person. He enthused one day, 'Och Liberathur, I have an illigant new beagle. He's a splendid dog, a huge slaughtersome beast! Och! I wish you saw him! He's the slaughteringest dog that ever followed a hare!'

'And what do you call this killing dog of yours?'

'Troth, Liberathur, I've no particular name for him yet. Or, rather, I have two names, Savage and Cannibal.'

'But, my dear Theig, are you not very extravagant in these hard times to squander two names on one dog? Couldn't you keep one of them for yourself?'

But all good things come to an end. Back he had to go to the political grind.

Fortunately John took a lot of the burden from him, and much of his correspondence was devoted to coaching his son. John must beware of running foul of the 1793 Irish Convention Act by 'assuming *any species of representative capacity*'. The Repeal Association represented only its own members and spoke only for itself. 'You will not, my beloved John, mistake me. I say this to you not by way of reproach but simply by way of caution.' John

---

*Tim of the Stick – a tribute, presumably, to his pugnacity.

was given long lists of men to see, men to sound, men to beware of and men to conciliate; of newspapers to contact and motions to move at Repeal Association meetings.

> That which I am most anxious about is that you should *cut a figure* at the Association. It is the best opportunity you could have of introducing yourself quietly and discreetly into public life, especially by showing yourself a man of business. The facility of being so will grow upon you though you should feel awkward at first. I implore you to try. Begin manfully on Monday.

He must learn the art of man-management: 'I entirely approve of what you have done ... Conciliate everybody, *good*, *bad* and indifferent without *yielding any principle* and without failing to make the *good* feel the preference of your kindness to them.'

With the ministry drifting in and out of coma, a general election could not be long delayed, and the Repeal Association was in bad shape for it. O'Connell's own leadership was doubtful and hesitant; he feared and half expected defeat. It was not until early January 1841 that the first move was made to appoint Repeal Wardens to collect the Repeal Rent, so funds were very low. There was general public apathy, not at all conducive to agitation. His own plans were uncertain: he wished to be elected for Dublin, but to have a bolt-hole in Kilkenny if things went wrong in Dublin. To Edmond Smithwick, his man in Kilkenny, he wrote on 21st May, 'My first object was to get my son John returned for Athlone and myself for Kilkenny, subject to my removal if I succeed in Dublin, and then having John for Kilkenny as I had provided a substitute for him in Athlone.' If this plan seemed too audacious, John would stand for Kilkenny, announcing himself as candidate as soon as possible.

> The difficulty is just this. He cannot publicly renounce Athlone until another liberal candidate is found for that town. The instant *that* is done he will address your electors as a Repealer and the son of a Repealer - one of those who prefer Ireland to everything else.

On the same day he wrote again to Smithwick, 'I will be *most impatient* to know how my dearest John is likely to be received by the "boys of Kilkenny". I look upon Dublin as safe. If not,

John would resign in my favour, if permitted by the Kilkenny constituency.'²⁵

These were not the sort of battle orders to inspire confidence in the troops in Kilkenny, Athlone or Dublin.

In June Melbourne's ailing ministry breathed its last, resigning after the loss of a vote of confidence. Writs for a general election were issued for 23rd June.

O'Connell was tired, feeling his age, and admitted to Pierce Mahony on 22nd June, 'I wish I was fairly rid of the toil, tumult and expense of Dublin.' Especially the expense. He had not merely to finance his own election campaign – and Dublin was notoriously expensive – but also Maurice's for Tralee, John's for Kilkenny and Dan's maiden effort at Carlow: 'It will be very hard on me to have to bear the cost of so many elections.' From all sides came reports of shortage of money; also, John regretted to say, of idleness, hesitation, irresolution, 'and I will plainly say something of incapacity'. What was most lacking was leadership.

The only bright feature was that, partly owing to the death of Bishop Doyle and his replacement by an out-and-out repealer, the priests were more zealous and active in the cause than at any time since 1829. O'Connell was particularly anxious for success in Carlow, and spent a lot of time helping Dan there. 'My great object is to make Carlow the Clare of the Repeal.' Surely Lord Milton (a Liberal) could be written to about his recalcitrant Protestant tenants there: 'he can *command* them.'²⁶

'The want of funds', O'Connell told John, 'is a decisive reason for not urging the Repeal as we otherwise would. This really is the secret of our weakness. I will press for the appointment of Repeal Wardens until every parish is provided with the machinery.' He should, of course, have done that months ago.²⁷

In the end the election was a disaster. O'Connell himself lost Dublin. Having been offered safe seats, without opposition, for County Meath, Clare, Kilkenny and County Cork, he finally settled for County Cork. But it did not make up for losing Dublin. Ireland returned only eighteen repealers, fewer than half the 1832-3 number, forty-seven Liberals and forty Conservatives. In Westminster Peel had a safe majority of between eighty and ninety.

The days of dutiful co-operation with a well-disposed government were over. It must be back to mass agitation.

13

*The Return of Hurlothrumbo**

In Westminster the new Tory government gave Ireland a low priority. The danger of a Chartist rising and the agitation of the Anti-Corn Law League seemed more pressing problems. O'Connell himself believed, not without a touch of complacency, that England was nearer than Ireland to revolution. In June 1842 he assured his Kilkenny friend, Edmond Smithwick, that the Tories would not last long, but

> there is a danger of a convulsion. You have no idea of the total and hopeless destitution of the English working classes in the great manufacturing towns. It is really awful ... Toryism is likely to get a vital blow. Heaven protect us from seeing it go out in blood.

He warned FitzPatrick that in England the

> destruction of lives and property are imminent ... If matters proceed to any extremity Ireland is my post to keep the people from any outbreak. It will be enough for the Irish to watch events and guard against anarchy or outrage and to contrast

---

*Hurlothrumbo was a Dublin Tory nickname for O'Connell, a reference presumably to his rabble-rousing oratory.

favourably with any violence at this [the English] side of the Channel.

He rejoiced that Ireland would remain quiet.[1]

Unlike many Irish repealers, who wanted continued protection for Irish agriculture, he gave strong backing to Richard Cobden's Anti-Corn Law League, denouncing in speech after speech in the English manufacturing towns the Corn Laws by means of which 'the landlords' venison was sweetened with widows' tears and their claret dyed with orphans' blood.' He linked the Corn Laws with the union, believing (wrongly) that Peel was the prisoner of the landlords and that if their power were weakened, parliament would grant repeal. But he got no thanks from Cobden who, English through and through, viewed the great Irishman with abhorrence. O'Connell, he said,

> always treated me with friendly attention, but I never shook hands with him nor faced his smile without a feeling of insecurity. And as for trusting him on any public question where his vanity or his passions might interpose, I would have as soon thought of an alliance with an Ashantee chief.[2]

O'Connell did not at once plunge into agitation for repeal, for on 1st November 1841 he was elected, unopposed, Lord Mayor of Dublin,[3] the first Catholic to hold that office for a hundred and fifty years and surely the most unlikely Lord Mayor since Wilkes was Lord Mayor of London. In that office he promised, and on the whole kept his promise, to abstain from partisan politics. It was a signal honour, and his people at Derrynane shouted their joy at the news. 'You have', John congratulated him, 'a legally recognised *lordship* from the people, utterly unconnected with court favour or aristocratic usage. In short a most democratic dignity.' It meant, however, no holiday in Derrynane that autumn:

> There was quite a *scene* upon the mountain yesterday when Denis McCrohan told the huntsmen you could not come. Two or three of them, led by Cormac, fairly sat down and cried ... Your hounds are quite well, but look lonely without you.

The Liberator was delighted with his success and, always a

showman, played up magnificently. In his crimson robes, embellished with a sable collar and white satin bows, crowned with an enormous cocked hat, he addressed the cheering multitude from his balcony in Merrion Square:

> A great revolution has this day been consummated ... I now address you as Chief Magistrate of this great metropolis. Let them tell you, if they dare, that I won't carry the Repeal of the Union ... Yes, I shall yet address the Speaker of the Irish Parliament in College Green. [Tremendous cheers.]

He had for years been an ardent supporter of Father Mathew's temperance campaign, without going so far as personally to take the pledge, and in this, his first speech as Lord Mayor, he promised to do his utmost in the temperance cause: 'Oh, give me my honest teetotaller!! ... Let your triumph be unstained by any breach of the law or of the peace. Remember, I am now your Lord Mayor, and must have every man punished who breaks the peace.'

With perfect propriety he attended, in his robes, the levée of the Conservative Lord Lieutenant, Lord de Grey. With somewhat less propriety he had announced his intention of doing so in a speech at the Corn Exchange:

> In my official capacity of Lord Mayor, and in such *only*, I feel it my duty to pay every token of respect to the representative of Her Majesty ... In fact I feel no respect at all for Lord de Grey ... If I went there in my private capacity, I should richly earn contempt for paying the slightest mark of respect to so paltry, pitiful, delusive and hypocritical an administration.

But he would not attend Mass in his robes: 'for the Lord Mayor can be a Catholic, but his robes must be Protestant'. Ironically his first case as Chief Magistrate was a lawsuit by a priest's servant for unpaid wages. His Lordship issued a decree against the priest.

Indeed the glory of being Lord Mayor went a little to his head and aroused military ambitions which had slumbered for forty years. If, as he expected, there was revolution in England with the rebels out in force, sabotaging the railways to prevent the movement of troops, Her Majesty would look to Ireland as a haven of peace and – who knows? – a refuge. 'In such a case as that I, as Lord Mayor, should go to the Castle, and armed with the government authority, I should forthwith organise a city militia.'

'Queen Victoria might have to run over here for protection,' said Fitz-Simon.

O'Connell went on, 'I should have two as fine battalions as ever took the field. As Lord Mayor I should be entitled to be Colonel. I would say to the ranks, "You must die if necessary, but you must not be defeated."' He paused for a moment, and then added, 'What we are saying now is mere after-dinner table-talk; yet it *might* be a reality ere this time tomorrow.' And part of him hoped it would.

But he had instead to put up with the endless drudgery of hearing the sort of petty cases in which, long ago, he had so often acted for the defence. To each he gave as much attention as to the Doneraile Conspiracy. He undertook also the Herculean task of going through the Burgesses' Roll and verifying, after hearing rival pleas, the right to vote of 18,000 men on it. There were wagers that he would not complete it, but he did, ticking off the last name on his last day in office.

The Lord Mayoralty had a bad effect on his finances. Expenses were heavy and the Tribute and Rent for 1842 totalled only £5,705. 'Want is literally killing me,' he wrote to FitzPatrick in July, 'I have grown ten years older from my incessant pecuniary anxiety' ... 'I write overwhelmed with affliction.' As usual, he had no idea of the amount of his debts: FitzPatrick must see to them.[4]

By the end of the year he was fed up with the boredom and frustration of the job and his absence from active politics. 'In another fortnight,' he rejoiced, 'I'll have the privilege of knocking down anyone who calls me My Lord.'

Another privilege was his holiday in Derrynane. 'I have', he informed FitzPatrick,

> greatly enjoyed my hunting scenes and I really feel a restoration of health and energy ... My pack is beautiful, and they hunt admirably. They kill with ease full six and even seven hares in a day, and this amid the finest scenery, the most *majestic* in the world. How I wish you saw this place and saw

my hounds hunt, because it is not the men but the dogs who hunt with me.

Ever since Catholic emancipation he had been involved in the anti-slavery movement which he promoted with unusual single-mindedness,[5] offending many Americans as he contrasted their professed devotion to liberty with their treatment of negroes. 'In the midst of their laughter and their pride,' he thundered at a meeting in Cork,

> I point to the negro children screaming for the mother from whose bosom they have been torn. America! It is a foul stain on your character! ... Let them hoist the flag of Liberty with the whip and rack on one side and the star of freedom on the other!

Greeted with outstretched hand by an American supporter of repeal, he asked, 'A Southerner, sir?' 'Yes, sir.' 'A slaveholder, I presume?' 'Certainly, sir.' 'Then,' said O'Connell, 'I have no hand for you.'

'Your slave-system', he told an advocate of slavery, 'is abominable. It cuts at the root of Christianity, which teaches us to do to others as we would they should do to us; but you inflict on the slaves that which you would rather die than suffer yourselves.' To a group of slave-breeders he wrote:

> As to the odour of the negroes, we are quite aware they have not as yet come to use much of the otto of roses or eau de Cologne. But we implore of your fastidiousness to recollect that multitudes of the children of white men have negro women for their mothers; and that our British travellers complain, in loud and bitter terms, of the overpowering stench of stale tobacco-spittle as the prevailing odour among native free Americans ... The negroes would certainly smell at least as sweet being free, as they do now, being slaves.

Various devious motives have been attributed to him over this question: he wished to curry favour with English radicals by embracing one of their favourite causes; he wished to imply the superiority of monarchical to American republican constitutions;

he wished to acquire a general reputation for philanthropy. It seems unnecessary to look further than a simple disgust at 'the peculiar institution'. But the issue was not always simple, for there could be a conflict between the principles of anti-slavery and of free trade. What should be a patriot's choice between importing expensive sugar grown by free men and cheap sugar grown by slaves? After a heated debate in the Repeal Association the Liberator, having preserved throughout an uncharacteristic silence, was afflicted by a headache and had to leave before the vote.

He even denounced George Washington for having been a slave-owner, and the American Ambassador for being a slave-breeder, for which the ambassador challenged him, unsuccessfully, to a duel.

His attitude was not popular with Irish-Americans who, in general the poorest of free Americans, feared negro competition. The Irish-born Catholic bishop of New York attacked O'Connell for unwarranted interference in American affairs. It had a damaging effect on Irish-American support for repeal. O'Connell refused to accept subscriptions from America if these were given on condition that he held his tongue about slavery. In the line he took O'Connell had very little support in Ireland and was opposed even in the Repeal Association. But on this issue, where expediency argued the prudence of sitting on the fence, the arch-pragmatist acted on principle.

Generally Irish-Americans have remained unsympathetic to the aspirations of American blacks, as have most nationalist politicians in Ireland who have always had to rely on American support. Honourable exceptions are O'Connell and Mrs Bernadette Devlin McAliskey.

While O'Connell as Lord Mayor was in baulk, the Dublin headquarters staff of the Repeal Association – notably John, Steele, O'Neill Daunt, FitzPatrick and the General Secretary Thomas Matthew Ray – had been preparing a campaign more effective than that of 1841, with a special emphasis on appointing Repeal Wardens in almost every Irish parish and in many English, Scottish and American towns. In October 1842 there appeared the first number of the *Nation*, strongly repealist but more intellectual and a great deal more independent of O'Connell than the *Pilot*. 'The Great Dan' took charge of the Association early in 1843, responding magnificently to the challenge and displaying for the last time – he was sixty-eight – all his splendid powers as orator, organiser and agitator.

The Association was his creation and his instrument, John his deputy. It was modelled on the Catholic Association of 1828 with wardens, clubs and, of course, Repeal Rent. 'Repeal volunteers' paid £10 a year, members £1, and associates one shilling. Its executive council in Dublin, 180 strong, was too large for day-to-day business and delegated most of the work to committees, which sat several times a week. O'Connell made all the important and most of the less important decisions. O'Neill Daunt gives a good picture of him at work: a massive figure wearing a fur tippet and a broad-brimmed top-hat, seated at the head of a long table in a gaslit room, with committee members sitting along both sides perusing papers and taking part in debate.

Difficult questions are submitted for his guidance, disputes in remote localities are referred to his adjudication, reports are confided to his care to be drawn up ... He originates rules and regulations. He creates a working staff throughout the country, he renders the movement systematic. He cautiously guards it from infringing in the smallest particular upon the law. And every now and then he lightens proceedings by a flash of wit or a hilarious anecdote from his past.

Ray, as secretary, submitted matters to him. 'Here is an application, Liberator, from a Presbyterian clergyman for pecuniary aid to enable him to go on a repeal mission.'

'Does anyone here support that application, Ray? I will oppose it, because I saw the reverend gentleman as drunk as Bacchus at a public dinner.'

'But he is quite reformed, Liberator, and has taken the pledge.'

'No matter. After such a public *exposé* of himself, we ought to have nothing to do with him.'

'Very well, sir. Here's a letter from the Ballinakill repealers, wanting Mr Daunt to go down to address a meeting there.'

'I'm glad of it. I suppose Daunt will have no objection.'

'Not in the least,' said Daunt.

'And here's a letter from the people of Kells, wanting Mr John O'Connell to attend a meeting there next week.'

'My son John will go, won't you, John?'

'Yes, father.'

'Then write and tell 'em so.'

'Counsellor Clements has made an objection to the words, "We pledge ourselves" in the Irish Manufacturer's Declaration. He's afraid of their being illegal.'

'Then alter the passage thus: "We pledge ourselves *as individuals*". If there be any difficulty, that will obviate it ... What's that large document? ... Umph, let's see what sort of affair it is ... What a waste of industry! There is absolutely nothing in that voluminous paper that would be of the slightest utility.'

'I think the last two pages contain a few good facts.'

'Then print the last two pages and throw away the rest.'

There was an element of blarney in his handling of committee meetings which did not escape parody by the irreverent. 'I have the distinguished honour and satisfaction', he would say, 'of moving that we enrol among our members my esteemed friend, the worthy and patriotic Mr ...' Then, *sotto voce* to the secretary, 'What's his name, Ray?'[6]

In his abortive campaign for repeal in the early 1830s O'Connell had allowed himself to be diverted away from the main issue towards a number of other matters – reform of the franchise, tithes, municipal reform and so on. Now he reverted to his earlier tactics, which had achieved emancipation, concentrating on the main issue and relating to it all subsidiary and local issues, mainly agrarian grievances. Again and again he insisted that only repeal of the union would remedy Irish ills; only an Irish parliament could ensure fixed tenures at fair rents with compensation for improvements, or reduce the tax burden on Ireland, or abolish tithe-rent charges, or protect native industry against English competition, or introduce the secret ballot and one man one vote, or change the unpopular Poor Law and end the hated workhouse means test. His propaganda was directed mainly to tenant farmers and cottiers, and his agitation had at first less urban, middle-class and Protestant support than his campaign for emancipation.

At the end of February 1843 he instituted in the Dublin Corporation a full-scale debate on repeal of the union.[7] It was a bold trial of strength because there were many Protestants in Dublin and the 'Macedonian phalanx' of Protestant Freemen was deemed impregnable. Ireland, he insisted, was a perfectly viable state:

> Five independent kingdoms in Europe possess less territory or people; and her station in the Atlantic between the old world and the new design her to be the *entrepot* of both, if the watchful jealousy of England did not render her natural advantages nugatory.

He quoted Locke, apostle of the glorious revolution of 1688: 'A legislature cannot transfer the power of making laws into other hands for, being but a delegated power from the people, they who have it cannot pass it over to others.' The Irish parliament could not, therefore, extinguish itself, and indeed it was not dead but only slept. So the union was unconstitutional. It was procured by fraud, intimidation and wholesale bribery, and like any other compact procured by criminal means it was not binding.

He reeled off, without a note, a wealth of statistics – such as the consumption *per capita* of tea, coffee and wine before and after 1802 – to prove that the union had condemned the country to economic decline. It robbed the people of their control over the executive and the judiciary; it robbed them by imposing on Ireland a disproportionate share of the kingdom's taxation; it forced them to submit to imperfect representation in the House of Commons, and to see jobs on the public payroll handed out to Englishmen and Scots.

He stressed the importance for Ireland of keeping a constitutional link with England, and claimed that unless repeal were granted that link would be broken. Protestants would have nothing to fear and much to gain from repeal. In a passionate peroration, he rhapsodised over the beauty of Ireland,

> the loveliness of her green valleys, the luxurious fertility of her plains, the multitude of her ever-flowing streams capable of turning the machinery of the world! Yes, ours is a country for a man to delight in, and for superior beings to smile upon, while her people are foremost in every physical and social quality, temperate, moral, religious, hospitable and brave. Yes, that people shall be what they ought to be! The star of liberty shall beam above them! The blessing of self-government and

self-legislation shall be revived amongst them! Their allegiance to the throne is pure and unbroken, but their love of liberty is unextinguishable and unconquerable.

The Conservative leader, Isaac Butt, could not match this sort of thing: his reply was quite inadequate, and by forty-five votes to fifteen the Dublin Corporation, the governing body of the capital, voted for repeal. It was a famous victory, and it seemed to be an event of great significance, giving repeal both respectability and credibility; it brought over many middle-class Catholics and even a few Protestants.

O'Connell expected great things from the Dublin Protestants, who forty years earlier had been so strong against the union. But he was to be disappointed. Of 509 Dubliners, mainly upper and middle class, who are recorded as regularly attending meetings of the Repeal Association between 1840 and 1849, only three are known to have been Protestants. The capital had a strong concentration of working-class Protestants who from 1839 to 1842 suffered from a severe depression with much unemployment, for which it was easy to blame the parliament in Westminster and unfair English competition. But instead of supporting repeal, Dublin working-class Protestants fell completely under the domination of the Reverend Tresham Dames Clegg, a populist pastor and a forerunner of Mr Ian Paisley, who had no idea in his mind – or at least never voiced one – other than 'To hell with the Pope!' Clegg's Dublin Protestant Operatives Association bears an uncanny resemblance to Paisley's Democratic Unionist Party. He came to prominence at a time when working-class Protestants were bitterly resentful of Catholic emancipation, for unlike Protestants of the upper and middle classes they had no economic cushion against the shock. O'Connell's triumph meant for them simply the loss of many of the privileges which had set them apart from the despised Papist majority. Then the Municipal Reform Act removed the municipal franchise from 4,000 Protestant Freemen and gave it instead to all £10 householders, among whom Catholics were in a majority of two to one. With the loss of their municipal franchise and their privileged status, their city council lost most of its police, judicial and fiscal powers. So Dublin working-class Protestants, whose fathers had prospered under a Protestant parliament in Dublin, were in no mood to support any proposals which would deliver them over to a parliament of Papists. When the Reverend Tresham Clegg informed them that all their troubles were due to the Anti-Christ in Rome and his demons in Conciliation Hall, they believed him.[8]

Another disappointment was the paucity of support for repeal from English Catholics. There was, however, one useful convert to the cause – Frederick Lucas, first editor of the English Catholic paper, the *Tablet*, founded (with a good deal of help from O'Connell) in 1840. Lucas was always friendly to O'Connell and sympathetic to Ireland, and in 1843 he was at last converted to repeal.

Nevertheless O'Connell was confident that he could win repeal without the Dublin working class Protestants, and set off after Easter 1843 on his grand tour of Ireland, addressing forty public meetings, including many 'monster' meetings at which he claimed audiences of hundreds of thousands. His troops at first needed animating. 'What is Tipperary doing?' he demanded of Charles Bianconi, the famous mail-coach contractor.

What the double-deuce is Clonmel doing? ... What is Charles Bianconi doing? A vivacious animal in himself, but now ingly as torpid as a flea in a wet blanket. So much for scolding you all. And now, my good friend, I want to see 60,000 to 100,000 Tipperary boys meeting peacefully and returning home quietly ... Though you are a foreigner, you have brains in your noddle. What will you do for the Cause, eh?

At sixty-eight he was at the top of his form. He inspired every meeting with a terrific sense of urgency: *now* was the time for repeal, 1843 was Repeal Year! A fanatic for toleration, a berserker for non-violence, he worked up his vast audiences to the highest pitch of belligerent excitement – and held them there, a consummate tactician who combined the advantages of physical force with the legal safety of disclaiming its exercise. The discipline and good order of the huge crowds were, to the Castle, horribly ominous.

Every meeting of O'Connell's was attended by the Castle's shorthand writers, alert for any slip which would put him within reach of the law. He treated them always with distinguished consideration. At Skibbereen he saw them ushered to places of honour in the front row, satisfied himself that they had every facility – and then, when their note-books were open and their pencils poised, addressed the meeting in Irish.

The Repeal Rent, an infallible barometer of his power, rose during April and May from £60 to £700 a week, so that the total for 1843 was a record £48,706. The Liberator looked forward to taking his seat in the Irish House of Lords as the Earl of Glencara, in anticipation of which he had a new seal cut, the O'Connell arms surmounted by an earl's coronet.[9]

The new repeal weekly, the *Nation*, was the mouthpiece and rallying-point of a pressure group of younger members of the Repeal Association. Their leading lights were Charles Gavan Duffy, a 37-year-old Catholic journalist; John Mitchel, a Belfast Protestant in the United Irishmen tradition; John Blake Dillon, a Spanish-looking Mayo man, a Catholic but a graduate of Trinity; and Thomas Davis, thirty-nine years old, son of an English army surgeon and an Irish mother. Known as 'the gentle Davis', he was in fact rather abrasive and formidable. They called their group 'Young Ireland'.

The ideas of Young Ireland were subtly different from those of the old Liberator. They had a concept of the Irish nation which rejected pragmatic compromise with England. They tended to be urban, intellectual, middle-class and élitist, disliking O'Connell's populist, Hurlothrumbo style and his emphasis on agrarian grievances. They saw the Repeal Association as too Catholic and, giving O'Connell no credit for his great efforts in that direction, pursued that will-o'-the-wisp of Irish politics that had eluded the Liberator and was to elude all nationalist politicians – persuading Protestants to play a full and active part, without regret or reservation, in the public life of a country which was overwhelmingly Catholic. But in this they were far from consistent. Davis, more in tune with his Catholic grandmother than his Protestant parents, while proclaiming no less frequently than O'Connell that the Irish nation comprised all races and all religions in Ireland, in three editorials in the *Nation* described landlords, by implication Protestants, as 'alien in race and religion' to the people of Ireland.

Young Ireland resented O'Connell's censorship of the nationalist press and did not hesitate, through the *Nation*, to criticise his minor tactics, though not his strategy. They disapproved of

273

his scurrilous abuse of political opponents, even of political friends who were temporarily at variance with him. 'We dislike', wrote Davis,

> the whole system of false disparagement. The Irish people will never be led to act the manly part which liberty requires of them by being told that 'The Duke', that gallant soldier and most able general, is a screaming coward and doting corporal.

O'Connell's leadership they described – as yet only among themselves – as a 'base *mélange* of mendicancy and tyranny'. They admired the Chartists, whom he abhorred, and approved the Poor Law, which he disparaged. Most of them disagreed with him on slavery, thinking it vital to gain American support. 'We deny', said Mitchel some years later,

> that it is a crime, or a wrong, or even a peccadillo to hold slaves, to buy slaves, to keep slaves to their work by flogging or other needful correction. We wish we had a good plantation well-stocked with healthy negroes in Alabama.

In June 1843 the *Nation* published an article by Davis on 'The Morality of War' which, by implication and naming no names, challenged the Liberator's principle of relying solely on moral force and eschewing secret plots and physical force. Thereafter the *Nation* published an increasing number of articles extolling the use of arms and urging patriots to practise in their use. O'Connell always thought of 1798 as a tragic, bloody blunder, without which England could never have got away with the union. Young Ireland's view of 1798 was put in an anonymous poem in the *Nation* which the Liberator cannot have been pleased to read:

> Who fears to speak of '98,
> Who blushes at the name,
> When cowards mock their country's fate,
> Who hangs his head in shame?
>   He's all a knave
>   Or half a slave
> Who slights his country thus.

> But true men, like you men,
> Will fill your glass with us.

'The Great Dan' much disliked criticism from his own side. 'Is O'Connell jealous of us?' asked Gavan Duffy. 'Jealous of us?' replied Dillon, 'Why, he's jealous of Brian Boru.'[10]

Nevertheless, in the spring and summer of 1843 Young Ireland was part of O'Connell's movement, acknowledging his leadership and significantly increasing his middle-class support.

It was this, together with the discipline of his huge meetings, which most alarmed the government. No one could now claim that the cause of repeal attracted only the *canaille* and a handful of uppity lawyers and priests. By May the ministry was seriously alarmed. Peel made a very strong statement in the House, declaring that he was authorised by the queen to say that she would do all in her power to preserve the union; even civil war, he said, would be better than a break-up of the Empire. Troop reinforcements were poured in, magazines and military stores were stocked up.

O'Connell reacted sharply. What was illegal in Her Majesty's loyal subjects assembling, in however large numbers, to petition her parliament? 'I will observe the spirit of the law, the letter of the law. I will, to be sure, shear it to its closest limits, but I will obey, and I set their blustering at defiance!' To thousands of Longford men he confided, 'I tell you what, if they attack us, then,' he thumped his ample chest to fierce yells of exultation, 'who will then be the coward?' (More cheers.) 'We will fight for Repeal and Liberty. Go home quietly, tell your friends of this day's work, and when I want you again, I'll let you know the day.'

At Kilkenny he trod closer to the brink.

> I stand today at the head of a group of men sufficient, if they underwent military training, to conquer Europe! Wellington never had such an army. [Cheers.] There was not at Waterloo on both sides as many brave and determined men as I see before me today. Tell them what to do and you will have them disciplined in an hour. [Cheers.] They are as well able to walk in order after a band as if they wore red coats.[11]

Three days later, in his 'Mallow Defiance', he went within a hair's breadth of incitement to rebellion.[12] Every word was calculated and premeditated; lest he be misreported he assembled the press reporters and instructed them to note exactly what he said, to make verbatim reports of it. At the meeting in the afternoon he spoke in his most temperate, moderate style. The public dinner was a festive occasion, but O'Connell was not elevated by liquor. He might not always mean what he said, but he always said exactly what he meant to say. After dinner in the jam-packed hall, a singer obliged with a patriotic song of Moore:

> Oh, where's the slave so lowly,
> Condemned to chains unholy,
> Who, could he burst
> His bonds accursed,
> Would pine beneath them slowly.

The Liberator leaped to his feet and bellowed, 'I am not that slave!'

'We are not slaves! We are not slaves!' they roared.

O'Connell swept into full flood of oratory.

Gentlemen, you may soon have the alternative to live as slaves or die as freemen. [Prolonged cheers.] In the midst of peace and tranquillity our Saxon traducers are covering the land with troops. [Groans and hisses.] On Thursday the Cabinet was considering what to do, not for Ireland but against her. [We are ready to meet them!] Of course you are. Do you think I suppose you to be cowards or fools? Are we to be called slaves? [No! No!] Have we not the ordinary courage of Englishmen? [Let them try!] Are we to be trampled under foot? [No! No!] Oh, they shall never trample on me at least! [Tremendous cheering for several minutes.] I was wrong, they may trample me under foot. [No! They never shall!] I say they may trample on me, but it will be my dead body they trample on and not the living man! [Hear! Hear! and tremendous cheering.] Cromwell, the only Englishman who ever possessed Ireland, sent 80,000 Irishmen to work as slaves, and every one perished beneath the ungenial sun of the Indies. Peel and Wellington may be second Cromwells. They may get his blunted truncheon and enact – Oh Sacred Heaven! – on the fair occupants of that gallery, Cromwell's massacre of the women of Wexford. But I am wrong. By God, they never shall! [Tremendous cheering and waving of handkerchiefs by the ladies.] Remember that deed! Three hundred women, the beauty and loveliness of Wexford, the young and the old, the maid and the matron. When Cromwell entered the town, these three hundred inoffensive women, of all ages and classes, were collected around the cross of Christ, erected in the part of the town called the Bull Ring. They prayed to Heaven for mercy, and I hope they found it. They prayed to the English for humanity, and Cromwell slaughtered them. [Cries of Oh! and a great sensation.] I repeat it. Three hundred of the grace, the beauty, the virtue of Wexford slaughtered by those English ruffians. [Oh! Oh!] Sacred Heaven! [Oh! Oh! Many of the ladies screaming in terror.] But, I assert, there is no danger to the women of Ireland, for the men of Ireland would die to the last in their defence. [Wild cheering, the entire company on its feet.] We were a paltry remnant in Cromwell's time. We are nine millions now!

How eagerly the Crown lawyers must have perused his speech! But what more did he in fact say than, '*If* Peel and Wellington behave in Cromwell's shocking manner, we will defend our women to the last'? Not even the best of handpicked juries could find him guilty on that. Yet the effect was terrific – and all from a man who repeated time and time again that repeal was not worth one drop of human blood, that he would shed no blood for it except his own, and that one live repealer was worth a whole graveyard of dead repealers.

The government's next move was to dismiss a number of magistrates including, on 23rd May, O'Connell himself, on the grounds that, although repeal meetings were not in themselves illegal, they tended to result in outrages. This, however, recoiled against them, for several magistrates of the highest repute, who were not repealers, resigned from the Bench in protest. These included O'Connell's old County Clare antagonist, William Smith O'Brien, who, with Thomas Wyse and John, conducted during the Liberator's absence from Westminster a spirited opposition in the Commons to the government's Irish legislation,

277

especially a draconian Arms Bill which they succeeded in weakening.

O'Connell's response to the dismissal of repeal magistrates was to set up Repeal Courts to judge disputes voluntarily submitted to them. Seventy-seven years later Sinn Fein was to adopt the same tactic, with considerable success; but O'Connell's courts were a flop, largely because of the poor quality of the unofficial magistrates. He also proposed a 'Council of Three Hundred', not elected or representing anyone (because that would have cut across the law) but consisting of men in whom the people had 'expressed their confidence'. It would assemble in Dublin, ostensibly to bring in the Repeal Rent but actually to operate as a sort of unofficial parliament. (Another idea of O'Connell's which was exploited with more success by Sinn Fein.) In a moment of euphoria he even hoped the Westminster parliament might recognise the Council's parliamentary status and transfer power to it. But this idea also flopped: the Council never assembled.[13]

But although the Repeal Courts and the Council of Three Hundred were not particularly happy inspirations, by midsummer the repeal campaign seemed to be a roaring triumph. That was how foreign observers saw it. O'Connell's fame on the continent was terrific.[14] It was fuelled, of course, by anglophobia, particularly in France, and a widespread jealousy of English commercial and political domination. Statesmen like Cavour and Mazzini, who hoped for English support in the liberation of Italy, were prudently non-committal about him. But elsewhere, from France to Hungary and Poland, European liberals revered him as the man of the people who was challenging and looked like defeating the immensely powerful British aristocracy; nationalists saw him as the man who had taught the Irish to be a nation; Catholics saw him as the man who had wrung Catholic emancipation from a government of Protestant bigots; liberal Catholics saw him as the man who had wedded Catholicism and liberalism, who had 'baptized liberalism and made it Christian' and 'sprinkled the first drops of baptismal water upon that savage power which we call Democracy'. Above all, as Lamartine said, O'Connell taught European democrats that government could be shaken and brought down not by bloody revolution, but by the power of massive, peaceful agitation. European travellers flocked to Ireland to write their Irish books, and all made the obligatory pilgrimage to Merrion Square or Derrynane: no travel book would be complete without an interview with and an assessment of the Liberator. No Englishman could cross the Channel without being asked how the government proposed to deal with him. A stock exchange expert remarked that O'Connell, 'as far as the money market is concerned, is one of the Great Powers of Europe. His movements have a sensible effect on the Funds.' He was pleased to bestow upon the liberal king of Bavaria his autograph, but refused it to the Tsar who ill-treated the Poles.

His fame crossed the oceans.[15] American slave-owners had their reservations about him, but most Americans approved of his tweaking the lion's tail, and Irish-Americans took immense pride in his achievements. French Canadians looked to him as their champion, and in log cabins in Quebec and Montreal hung framed engravings of the Liberator and the Virgin Mary standing by the crucifix. Irish-Australians liked more his fervent admiration for the Empire and the Crown, and his insistence that free settlers and emancipated convicts should be treated as equal citizens. He took considerable interest in Australian affairs, particularly in securing jobs there for Irish Catholics.

It was his second repeal agitation which, even more than emancipation, made him a Gaelic folk hero, the subject of innumerable stories and songs with no basis in fact.[16] His birth was marked by supernatural phenomena in Kerry; his swaddling clothes had curative properties; he was born with the mark of a cross on his back. As a young lad he displayed a precocious aptitude for resolving complex legal disputes by a few shrewd words.

Many of the legends hark back to his cunning at the Bar: he is constantly confounding opponents who are English or affluent.

> One day through the street as brave Daniel was walking
> A party of cockneys for to view him they stood:
> In order to humbug the monarch of Ireland
> One pulled out a note and said, 'Sir, is that good?'

> For to answer the question brave Dan was not lazy,
> The note to his pocket conveyed in a trice.
> When asked to return it, he says to the fellow,
> 'Sir, I am a lawyer that's paid for advice.'

In his non-violent agitation for repeal, he is portrayed by Gaelic bards as the hero with flashing sword who will lead the hosts of Gaeldom and drive the descendants of Luther and Calvin into the sea. Naturally the treacherous Saxons try to assassinate him, but he is always given timely warnings in his native tongue. At an English host's dinner-table an Irish servant girl asks him, 'Daniel O'Connell, do you understand Irish?' 'I do, my girl, what is the matter?' 'There's poison in your cup that would kill hundreds.' 'Bless you, my girl, and I will give you a dowry.' An Englishman engages him in a sword duel. Time and again his unerring blade penetrates the villain's defences, but the caitiff is wearing armour under his shirt. A boy, watching, calls out in Irish, 'Daniel, how would you kill a pig at home?' Dan takes the hint and runs the fellow through the throat.

His powers of locomotion were supernatural: to defend some Kerry fishermen charged in Belfast with smuggling, he rode from Derrynane to Belfast in a couple of days, and when he arrived his horse fell dead under him.

An Englishman bet Dan that his two cats would hold up two candles all during dinner; Dan took the bet and produced two mice from his pocket. When Dan was practising his speech in a garden, the very birds fell silent to listen.

Naturally Orangemen had a different view of O'Connell.

> Dan O'Connell he may boast of his great big rebel host,
> He can swear they're ten million in number.
> But half of them, you'll find, they are both lame and blind,
> But we're the bold Orange heroes of Comber.

Whereas he invariably got the better of Englishmen, landlords, judges and merchants, he was sometimes outwitted by his own kind. An old woman is charged with selling the same calf to three purchasers. The counsellor advises her that her only hope of acquittal is to pretend to be mad, throwing her coat over her head and saying, 'Bow-wow-wow'. She was duly acquitted, but when he went to claim his fee from her she threw her coat over her head and said, 'Bow-wow-wow'. He knew, then, that he was beaten at his own game.

His sexual prowess was heroic, his mistresses legion, including Queen Victoria. Rathkeale in County Limerick is infamous as the only village in Ireland which failed to provide him with home comforts. If the queen was short of soldiers for her army, all she had to do was apply to Dan to produce them. His procreative powers were so phenomenal that a Dublin pub-balladeer, familiar with the marvels of modern technology, sang, 'He's now making children in Dublin by steam.'

O'Connell thrived on praise. 'Was not that a good speech?' he would say to someone on whom he could rely for the right sort of answer. He must have relished being called 'Liberator' by everyone, even in his own family, for he did nothing to stop it, and even used to sign papers 'Daniel O'Connell, Liberator of Ireland'. But though he lapped up adulation, he took it with a pinch of salt. At a public meeting in Tralee, one bitter winter's day, there was an old harper, plucking away with frozen fingers at his harp between speeches. Betsey, who happened to be present, said to Tom Steele, 'Pray do something for that poor harper, Mr Steele, he looks miserable.'

Steele boomed back, at his most grandiloquent, 'Make your mind easy about him, daughter of Ireland's Liberator. I have taken care of the bard. I have made him immortal. In virtue of my office of Head Pacificator of Ireland, I have made him O'Connell's Chief Musician.'

'And I', said Ireland's Liberator, with a firmer grasp of reality, 'have given him half a crown.'

Through the summer the monster meetings continued, thirty-five of them drawing crowds of over 100,000. In August a million people assembled to hear – or see – him speak at Tara, once the seat of the High Kings of Ireland. The estimate is that of *The Times;* O'Connell's was one million, two hundred thousand. Even if only a quarter were there, and one in a hundred heard him, it was a stupendous effort of organisation, given the communications of the day, to bring such huge numbers together – and all without a shot fired, a stone thrown, or a head broken by a blackthorn stick. Was it to be peace or civil war? The question seemed to rest with the whim of one man who held Ireland in the palm of his hand.

The Chief Secretary, Lord Eliot, and the Home Secretary, Sir James Graham, thought that they detected in O'Connell signs of moderation and that 'the heat of Repeal has somewhat abated'. Lord de Grey, the Lord Lieutenant, didn't, and seemed to be proved right when O'Connell announced in August the greatest monster meeting of all time, at Clontarf, near Dublin, where Brian Boru had defeated the Danes, for 8th October 1843. Moreover in a notice issued by the Repeal Association in connection with the meeting military terms were used, such as 'Repeal cavalry'. O'Connell was quick to disavow these injudicious words, but de Grey insisted that something must be done. The question was, what?

But O'Connell had grievously miscalculated. He had worked up such warlike feelings that he could not retreat without humiliation for himself and disillusion for his people. As he would not make, perhaps could not make and certainly *had* not made any preparations for rebellion, retreat he must as soon as the government stood up to him. Moreover, hating and despising Peel, O'Connell had underestimated him.

For Peel was a master-politician, as crafty as he was tough, or flexible when that served his purpose. He had a keen sense of timing. Others might think O'Connell had the government on the run, but Peel thought O'Connell was bluffing and was determined to call the bluff. If the Clontarf meeting was not illegal it could be made so. On 7th October, the day before it was to take place, a proclamation declared it to be an unlawful assembly.

This, as Peel intended, put O'Connell in a hideous dilemma. Either he must obey the law, call off what was to be his greatest triumph, and suffer a humiliating loss of face; or he must defy the law and be responsible for whatever consequences might ensue when horse, foot and guns, already in position at Clontarf, were ordered to disperse a hundred thousand wildly excited Irishmen, spoiling for a fight.

O'Connell called it off. It was common sense to do so, and the only course compatible with his principles of non-violence and legality. But to his followers it was a shattering anti-climax. According to Gavan Duffy the retreat was most resented by the Young Irelanders: 'The power they had helped to create was being recklessly squandered; the policy to which they stood pledged was practically relinquished.' But there is not the slightest contemporary evidence that the Young Irelanders advocated defying the law and going ahead with the Clontarf meeting. Some people, not specifically Young Irelanders, while recognising that a mass defiance of the law was imprudent, blamed O'Connell for tamely submitting to Peel without testing the legal question of whether the right to petition parliament must give way to a Castle proclamation. This he could have done by proceeding peacefully, with a few colleagues, to the meeting place, and then bringing an action for assault against anyone who presumed to lay hands on him. It is strange that he, a lawyer, did not think of this. Wilkes would have done so.[17]

But what could his critics do? They could not put the boot into the only possible leader of the repeal movement, but must endure what exasperated them and wait for better times. Besides, as members of the committee of the Repeal Association they had acquiesced in the decision to call off the meeting and could not now plausibly repudiate it. But after Clontarf, O'Connell's course ran downhill all the way.

14

The Exhausted Volcano

If the damage to O'Connell's reputation was severe, even greater was the damage to his self-confidence. He began to hedge on repeal, suggesting tentatively that an acceptable substitute would be some federal arrangement, with the Westminster parliament (including, of course, M.P.s from Ireland) dealing with defence, foreign affairs and the Empire, while a parliament in Dublin busied itself with purely Irish affairs. Ten years ago, during his negotiations with Dr Boyton, he had flown that kite and it had been ignored; it did not receive much more attention now.

O'Connell thought he might even be charged with high treason, for which the penalty was death. If the government were to try him on such a charge, with a packed jury, 'I shall make my confession and prepare for death.' It was a relief when, on 14th October 1843, he, John, Steele, Ray, Gavan Duffy and four others were arrested and charged with conspiring to change the government by intimidation and demonstrations of great physical force. He told John, 'I do not think two years' imprisonment would kill me; I would keep constantly walking about, and take a bath every day.'

His enemies were delighted. Lord Clarendon, formerly George Villiers, gloated to Philip Crampton:

The government may reckon to the nth + 1 where there is an infinite upon the pure unadulterated cowardice of O'Connell and that under fear of either collision or prosecution he will

284

eat dirt and more dirt and try to cram the same unsavoury *palulum* down the throats of all the followers he can re-dupe. His milkandwateryness and his federation and his anglomania and all the rest of his recreant garbage since the Government gave its little sign of non-abdication really place him beneath contempt ... In any other country but Ireland a leader like O'Connell would at once lose all chance of future prestige and profit, but the people are so blarney-ridden and priest-ridden that no such thing will probably occur. He will get an acquittal, an ovation and a subscription, and then be cautious for a while; but I hardly understand how the enormous head of steam he has got up can be turned off quietly, or how the concentration of bitterness against England and all the hierarchical and agrarian hopes that have been excited are to subside.[1]

The repercussions of the Clontarf fiasco and his arrest were not all to O'Connell's disadvantage. They brought him sympathy from non-repeal liberals, and Smith O'Brien took the plunge and joined the Repeal Association. A wealthy and respected landowner, of old Irish stock claiming descent from Brian Boru, of the highest integrity but cold in manner, without a trace of charisma or popular appeal and a poor public speaker, 'more Smith [it was said] than O'Brien', he was O'Connell's most valuable recent acquisition. 'You are', the Liberator informed him, 'literally a living treasure to the cause.' 'O'Brien certainly merits to be enrolled among the most pure benefactors of his native land.' The new recruit's great value was that he was a Protestant, and of far higher repute for level-headedness than 'mad Steele'.

> Even the casual fact of your religion is most useful to the Repeal cause. It is impossible that any Protestant who calmly thinks can imagine that you would be a party to any political movement which could deprive Protestants of their legitimate station and due sway in the state. Politically speaking I am delighted that you are a Protestant. Protestantism can never want just protection where you advise and direct.[2]

How could O'Connell reconcile these sentiments with a letter he had written just two years earlier to the Reverend Paul Cullen,

Rector of the Irish College in Rome?* In it he listed sixteen ways in which repeal would strengthen the Catholic Church at the expense of the Church of Ireland. They included:

> The Protestants in Ireland are not so much religionists as politicians. They are ... Protestants by reason of ... political power being almost entirely confided in them ... If the Union were repealed and the exclusive system abolished, the great mass of the Protestant community would with little delay melt into the overwhelming majority of the Irish nation. Protestantism would not survive Repeal ten years. Nothing but persecution would keep it alive and the Irish Catholics are too good and too wise to persecute ... The Repeal of the Union would free the Catholic people of Ireland from the burden of supporting the useless Protestant Church ... The Repeal of the Union would at once disengage the [Protestant] Church lands from the hands to which they have been unjustly transferred by means of the so-called Reformation.

With the funds thereby acquired, the Catholic Church could suitably endow the hierarchy and priesthood and carry out a whole programme of works highly advantageous to Catholics. 'However,' he warned Cullen, 'I am prevented from presenting it [Repeal] in its true colours to the British people lest it should have the effect of increasing hostility to that measure.'[3]

Not even O'Connell could argue that the two letters, to the Protestant landlord and the Catholic priest, are compatible. So which of them, in spirit miles apart, represented his real opinion?

Over the past thirty years he had tried again and again to attach Protestants to whatever cause he was supporting at the time. Except during his campaign for Catholic emancipation, his success had been negligible, and confined mainly to middle- and upper-class Protestants who could contribute little but money and zeal to a mass agitation. 'The moment Protestants forget Ascendancy and consent to endure equality with good temper, we shall be too strong for our enemies.' But they would never do so, and it was only natural for him to be sometimes exasperated

---

* Later Archbishop of Dublin, of Armagh and Cardinal.

by their obduracy. He could never regard Protestantism as a religious thing: he saw it purely as a rationalisation for the defence of privilege. He said frankly to O'Neill Daunt, '*The* difficulty [about Repeal] is Protestantism.' So did the letter to Cullen express his inmost thoughts?

He was writing to Cullen with a specific purpose, to dissuade the Pope from obliging the British government by ordering Irish bishops and priests to withdraw from repeal. What he said to Cullen was at variance with everything – well, nearly everything – he had said on that subject for his whole political life. It is difficult to know with someone as devious as O'Connell, but on the whole it seems probable that his letter to Smith O'Brien set out his real views, albeit exaggerated by the flattery which came naturally to him. He was being less than honest in his letter to Cullen.

It is odd that the disciple who followed him with the most unswerving, dog-like devotion was the Protestant Tom Steele. 'My revered leader, my beloved friend, the Liberator,' Steele would begin his letters. Maurice said of him, 'If the Liberator ordered him to stand to his chin in a barrel of gunpowder smoking a cigar, he would delightedly comply, and feel cruelly disappointed if the explosion did not take place.' But, devoted as he was, as a political asset Steele could not compare with the cold, aristocratic Smith O'Brien.[4]

O'Connell and his fellow-martyrs were, of course, released on bail pending trial, and he went down to Derrynane for Christmas. He lost some noble hounds from distemper, but the rest gave him splendid sport. To FitzPatrick he wrote:

I already feel the immense benefit of my native air and my delightful exercise. I am regaining strength and vigour to endure whatever the sentence may be. You will believe that I shall endure it without shrinking or compromise, come what may.

And to Pierce Mahony:

What a tasteless fellow the Attorney General was not to allow me another fortnight in these mountains! I can forgive him anything but *that*. Why, yesterday I had the most delightful

day's hunting. I saw almost the entire of it – hare and hounds.
We killed five hares – the dogs ran without intermission five
hours and three quarters. In three minutes after each hare was
killed we had another on foot and the cry was incessant. They
were never at more than a momentary check and the cry, with
the echoes, was splendid. I was not in such wind for walking
these five years, and you will laugh at me when I tell you the
fact that I was much less wearied than several of the young
men.

Then he must go back to Dublin to face the music. 'The tone
of O'Connell is doubtless lowered,' wrote Lord Clarendon before
Christmas, 'and the fear of being shut up has caused him to
display quite a large crop of white feathers. But ... can twelve
jurymen so utterly regardless of their lives as to convict
O'Connell be found?'

They could. The Castle took care of that. When he came up
for trial on 15th January 1844, the prosecution challenged eleven
Catholic jurymen on the ground that they were repealers, and
eventually achieved a jury composed entirely of Protestants,
largely of Orangemen.[5] Despite a vigorous defence by a team of
Irish lawyers, including Sheil, all but one of the accused were
found guilty and remanded on bail for sentence. Not having set
foot in the Commons for the whole of 1843, O'Connell went over
to London to put in an appearance and whip up support among
English radicals. Smith O'Brien was left in charge of the Repeal
Association in Dublin.

It lay very low. Davis predicted, 'O'Connell will run no more
risks. Even when this judgement shall be set aside, and he will
come out in triumph, he will content himself with imposing
demonstrations.' In fact O'Connell advised against imposing demonstrations: parish meetings were in future to be the vehicle of
propaganda. He even suggested closing down the Repeal Association. He had, after all, closed down most of his associations at
one time or another, to avoid prosecution, and revived them
under other names. But he did not press this suggestion in the
face of strong protests from Young Ireland and Smith O'Brien.
So, with O'Connell out of action, the Association carried on,
rather diminuendo, with Smith O'Brien in the chair. Its most
surprising resolution during this bleak period was to

view with satisfaction the permanent location in this country of whatever naval and military establishments may be required for the general defence of the Empire. Their expenditure gives a stimulus to our home markets and their presence enlivens our social meetings.[6]

In January O'Connell had written to Charles Buller, an English Liberal M.P., a summary of what the government should do if it wished to conciliate Ireland and weaken the demand for repeal. There must be perfect religious equality, with the state either paying the clergy of all denominations or paying none of them. He preferred the latter, with no established church. Post-union legislation enhancing the landlords' powers of eviction and distraint must be repealed. The franchise must be reformed, preferably by introducing the secret ballot but, if that were impossible, by a great increase in the number of rural voters. Irish Corporations should be placed on the same footing as English and Scottish Corporations. The qualifications for the vote in boroughs must be lowered, and the voting privileges of Freemen, 'an ancient Protestant nuisance', must be abolished. The income tax on absentee landlords should be increased five-fold. Fixity of tenure should be given serious consideration. The present humbug committee* should be turned into a real, efficient, searching inquiry, and the commission entrusted with that inquiry should be composed of tenants as well as landlords.

I have thus, my dear Buller, candidly given you the elements of the destruction of my political power and for the diminishing of the demand for the Repeal. But I do not expect any important result from your exertions ... You cannot succeed – it is impossible – your countrymen are too deeply embued in national antipathy to the Irish. You have injured us too deeply, too cruelly, ever to forgive us. And then there is a bigoted anti-Catholic spirit embittering, enhancing and augmenting the English hatred of the Irish nation.[7]

In the event he found in England a surprising degree of sym-

* The Royal Commission under the Earl of Devon appointed in November 1843 to inquire into the law and practice of the occupation of land in Ireland. Usually known as the Devon Commission.

pathy and much indignation at his being found guilty by a jury so blatantly packed. Whigs in general, Irish Whigs in particular, spoke up for him in the Commons and his own references to recent events were moderate and free from rancour. Pierce Mahony, dining with Lord Anglesey, brought O'Connell a message from the man with whom his relations had been so chequered: 'I greatly regret any differences between me and O'Connell and let him know that I sincerely wish him success and if I had power I would exert it on his behalf.'[8] It seemed as though, when the Liberals regained office, another concordat with them might be possible.

Returning to Dublin, O'Connell was sentenced to twelve months' imprisonment and a fine of £2,000, and bound over for £5,000 to keep the peace for seven years. His associates were sentenced to nine months' imprisonment and fined £50 each. Having won that round, the government was not vindictive, and allowed them to choose their place of detention. They presented themselves, with suitable ceremony, at the Richmond Bridewell, the governor of which welcomed them rather in the spirit of a host at a country house party. It was not a very vile durance: each prisoner was allotted a large, well-furnished apartment, and at a dining-table laden with gifts of salmon, venison, poultry and game, they could entertain as many visitors as they pleased.

O'Connell declared that his greatest hardship was anxiety lest the people rebel in protest at his treatment. He issued a message to his fellow-countrymen urging them most strictly to keep the peace. 'Obey my advice. NO RIOT. NO TUMULT. NO BLOW. NO VIOLENCE. Keep the peace for six months, or at the utmost twelve months longer, and you shall have the Parliament in College Green again.' Greatly to his relief, they obeyed him.

While in prison he had a pathetic, old man's love affair with a 23-year-old girl who occasionally, suitably chaperoned, visited him. She was Rose McDowell, daughter of a Belfast Protestant merchant, 'one of the most superior women I ever met with, with intellect, sound judgement and fascinating sweetness.' His family managed to hush it up, and little is known of it because she kept her mouth shut for sixty years and he, shortly before his death, instructed FitzPatrick to destroy all his correspondence with the lady – 'which you may read yourself because it contains nothing disreputable'. There is no food for scandal here: his hopeless passion did not last long, and he seems to have seen her only once after his release; but it cannot have made his imprisonment any easier.

He and his colleagues were treated with every possible consideration. He assured Betsey, 'We all enjoy excellent health and spirits. We are quite gay and cheerful as larks.' From the governor and his family they received 'the kindest and most constant attention during our unjust imprisonment. Everything that could be done to alleviate the irksomeness of confinement was done by this excellent and amiable family.' Nevertheless the fact of confinement, the restriction and lack of exercise imposed on a somewhat overweight, elderly man undermined his excellent constitution. When he was released he seemed to have aged years.

His release came much earlier than he expected. On 4th September, just over three months after they had entered prison, the House of Lords reversed the judgment against the eight on the grounds that the trial had not been fair, and on 6th September they were free. Their triumphal procession through the streets amid the thunderous cheering of the crowds, with a mounted escort of top-hatted gentlemen carrying imitation lances and with the Liberator on a huge, lofty, ornamental chariot, was one of the greatest spectacles the capital had ever seen.[9]

As soon as possible he was back in Derrynane, finding everything in the best of order. 'I am in truth a great farmer and have certainly the best crop of hay ... in the province.' The potato crop too was excellent and his pack 'in high pride of beauty'. John had suffered most from imprisonment, but quickly recovered in the Kerry air. Like any man of sixty-nine, O'Connell knew that his hunting days were numbered, but squeezed every last minute of enjoyment out of them. He might no longer be able to keep up with hounds, but he could still watch them hunting across the mountainside and hear their glorious cry. Nothing made him more cross than well-meaning strangers offering to help him over a ditch or wall.

Although the Agitator himself was in eclipse, Peel saw the political forces he had conjured up as still very dangerous. The Catholic Church was even more politically conscious and more liberal in its politics than during the emancipation campaign. The vast majority of the parish clergy, especially the curates, were active propagandists for repeal. Father Mathew's spectacular, revivalist Temperance Movement was almost a subsidiary of the Repeal Association. So, coercion having failed, Peel set out to pare away Catholic support for repeal by a series of conciliatory measures. With their leader in prison or in disrepute, he thought Catholics would be grateful for any crumb he might toss them. In this he erred.[10]

There was a board, set up by the now defunct Irish parliament, to adjudicate in cases of disputes about legacies to charitable institutions, which in fact meant schools, hospitals, asylums, etc. run by one or other of the Churches. Since there were fifty gentlemen on the board, nearly all Protestants, it was both unwieldy and biased. A Catholic charity, aggrieved by its decision, had no redress in the courts which would not ratify bequests for 'superstitious' purposes. Would it not be a perfectly harmless measure, gratifying Catholics and annoying nobody, to replace the board by one of thirteen members, appointed by the Crown, of whom five would be Catholics? It seemed a piece of minor do-goodery which in Victorian England would have been acknowledged with a finger to the hat-brim and a 'Thankee kindly, Zurr.'

Unfortunately Her Majesty's government made one of the classic mistakes in Anglo-Irish relations, legislating for Ireland without consulting a single Irish Catholic, except one widely regarded as a renegade. So the Charitable Bequests Bill, first put before the Lords in June 1844 as an olive branch proffered to Catholic Ireland, turned out instead to be a bone of furious contention. Two-thirds of the hierarchy followed the lead of the militant Dr John MacHale, Archbishop of Tuam, in attacking it with unmeasured invective because a well-intentioned but ill-advised clause rendered invalid any bequest of real property made within three months of the testator's death. This, said Dr MacHale, impugned the integrity of Catholic priests by assuming that they would cajole and bully a dying man, could be inspired only by a 'deadly hatred' of the Catholic Church, and surpassed 'in its odious provisions the worst enactments of penal days'. O'Connell from his suite in Richmond Jail denounced the bill as legally unsound, 'worse than humbug', an insidious attempt to increase the Castle's patronage and influence the doctrine, usage and discipline of the Catholic Church. On his release he held mass meetings of protest against it. Peel then made matters worse by enlisting the aid of the Pope in controlling his turbulent priests, thus giving the Hierarchy and the Agitator occasion to rail, in terms worthy of Exeter Hall, against a concordat between the Government and the Papacy and against Papal interference in the affairs of the United Kingdom. Nevertheless, on advice from Rome, Dr Crolly, Archbishop of Armagh, and Dr Murray, Archbishop of Dublin, did accept nomination to the new board which did useful work in a modest way for the next eighty years. Peel had achieved something, in bringing about an open split between O'Connell and a strong minority of the hierarchy led by Crolly and Murray. Moreover some of the Young Irelanders, notably Smith O'Brien who saw nothing much wrong with the Charitable Bequests Bill, objected to O'Connell involving the Repeal Association in agitation against a purely Catholic grievance, and a minor one at that.[11]

The Young Irelanders were also incensed by O'Connell declaring, rather precipitately, in favour of a federal constitution for Ireland and England. During October 1844, in private letters to Smith O'Brien, FitzPatrick, Pierce Mahony and others, and in an open letter to the Repeal Association, O'Connell argued that an Irish parliament dealing with domestic matters would give Ireland all the essentials of self-rule, while adequate representation in the Westminster parliament would give her a share in framing defence, imperial and foreign policies. The necessary link with England would be safeguarded. By bringing respectable federalists into alliance with, if not membership of, the Association, irresistible pressure would be brought to bear on the government to grant the essentials of repeal while avoiding its dangers. All that was needed was for the federalists to lay their cards on the table so that he could play their hand.

Even O'Neill Daunt was shocked, writing to O'Connell in pained protest, 'Federalism is not new in the Association, but a *preference* for it on the part of our leader is new.' The Young Irelanders were appalled, and Gavan Duffy replied with a broadside in the *Nation*.[12] The Association, he argued, could no more renege on its commitment to repeal than the Irish parliament could legally abolish itself in 1800. To dilute the demand for 'simple Repeal' would delight all its enemies, and the Repeal Association would disintegrate as its more ardent members resigned in disgust. Reputable federalists like Wyse and Sharman Crawford would never accept O'Connell's leadership: he was personally obnoxious to too many of them. An Irish parliament with powers approximating to those of a Grand Jury was no substitute for a real, sovereign, independent parliament. It would perpetuate both Ireland's subordination to England and the curse of absenteeism as wealthy, able Irishmen looked to London as the focus of their ambition. His diatribe aimed at O'Connell was summarised by an acute critic as, 'Your proposal will ruin Federalism and ruin Repeal; and though you are our leader, you should not lead us to destruction.'

Because the federalists ignored the fly O'Connell had cast over them, the issue faded out. But it added to the suspicions and jealousies which plagued the Association. There was the generation gap between Old Ireland and Young Ireland; the conflict in style between the populist, rural, emotional and Catholic approach of O'Connell and the élitist, urban, intellectual and slightly anti-clerical approach of Young Ireland; and the conflict between a pragmatic readiness to accept a federal compromise and an insistence on 'simple Repeal'. Moreover O'Connell was determined that his son John, a smart little fellow with some political skill but not much depth, should succeed him as boss of the Repeal Association, while the Young Irelanders thought the throne should be elective, not hereditary.[13]

They suspected that O'Connell would, at the drop of a hat, abandon the cause of repeal and enter a new compact with the Whigs. They were not far wrong. Indeed the publication of the Devon Commission Report in January 1845 extracted from him an admission that even Peel might be sincere in wishing to do good for Ireland.

Not that he approved of the report, which was all that could be expected from a body composed only of landlords' representatives. It recommended neither a punitive tax on absentee landlords, nor fixity of tenure for tenants, nor the tenant's right to reimbursement for any permanent improvements he had installed; all of which, although unpalatable to landlords, O'Connell thought essential lest the people 'operate a "fixity of tenure" for themselves with a vengeance'. But the report did some good in calling attention to the plight of cottiers and landless labourers, and made it clear that there were other problems besides the relations between landlord and tenant farmer,[14] notably those between tenant farmers and labourers.

To most Tories it seemed that the root of the Irish problem was the Royal College of Saint Patrick at Maynooth. Founded and financed by the government to provide a supply of priests untainted by Jacobinism and democracy, it now seemed to be a forcing-house of sedition. As we have seen, it was not true, though frequently alleged, that the average Maynooth priest was of disreputable social origin; in fact he came from the respectable middle and upper-middle classes. But he was politically aware, and almost certainly an ardent repealer. When, therefore, Mac-Hale asked for an increase in the annual Maynooth grant, for the college was heavily in debt and needed to increase its output, some ministers saw this as a Heaven sent opportunity to control these troublesome young men, perhaps even by putting them on the government payroll. The Cabinet, however – this time after consulting Irish Catholic opinion – decided on the wiser course: an increase in the grant would be without strings, an act of pure benevolence. The benevolence was duly acknowledged in Ireland, even by the Presbyterians. The formidable 'John of Tuam' publicly praised it, and O'Connell at a public meeting declared that 'nothing was ever more fair, manly and excellent in all its details.'[15]

In May 1845, there was introduced the Academical Institutions (Ireland) Bill. The government's intentions were again excellent. It was, and is, the conviction of most English and some Irish laymen that education which segregates young Catholics from young Protestants, inculcating in both a tribal concept of history and politics, is a principal cause of envy, hatred and all uncharitableness. (This is not a view shared by the clergy of any denomination, who wish to protect their young from contamination.) So the third of Peel's conciliatory measures was this legislation, which set out to provide Catholics and Dissenters with university education and degrees by setting up non-denominational colleges in Cork, Galway and Belfast, leaving Anglicans in undisturbed possession of Trinity College. He hoped to evade the most thorny problem by providing only the facilities for the teaching of divinity, the chairs for which must be privately endowed. He deliberately omitted to consult the Catholic hierarchy, assuming, no doubt, that their reactions would be unfavourable. They were indeed. MacHale denounced in an open letter this 'infidel and slavish and demoralising scheme' while the equally uncompromising Dr Cantwell, Bishop of Meath, predicted that the colleges would be so exploited by Protestant proselytisers that 'the harvest of immorality, irreligion and infidelity among the youth of Catholic Ireland will be quick and abundant.' The hierarchy would have nothing to do with the scheme unless the teaching of history, logic, metaphysics, moral philosophy, geology and anatomy was solely in Catholic hands. (One cannot quite see the relevance of the last two subjects to their fears.) But some prelates, including Doctors Crolly and Murray, were not wholly opposed to the bill, so to meet their fears it was agreed that the Crown should appoint three visitors to the colleges, Catholic, Anglican and Presbyterian, who should keep an alert watch for proselytising and other abuses. This olive-branch was spurned by MacHale. O'Connell, who had in the past cautiously favoured mixed education in secular subjects, now followed MacHale's line of outright rejection of the 'Godless Colleges'. The private endowment of religious education would give an enormous advantage to the Protestants 'who are rich over the Catholics who are poor', and among the visitors there would always be two Protestant voices to one Catholic.[16]

Well might Peel have thought, 'You can't win'; and the problem of providing young Irish Catholics with university education, in their own country, without polluting the pure Anglican fount of Trinity, was to bedevil Irish politics for the next sixty years.

The Young Irelanders, with their intellectual, middle-class, slightly anti-clerical bias, had welcomed the bill as bringing together (in Wolfe Tone's oft-quoted words) 'Catholic, Protestant and Dissenter in the common denomination of Irishman'. There is some evidence (besides Gavan Duffy's spiteful allegation) that John O'Connell, in order to discomfit the Young Irelanders and embroil them with the Catholic Church, stoked up his father's hostility to the 'Godless Colleges'.[17]

In a bad-tempered debate in the Repeal Association on 26th May O'Connell complained of this perfectly well-meaning measure that 'a more nefarious attempt at profligacy and corruption never disgraced a Minister'. He cheered and waved his cap when one of his acolytes charged the Young Irelanders with indifference to religion; and he got involved in an unseemly exchange with Davis, a supporter of the bill, whom he accused of sneering at Catholics. Finally he lambasted for their inordinate ambition

> the section of politicians styling themselves the Young Ireland Party ... There is no such party as that styled Young Ireland ... I am for Old Ireland. 'Tis time this disillusion should be put an end to. Young Ireland may play what pranks they please. I do not envy them the name they rejoice in. I shall stand by Old Ireland; and I have some slight notion that Old Ireland will stand by me.

It all ended in tears and reconciliation, with O'Connell sobbing, 'Davis, I love you!' But the damage was done, the split was exposed to public view. It was widened by Davis's death in September. He was the most able and most respected of the Young Irelanders, and O'Connell was genuinely grieved:

> His loss is indeed irreparable. What an example he was to the Protestant youth of Ireland! What a noble emulation of his virtues ought to be excited in the Catholic young men of Ireland! And his heart, too, was as tenderly kind as his judgement was comprehensive and his genius magnificent.[18]

Thereafter Gavan Duffy, far more hostile to O'Connell, assumed the intellectual leadership of Young Ireland.

In the autumn of 1845 the potato blight was observed in at least eleven counties. With his intimate knowledge of rural Ireland, O'Connell saw the prospect of disaster far sooner than the Young Irelanders, and more or less took over the Mansion House Committee set up by the Dublin Corporation as a clearing house for information on the spread of the disease and a pressure group for relief measures.[19]

The first consequence of the partial crop failure was a political crisis in England. Peel was as quick as O'Connell to see the significance of the potato blight, and it confirmed his growing conviction that the Corn Laws should be repealed so as to allow corn to be imported free of duty. 'Rotten potatoes put Peel in his damned fright,' said the Duke. This split the Conservative government, and on 5th December Peel resigned. It was assumed that Lord John Russell would form a government, and O'Connell was again tempted by the prospect of an alliance with the Whigs. Smith O'Brien warned him against this; he believed it to be

> for the interest of Ireland that administration after administration should be shipwrecked until England shall have learned that it would be wise on her part as well as just to conform to the wish and the determination of Ireland by acceding to our demand for a national parliament.

He suspected that the Whigs, by promising to repeal the Corn Laws, were baiting a trap for O'Connell. He himself was in favour of reducing the import duty on corn but not of abolishing it altogether which, he argued, would ruin Irish agriculture and was not desired by Irish voters.[20]

O'Connell would have none of this. He was opposed in principle to duties on imported food. More important, he *knew* that a serious famine was approaching. The effects could only be alleviated by the government acting promptly to provide work for all those whose crops had failed, and cheap food for them to buy.

> Unless the Government comes forward energetically with some plan of this kind, it is impossible to calculate the number of people who will perish in Ireland within the next twelve months of famine and pestilence. But how can we insist on the Government finding employment and food ... if we vote in favour of the Corn Laws and thereby prevent food being as cheap as it would otherwise be? How can we on one hand complain of starvation and on the other vote against provisions being as cheap as they might otherwise be?[21]

In the event Lord John Russell was unable to form a government, so Peel carried on, pledged to repeal the Corn Laws with the aid of Whig free traders in the face of bitter opposition from most of his own party. Peel was not a bigoted adherent of *laissez faire* economics: he arranged for Treasury grants to be issued to local relief committees (charged with organising relief schemes) which were to match pound for pound local contributions; and for Indian corn to be imported from America on the government account and sold to the people, through the relief committees, at a reasonable price. There were unexpected problems in milling the Indian corn, which is far harder than any grain used in Ireland and which in the United States was chopped up in steel mills; the country people did not know how to cook it, or indeed how to cook any food but the potato. The local relief committees were far from efficient or energetic. Throughout the winter of 1845–6, with famine inexorably approaching, wheat, oats and livestock were being exported, necessarily under heavy military escort. Whatever the economic justification for this, nothing in Irish history has caused more bitterness against England. Nevertheless Peel's policy was fairly successful in alleviating the effects of what was still only a partial failure of the potato crop. Worse, far worse, was to come.

While with one hand Peel proffered a bunch of carrots – the Charitable Bequests Bill, the Maynooth grant, the 'Colleges' Bill, repeal of the Corn Laws, anti-famine measures – with the other he flourished a heavy stick. His Protection of Life (Ireland) Bill, commonly known as the (latest) Coercion Bill, was drafted to meet the complete breakdown of law and order which was expected to be the first result of the famine. O'Connell with his repealer 'Tail' and Liberal allies fought this tooth and nail, using every device to obstruct, filibuster and delay. 'There is', complained Peel,

> an Irish party, a determined and not insignificant one, for which British indignation has no terrors. Their wish is to disgust England with Irish business and Irish members, and to induce England ... to listen to a Repeal of the Legislative Union for the purpose of purging the House of a set of troublesome and factious members who equally obstruct legislation for Ireland and for Great Britain.

O'Connell's campaign against Peel's Coercion Bill, which Parnell was to copy in exact detail, was the Liberator's last parliamentary victory. On 25th June 1846, the very day on which the Corn Laws were repealed, a combination of repealers, Liberals and vengeful Tory protectionists threw out the Coercian Bill and Peel resigned. Lord John Russell did then form a government.[22]

Meanwhile O'Connell suffered from an annoying distraction,

an all too successful attempt by *The Times* to discredit him as a landlord, a role in which he particularly prided himself.[23] Late in 1845 the editor commissioned a special reporter, T.C. Foster, to report on the agricultural scene in Ireland. He visited O'Connell's estates and denounced him as a negligent and harsh landlord. The Liberator, he wrote, courting easy popularity and in order to maximise his rents, allowed his tenants to sub-divide their holdings *ad infinitum*; and he animadverted on the condition of Cahirciveen, its dirty, unpaved streets and old-hat-mended windows. Stung to the quick, O'Connell retorted with character-istic vigour, itemising the £4,000 he had spent on Cahirciveen and describing Foster as a boundless liar and gutter com-missioner of the infamous *Times*. Foster replied that O'Connell's father was a huckster shopkeeper and his family of disreputable origin.

The editor then sent William Howard Russell, soon to be famous for his reports on the Crimean War, to check up on Foster's allegations. Broadly speaking, he confirmed them. In the rocky townland of Derrynanebeg (609 acres), close to the Liber-ator's house, there were sixty-two holdings, for which he received rents varying from two shillings to £7 a year. (Today in that townland are six holdings, none economically viable.) O'Connell called upon Lord Cloncurry and the Knight of Kerry to testify that he was a good landlord, which they duly did.

Many years later, in his memoirs, Russell returned to the subject.

> I believe the tenants of Derrynane Beg were squatters, the evicted refuse of adjoining estates, who flocked to the boggy valley where they were allowed to run up the hovels of sod-dened earth and mud, with leave to turn out their lean kine and cultivate patches of potatoes on the hillside, paying as many shillings as the agent could squeeze out of them.

In September 1846 the young English Quaker, W.E. Forster, investigating famine conditions, stayed with O'Connell at Der-rynane and wrote in a private letter:

> I have made a great deal of inquiry in all quarters respecting his tenantry and am convinced that the impression made by

the report in *The Times* is most unfair and untrue. I should say he is decidedly the best landlord in the district, but owing to his having allowed rejected tenants from other estates to squat on his estate at nominal rents, there are, of course, some wretched cabins.

The truth was that O'Connell was by no means an 'improving' landlord; he was too kind-hearted, too politically vulnerable, and he understood too well the peasant's point of view that land is not just something to make money out of, but is the one thing that keeps a man and his family from actual starvation, or at best from begging from door to door. Except in Cahirciveen, of which he was proud, he did not invest much capital in his estate; he had little capital to invest. He, or his agent John Primrose, reputedly a hard man, was strict over payment of rent in good years and did not hesitate to evict defaulters, but in bad years he was generous over remissions of rent, and during the famine he exerted himself and Maurice to the limit to ensure that, however others fared, his own people did not starve. He should not, perhaps, have allowed all those squatters, but in the circumstances of the winter of 1845-6 it was very difficult for him to say, 'No. Go away.'

O'Connell expected Lord Russell's government to be a good thing for Ireland. It turned out to be a catastrophe. For Russell, and even more for the Secretary to the Treasury, Charles Edward Trevelyan, who was in charge of the famine relief, it was an article of faith, irrefutable, that private enterprise could cope with any situation; and that if only the government refrained from interfering, private traders in grain would solve all the problems of the famine. So Trevelyan stopped the import of grain on the government account except for the counties along the west coast where even he realised there *were* no traders in grain; he stopped the Treasury grants of half the cost of relief schemes and substituted loans to be repaid out of Poor Rates; and he insisted that the export of wheat, barley and oats should continue unimpeded because, out of the profits they made, the private traders would import Indian corn. 'Perfect Free Trade', he laid down *ex cathedra*, 'is the right course.' At the same time he imposed the strictest Treasury control over all relief schemes, lest they breach the rule that they must not benefit one landlord more than another.

(This disqualified drainage schemes from relief loans because they were bound to benefit more those landowners through whose properties they passed.) Every application by a local relief board for a scheme had to be personally examined and authorised by himself; and although he slaved away twelve or fifteen hours a day, there were weeks of delay between the application for a scheme and final Treasury approval. Moreover, except in Dublin, Belfast and Cork, corn chandlers such as operated in every English town hardly existed. The trade in foodstuffs fell into the hands of that scourge of nineteenth-century Ireland, the rapacious 'gombeen man', huckster and money-lender, who made outrageous profits out of starvation. And such merchants in grain as existed were geared to exporting corn and could not rapidly improvise an import business.[24]

However, confident that he could sway the government's policy as he had ten years earlier, O'Connell bombarded ministers and civil servants with advice, admonition and desperate pleas – all perfectly sensible and all ignored. In vain he called Russell's attention to the 'frightful state of famine by which the people of this country are not merely menaced but actually engulfed' and appealed in anguished words for the most urgent action.

I respectfully submit that the forms of law and of constitutional guarantees must yield to the pressure of a death-dealing famine. And I also submit whether Her Majesty's Government may not feel, at such an awful crisis, it right to consider whether Parliament may not ... confer upon the Government extraordinary powers of directing, *without any delay*, the execution of works of public utility and of supplying the immediate means of paying the wages of the labourers employed.

Although works had been designed and authorised, 'ten days elapsed and not a single labourer has been taken into employment. Can I implore you to take the trouble of getting the matter remedied and to insist that the people should be set to work as speedily as possible?'

In this county they have employed the county surveyor ... but he cannot multiply himself eightfold and therefore the want of promptitude in commencing employment is distinctly traceable to the Board of Works ... A sum of not less than one million ought to be immediately placed under the Lord Lieutenant to employ at his discretion.

For all the effect his letters had, he might have been whistling jigs at milestones. At the same time, and with more effect, he badgered Maurice, not the most energetic of men, into organising work in the Derrynane area and importing Indian corn and American 'saved beef'.[25]

Meanwhile, as though not a single Irish child was hungry, the Young Irelanders were concerned solely with their challenge to O'Connell. The *Nation* openly declared that his leadership would make it 'certain as fate that this generation would accomplish nothing'. In his absence there had been 'malevolent' anti-O'Connell speeches in the Repeal Association by Thomas Francis Meagher, a young man about town from a well-to-do Waterford family, who claimed to speak for the 'people of Ireland' in opposition to the old men of the Association. Ray warned O'Connell that Smith O'Brien, who had not yet joined Young Ireland, was nevertheless in full agreement with them and at the first opportunity would say something 'unpleasant' which 'could not be let to pass'. Smith O'Brien was further offended by the coolness with which the Liberator regarded his incarceration in the Clock Tower for contempt of the House, in that he had deliberately disobeyed a summons to attend a Commons committee. (Privately 'the great Dan' expressed his opinion that it was a foolish thing to run amuck at the House.) O'Brien got far warmer support from the *Nation*, and his sympathy with Young Ireland was thereby strengthened; but O'Connell regarded the *Nation's* praise of O'Brien as an implied attack on himself.[26]

The revolt against O'Connell's leadership was based on the suspicion that he was again preparing to drop repeal for any scraps Lord John Russell might toss him from Westminster. So he was. The scraps included a wider franchise, more thorough municipal reform, freedom of education along denominational lines, elected county boards to perform the functions of the landlord-dominated Grand Juries, a 20 per cent tax on the incomes of absentee landlords, and a radical reform of landlord-tenant relationships giving fixity of tenure, compensation for improvements and the abolition of the landlord's power to distrain a tenant's property if he were behind with the rent. Such mundane matters were of little interest to Young Ireland romantics, but O'Connell had cleared his flank by getting them formally adopted as Repeal Association policy, and evidently they could be achieved only by co-operation with a Whig government. This did not stop Meagher in the Repeal Association describing the last Whig government as 'little else than a State Relief Committee for the beggarly politicians that beset the country'.[27]

In June 1846 O'Connell, in London, showed his teeth, instructing his man in Kilkenny, Edmond Smithwick, that at the forthcoming by-election Kilkenny 'must return a Repealer, and I cannot possibly permit it to return either a Tory or a Whig, or an animal more mischievous than either of the others, called a Young Irelander'. He decided on a showdown, on an issue and at a time chosen by himself. 'Father of your Country,' wrote the faithful Tom Steele, 'it has given your Old Ireland people joy beyond measure that on your return you intend putting these scamps in their proper place.'[28]

The issue he chose with care. It was a matter at the very heart of his political creed, that repeal could and must be achieved by moral force alone. Gavan Duffy and Mitchel had actually been urging Repeal Wardens to study how to sabotage railways, to stop the government using them for troop movements at a time of insurrection.[29] It was intolerable! Either they must stop this sniping at what was and always had been a basic principle of the Repeal Association, and at his leadership, or the Association would be better off without them.

At a committee meeting of the Repeal Association on 11th July 1846, O'Connell referred to 'Peace Resolutions' which had been passed by the Association in 1841, 1843, 1844, January 1846 and June 1846, and proposed yet another affirmation of that great principle:

That to promote political amelioration peaceable means only should be used, to the exclusion of all others, save those which are peaceable, legal and constitutional. It has been said very unwisely that this principle prohibits the necessary defence against unjust aggression on the part of a domestic government or a foreign enemy. It does no such thing; it leaves the right of self-defence perfectly free to the use of any force sufficient to resist and defeat unjust aggression. We emphatically announce our conviction that all political amelioration, and the first and highest of all – the Repeal of the Union – ought to be sought for, and can be sought for successfully, only by peaceable, legal and constitutional means, to the utter exclusion of any other ... By such means *alone* we can, we ought, and, with the blessing of Almighty Providence, we will obtain the Repeal of the Union.

In the subsequent discussion O'Connell insisted that all members of the Association adhere to this resolution. The committee adopted his statement with two abstentions – Mitchel and Meagher.

Two days later, at a full Association meeting, O'Connell repeated his insistence. 'I want you either to declare for me or for that fiendish nonsense which suggests physical force ... I want you to banish from you all idea of physical force.' After loud applause, he referred again to all the past resolutions of the Repeal Association on loyalty to the Crown, non-violence, and gaining their point by legal and constitutional means alone without the slightest use of physical force. Mitchel protested that he could not repudiate the principles of his father, who had been out in 1798. 'The men on '98 thought Liberty worth some bloodletting!'

'He speaks of '98!' roared O'Connell in a fury. 'Their struggle was of blood and defeated in blood. The means they adopted weakened Ireland and enabled England to carry the Union!'

Mitchel protested against the Association binding itself by 'some abstract and universal principle'. But the principle was neither abstract nor universal. It was fundamental, it was specific, and it applied only to the circumstances of Ireland at that time. O'Connell was certainly no universal pacifist; but as a countryman, a landowner, and a lawyer of many years' experience of defending clients against charges of murder, arson and assault, he knew a good deal more than Young Irelanders about Irish countrymen's propensity to violence, and insisted that the principle of non-violence be accepted 'in theory and in practice. I drew up this resolution to draw a marked line between Young Ireland and Old Ireland.' The statement was adopted by acclamation, only Meagher dissenting.

305

At another general meeting on 28th July, O'Connell having returned to London, his son, John, announced that anyone who refused to accept the Liberator's own interpretation of his policy of non-violence was opposed to his leadership. Meagher replied with pugnacious heroics and a romantic panegyric to the cleansing virtues of the Sword, but was cut short by John O'Connell saying with the plenary authority of his absent father that he could not allow this to go on. With much angry spluttering Smith O'Brien, Mitchel, Meagher, Gavan Duffy and several others walked out.[30]

O'Connell summarised these differences with uncharacteristic fairness and objectivity in a letter to Dr Blake, Bishop of Dromore.

> The point hinges on this. We, the sincere Repealers, have placed the basis of our exertions on this: the carrying the Repeal by peaceable, legal and constitutional means and by *none other*. The seceders, on the contrary, insist that, in case we do not succeed by peaceable and legal means, we should reserve to ourselves the use in any favourable opportunity of the sword.

O'Neill Daunt observed coolly, 'Certainly if Meagher *must* flourish his sword, it is just as well that he should henceforth flourish it elsewhere than in Conciliation Hall ... The common sense seems to be, "Do not show your teeth unless you can bite." ' Swaggering and rhodomontades about the Sword were criminal folly on the part of people who had no means of waging war and had made no preparations, especially when the staple food of their potential army was rotting in the ground and the people depended solely on the government to save them from starvation. Later he wrote, 'O'Connell's doctrine "that no amount of political amelioration is worth one drop of human blood" is fudge, but perfectly safe and legal fudge. The opposite doctrine might involve one in the toils of the Attorney General.' O'Connell too saw this risk and put the point to Dr Blake, who had some sympathy with the Young Ireland position and urged a reconciliation:

> I solemnly, as a lawyer of many years' standing, assure your

Lordship, with the most perfect truth, that the plan of the seceders would, if we were to accede to or even tolerate it in the Association, involve every member of the Association, inclouding your Lordship, in the guilt of high treason ... If we were tomorrow to admit the seceders upon their own position, we should either dissolve the Association or render ourselves, in point of law, liable to at least imprisonment with the greatest risk of incurring actual execution on the scaffold.[31]

The essence of the quarrel between O'Connell and Young Ireland was that they knew when they joined the Repeal Association that it was committed to the use of moral force only; they tried to change this, and O'Connell would not let them. Long after his death Gavan Duffy in *Young Ireland* and Mitchel in *Jail Journal* were to wreak a terrible revenge on his reputation. But though O'Connell's rejection of the *use* of violence was total, he had never been reluctant to exploit the fear of it. As O'Neill Daunt shrewdly observed:

The great Dan boasts that the Catholic Association is a signal instance of the efficacy of moral force. But it was really a triumph of physical force which was never brought into the field but was none the less potential. On the other hand Young Ireland eloquence about the results obtainable by our valour and French assistance is moonstruck madness.

Daunt wanted at least Smith O'Brien back in the fold and wrote to him pointing out the damage done by the split. Repeal, he argued, could never be achieved by anyone else while the Liberator was still alive. O'Connell was with difficulty persuaded to try to woo the seceders back. But nothing came of it; the breach was final and, together with the famine, destroyed whatever hope there was of repeal.[32]

The winter of 1846-7 was the most miserable period of O'Connell's life. He was slowly dying, and knew it, of what was probably a tumour on the brain. This did not affect him mentally: his letters and recorded utterances were, to the end, perfectly sensible; but it affected him physically. His gait was shambling, his balance unreliable. As early as April 1846 that magnificent voice had begun to fail him. Disraeli described him appealing to

the Commons for urgent action to forestall catastrophe. He spoke
for nearly two hours in a voice audible only to those near him,

> a strange and touching spectacle to those who remembered the
> form of colossal energy and the clear and thrilling tones which
> had once startled, disturbed and controlled Senates ... To the
> House generally it was a performance of dumb show, a feeble
> old man muttering before a table; but respect for the great
> parliamentary personage kept all as orderly as if the fortunes
> of a party hung upon his rhetoric.

'I feel the feebleness of age upon me,' he told O'Neill Daunt. Yet
he was only seventy-two, an age at which many a politician has
been full of energy. More and more of his letters had to be
written in another hand, only signed by himself. Politically he
was in the doldrums, for the government did not need the votes
of a handful of repealers. Yet the suspicion that he was in with
the Whigs and suborned by a few civilities from the Castle cost
him much support. He was widely blamed for the breach with
Smith O'Brien, who now joined Young Ireland – driven into it,
people said, by the old man's wretched jealousy of anyone near
the throne.[33]

His finances had never been in a more hopeless state. He was
spending at a rate of £8,000–£10,000 a year, but nothing was
coming in. His famished tenants could pay no rents, and 'it would
be the absurdest of all absurd things to think of a Tribute in
such times as these.' 'He has always', observed Daunt in February 1846, 'spent the Tribute as fast as it came in, living from
hand-to-mouth, with no savings, not a farthing saved for a rainy
day. How does he keep afloat?'[34]

Overshadowing all else, his beloved country was engulfed in
the worst disaster of modern European history, and, except for
his own people at Derrynane, he could do nothing to alleviate it.
The 1846 potato crop, of which there had been high hopes in the
summer, was a total failure and, to add to the misery, the winter
of 1846–7 was one of the coldest and wettest of the century. The
local relief committees, which had not done too badly during the
previous winter when the crop failure was only partial, proved
totally inadequate when swamped with applications for work.
Nothing but time, weeks and weeks during which people were

dying by the thousand, could squeeze works schemes through first the bottleneck occasioned by the shortage of surveyors and trained staff, then the bottleneck of Trevelyan exercising rigid Treasury control. Private enterprise was quite incapable of coping as English economists had expected of it. The eastern counties were the worst hit by the famine; but along the west coast the government's undertaking to keep the people alive had to be modified by a cautious qualification, 'if possible'. The most useful thing a landlord could do was to remit rents, so that tenants could eat the corn, butter and pigs they produced instead of selling them for export to pay the rent and escape eviction. Some did. Others, whose rents were their only source of income, didn't. Some exploited the famine as an opportunity to improve the viability of their estates by wholesale evictions. Economically and logically it might be the best thing to do, but at what a cost in human misery and generations of hatred!

'A NATION', wrote O'Connell, agonised, in December 1846, 'is starving ... and to the all prevalent famine is now added dysentery and typhus in their worst shapes ... What is to be done? What is to be done?' The dying Liberator did his best, which is more than can be said of Young Ireland which retreated into intellectual and literary politics. His appeals to authority seemed to be ignored, but at least he could stimulate Maurice into further efforts to save his people at Derrynane. Had the Indian corn arrived? What was Maurice doing to ensure that the men employed by the Board of Works on repairing the sea-wall were paid regularly? Was he being pressed for payment for the ten tons of oatmeal? 'Of course you should get as much money as you possibly can for the corn and bread. If it were nothing else but to help you pay off the rascally bills. But I know you will not be harsh to the people.' His last speech in the House of Commons, almost inaudible, was made on 8th February 1847. Only a great national act of charity, he told those who could hear him, 'can save the lives of a quarter of the Irish population.' Food must be procured for the people wherever it could be got at whatever expense. England ought to use her power generously and magnificently to rescue that country. The Irish at present could do nothing for themselves. But to FitzPatrick he wrote despondently, 'At a period when Parliament could not do half enough for Ireland, it is not disposed to do half as much as it can.'[35]

309

His doctor was 'so anxious to have me well that he mistakes his wishes for his opinions. May God's holy will be done.' He determined to make a pilgrimage to Rome, knowing he would never reach the Holy City, and was delighted to hear of his dear Father Miley's kind, kind intention to accompany him. FitzPatrick was charged, 'Take care not to say anything that might induce him to incommode himself, but do everything quietly to facilitate his coming.' His last letter, written on 1st March 1847, was to FitzPatrick, tying up all the loose ends – or at least some of them – of his private affairs. 'They deceive themselves, and consequently deceive you, who tell you that I am recovering. God's holy will be done.'[36]

On 22nd March, accompanied by Father Miley and a valet, he set off on his journey across a continent still gripped by winter. The French treated him with all honour, as though he were still the man he had once been. In Genoa he refused to go further. There O'Connell died, on 17th May 1847.

15

Post-Mortem Report

Thanks to the literary articulacy of Young Ireland and its successors in the physical force tradition, far more attention has been focused on O'Connell's failure to win repeal than on his success in winning Catholic emancipation. Yet the latter was the biggest single step forward in modern Irish history, the indispensable starting-point for all subsequent advances to nationhood. O'Connell achieved it almost single-handed against a Protestant Ascendancy bent on self-preservation and, across the water, a deadweight of anti-Irish, anti-Papist prejudice. He achieved it by inspired leadership, political flair, showmanship, organising ability and an incomparable understanding of Irish countrymen. The Catholic Association which he created was used as a model by English agitators for reform and opponents of the Corn Laws, and by liberals and nationalists in Europe; and across the Atlantic his methods put his pupils in control of nearly every big city in the eastern states.

Some critics, even in his native Kerry, disparage his achievement. Emancipation, they say, would have been conceded in any case, without any agitation by O'Connell, who would have done better to concentrate on repeal. They are egregiously mistaken. If emancipation had not been conceded during the Age of Reason, when the ruling class was tolerant to the point of indifference in its Anglicanism, it was far less likely to be conceded fifty years later when the Church of England, and the Cabinet itself, was full of anti-Papist evangelicals.

311

The fascination of O'Connell's character and career lies in his many-sidedness or, to speak frankly, his deviousness. Of the many causes which he espoused, he was consistent and whole-hearted only in Catholic emancipation, anti-slavery and the rejection of the use of violence for political ends. In the cause of franchise reform he was remarkably ambivalent; on repeal he blew hot and cold in bewildering succession. Was he a democrat? Certainly, when it suited his purpose; but he was up to every trick in the political game, and did not hesitate to exploit in one election the landlord influence which he denounced in another.

Too little attention has been paid to his terrific efforts to alleviate the famine, for all his countrymen if possible, and if not, for his own people in Derrynane and Iveragh. In the last nine months of his life his best qualities shine like a beacon through the surrounding darkness. Frail and dying, he was a human dynamo. The 'ifs' of history lead down by-ways which are none the less fascinating for being cul-de-sacs. If there had been an Irish parliament and O'Connell in a commanding position in it, how differently the prolonged horror would have been handled! There would have been sympathy and understanding rather than exasperation at the perversity of the Irish who preferred charity to self-help; pragmatism instead of reliance on an economic theory which could not be applied to Ireland; and improvisation instead of red tape and rigid Treasury control. Famine relief would have been handled in an Irish, rather than in the most unimaginative English way.

If repeal had been granted at a time when no one dreamed of partitioning the country, Ireland would surely have been united, free and independent but linked to her nearest neighbour in a fruitful and amicable relationship.

Alas, there was in O'Connell's time not the slightest chance of repeal being conceded, either to his moral force or to the physical force of Young Ireland. Repeal, or Home Rule, was possible only if it were adopted by one of the major parties in parliament for its own ends; or if the British people were war-weary and in no mood for a fight against what they half-recognised as a reasonable cause. One condition applied from 1910 to 1914, the other from 1918 to 1922; neither was present during O'Connell's lifetime. It indicates a flaw in his political awareness that he did not properly realise this.

But the reputation of this greatest of Irishmen deserves to rest not on what he might have done, nor on what he failed to do, but on his wonderful achievement in 1828 which raised his people's heads and straightened their backs after generations of subjection and failure.

References

Unless these are of unusual or controversial interest, I have not thought it necessary to give references for well-known anecdotes or incidents in O'Connell's life. Those who wish to trace their origin can find them in the very long, early biographies of the Liberator by William Fagan, Mary Cusack and others.

Nor have I given references to details of O'Connell's private and family life, except to matters of particular interest. Apart from his daughter Ellen's short unpublished memoirs in the National Library of Ireland, the source for all these is *The Correspondence of Daniel O'Connell* which contains in eight volumes every extant letter written to or from him.

The *Correspondence* is by far the most useful, indeed indispensable, source for any book about him. I, and later biographers, owe an immeasurable debt to Professor Maurice R. O'Connell and Mr Gerard J. Lyne for collecting, editing and annotating over 3,500 letters. I have referred to these by the letter number (e.g. O'C. Corr. 2223), not by page and volume.

The following books, articles, pamphlets and unpublished manuscripts are cited in the chapter references in the shortened forms listed.

Cited as	Author and Full Title
Anglesey Letters	Public Record Office, Northern Ireland, D619/27B, letters of Lord Anglesey to Lord Holland, Chancellor of the Duchy of Lancaster.

References

Anglesey Memo — Public Record Office, Northern Ireland, D619/32B, memoranda of interviews given by Lord Anglesey to Archbishop Murray and O'Connell; and on the Catholic Association.

Anglesey, *One-Leg* — Marquess of Anglesey, *One-Leg, The life and letters of William Henry Paget, first Marquess of Anglesey, KG, 1768–1854* (London, 1961).

Atkins — J.B. Atkins, *Life of Sir William Howard Russell*, 2 vols (London, 1911).

Barlow — R.B. Barlow, *Citizenship and Conscience* (London, 1962).

Barrow, *Mirror* — J.H. Barrow (ed.), *The Mirror of Parliament ... for the Session ... commencing 29th January 1828*, 36 vols (London, 1828–37).

Beames — Michael Beames, *Peasants and Power* (Brighton, 1983).

de Beaumont — Gustave de Beaumont, *Ireland: Social, Political and Religious*, trans. W. Cooke-Taylor, 2 vols (London, 1962, 1964).

Clark — Samuel Clark, *Social Origins of the Irish Land War* (Princeton University, 1979).

Clarke — R. Clarke, 'The Relations between O'Connell and the Young Irelanders', *Irish Historical Studies*, vol. III (1942).

Courtenay — Ellen Courtenay, *A Narrative of the Most Extraordinary Cruelty, Perfidy and Depravity Perpetrated against Her by Daniel O'Connell Esq.* (London, 1837).

316

References

Crampton 4177 and Crampton 3278 Misc. Box III	Trinity College, Dublin, MS 4177; and 3278 Misc. Box III.
Cusack	Mary F. Cusack, *The Liberator, His Life and Times* (London, 1872).
D'Arcy	F.A. D'Arcy, 'The Artisans of Dublin and Daniel O'Connell, 1830–47', *Irish Historical Studies*, vol. XVII (1970).
Daunt Journal	National Library of Ireland, MS f3040, W.J. O'Neill Daunt's Journal.
Daunt, *Recoll.*	W.J. O'Neill Daunt, *Personal Recollections of the Late Daniel O'Connell, M.P.*, 2 vols (London, 1848).
Donnelly	J.S. Donnelly, *The Land and People of Cork in the Nineteenth Century* (London, 1975).
Duffy	Charles Gavan Duffy, *Young Ireland: A Fragment of Irish History, 1840–50* (London, 1880).
Edwards, 'American'	Owen Dudley Edwards, 'The American Image of Ireland', *Perspectives in American History*, vol. IV (1970).
Edwards, *O'Connell*	R. Dudley Edwards, *O'Connell and His World* (London, 1975).
Fagan	William Fagan, *The Life and Times of Daniel O'Connell*, 2 vols (Cork, 1847–8).
Fitz-Simon	National Library of Ireland Neg. 2720, Pos. 1624, Ellen Fitz-Simon's memoirs.

317

References

Graham   A.H. Graham, 'The Lichfield House Compact, 1835', *Irish Historical Studies*, vol. XII (1961).

Greville   Charles Greville, *The Greville Memoirs: A Journal of the Reigns of King George IV, King William IV and Queen Victoria*, 8 vols (rev. edn, London, 1938).

Gwynn, *Courtenay*   Denis Gwynn, *O'Connell and Ellen Courtenay* (London, 1932).

Gwynn, *Daniel O'C.*   Denis Gwynn, *Daniel O'Connell, the Irish Liberator* (London, 1929).

Gwynn, *O'Gorman Mahon*   Denis Gwynn, *The O'Gorman Mahon: Duellist, Adventurer and Politician* (London, 1934).

Hill, 'Nationalism'   J. Hill, 'Nationalism and the Catholic Church in the 1840s: Views of Dublin Repealers', *Irish Historical Studies*, vol. XIX (1975).

Hill, 'Protestant'   J. Hill, 'The Protestant Response to Repeal: the Case of the Dublin Working Class', in F.S.L. Lyons and R.A.J. Hawkins, *Ireland under the Union: Varieties of Tension* (Oxford, 1980).

Irish Education   *Eighth Report of the Commission on Irish Education* (1827).

Kerr   Donal Kerr, *Peel, Priests and Politics* (Oxford, 1982).

Lecky   W.E.H. Lecky, *Leaders of Public Opinion in Ireland*, 2 vols (London, 1912).

318

McCartney

Donal McCartney (ed.), *The World of Daniel O'Connell*, 14 essays (Dublin, 1980).

MacDonagh, *Life*

Michael MacDonagh, *The Life of Daniel O'Connell* (London, 1903).

MacDonagh, 'O'Connell'

O. MacDonagh, 'The Contribution of O'Connell', in B. Farrell, *The Irish Parliamentary Tradition* (Dublin, 1973).

MacDonagh, 'Politicization'

O. MacDonagh, 'The Politicization of the Irish Catholic Bishops, 1800–50', *The Historical Journal*, vol. XVIII (March 1975).

MacHale

John MacHale, *Letters of the Most Reverend John MacHale, 1820–34* (Dublin, 1893).

MacIntyre

Angus MacIntyre, *The Liberator: Daniel O'Connell and the Irish Party, 1930–47* (London, 1965).

Madden

D.O. Madden, *Ireland and Its Rulers since 1829* (London, 1844).

Morley

J. Morley, *Life of Richard Cobden* (London, 1903).

Nowlan

Kevin Nowlan, *The Politics of Repeal* (London, 1965).

O'C. Corr.

The Correspondence of Daniel O'Connell, ed. Maurice R. O'Connell, 8 vols (Dublin, 1972–9).

O'C. Journal

Daniel O'Connell, His Early Life and Journal, 1795–1806, ed. Arthur Houston (London, 1906).

O'C. Speeches   John O'Connell (ed.), *The Life and Speeches of Daniel O'Connell*, 2 vols (Dublin, 1846).

O'Connell, *Last Colonel*   Mrs M.J. O'Connell, *The Last Colonel of the Irish Brigade*, 2 vols (London, 1892).

O'Connell, 'Lawyer and Landlord'   M.R. O'Connell, 'O'Connell as Lawyer and Landlord', Thomas Davis Lecture for Radio-Telefis Eireann, spring 1975.

O'Connell, 'Reconsidered'   M.R. O'Connell, 'O'Connell Reconsidered', *Studies*, vol. LXIV (1975).

O'Faolain   Sean O'Faolain, *King of the Beggars* (London, 1938; paperback edition, Dublin, 1980).

O'Ferral, *Daniel O'C.*   Fergus O'Ferral, *Daniel O'Connell* (Dublin, 1981).

O'Ferral, *O'Connellite Politics*   Fergus O'Ferral, *O'Connellite Politics and Political Education*, Trinity College, Dublin, PhD thesis, 1978.

O Tuathaigh   Gearoid O Tuathaigh, *Ireland before the Famine, 1798–1848* (Dublin, 1972).

Popery   *Report by His Grace the Lord Primate for the Lords Committee Appointed to Enquire into the Present State of Popery in the Kingdom* (Dublin, 1732).

Reid   T. Wemyss Reid, *Life of the Hon. W.E. Forster*, 2 vols (London, 1888).

Repealer Repulsed   *The Repealer Repulsed* (Belfast, 1841).

Scully   Denys Scully, *A Statement on the Penal Laws*, 2 vols (Dublin, 1812).

References

Sheil   Richard Lalor Sheil, *Sketches Legal and Political*, 2 vols (London, 1955).

Wall   Maureen Wall, 'The Penal Laws', *Irish Historical Series*, no. 1 (Dundalk, 1976).

Woodham-Smith   Cecil Woodham-Smith, *The Great Hunger: Ireland, 1845–9* (London, 1962).

Wyse, *Catholic Association*   Thomas Wyse, *A Historical Sketch of the late Catholic Association*, 2 vols (London, 1829).

Wyse 15019
Wyse 15020
Wyse P. 5078   National Library of Ireland, MS 15019 (5) and (6), 15020 (1), (2) and (3), letters of Thomas Wyse and his brother George; MS P.5078, T. Wyse's Diary.

Newspapers Cited

The *Clare Journal*
Dublin Evening Post
Freeman's Journal
The *Nation*
The *Pilot*
The Times
The *Waterford Mirror*

Chapter References

2 *The O'Connells of Kerry*

1 English parliament, 3 W & M, ch. 2; Scully, vol. I, p. 62.
2 Irish parliament, 2 Ann, ch. 6; 9 Ann, ch. 6; 2 George II, ch. 26; Scully, vol. I, p. 135.
3 Irish parliament, 1 George II, ch. 9; Scully, vol. I, pp. 88–101.

4 Irish parliament, 2 Ann, ch. 7; Wall, pp. 12, 15–16, 49.
5 *Popery.*
6 Irish parliament, 2 Ann, ch. 6; 8 Ann, ch. 3.
7 Irish parliament, 2 Ann, ch. 6.
8 Ibid.
9 O'Connell, *Last Colonel*, vol. I, p. 56.
10 Irish parliament, 7 William III, ch. 5.
11 Trinity College, Dublin, MS 3346, no. 6.
12 Irish parliament, 7 William III, ch. 5.
13 Irish parliament, 2 Ann, ch. 6; 1 George II, ch. 20.
14 O'Connell, *Last Colonel*, vol. I, pp. 207–8.
15 Barlow, pp. 76, 205, 211.
16 Irish parliament, 18 George III, ch. 49.
17 O'Connell, *Last Colonel*, vol. I, p. 207.
18 Irish parliament, 18 George III, ch. 13.
19 O'Connell, *Last Colonel*, vol. I, pp. 265–6.
20 Irish parliament, 31 & 22 George III, ch. 24.

3 Young Dan

1 Irish parliament, 33 George III, ch. 31.
2 Clark, p. 88.

4 Dublin and 1798

1 Donnelly, p. 17.
2 O'C. Corr. 2903.
3 O Tuathaigh, p. 9; MacIntyre, p. 29.
4 O'C. Corr. 3340.
5 Ibid. 3332a.

5 Paterfamilias

1 O'C. Corr. 3380.
2 Ibid. 85.
3 Ibid. 237.
4 *Dublin Evening Press*, 14th January 1800.
5 Daunt, *Recoll.*, vol. I, p. 203.
6 O'C. Speeches, vol. II, p. 380; Fagan, vol. I, p. 116; O'C. Corr. 1372, note 2.

7 Ibid. 1237.
8 Ibid. 1663a.
9 Fitz-Simon, ff. 76-7.
10 O'C. Corr. 97.
11 Ibid. 3381.
12 Daunt, *Recoll.*, vol. I, pp. 14-15.
13 Edwards, *O'Connell*, p. 86.
14 O'C. Corr. 1136.
15 Ibid. 101.
16 O'C. Speeches, vol. I, pp. 50-1.

6 The Counsellor

1 Madden, pp. 22-5.
2 O'C. Corr. 548; MacDonagh, *Life*, p. 87.
3 MacDonagh, *Life*, pp. 84-7; O'C. Speeches, vol. I, p. 426.
4 MacDonagh, *Life*, pp. 89-90; O'C. Speeches, vol. I, pp. 447-8.
5 Daunt, *Recoll.*, vol. I, p. 82.
6 Ibid, vol. I, pp. 245-56, 303, 331; vol. II, pp. 1-5, 98-100, 135.

7 The Counsellor in Trouble

1 O'C. Corr. 953.
2 Ibid. 544.
3 Ibid. 841, note 1.

8 The Agitator

1 MacHale, pp. 92-5.
2 *New Monthly Magazine*, October 1928.
3 O'C. Corr. 1024, 969, note 1; O'C. Speeches, vol. II, p. 404.
4 O'C. Corr. 1023.
5 De Beaumont, vol. II, p. 61; O'Ferral, *O'Connellite Politics*, f. 1759.
6 In possession of Mr Brian MacDermot.
7 MacDonagh, 'Politicization', p. 42; Kerr, p. 6.
8 Wyse, *Catholic Association*, vol. I, pp. 282-3.
9 *Irish Education*, pp. 9, 58; MacHale, pp. 104-6.
10 O Tuathaigh, pp. 147-8.

11 MacDonagh, 'Politicization', pp. 40–2; Wyse, *Catholic Association*, vol. I, pp. 280–1.
12 Daunt Journal, ff. 14–15.
13 O Tuathaigh, pp. 69–71; Wyse, *Catholic Association*, vol. II, p. 107.
14 O'C. Corr. 1191.
15 Ibid. 1270, 1271.
16 Lecky, vol. II, p. 242; Daunt, *Recoll.*, vol. I, pp. 56, 224–5.
17 O'C. Corr. 1482.
18 National Library of Ireland, MS 5241.
19 O'C. Corr. 1362.

9 The Liberator

1 Daunt Journal, ff. 39–40.
2 *Clare Journal*, 30th June 1828.
3 MacDonagh, 'Politicization', p. 43.
4 Wyse, *Catholic Association*, vol. II, pp. 1–20; de Beaumont, vol. II, p. 132.
5 Wyse, *Catholic Association*, vol. I, pp. 411–16; O'C. Corr. 1500, note 2.
6 O Tuathaigh, pp. 90–2; Wyse, *Catholic Association*, vol. II, p. 90.
7 Wyse, *Catholic Association*, vol. II, pp. ccxiii–iv; Anglesey, *One-Leg*, p. 214.
8 Anglesey, *One-Leg*, p. 201.
9 Anglesey Memo. 4/2, 3/2.
10 Ibid. 2/2.
11 O'C. Corr. 1544.
12 Ibid. 1529.
13 Ibid. 1485.
14 Quoted in O'Faolain, p. 242.
15 O'C. Corr. 1525–6, 1531, 1534.
16 Wyse, *Catholic Association*, vol. II, p. 107; O'C. Corr. 1529.
17 Ibid. 1551.
18 Ibid. 1572, note 2.

10 The Member of Parliament

1 MacDonagh, 'O'Connell', p. 160; Crampton 4177, ff. 143, 144.

2 Wyse 15019 (6); O'C. Corr. 1851.
3 Daunt, *Recoll.*, vol. I, pp. 150–1; O'C. Corr. 1722, 1751, 1781, 2034, 2055.
4 Crampton 4177, f. 170b.
5 O'C. Corr. 1795, 1917; MacIntyre, p. 121; *Freeman's Journal*, 22nd January and 15th April 1831.
6 Wyse 15020 (1), 15020 (2).
7 Crampton 4177, f. 174.
8 O'C. Corr. 1593, note 2.
9 Ibid. 1593.
10 Ibid. 1585.
11 Ibid. 1601.
12 Ibid. 1668.
13 Ibid. 1670.
14 Ibid. 1678.
15 Ibid. 1684, note 4.
16 Ibid. 1687.
17 Ibid. 1689.
18 Ibid. 1690.
19 Ibid. 1693. *Waterford Mirror*, 28th July 1830.
20 O'C. Corr. 1921, 3420, note 5; Fagan, vol. II, pp. 49–50; Gwynn, *O'Gorman Mahon*, p. 113.
21 O'C. Corr. 1809.
22 Ibid. 1808, 1809.
23 Ibid. 1815.
24 Ibid. 2121 and note 4, 2122.
25 Ibid. 2123.
26 Ibid. 1583, 1696; Wyse 15020 (1), 6th July 1830; O'C. Corr. 1711; *Waterford Mirror*, 25th July 1830; Wyse P. 5078, October 1830; Wyse 15020 (3), 7th October 1830.
27 O'C. Corr. 1616 and notes 2–4, 2016, 1705.
28 Ibid. 1720a, note 1; Greville, vol. II, p. 147; Crampton 4177, ff. 143, 170a, 172.
29 Knight of Kerry to Croker, 23rd February 1831; quoted in MacDonagh, 'Politicization', p. 44, note 18.
30 MacDonagh, 'Politicization', pp. 43–4.

11 The Repealer

1 O'C. Corr. 3404.
2 Ibid. 1740.

3 Ibid. 1957.
4 Ibid. 1854.
5 Ibid. 1863; Anglesey Letters, f. 5.
6 O'C. Corr. 1957.
7 Crampton 4177, f. 174.
8 Ibid. f. 177.
9 O'C. Corr. 2799, note 1; 1774, notes 1 & 2; *Repealer Repulsed; Freeman's Journal*, 27th January 1831; *Dublin Evening Press*, 10th February 1831.
10 O'C. Corr. 1716.
11 O Tuathaigh, pp. 165-6.
12 O'C. Corr. 1297.
13 Ibid. 1727, 1735, 1736, 1744, 1737.
14 Ibid. 1784.
15 Crampton 4177, f. 174.
16 O'C. Corr. 1822, 1757, 1860.
17 Anglesey Letters, 1.
18 Ibid. 2, 3, 19; MacIntyre, pp. 23-5, quoting Home Office Papers 100/236.
19 Barrow, *Mirror*, 1831, vol. I, pp. 727-34; O'C. Corr. 1782, note 7, 1784.
20 Anglesey Letters, 7, 8.
21 Quoted by MacIntyre, p. 27.
22 Anglesey Letters, 14.
23 For the tithe problem: Anglesey Letters, 34, 42; O'C. Corr. 1757, 1854, 1955a; MacIntyre, pp. 36-7, 170-6, 190; Beames, pp. 115-16.
24 O'C. Corr. 1723, 1738, 1740, 1744.
25 Ibid. 2010, 2011, 1757, 1957, 1822; Anglesey Letters, 9.
26 Ibid. 13.
27 Ibid. 12, 18, 20, 29.
28 Crampton 3278 Misc. Box III.
29 Wyse 15019 (5).
30 O'C. Corr. 1851, 1853, 1893.
31 Ibid. 1929, 1915.
32 Ibid. 1895a, 1859, notes 2 & 3; MacIntyre, pp. 30, 33.
33 O'C. Corr. 2903; MacIntyre, p. 102.
34 MacDonagh, 'O'Connell', pp. 160-2; MacIntyre, pp. 74-8, 146-7, 157-8.
35 O'C. Corr. 1972, 2010, 2011, 1921, 1980, 1984.

36 Fitz-Simon, f. 147.
37 O'C. Corr. 3414.
38 Ibid. 3404, 3405, 3407, 3408, 3409, 3410, 3411, 3412, 3413.
39 Daunt, *Recoll.*, vol. II, pp. 51–2.
40 Ibid. vol. II, pp. 126–8; O'C. Corr. 2057a.
41 O'Connell's relations with the Dublin trade unions are described in D'Arcy; O'C. Corr. 2058, 2485a, 2548.
42 O'C. Corr. 1639, 1653.
43 The Ellen Courtenay affair is described in Courtenay, and in Gwynn, *Courtenay*. See also O'C. Corr. 1848, 1852, 1871, 1889.
44 O'C. Corr. 735, 739.
45 Barrow, *Mirror*, 1833, vol. I, pp. 379 ff., 565 ff., 790 ff., 815, 872; MacIntyre, pp. 44–50, 151; Sheil, vol. II, pp. 135, 153; O'C. Corr. 1949, 1955a, note 1, 1966, 2033.
46 O'C. Corr. 1982, 1975a, note 1.
47 Ibid. 2747, 2750; MacIntyre, pp. 84–5.
48 Barrow, *Mirror*, 1834, vol. I, p. 1191 ff.
49 O'C. Corr. 2073, 2075, 2081.

12 The Wheeler-Dealer

1 MacIntyre, pp. 131–4; O'C. Corr. 2066, 2086, note 6, 2136, 2145.
2 O'C. Corr. 2118, 2186, 2187, 2191, 2196, 2201, note 1, 2216; MacIntyre, pp. 60–1; Graham, pp. 210–12.
3 MacIntyre, pp. 137, 141–2; O'C. Corr. 2214, 2216; Graham, pp. 212–21, 223; MacIntyre, p. 145.
4 Greville, vol. IV, p. 10; O'C. Corr. 2228, 2229.
5 MacIntyre, pp. 159–61; O'C. Corr. 2235.
6 O'C. Corr. 2234, note 3, 2240, 2241.
7 Ibid. 2247–2259, 2263–2272, 2311, note 1.
8 For municipal reform see MacIntyre, pp. 154, 228–39, 258–61; O'C. Corr. 2262a; Daunt, *Recoll.*, vol. I, p. 151.
9 O'C. Corr. 2330, 2331, 2333, 2334, 2229, note 4.
10 MacIntyre, p. 120 ff.
11 Ibid. pp. 122–3; O'C. Corr. 2440, 2449.
12 O'C. Corr. 2414; MacIntyre, pp. 62, 64, 154.
13 For O'Connell and the Poor Laws see: O'C. Corr. 2324; MacIntyre, pp. 209–10, 215–18, 225–6; Daunt Journal, vol. II, pp. 108–10, 275.

14 MacIntyre, pp. 192–8; O'C. Corr. 2369.
15 MacIntyre, p. 198.
16 O'C. Corr. 2503 and family legend.
17 O'C. Corr. 2542.
18 Ibid. 2552, note 1, 2554, 2558, 2582, note 4, 2583, note 3.
19 Ibid. 2611.
20 Ibid. 2618, 2620, 2657, 2682, 2643, 2688.
21 Daunt Journal, f. 44.
22 O'C. Corr. 2665.
23 Ibid. 2658, 2700, 2724, 2807, 2816, 2817, 2645, 2646, 2648.
24 Ibid. 2699, note 1, 2704.
25 Ibid. 2853, 2877, note 4, 2862, 2863, 2864.
26 Ibid. 2894, 2874, 2890, 2899, 2891, 2892, 2877, 2903.
27 Ibid. 2877.

13 The Return of Hurlothrumbo

1 O'C. Corr. 2965, 2967, 2968.
2 Ibid. 2597, 2599, 2668; MacIntyre, p. 265; Morley, pp. 491–2.
3 For O'Connell as Lord Mayor: Daunt, *Recoll.*, vol. II, pp. 13, 19, 22–3, 45–6, 73–4, 84–8; MacIntyre, p. 121.
4 MacIntyre, p. 121. O'C. Corr. 2967, 2969.
5 For O'Connell and slavery: D.C. Riach, 'O'Connell and Slavery' in McCartney, pp. 175–85; Daunt, *Recoll.*, vol. II, p. 282; O'C. Corr. 3005a, 3011, 3027a, note 1; Edwards, 'American', pp. 255–70.
6 Daunt, *Recoll.*, vol. II, pp. 64–7; Duffy, p. 27.
7 Nowlan, pp. 39–40; MacDonagh, *Life*, p. 257; Duffy, pp. 76–82; O'C. Corr. 3002a, note 2.
8 Hill, 'Nationalism', p. 375; Hill, 'Protestant', pp. 36–47, 63.
9 Duffy, p. 169; Daunt Journal, f. 460; O'C. Corr. 3006.
10 Clarke, pp. 19–20, 26.
11 *Nation*, 20th May 1843; Duffy, p. 121; *Longford Journal*, 3rd June 1843, quoted in O'Faolain, p. 299.
12 MacDonagh, *Life*, pp. 314–17.
13 MacIntyre, p. 270; Nowlan, p. 54.
14 V. Conzemius in McCartney, pp. 143–62; Daunt, *Recoll.*, vol. I, p. 71; O'C. Corr. 2914.
15 P. O'Farrell in McCartney, pp. 112–23.
16 Gearoid O Tuathaigh in McCartney, pp. 30–43.
17 Duffy, pp. 181–2; Nowlan, pp. 56–7; Clarke, p. 21.

14 *The Exhausted Volcano*

1 Crampton 4177, f. 324.
2 O'C. Corr. 3124, 3037, 3061.
3 Ibid. 2959.
4 Ibid. 1976; Daunt Journal, ff. 29, 40.
5 Crampton 4177, f. 325; MacIntyre, pp. 271-2; O'C. Corr. 3039.
6 Clarke, p. 22; O'C. Corr. 3057.
7 Ibid. 3047.
8 Ibid. 3071.
9 MacDonagh, *Life*, pp. 294-308; MacIntyre, p. 272.
10 Kerr, pp. 4-6, 80-7, 54.
11 Nowlan, pp. 66-8, 76; Kerr, pp. 179-207, 218; O'C. Corr. 3083a, 3100, note 5.
12 O'C. Corr. 3092, 3100, 3100a, 3108; Duffy, pp. 107-12.
13 Daunt Journal, ff. 194-5.
14 O'C. Corr. 3141, 3142; Nowlan, pp. 90-1.
15 Nowlan, pp. 90-1; Kerr, pp. 249-51, 257, 263-5, 284-7; O'C. Corr. 3141.
16 *Nation*, 14th June 1845; Nowlan, p. 87; Kerr, pp. 309-11; O'C. Corr. 841, note 1, 3146, 3149.
17 Duffy, pp. 170-1, 125, 169; Nowlan, p. 88; O'C. Corr. 3309.
18 Duffy, pp. 173-6; O'C. Corr. 3169.
19 MacIntyre, p. 284.
20 Nowlan, p. 97; O'C. Corr, 3180.
21 O'C. Corr. 3181, 3189.
22 MacIntyre, pp. 287-8.
23 O'Connell, 'Lawyer and Landlord'; *The Times*, 18th November and 25th December 1845; Reid, pp. 178-81; MacIntyre, p. 287; Atkins, vol. I, pp. 33-4; O'C. Corr. 3427.
24 Woodham-Smith, pp. 123-9; Donnelly, p. 84.
25 O'C. Corr. 3264, 3290, 3297, 3271.
26 Ibid. 3232, 3227, 3228, 3203, notes 1 & 2, 3208, note 1; Daunt Journal, f. 194.
27 O'Connell, 'Reconsidered', p. 113; Clarke, pp. 28-9.
28 O'C. Corr. 3234, 3228a.
29 Ibid. 3216.
30 Daunt Journal, ff. 192-3; O'C. Corr. 3248, note 2; *Dublin Evening Post*, 14th July, 28th July, 30th July 1846.

References

31 Daunt Journal, ff. 197, 258–9; O'C. Corr. 3340.
32 O'Connell, 'Reconsidered', p. 119, note 8; Daunt Journal, ff. 260, 244; O'C. Corr. 3365, note 2.
33 MacIntyre, p. 290; Daunt Journal, ff. 272, 274, 286–7.
34 Daunt Journal, f. 283; O'C. Corr. 3206, 3299.
35 O'C. Corr. 3361, 3362, 3370, 3373 and note 1.
36 Ibid. 3376, 3377.

Additional Bibliography

The following material is of interest in relation to O'Connell's life and times.

Books

James C. Beckett, *The Making of Modern Ireland, 1603–1903.*

John Warren Doyle, Bishop of Kildare and Leighlin (nom-de-plume J.K.L.), *A Vindication of the Religious and Civil Principles of the Irish Catholics* (Dublin, 1823).

R. Dudley Edwards and T.D. Williams, *The Great Famine* (Dublin, 1956).

B. Farrell, *The Irish Parliamentary Tradition* (Dublin, 1973).

Norman Gash, *Mr Secretary Peel, The Life of Sir Robert Peel to 1830* (London, 1961).

Robert Kee, *The Green Flag: A History of Irish Nationalism* (London, 1972).

Elizabeth Longford, *Wellington, Pillar of State* (London, 1972).

Raymond Moley, *Daniel O'Connell, Nationalism without Violence* (New York, 1974).

J.R. O'Flanagan, *The Bar Life of O'Connell* (Dublin, 1875).

Additional Bibliography

Thomas Pakenham, *The Year of Liberty* (London, 1969).

J.A. Reynolds, *The Catholic Emancipation Crisis in Ireland, 1823-29* (New Haven, 1954).

P. Somerville-Large, *Dublin* (London, 1979).

Articles

'The County Clare Election', *New Monthly Magazine* (October 1828), pp. 289-303, 385-91.

B. Inglis, 'O'Connell and the Irish Press, 1800-42', *Irish Historical Studies*, vol. VIII (1952).

M.R. O'Connell, 'Daniel O'Connell: Income, Expenditure and Despair', *Irish Historical Studies*, vol. XVII (1970).

M.R. O'Connell, 'O'Connell and the Irish Eighteenth Century', *Studies in Eighteenth-Century Culture*, vol. 5 (1976), University of Wisconsin Press.

M.R. O'Connell, 'O'Connell, Young Ireland and Violence', *Thought*, vol. 52 (1977).

Unpublished Material

National Library of Ireland, MSS 3289-90, proceedings of the Catholic Association.

Index

Troy, John Thomas, Archbishop, 58, 119

Union with Britain, 48, 57–9; effects of, 60–1
United Irishmen, 33, 34, 35, 36, 39, 40, 41, 43, 44–5

Veto controversy, 81–97
Victoria, Queen, 251, 254–5, 256, 264–5
Villiers, George William Frederick, later Lord Clarendon, 171, 173, 188–9, 195, 284, 288
Volunteers, 11–12, 33, 34

Waterford, Henry de la Poer Beresford, 3rd Marquess of, 143
Wellesley, Richard, 1st Marquis of, 121, 237
Wellington, Arthur Wellesley, 1st Duke of: abused by O'Connell, 116, 163, 274; considers that his brother, the Marquis of Wellesley, should be castrated, 121; views on Ireland, 132–3, 145–7, 160–1; considered obnoxious by Catholic Association, 148, 152; alive to danger of civil war, 160; views on Marquis of Anglesey, 161, 164; dismisses Anglesey, 165; seen by O'Connell to be weakening in his opposition to Catholic emancipation, 165;

recommends Catholic emancipation as an unfortunate necessity, 165
Whiteboys, 33–4, 110–13, 182–3, 197, 202–3, 204, 230–1
Whitworth, Charles, 1st Viscount, 90
Wilkes, John, xv–xvi, 21, 92, 140, 263, 283
William IV, King, 238, 251; *see also* Duke of Clarence
Woulfe, Stephen, 85
Wyse, George, 175, 184
Wyse, Thomas: exaggerates low social status of Catholic priests, 126; leading Catholic emancipationist in Co. Waterford, 143; organises liberal clubs, 145; sees importance of Protestant support for Catholic emancipation, 159; resents and distrusts O'Connell, 160, 171, 184, 212, 294; approves of disenfranchisement of forty-shilling freeholders, 167; opposes repeal, 184, 194; resigns from bench in protest at treatment of O'Connell, 277; favours federation, 294

Yeomanry, 34, 39, 45, 192, 197, 208–10, 217
York, Frederick Augustus, Duke of, 135
Young Ireland, xvi, 272–5, 293, 296, 297–8, 303–7